D1528804

Perspectives on
STANLEY KUBRICK

Perspectives on
FILM

RONALD GOTTESMAN
University of Southern California
and
HARRY M. GEDULD
Indiana University

Series Editors

❖

Perspectives on
STANLEY KUBRICK

❖

edited by

MARIO FALSETTO

G. K. Hall & Co.
An Imprint of Simon & Schuster Macmillan
New York

Prentice Hall International
London Mexico City New Delhi Singapore Sydney Toronto

G.K. Hall & Co.
An Imprint of Simon & Schuster Macmillan
1633 Broadway
New York, NY 10019

Library of Congress Catalog Card Number: 96-15731

Printed in the United States of America

Printing number

1   2   3   4   5   6   7   8   9   10

Library of Congress Cataloging-in-Publication Data

Pespectives on Stanley Kubrick / edited by Mario Falsetto.
       p.   cm.—(Perspectives on film)
    Filmography: p.
    Includes bibliographical references and index.
    ISBN 0-8161-1991-0 (alk. paper)
    1. Kubrick, Stanley—Criticism and interpretation.   I. Falsetto, Mario.   II. Series.
    PN1998.3.K83P47   1996
    791.43'02333'092—dc20   96-15731
                                                                                  CIP

The paper used in this publication meets the requirements of ANSI/NISO Z39.49-1992 (Permanence of Paper).

For my parents
Mafalda and Settimio Falsetto

Contents

❖

Series Editors' Note

This series is devoted to supplying comprehensive coverage of several topics: directors, individual films, national film traditions, film genres, and other categories that scholars have devised for organizing the rich history of film as expressive form, cultural force, and industrial and technological enterprise. Each volume essentially brings together two kinds of critical and historical material: first, previously published reviews, interviews, written and pictorial documents, essays, and other forms of commentary and interpretation; and, second, commissioned writings designed to provide fresh perspectives. Each volume is edited by a film scholar and contains a substantial introduction that traces and interprets the history of the critical response to the subject and indicates its current status among specialists. As appropriate, volumes will also provide production credits, filmographies, selective annotated bibliographies, indexes, and other reference materials. Titles in this series will thus combine the virtues of an interpretive archive and a reference guide. The success of each volume should be measured against this objective.

The present collection, the first to bring together those essays and articles that have most enriched critical understanding of Kubrick's ten most crucial feature films, also makes clear the powerful controversies that these films have generated.

Foregrounded by several of Kubrick's key interviews, the body of the book provides a series of contrasting commentaries on each of his films. Thus Mark Crispin Miller explores the enigmatic, and richly innovative narrative strategies of *Barry Lyndon*, while Alan Spiegel's essay offers insightful comparisons between the aesthetics of that film and Robert Altman's *The Long Goodbye*. The reader is especially referred to the analyses of *The Shining* by Richard T. Jameson and Paul Mayersberg for a keen sense of the thick texture of the discourse that characterizes the most informed and disciplined responses to Kubrick's creativity.

In his introduction, Falsetto tells us that Kubrick is "profoundly committed to the uniqueness of the film medium. His films challenge our understanding of the world, and sometimes force us to think in ways we would prefer not to." Appropriately, this collection will challenge many critical superficialities and assumptions, while providing, we think, the most searching and revealing perspectives to date on a body of work that ranks among the most provocative and disquieting of our century.

Ronald Gottesman
Harry M. Geduld

Publisher's Note

Producing a volume that contains both newly commissioned and reprinted material presents the publisher with the challenge of balancing the desire to achieve stylistic consistency with the need to preserve the integrity of works first published elsewhere. In the Perspectives series, essays commissioned especially for a particular volume are edited to be consistent with G. K. Hall's house style; reprinted essays appear in the style in which they were first published, with only typographical errors corrected. Consequently, shifts in style from one essay to another are the result of our efforts to be faithful to each text as it was originally published.

Acknowledgments

One of the pleasures of editing this anthology was that I was able to reacquaint myself with the rich literature on Stanley Kubrick, and to commission several provocative new pieces. I would like to acknowledge the assistance of Concordia Aid to Scholarly Research at Concordia University (Montreal) for its generous support of this project. All the stills are courtesy of the Museum of Modern Art, Film Stills Archive. Special thanks to Carole Zucker, for her unending patience and support.

INTRODUCTION

Stanley Kubrick:
An Overview

MARIO FALSETTO

Stanley Kubrick began his career in the early 1950s making several documentaries and two independent features, *Fear and Desire* (1953) and *Killer's Kiss* (1955). Although he would eventually become a key artist within the studio system, the lack of early studio support proved crucial in shaping the pattern of creative autonomy that has characterized his career ever since. Kubrick has created an impressive body of work in a career that now spans over forty years, and his place in contemporary film history is assured. Despite this independence and secure reputation, however, Kubrick's films have often proved difficult for film reviewers and scholars.

Since the release of *2001: A Space Odyssey* (1968), Kubrick's work has generated strong defense from his admirers and equally hostile attack from his critics. Also, the critical standing of a Kubrick film seems to undergo extensive revision over the course of time. The initial release of a Kubrick film is generally an unreliable barometer of how the film will be perceived years after its initial release. This idea is echoed in an article on *The Shining* (1980) by P. L. Titterington:

> It is becoming commonplace that a first viewing of a new Kubrick film is likely to be a baffling experience (of recent work, probably the only exception is *A Clockwork Orange*, and that only because it can more easily be understood at the simple plot level alone). Time has to be allowed for one to become familiar with such a complex style, and one would suspect that Kubrick (who suggested that two viewings of *2001* would probably be necessary) would also want to say that a lot depends on what is communicated

directly and subconsciously, even if the audience cannot articulate what they have seen.[1]

The Kubrick filmography consists of three short films and twelve features, the first two of which he considers apprentice works. Kubrick's reputation rests essentially on ten feature films beginning with *The Killing* (1956) through to his most recent production, *Full Metal Jacket* (1987).

Kubrick enjoys perhaps the most autonomous and commodious arrangement with the studios of any major filmmaker alive. He freely chooses whatever project interests him and can apparently take as much time and money to complete his films as is needed. Despite this remarkable studio support, Kubrick has produced only four films since *2001: A Space Odyssey* (1968). His approach is careful and methodical.

Kubrick takes as long as he does between projects partly because he spends a great deal of time searching for a new project after he completes a film, a phase that may last over a year. He is, of course, also involved in every stage of production. This not only includes the expected writing, producing and directing chores, but also his working closely with fellow artists such as cinematographers, editors, and art directors, and even helping to plan the film's release and ad campaign. This involvement inevitably makes the production process longer than that of many other directors. Michel Ciment has commented on some of Kubrick's working methods:

> He prefers to prepare a project, collect material for it over a period of months, even years, pore over books and magazines with the systematic curiosity of an autodidact, monitor the seating capacity and average takings of cinemas in each foreign capital or the design and deployment of posters or even the distance between seats and screen at press shows, not to mention the size of newspaper ads and the rates of currency exchange. He also has the subtitles of every foreign version of his films completely re-translated into English to make certain that nothing crucial has been omitted, supervises all dubbed versions, and checked out the quality of the seven hundred prints of *The Shining* which were released the same day in the United States.[2]

This need to control all aspects of his productions has contributed to a certain mythology about Kubrick. Those who work with him, however, seem to agree that his perfectionism is a positive, if occasionally trying, quality. Ken Adam, set designer on several Kubrick films, stated in a 1964 interview that "Stanley is an extremely difficult and talented person. We developed an extremely close relationship and as a result I had to live almost completely on tranquillizers."[3] Kubrick seems genuinely open to other people's contributions and instills a high degree of loyalty among his collaborators. All reports indicate that he is not dictatorial on the set and is endlessly patient with his collaborators. He has a reputation for making actors do numerous retakes (as many as fifty, we are told, for a simple scene), yet most actors who have worked with Kubrick speak highly of the experience, appreciative, no doubt, of the opportunity to work closely with a director sensitive to film performance. In a 1975 interview, Malcolm McDowell stated:

> This is why Stanley is such a great director. He can create an atmosphere where you're not inhibited in the least. You'll do anything. Try it out. Experiment. Stanley gives you freedom and he is the most marvelous audience. I used to see him behind the camera with the handkerchief stuffed in his mouth because he was laughing so much. It gave me enormous confidence.[4]

The myths associated with Kubrick, of course, extend beyond the film set. Tim Cahill summarizes some of the more extreme ones in a 1987 interview:

> TIM CAHILL: Stanley Kubrick is a perfectionist. He is consumed by mindless anxiety over every aspect of every film he makes. Kubrick is a hermit, an expatriate, a neurotic who is terrified of automobiles and who won't let his chauffeur drive more than thirty miles an hour.
>
> STANLEY KUBRICK: Part of my problem is that I cannot dispel the myths that have somehow accumulated over the years. . . . In fact, I don't have a chauffeur. I drive a Porsche 928S, and I sometimes drive it at eighty or ninety miles an hour on the motorway. . . .
>
> T.C.: I've heard rumors that you'll do a hundred takes for one scene.
>
> S.K.: It happens when actors are unprepared. You cannot act without knowing dialogue. If actors have to think about the words, they cannot work on the emotion. So you end up doing thirty takes of something. And still you can see the concentration in their eyes; they don't know their lines. So you just shoot it and shoot it and hope you can get something out of it in pieces. Now, if the actor is a nice guy, he goes home, he says, "Stanley's such a perfectionist, he does a hundred takes on every scene." So my thirty takes become a hundred. If I did a hundred takes on every scene, I'd never finish a film.[5]

The major events in Kubrick's biography are well documented. Born in the Bronx in 1928, he went directly from high school—where his passions included still photography, jazz drumming, and chess—to a job at *Look* magazine at the age of sixteen. He stayed five years working as a photojournalist before leaving to make his first short film. In an interview with Joseph Gelmis, Kubrick said, "I'd keep seeing lousy films and saying to myself, 'I don't know anything about moviemaking but I couldn't do anything worse than this.'"[6] The first film, a documentary entitled *Day of the Fight* (1951), had as its subject the boxer Walter Cartier, the subject of an earlier photo-layout by Kubrick. A second film, *Flying Padre* (1951) concerned a priest in New Mexico who flew from one end of his parish to the other in a Piper Cub airplane. This was followed in 1953 by a final documentary, *The Seafarers*.

Though these films did not make Kubrick any money, he was encouraged enough to embark on his first feature, *Fear and Desire* (1953), an antiwar allegory made for less than $40,000, borrowed mostly from his family. The film was not a financial success, but it garnered some critical attention, and soon after, Kubrick made a second feature, *Killer's Kiss* (1955). A highly atmospheric film noir, *Killer's Kiss* marked the end of the apprentice phase of Kubrick's career.

These initial experiences proved to be a perfect training ground, since Kubrick had no background in theater, television, or film school. He learned every aspect of the mechanics of filmmaking, handling virtually every major task on the films himself, including the photography. Apart from this practical experience, Kubrick's aesthetic sense was shaped by frequent film screenings, including many at the Museum of Modern Art, which acted as a kind of film school for the young, aspiring artist. He read books about film by such people as Eisenstein and Pudovkin, decidedly preferring the latter to the former.

With this particular background, it is not surprising that Kubrick rates editing as the most creative aspect of filmmaking: "It's the nearest thing to some reasonable environment in which to do creative work . . . editing is the only aspect of the cinematic art that is unique. It shares no connection with any other art form: writing, acting, photography, things like that are major aspects of the cinema, are still not unique to it, but editing is."[7]

After *Killer's Kiss*, Kubrick directed *The Killing* (1956), a highly inventive heist film that Alexander Walker calls Kubrick's "graduation" piece. This was the first film made in partnership with James B. Harris—an association that lasted through the making of *Lolita* (1962). The complexities of *The Killing* are primarily revealed in its innovative narrative structure. It also featured fine performances by character actors generally not given the chance to display their craft. Around this time, Kubrick began to attract the attention of the film world. In a 1957 *Newsweek* article, Kubrick is referred to as the latest Hollywood "boy wonder,"[8] a description amply confirmed by the release of his next film, *Paths of Glory* (1957), still regarded as one of the best antiwar films ever made.

Paths of Glory announced that Kubrick was indeed a world-class filmmaker. The film displayed a bold, stylistic system, especially in its use of moving camera and complicated spatial strategies, as well as a depth of characterization not apparent in Kubrick's earlier work. The handling of sensitive moral issues and involving dramatics elevated Kubrick to the front ranks of Hollywood directors. In his *Sight and Sound* review, Gavin

Lambert called *Paths of Glory* "not only a film of unusual substance but a powerfully realized and gripping work of art."[9]

After an unproductive period in Hollywood working on several projects, including *One-Eyed Jacks* for Marlon Brando, Kubrick was hired to replace Anthony Mann on *Spartacus* (1960), a film that proved Kubrick could handle the complicated logistics of a massive Hollywood epic. Although remarkable in many ways, the film is viewed as something of an exception in the director's oeuvre—Kubrick did not write any part of the screenplay, had no input in the film's casting, and has referred to himself as a "hired hand" on the film. Although he has complained of the experience, *Spartacus* is an intelligent, if somewhat conventional, epic. It was generally well received, with Stanley Kauffmann remarking in *The New Republic* that Kubrick's "direction will probably be under-rated, but by and large he has done a penetrating and imaginative piece of work."[10] Perhaps more than any other experience, the making of *Spartacus* highlighted to Kubrick the importance of being involved at every stage of production.

Spartacus was followed by *Lolita* (1962), the first Kubrick film to be shot in England where the director has continued to work to this day. The adaptation of Nabokov's controversial novel received something of a mixed reception, although it was almost universally praised for its fine performances. Most of the negative reaction centered on the differences between the film and the book. Some critiques focused on the choice of Sue Lyon who played Lolita, often ignoring the other aspects of the film. Some responses, such as Raymond Durgnat's review in *Films and Filming*, were more perceptive. Durgnat claimed that "Sue Lyon gives an expert performance," and declared that "paradoxically, Kubrick's film is totally unerotic. Lolita wriggling in a hula-hoop, the credit-sequence of a male hand lacquering the toe-nails of a (podgy) female foot, are erotic ideas coldly staged, cerebral and emblematic."[11]

The film's (understandable) differences with the novel did not seem to bother Vladimir Nabokov, who, nevertheless, was surprised to discover that most of the script he had written for the film had not been used. He has commented on the film:

> A few days before, at a private screening, I had discovered that Kubrick was a great director, that his *Lolita* was a first-rate film with magnificent actors, and that only ragged odds and ends of my script had been used. The modifications, the garbling of my best little finds, the omission of entire scenes, the addition of new ones, and all sorts of other changes may not have been sufficient to erase my name from the credit titles but they certainly made the picture as unfaithful to the original script as an American poet's translation from Rimbaud or Pasternak. I hasten to add that my present comments should definitely not be construed as reflecting any belated grudge, any high-pitched deprecation of Kubrick's creative approach.[12]

As with most other Kubrick films, *Lolita*'s status continues to be elevated with the passage of time. Kubrick followed up *Lolita* with one of his greatest commercial and critical successes, *Dr. Strangelove, or How I Stopped Worrying and Learned to Love the Bomb* (1964). This nihilistic satire, based on the novel *Red Alert*, was originally intended to be a straightforward drama about the cold war, but it eventually evolved into what Kubrick calls a "nightmare comedy." Here is the director discussing the evolution of the film's tone in a 1963 article that appeared in *Films and Filming*:

> Now *Red Alert* is a completely serious suspense story. My idea of doing it as a nightmare comedy came when I was trying to work on it. I found that in trying to put meat on the bones and to imagine the scenes fully one had to keep leaving things out of it which were either absurd or paradoxical, in order to keep it from being funny, and these things seemed to be very real. Then I decided that the perfect tone to adopt for the film would be what I now call nightmare comedy, because it most truthfully presents the picture.[13]

Most reviewers thought *Dr. Strangelove* had admirably achieved its ambitions, and reacted favorably to the film, although responses often depended on the reviewer's political orientation. Typical of the positive evaluation of the film was director Bryan Forbes' review in *Films and Filming*, which described the film as "a tragic-comic masterpiece—the first truly moral film of our time: courageous, outrageous, borrowing nothing, admitting of no compromise, very naked and very unashamed: a shattering, womb-trembler of a film."[14] Stanley Kauffmann, writing in *The New Republic*, described Kubrick's film as "the best American picture that I can remember since Chaplin's *Monsieur Verdoux* and John Huston's *Treasure of the Sierra Madre* (both 1947)."[15] On the other hand, as Charles Maland points out in a highly perceptive piece written in 1979, "the critic for the right-wing *National Review* . . . suggested that *Dr. Strangelove*'s theme was that ideology should be abandoned. . . . Closing with a hope that Kubrick might make a film criticizing Stalinism."[16] The film was extensively debated, often by commentators who generally did not write film reviews. In an essay reprinted in this collection, Robert Brustein called *Dr. Strangelove* . . .

> a work of comic anarchy, fashioned by a totally disaffected and disaffiliated imagination: it is thus the first American movie to speak truly for our generation. . . . For although *Dr. Strangelove* is about a political subject, its only politics is outrage against malevolence of officialdom. Conservatives will find it subversive, liberals will find it irresponsible, utopians will find it bleak, humanitarians will find it inhuman—*Dr. Strangelove* is all these things. But it also releases, through comic poetry, those feelings of impotence and frustration that are consuming us all; and I can't think of anything more important for an imaginative work to do.[17]

Kubrick's next film, *2001: A Space Odyssey* (1968), was something of a watershed in the director's career. The film is now generally acknowledged as a great masterpiece of modernism, but its acceptance was by no means universal or immediate. With the reception accorded *2001*, there is a clear shift in critical response to Kubrick's work. Many of the initial reviews were shortsighted and hostile. The film proved baffling to some reviewers and older audiences.[18] One of the most caustic reviews came from Andrew Sarris, the doyen of American film critics. Sarris has generally been unsympathetic to Kubrick's work, as well as the avant-garde and anything resembling "ambiguous" narrative. In a review of the film, Sarris wrote that "*2001: A Space Odyssey* also confirms Kubrick's inability to tell a story on the screen with coherence and a consistent point of view."[19]

2001 is a key film for Kubrick in many ways, especially in its radical narrative experimentation. Additionally, the film again exemplified Kubrick's ability to tap into the most important issues of the time, something he had already done with *Dr. Strangelove*. Robert Kolker has commented on this aspect of the director's work:

> The films of his trilogy—*Dr. Strangelove, 2001: A Space Odyssey* (1968), *A Clockwork Orange* (1971)—were commercially successful and demonstrated an unerring ability to seize upon major cultural concerns and obsessions— the cold war, space travel, the ambiguities of violence—and represent them in images and narratives so powerful and appropriate that they became touchstones, reference points for these concerns: myths.[20]

2001 illustrated another aspect of Kubrick's talent that we now take for granted: his interest in technology. The film's exhilarating special effects, which Kubrick designed and conceived, remain a standard to which films are still compared. Current big-budget spectacular films may be technically more sophisticated, but they are by no means more aesthetically interesting or accomplished than *2001*. Michel Ciment has commented on Kubrick's interest in the mechanics of filmmaking as follows:

> Kubrick, more than any other contemporary film-maker, has immersed himself in the problems of art and technology. Like the medium's pioneers (Griffith, Murnau), and with a zeal comparable to theirs, he recognized that the intensification of realism on the screen was dependent on the development of technological artifice. His experiments with transparencies, models and other special effects for *2001*, with direct sound recording on lightweight microphones for *A Clockwork Orange* and with lighting for *Barry Lyndon* have all engendered technological improvements and accentuated the impression of reality. They can be compared with Griffith exhorting cameraman Billy Bitzer to improve the lighting of his films or Murnau forcing Karl Freund to invent a more mobile camera.[21]

John Alcott, cinematographer on several of the director's films has also discussed Kubrick's skill as a photographer: "He knows exactly what he wants. If he were not a director, he would probably be the greatest lighting cameraman in the world. On the set, he works at the camera and you can learn a lot from working with him."[22]

2001 also highlighted, as never before, Kubrick's conceptual talent. Alexander Walker has perceptively observed that . . .

> only a few directors possess a conceptual talent—that is, a talent to crystallize every film they make into a cinematic concept. It is a skill that goes far beyond the mere photographing of a script, however cinematic the script may be in itself. It transcends the need to find a good subject, an absorbing story, or an extraordinary premise to build on. Essentially, it is the talent to construct the form that will exhibit the maker's vision in an unexpected way, often a way that seems to have been the only possible one when the film is finally finished. It is this conceptual talent that strongly distinguishes Stanley Kubrick.[23]

2001 confirmed that Kubrick's films were always more than accomplished entertainments. It was now obvious that Kubrick was an artist very much interested in ideas. Alexander Walker has commented on Kubrick's wide-ranging interests, both in his films and in his every day life:

> An evening's conversation with him has covered such areas as optical perception in relation to man's survival; the phenomenon of phosphene; German coastal gun placements in Normandy; compromised safety margins in commercial flying; Dr. Goebbels' role as a pioneer film publicist; the Right's inability to produce dialecticians to match the Left's; the Legion of Decency's pressures during the making of *Lolita*; S.A.M.-3 missiles in the Arab-Israeli conflict; Irish politics and the possibility of similarities in the voice prints of demagogues; and, of course, chess.[24]

This intellectual curiosity has found its way into Kubrick's films, and, at their most speculative such as in *2001*, they are embedded with intricate meaning and formal elegance. *2001* represents Kubrick at his most ambitious and curious. The film constitutes the director's greatest meditation on the self and individual consciousness. It attempts to create an involving subjective experience that strains not only the limits of narrative cinema, but the audience's understanding of filmic subjectivity. In an unusually thoughtful analysis that first appeared in *Sight and Sound*, Don Daniels called *2001* ". . . a study of various capacities for consciousness, an attempt to suggest through spectacle the possibilities and limitations of the powers of Mind for perception, intellection and feeling.[25]

More than any other Kubrick film, *2001* attempts to create a nonverbal cinematic experience. Kubrick has stated that he thinks of the experience of watching a film as something akin to dreaming, and this idea is well illustrated in *2001*: "I think an audience watching a film or a play is in a state very similar to dreaming, and that the dramatic experience becomes a kind of controlled dream . . . the important point here is that the film communicates on a subconscious level, and the audience responds to the basic shape of the story on a subconscious level, as it responds to a dream."[26]

The nonverbal nature of *2001* is most apparent in the way it foregrounds the sense of sight (at the expense of language). The film's emphasis on the visual and the abandonment of traditional narrative is evident in the fact that its 141-minute running time contains little more than forty minutes of dialogue. As Kubrick stated: "Film operates on a level much closer to music and to painting than to the printed word, and, of course, movies present the opportunity to convey complex concepts and abstractions without the traditional reliance on words."[27] In a more theoretical vein, Annette Michelson situates this aspect of *2001* within a phenomenological reading: "Experience as vision ends in the exploration of seeing. The film's reflexive strategy assumes the eye as ultimate agent of consciousness, reminding us, as every phenomonological esthetic, from that of Ortega to that of Merleau-Ponty has, that art develops from the concern with 'things seen to that of seeing itself.'"[28]

Though the radical nature of Kubrick's accomplishment was not apparent to everyone, *2001*'s spiritual and metaphysical aspirations seemed to be precisely what attracted young audiences to the film. There has rarely been a film that seemed so perfectly attuned to its historical moment. The film would probably have been unthinkable ten years earlier or ten years later, but in 1968 all the elements seemed to converge in an ideal confluence of perfect timing and artful creation.

The cerebral nature of Kubrick's achievement, combined with an intensely involving cinematic experience, distinguished *2001* from most other recognizable "art" films of the period. But the nature of Kubrick's intellectual accomplishment is one of the most contentious aspects of Kubrick scholarship. P. L. Titterington, in discussing the intellectual nature of Kubrick's work, argues that

> Kubrick's search is for a language of film that will convey complex ideas directly and the cinema he is trying to create is very much a cinema of ideas. "Metaphysical" is an adjective that has often been used to describe his films, and justifiably. It captures something very important in the work—the philosophical nature of the ideas explored and the way they are presented. But in the area of style it suggests too "one-dimensional" an approach. It does not begin to do justice to the interplay Kubrick has been able to achieve between the simplistic naturalistic scene (the job interview in *The Shining*; Haywood Floyd's address to the moon station in *2001*) and the resonance such a scene takes on in relation to the deeper levels of the film.[29]

Related to the notion of the "metaphysical" described by Titterington is another quality central to Kubrick's complex, late work: the gap between the surface meaning of a scene and its deeper, subtextual meaning. The films' formal intricacies and complex organization contain rich layers of meaning, which may not always be apparent to casual viewers.

Despite Kubrick's intellectual aspirations, Robert Kolker has observed that it is in their emotional power that Kubrick's films will be judged. Kolker has observed that

> Kubrick is an ironist whose films are both controlled and open, inviting emotional more than intellectual engagement (even though they are intellectually more rigorous than the work of any other American filmmaker). They are considerably more declarative than are the films of Godard, stating more than they question. Even though they offer room to observe and draw conclusions while attacking the core ideological structures of the culture, the conclusions drawn are always the same. The viewer is invited to watch the spectacle of the characters losing and perhaps consider some ramifications of the loss, but little more. His powerful spectacles and intriguing, intricate formal structures open a cavern of mirrors which reflect either our own worst fears of ourselves or our most passive inclinations to remain as we are.[30]

Part of the problem academics have had in dealing with Kubrick is related to the question of auteurism, and its uncomfortable place within current film studies practice. In his original essay for this collection, Dennis Bingham has perceptively noted that

> Kubrick's films lent themselves perfectly to auteurist sensibilities and analysis, with one exception. The auteur himself was nowhere to be found in films which appeared to have been handed down from on high, with interior meaning buried so far beneath the spectacular surfaces (in *2001* and *Barry Lyndon* in particular) as to keep the essentially New Critical method of auteur analysis busy indefinitely. Kubrick's films announce themselves as creations, but without the palpable presence of a creator. This, I feel, is at the heart of the confused critical receptions of his films beginning with *2001*.

Bingham goes on to argue that: "Kubrick is a problematic figure for academics, only partly because of the discredited auteurist baggage his reputation has carried. The film studies reception shows the problems the new academic profession has had reconciling what Fredric Jameson calls 'classical modernist' auteurism with post-structuralist approaches that find the auteur irrelevant to concerns of ideology and signification."

2001 was to have been followed by a film about Napoleon that has thus far not been made. Instead, Kubrick followed up his science-fiction epic with his 1971 adaptation of Anthony Burgess' novel, *A Clockwork Orange*, one of his most brilliant if controversial films. The exaggerated, stylized decor and experiments with first-person point of view contribute to the film's highly determined, theatrically distanced stylistic system.

Although *A Clockwork Orange* received a high degree of praise and numerous awards, it was unfortunately caught in the debate about on-screen violence raging at the time. Most critics who came to the defense of the film understood that its stylized presentation formed an argument about violence, but some reviewers claimed that the presentation of Alex (Malcolm McDowell) was too sympathetic for the argument to be effective. In the film's defense, Kubrick has compared Alex to literary characters such as Shakespeare's Richard III: "Alex, like Richard, is a character whom you should dislike and fear, and yet you find yourself drawn very quickly into his world and find yourself seeing things through his eyes."[31] It is true that Alex is presented with a degree of charm absent in the film's other characters, but this kind of negative character functioning is not unusual in Kubrick's work. Alex is not presented with complete sympathy, of course, but the film does argue that there is something admirable in the way the character channels his creativity. Kubrick has stated that "what we respond to subconsciously is Alex's guiltless sense of freedom to kill and rape, and to be our savage natural selves, and it is in this glimpse of the true nature of man that the power of the story derives."[32] In the same interview, Kubrick claimed that

> one of the most dangerous fallacies which has influenced a great deal of political and philosophical thinking is that man is essentially good, and that it is society which makes him bad . . . Rousseau transferred original sin from man to society, and this view has importantly contributed to what I believe has become a crucially incorrect premise on which to base moral and political philosophy.[33]

A Clockwork Orange, though caught up in controversy, earned generally positive reviews, as well as the approval of Anthony Burgess, who called it "very much a Kubrick movie, technically brilliant, poetic, mind-opening."[34] Despite some major differences between novel and film, Burgess concurred that the film communicated much the same moral point as his novel: "What my, and Kubrick's, parable tries to state is that it is preferable to have a world of violence undertaken in full awareness—violence chosen as an act of will—than a world conditioned to be good or harmless."[35]

Kubrick followed the critical and commercial success of *A Clockwork Orange* with his most ambitious film to date, *Barry Lyndon* (1975). An historical epic set in the eighteenth century, it is also one of his most personal films. True to form, the film divided critics once again, with the most negative reviewers arguing that the film was visually stunning but "undramatic," or more disparagingly, something akin to "a three-hour slide show." Certainly the film was slowly paced, detached, and painterly. But the de-dramatized presentation was a crucial aspect of the film's ambition. Once again, the complex stylistic system of *Barry Lyndon* went unappreciated by many of the same critics who were perfectly capable of appreciating the art cinema of Bresson or Antonioni.

Still, there were many who did appreciate Kubrick's daring study of human weakness. Michael Dempsey, writing in *Film Quarterly*, claims "*Barry Lyndon* is not drama or a character study or even a satire on the abundant human corruption which it portrays. It is, like Ozu's films though in a different way, a meditation on the transience of life."[36] Despite the film's surface beauty, the characters are filled with pettiness and human failings. The painterly world of *Barry Lyndon* is revealed to be shallow and ephemeral. The seemingly rational, ordered universe masks a chaotic, cruel world.

Kubrick continued his experiments with visual style (especially in his use of the zoom lens), characterization, and voice-over commentary. The film relies on complex spatial strategies of camera movement, slow zooms, long takes, camera position, long shots, rhythmical editing, and character placement within the frame for much of its impact. The framing devices, the precise use of the zoom, and the careful camera movements call attention to the spatial and temporal rigidity and orderliness of this world. The film's characters seem trapped within the two-dimensional space of the image.

Barry Lyndon contains the most sympathetic portrayal of character in all Kubrick's work. There is a depth of feeling for the flawed but noble Barry (Ryan O'Neal) that contrasts markedly with the unemotional style of the film. It is a remarkable accomplishment that Kubrick achieves this high degree of character sympathy within one of the most stylized and distanced presentations of any of his films.

Barry Lyndon's view of the eighteenth century, beneath the surface beauty of the image, is ultimately a negative one. The film paints a portrait of a society that values wealth, position, marriages of convenience, philosophy, art, music, fine clothes, grand architecture, and good breeding. But while achieving what many consider an apogee of civilization, this society has lost its energy, passion, and intensity. It has been aestheticized into numbness and atrophy. The film seems to argue that it matters little what an era may accomplish if in the process we lose such essential components of humanity as emotion and free will.

Barry Lyndon is Kubrick's most profound statement on art and human relationships. It is his most fully rounded work. As much as it is about the eighteenth century, it is also about contemporary society. It offers the director's most sustained analysis of male/female relationships, aesthetics, morality, and social institutions. It also represents Kubrick's most focused attempt at creating a sympathetic character.

One of the most striking features of Kubrick's next film, a screen adaptation of Stephen King's *The Shining* (1980), is its visual style. This is achieved in part by the innovative use of Steadicam photography, which facilitates the extensive choreography of character and camera movement. The film may be an instance of an innovative technological development determining a film's style. What is also of interest in the film is the relatively objective way many subjective encounters are presented—the film is a horror tale with many ghostly encounters. The line between objective reality and the subjective, interior life of the characters becomes blurred. *The Shining* raises some of the most intriguing questions of character subjectivity in Kubrick's work. It is one of the director's most open filmic texts and offers the spectator an almost endless array of interpretive possibilities.

The Shining is also notable because it features a wildly inventive and emotionally charged performance by Jack Nicholson in the leading role. The performance is striking for its physicality and expressiveness. Nicholson's performance is wild and extreme, verging on the hysterical. At times, the actor gives the impression of being out of control. The performance relies heavily on the physical and the comic for its effect. It is not a very "respectable" performance and may strike some as overbearing, vulgar, and just plain "too much." In fact, it is precisely these risky, over-the-edge qualities that make the performance and the film so invigorating.

Full Metal Jacket (1987), Kubrick's long-awaited follow-up to *The Shining*, is an emotionally distanced, ironic, and unsentimental work. As in Kubrick's earlier forays into the combat-film genre, it is concerned with the irrationality of war. Despite the film's attention to accurate details of presentation, it offers a somewhat abstracted view of war. Although it concentrates specifically on the Vietnam experience, the film's primary concern is to examine aspects of human behavior that any war or conflict might generate.

Full Metal Jacket contains a meticulously detailed recreation of war-ravaged Vietnam. An unusual aspect of the film's look creates a locale that seems like a realistic portrayal of Vietnam, but at the same time, feels unreal. An abandoned concrete city (Beckton-on-Thames) and gasworks were demolished to lend verisimilitude to the film. Beyond this accuracy, the film achieves a kind of hyperrealism because of an almost over-aestheticism in the decor and production design. The inferno of war has never seemed at once so accurate and yet so removed and distant.

The essays collected in this volume are comprised of a wide range of material that illustrates how Kubrick's work appeals to highly disparate audiences. The essays span the last thirty-five years of Kubrick scholarship and are arranged film by film in chronological order. Because this is the first anthology devoted solely to Kubrick, it was a challenge to decide what essays to include and what to exclude from the collection.

Some of the most interesting articles in the Kubrick bibliography have been in the form of interviews, both with the director and with his many collaborators. Unfortunately, it was not possible to reprint any of the Kubrick interviews found in Michel Ciment's *Kubrick*, all of which were carefully edited and approved by the director before publication in 1982. The reader is directed to Ciment's book for invaluable interviews with Kubrick on *A Clockwork Orange*, *Barry Lyndon*, and *The Shining*. The flavor of Kubrick's insights, nonetheless, can be found in the *Playboy* interview, as well as some of the other statements by the director reprinted in this collection. Joseph Gelmis' interview, for example, gives some intriguing glimpses into Kubrick's working methods.

Because Kubrick is so concerned with the mechanics of filmmaking, his work is of particular interest to those working in the film industry, as well as students making films. With this in mind, I have included several pieces that originally appeared in *American Cinematographer*. Those articles include interviews with cinematographer John Alcott on the making of *Barry Lyndon* and *The Shining*, and an article by Garret Brown, the developer of the Steadicam, on the use of this equipment in *The Shining*. I have also included two articles on the special effects of *2001*, which are so crucial to the overall aesthetic of that film. This kind of empirical research is important to include in a scholarly collection because the field of film studies has tended to cut itself off from the realities of filmmaking. I have included these more technical articles in an effort to bridge the gap that I believe exists between those engaged in analyzing films and those who make them.

Some of the essays oriented towards close analysis include my article on *The Killing* and *Lolita*. I felt it important to include an examination of the intricacies of narrative organization found in Kubrick's work, especially since the Kubrick bibliography has tended in the past to favor thematic over stylistic analysis. This essay has been adapted from my recent book, *Stanley Kubrick: A Narrative and Stylistic Analysis*. Along these lines, Dana Polan's reading of *Killer's Kiss* illustrates that Kubrick's later work is strongly linked stylistically and thematically to his early films. Dennis Bingham's article on *The Shining* examines some of the problems associated with the reception of Kubrick's films, especially by the academic community.

Two of the best Kubrick scholars are represented by extracts from their books. From Thomas Allen Nelson's *Kubrick: Inside A Film Artist's Maze*, I have excerpted an essay on *Paths of Glory*. Nelson argues that Kubrick's formal mastery of the medium develops an "ironic structure of oppositions and parallels between the chateau and the trenches, through which Kubrick will turn a system of clearly defined conflicts into a maze of paradoxical associations."[38] Robert Kolker's fine book *A Cinema of Loneliness*, devoted to five directors including Kubrick, is represented by extracts on *Dr. Strangelove* and *2001*.

Some of the best writing on Kubrick over the years has appeared in periodicals, some that specialize in film and others that do not. An article on *A Clockwork Orange* by Robert Hughes that first appeared in *Time*, explores the film in terms of its cultural context. Hughes argues that "no movie in the last decade (perhaps in the history of film) has made such exquisitely chilling predictions about the future role of cultural artifacts— paintings, buildings, sculpture, music—in society, or extrapolated them from so undeceived a view of our present culture."[39] Robert Brustein's review of *Dr. Strangelove* from *The New York Review of Books* is another example of a critic writing for a decidedly non-film audience. I have also included an article by Anthony Burgess that offers an interesting response to a Kubrick film from the perspective of one who supplied the original source material. This article originally appeared in *Rolling Stone*, a magazine not known for incisive film analysis but, nevertheless, important to popular culture. The interview with Kubrick on *Full Metal Jacket* is also reprinted from this magazine. It is a mark of the director's continuing appeal to young audiences that there has always been a high degree of interest in Kubrick's work in such venues. Such topical responses offer a different perspective from the more academically-oriented view generally found within film studies.

Among the articles included in this collection are Stephen Mamber's piece on *A Clockwork Orange*, which originally appeared in *Cinema* (USA). Mamber explores one of the most important aspects of Kubrick's sensibility: parody, and more generally, the ironic mode. Hans Feldmann's sympathetic reading of *2001*, *A Clockwork Orange*, and *Barry Lyndon*, which first appeared in *Film Quarterly*, is also included in this collection. Feldmann refers to the films as "a trilogy on the moral and psychological nature of Western man and on the destiny of his civilization."[40] Interestingly, Feldmann reads the three films as optimistic despite their perceived negative view of the world: "Yet for all the bleakness the critics have argued informs Kubrick's view of man, for all his negativism and pessimism, Kubrick is nevertheless struggling to strike an affirmative note."[41] He concludes that "Stanley Kubrick is a critic of his age, one of its interpreters and one of its artists."[42]

Alan Spiegel's reading of *Barry Lyndon* explores some of the complexities of the film and how it "constructs a shape that is a model of unity, symmetry, and abstract formal relationship."[43] He places the film in the context of some other unconventional American films of the 1970s. Mark Crispin Miller, in an article entitled "Kubrick's Anti-Reading of *The Luck of Barry Lyndon*," compares Kubrick's film with Thackeray's novel and offers some observations on the voice-over commentary. Miller argues that the commentary is an unreliable narration that "speaks for the audience within the film, and to the audience in front of the film, bridging the gap between the most superficial viewers in each."[44]

Kubrick's most recent film, *Full Metal Jacket*, is examined from somewhat different perspectives by two writers. Thomas Doherty places the film firmly within the combat-film genre. He examines some of the more unique aspects of the film such as its assaultive language, which he calls "a lyric bombardment of raw Marine obscenity—homophobic, misogynistic, sado-masochistic, racist, and exuberantly poetic."[45] Like Feldmann, Doherty sees in Kubrick's film an optimistic note behind the cynical surface: "*Full Metal Jacket* is far more complex and, yes, affirmative than

Hasford's bitter novel."[46] On the other hand, Michael Pursell finds Kubrick's Vietnam film "optimistic about nothing,"[47] and "uncompromisingly avoids the characters, situations and techniques of the genre in order to cut through the role-playing and the clichés."[48]

Stanley Kubrick has created some of the most powerful cinematic artworks in contemporary cinema. The director is intensely concerned with finding the appropriate cinematic shape for his artistic and human concerns. He has fashioned consistent and strongly recognizable elements as part of his style. Viewers always know when they are watching a Kubrick film. Many filmic elements contribute to the notion of a "Kubrickian" world view.

An understanding of Kubrick's late work demands an appreciation of ironic, distanced, and reflexive filmmaking: yet, despite this, his films continue to be popular. With the notable exception of *Barry Lyndon*, which proved a commercial disappointment, Kubrick has been able to reconcile his position as an artist of complex *and* popular work. Perhaps that is what makes him so unique and worthy of close attention.

Kubrick's films are made with great artistry and craftsmanship, and the director is profoundly committed to the uniqueness of the film medium. His films challenge our understanding of the world and sometimes force us to think in ways we would prefer not to. If we are, at times, made uncomfortable when we view a Kubrick film, we are just as often exhilarated by the experience. My hope is that this collection will illuminate Kubrick's impressive body of work and contribute to a better understanding of his accomplishment. I also hope the reader will want to rediscover the films, since without them, there would be no need for such an anthology.

Mario Falsetto
Concordia University, Montreal

Notes

1. P. L. Titterington, "Kubrick and *The Shining*," *Sight and Sound* (Spring 1981): 121.
2. Michel Ciment, *Kubrick*, trans. Gilbert Adair (London: Collins, 1983): 41.
3. *Ibid.*, 38.
4. *Ibid.*, 38.
5. Tim Cahill, "The Rolling Stone Interview: Stanley Kubrick," *Rolling Stone*, 27 August 1987, 36, 182.
6. Joseph Gelmis, "Stanley Kubrick" in *The Film Director as Superstar* (Garden City, New York: Doubleday, 1970): 315.
7. Philip Strick and Penelope Houston, "Interview with Stanley Kubrick," *Sight and Sound* (Spring 1972): 65.
8. "Twenty-Nine and Running: The Director with Hollywood by the Horns . . . Dissects the Movies," *Newsweek*, 2 December 1957, 96.
9. Gavin Lambert, "*Paths of Glory*," *Sight and Sound* (Winter 1958): 144.
10. Stanley Kauffmann, "It Needn't be Bad if it's Big," *The New Republic*, 14 November 1960, 19.

11. Raymond Durgnat, *"Lolita," Films and Filming* (November 1962): 35.

12. Vladimir Nabokov, Forward to *Lolita: A Screenplay* (New York: McGraw-Hill, 1974), X11-X111.

13. Stanley Kubrick, "How I Learned to Stop Worrying and Love the Cinema," *Films and Filming* 9, no. 9 (June 1963): 12.

14. Bryan Forbes, *Films and Filming* 10, no. 5 (February 1964): 26.

15. Stanley Kauffmann, *The New Republic*, 1 February 1964, 26.

16. Charles Maland, *"Dr. Strangelove* (1964): Nightmare Comedy and the Ideology of Liberal Consensus," *American Quarterly* (Winter 1979): 715-716.

17. Robert Brustein, "Out of this World," *The New York Review of Books*, 6 February 1964, 4.

18. As if to make amends for some of the initial hostile reviews, *2001* was recently named to the 1992 *Sight and Sound* poll as one of the ten best films of all time.

19. Andrew Sarris, *The American Cinema: Directors and Directions 1929-1968* (New York: E. P. Dutton, 1968): 196.

20. Robert Philip Kolker, *A Cinema of Loneliness*, 2nd ed. (New York: Oxford University Press, 1988): 79.

21. Ciment, 75.

22. *Ibid.*, 213.

23. Alexander Walker, *Stanley Kubrick Directs*, expanded edition (New York: Harcourt Brace Jovanovich, 1972), 7.

24. *Ibid.*, 10.

25. Don Daniels, "A Skeleton Key to *2001*," *Sight and Sound*, (Winter 1970–71): 29.

26. Bernard Weinraub, "Kubrick Tells What Makes *Clockwork* Tick," *New York Times*, 4 January 1972, 26.

27. Gelmis, 302.

28. Annette Michelson, "Bodies in Space: Film as Carnal Knowledge," *Artforum* (February 1969): 60.

29. Titterington, 121.

30. Kolker, 157-158.

31. Penelope Houston, "Kubrick Country," *Saturday Review*, 25 December 1971, 42.

32. Weinraub, 26.

33. *Ibid.*

34. Anthony Burgess, *The Listener*, 17 February 1972, 197.

35. *Ibid.*, 198.

36. Michael Dempsey, *"Barry Lyndon," Film Quarterly* 30, no. 1 (Fall 1976): 49.

37. Ciment, 154.

38. Thomas Allen Nelson, *Kubrick: Inside A Film Artist's Maze* (Bloomington, Indiana: Indiana University Press, 1982), 41.

39. Robert Hughes, "The Decor of Tomorrow's Hell," *Time*, 27 December 1971, 59.

40. Hans Feldmann, "Kubrick and His Discontents," *Film Quarterly* 30, no. 1 (Fall 1976): 12.

41. *Ibid.*, 13.

42. *Ibid.*, 19.

43. Alan Spiegel, "Kubrick's *Barry Lyndon*," *Salmagundi* (Fall 1977): 201.

44. Mark Crispin Miller, "Kubrick's Anti-Reading of *The Luck of Barry Lyndon*," *Modern Language Notes* 91 (1976): 1372.

45. Thomas Doherty, "Full Metal Genre: Stanley Kubrick's Vietnam Combat Movie," *Film Quarterly* 42, no. 2 (1988-89): 26.

46. *Ibid.*, 30.

47. Michael Pursell, *"Full Metal Jacket*: The Unravelling of Patriarchy," *Literature/Film Quarterly* 16, no. 4 (1988): 236.

48. *Ibid.*, 222.

INTERVIEWS

Kubrick on Kubrick

Director's Notes: Stanley Kubrick Movie Maker

STANLEY KUBRICK

Maybe the reason why people seem to find it harder to take unhappy endings in movies than in plays or novels is that a good movie engages you so heavily that you find an unhappy ending almost unbearable. But it depends on the story, because there are ways for the director to trick the audience into expecting a happy ending and there are ways of very subtly letting the audience be aware of the fact that the character is hopelessly doomed and there is not going to be a happy ending.

In a criminal film, it is almost like a bullfight: it has a ritual and a pattern which lays down that the criminal is not going to make it, so that, while you can suspend your knowledge of this for a while, sitting way back of your mind this little awareness knows and prepares you for the fact that he is not going to succeed. That type of ending is easier to accept.

One thing that has always disturbed me a little is that the ending often introduces a false note. This applies particularly if it is a story that doesn't pound away on a single point, such as whether the time-bomb will explode in the suitcase. When you deal with characters and a sense of life, most endings that appear to be endings are false, and possibly that is what disturbs the audience: they may sense the gratuitousness of the unhappy ending.

On the other hand, if you end a story with somebody achieving his aim it always seems to me to have a kind of incompleteness about it because

Reprinted from *The Observer*, 4 December 1960, by permission. Copyright © 1960 *The Observer*.

that almost seems to be the beginning of another story. One of the things I like most about John Ford is the anticlimax endings—anticlimax upon anticlimax and you just get a feeling that you are seeing life and you accept the thing.

It is sometimes supposed that the way to make pictures entirely as one wants to, without having to think about the box-office, is to dispense with stars in order to make them on a low budget. In fact, the cost of a picture usually has little to do with how much the actors get paid. It has to do with the number of days you take to shoot it, and you can't make a film as well as it can be made without having a sufficient length of time to make it.

There are certain stories in which you can somehow hit everything on the nose quickly and get the film shot in three weeks. But it is not the way to approach something of which you want to realise the full potential. So there often is nothing gained by doing without stars and aiming the film at the art houses. Only by using stars and getting the film on the circuits can you buy the time needed to do it justice.

I've often heard it asked whether it doesn't affect the reality and the artistic quality of a picture not to make it in actual locations. Personally I have found that working out of doors or working in real locations is a very distracting experience and doesn't have the almost classical simplicity of a film studio where everything is inky darkness and the lights are coming from an expected place and it is quiet and you can achieve concentration without worrying that there are 500 people standing behind a police line halfway down the block, or about a million other distractions.

I think that much too much has been made of making films on location. It does help when the atmosphere, circumstances and locale are the chief thing supposed to come across in a scene. For a psychological story, where the characters and their inner emotions and feelings are the key thing, I think that a studio is the best place. Working on a set provides the actor with much better concentration and ability to use his full resources.

When "Spartacus" was being made, I discussed this point with Olivier and Ustinov and they both said that they felt that their powers were just drifting off into space when they were working out of doors. Their minds weren't sharp and their concentration seemed to evaporate. They preferred that kind of focusing-in that happens in a studio with the lights pointing at them and the sets around them. Whereas outside everything fades away, inside there is a kind of inner focusing of psychical energy.

The important thing in films is not so much to make successes as not to make failures, because each failure limits your future opportunities to make the films you want to make.

People nowadays seem to have a great deal of difficulty deciding whether a character in a film is good or bad—especially the people who are making the film. It seems as if first they deal out twenty-five cents' worth of good and then twenty-five cents' worth of bad and at the very end of the story you have a perfect balance.

I think it essential if a man is good to know where he is bad and to show it, or if he is strong, to decide what the moments are in the story where he is weak and to show it. And I think that you must never try to *explain* how he got the way he is or why he did what he did.

I have no fixed ideas about wanting to make films in particular categories—Westerns, war films and so on. I know I would like to make a film that gave a feeling of the times—a contemporary story that really gave a feeling of the times, psychologically, sexually, politically, personally. I would like to make that more than anything else. And it's probably going to be the hardest film to make.

Interview With Stanley Kubrick

JOSEPH GELMIS

"A director is a kind of idea and taste machine; a movie is a series of creative and technical decisions, and it's the director's job to make the right decisions as frequently as possible."

The most controversial film of 1968 was Stanley Kubrick's *2001: A Space Odyssey.* It started out as a $6,000,000 science fiction movie and escalated into a $10,500,000 underground film. It polarized critical and public opinion. Most of its young admirers considered it a prophetic masterpiece. Its detractors praised the special effects but found it confusing and pretentious as drama.

Despite Kubrick's own ready interpretation of the action, the ending of *2001* was confusing to some people. The final scenes in the alien "zoo" or heaven and the metamorphosis of the astronaut into a star baby remained for many an enigmatic, purely emotional, nonverbal experience. Understanding became a function of the emotions, rather than one's reasoning powers.

Less than half the film had dialogue. It was a reorganization of the traditional dramatic structure. Process became more important than plot. The tedium was the message. It was a film not about space travel; it was space travel. "The truth of a thing is in the feel of it, not the think of it," Kubrick asserted.

Kubrick traces some of his fascination with the fluid camera back to Max Ophuls. His oeuvre, with the single exception of the optimistic transfiguration in *2001*, is a bleak skepticism and fatalism.

2001 was Kubrick's first experiment with restructuring the conventions of the three-act drama. It's quite possible it started out to be something entirely different. The book based on the original screenplay by Arthur C. Clarke and Kubrick is literal, verbal, explicit. The film, in its early stages, had a narrator's voice. It was cut bit by bit and then eliminated completely, by virtue of which *2001* evolved as a nonverbal experience.

In his next film, *Napoleon*, Kubrick says he plans to return to the use of a narrator and perhaps even animation or charts to illustrate and explain the battle tactics and campaigns. Kubrick's personal interest in the aesthetics of a well-staged campaign goes back to his days as a young chess hustler in Greenwich Village.

Born July 1928 in the Bronx, Kubrick was introduced to still photography as a hobby by his father, who was a physician. He achieved a certain youthful prominence as his class photographer at Taft High School. Later, with a sixty-eight average, he was unable to compete with returning GIs for a place in college. So, "out of pity," he recalls, *Look* magazine hired him as a photographer.

Kubrick's early training in movies was with two documentaries. At twenty-five, he made his first feature film, the 35-mm *Fear and Desire*, for $9000—plus another $30,000 because he didn't know what he was doing with the soundtrack. He didn't make any money on his first four feature films. He has never earned a penny on *The Killing* and *Paths of Glory*, which some of his early fans still consider his best films.

The only film he disclaims is *Spartacus*. He says he worked on it as just a hired hand. Every other film he's directed he has made to suit himself, within prescribed bounds of existing community standards. He wishes *Lolita* had been more erotic. The lag time between conception and completion of his films is now up to an average of three years. In part, this is the result of his wish to handle every artistic and business function himself.

To concentrate all control in his own hands, Kubrick produces as well as directs his films. He originates, writes, researches, directs, edits, and even guides the publicity campaigns for his films. Though he gets his financing from the major studios, he is as independent as he was when he was raising his money from his father and uncle.

The following interview is the outcome of meetings that took place in 1968 in New York and London and of correspondence that continued through 1969. Kubrick lives near London. His third wife is Suzanne Christiane Harlan, a German actress who appeared briefly at the end of *Paths of Glory*.

GELMIS: 2001 *took about three years to make—six months of preparation, four and a half months of working with the actors, and a year and a half of shooting special effects. How much time will* Napoleon *take out of your life?*

KUBRICK: Considerably less. We hope to begin the actual production work by the winter of 1969, and the exterior shooting—battles, location shots, etc.—should be completed within two or three months. After that, the studio work shouldn't take more than another three or four months.

G: *Where would the exteriors be shot? Actual sites?*

K: I still haven't made a final decision, although there are several promising possibilities. Unfortunately, there are very, very few actual Napoleonic battlefields where we could still shoot; the land

itself has either been taken over by industrial and urban development, preempted by historical trusts, or is so ringed by modern
buildings that all kinds of anachronisms would present themselves—like a Hussars' charge with a Fiat plant in the background.
We're now in the process of deciding the best places to shoot, and
where it would be most feasible to obtain the troops we need for
battle scenes. We intend to use a maximum of forty thousand
infantry and ten thousand cavalry for the big battles, which means
that we have to find a country which will hire out its own armed
forces to us—you can just imagine the cost of fifty thousand extras
over an extended period of time. Once we find a receptive environment, there are still great logistic problems—for example, a
battle site would have to be contiguous to a city or town or barracks area where the troops we'd use are already bivouacked. Let's
say we're working with forty thousand infantry—if we could get
forty men into a truck, it would still require a thousand trucks to
move them around. So in addition to finding the proper terrain, it
has to be within marching distance of military barracks.

G: *Aside from the Russian* War and Peace, *where they reportedly
used sixty thousand of their own troops, has there ever been a
film that used forty thousand men from somebody else's army?*

K: I would doubt it.

G: *Then how do you expect to persuade another government to give
you as many as forty thousand soldiers?*

K: One has to be an optimist about these things. If it turned out to be
impossible I'd obviously have no other choice than to make do
with a lesser number of men, but this would only be as a last
resort. I wouldn't want to fake it with fewer troops because
Napoleonic battles were out in the open, a vast tableau where the
formations moved in an almost choreographic fashion. I want to
capture this reality on film, and to do so it's necessary to re-create
all the conditions of the battle with painstaking accuracy.

G: *How many men did you use in the trench battle of* Paths of
Glory?

K: That was another story entirely. We employed approximately eight
hundred men, all German police—at that time the German police
received three years of military training, and were as good as regular soldiers for our purposes. We shot the film at Geiselgesteig
Studios in Munich, and both the battle site and the château were
within thirty-five to forty minutes of the studio.

G: *If you can't use the actual battle sites, how will you approximate
the terrain on the sites you do choose?*

K: There are a number of ways this can be done and it's quite important to the accuracy of the film, since terrain is the decisive factor
in the flow and outcome of a Napoleonic battle. We've researched

all the battle sites exhaustively from paintings and sketches, and we're now in a position to approximate the terrain. And from a purely schematic point of view, Napoleonic battles are so beautiful, like vast lethal ballets, that it's worth making every effort to explain the configuration of forces to the audience. And it's not really as difficult as it at first appears.

G: *How do you mean "explain"? With a narrator, or charts?*

K: With a narrative voice-over at times, with animated maps and, most importantly, through the actual photography of the battles themselves. Let's say you want to explain that at the battle of Austerlitz the Austro-Russian forces attempted to cut Napoleon off from Vienna, and then extended the idea to a double envelopment and Napoleon countered by striking at their center and cutting their forces in half—well, this is not difficult to show by photography, maps and narration. I think it's extremely important to communicate the essence of these battles to the viewer, because they all have an aesthetic brilliance that doesn't require a military mind to appreciate. There's an aesthetic involved; it's almost like a great piece of music, or the purity of a mathematical formula. It's this quality I want to bring across, as well as the sordid reality of battle. You know, there's a weird disparity between the sheer visual and organizational beauty of the historical battles sufficiently far in the past, and their human consequences. It's rather like watching two golden eagles soaring through the sky from a distance; they may be tearing a dove to pieces, but if you are far enough away the scene is still beautiful.

G: *Why are you making a movie about Napoleon?*

K: That's a question it would really take this entire interview to answer. To begin with, he fascinates me. His life has been described as an epic poem of action. His sex life was worthy of Arthur Schnitzler. He was one of those rare men who move history and mold the destiny of their own times and of generations to come—in a very concrete sense, our own world is the result of Napoleon, just as the political and geographic map of postwar Europe is the result of World War Two. And, of course, there has never been a good or accurate movie about him. Also, I find that all the issues with which it concerns itself are oddly contemporary—the responsibilities and abuses of power, the dynamics of social revolution, the relationship of the individual to the state, war, militarism, etc., so this will not be just a dusty historic pageant but a film about the basic questions of our own times, as well as Napoleon's. But even apart from those aspects of the story, the sheer drama and force of Napoleon's life is a fantastic subject for a film biography. Forgetting everything else and just taking Napoleon's romantic involvement with Josephine, for example, here you have one of the great obsessional passions of all time.

G: *How long a film biography are you contemplating?*

K: It's obviously a huge story to film, since we're not just taking one segment of Napoleon's life, military or personal, but are attempting to encompass all the major events of his career. I haven't set down any rigid guidelines on length; I believe that if you have a truly interesting film it doesn't matter how long it is—providing, of course, you don't run on to such extremes that you numb the attention span of your audience. The longest film that has given consistent enjoyment to generations of viewers is *Gone With the Wind*, which would indicate that if a film is sufficiently interesting people will watch it for three hours and forty minutes. But in actual fact, the Napoleon film will probably be shorter.

G: *What kind of research do you have going on right now?*

K: The first step has been to read everything I could get my hands on about Napoleon, and totally immerse myself in his life. I guess I must have gone through several hundred books on the subject, from contemporary nineteenth-century English and French accounts to modern biographies. I've ransacked all these books for research material and broken it down into categories on everything from his food tastes to the weather on the day of a specific battle, and cross-indexed all the data in a comprehensive research file. In addition to my own reading, I've worked out a consultant arrangement with Professor Felix Markham of Oxford, a history don who has spent the past thirty-five years of his life studying Napoleon and is considered one of the world's leading Napoleonic experts. He's available to answer any questions that derive from my own reading or outside of it. We're also in the process of creating prototypes of vehicles, weapons, and costumes of the period which will subsequently be mass-produced, all copied from paintings and written descriptions of the time and accurate in every detail. We already have twenty people working full time on the preparatory stage of the film.

G: *What movies on Napoleon have you gone back to see?*

K: I've tried to see every film that was ever made on the subject, and I've got to say that I don't find any of them particularly impressive. I recently saw Abel Gance's movie, which has built up a reputation among film buffs over the years, and I found it really terrible. Technically he was ahead of his time and he introduced inventive new film techniques—in fact Eisenstein credited him with stimulating his initial interest in montage—but as far as story and performance goes it's a very crude picture.

G: *What did you think about the Russian* War and Peace?

K: It was a cut above the others, and did have some very good scenes, but I can't say I was overly impressed. There's one in particular I admired, where the Tsar entered a ballroom and everyone scurried in his wake to see what he was doing and then rushed out of his way when he returned. That seemed to me to capture the reality of such a situation. Of course, Tolstoy's view of Napoleon is so far removed from that of any objective historian's that I really can't fault the director for the way he was portrayed. It was a disappointing film, and doubly so because it had the potential to be otherwise.

G: *Can you imagine yourself going down with just a cameraman and sound man and half a dozen people and shooting a film?*

K: Sure I can. In fact, any contemporary story is best done just that way. The only time you need vast amounts of money and a huge crew is when you require complex special effects, as in *2001*, or big battle or crowd scenes, as in the Napoleon film. But if you're just dealing with a story set in modern times, then you could do it very easily with both limited funds and a limited crew.

G: *In your own case,* Lolita *was set in America, and yet you shot it on an English sound stage. Couldn't that film have been shot in this way, with just a handful of people on location?*

K: Yes, it could certainly have been shot on location, although you'd still have needed more than a handful of people to do it.

G: *Would you have done it that way if you were making the film now?*

K: I would have done it at the time if the money to film had been available in America. But as it turned out the only funds I could raise for the film had to be spent in England. There's been such a revolution in Hollywood's treatment of sex over just the past few years that it's easy to forget that when I became interested in *Lolita* a lot of people felt that such a film couldn't be made—or at least couldn't be shown. As it turned out, we didn't have any problems, but there was a lot of fear and trembling. And filming in England we obviously had no choice but to rely mainly on studio shooting.

G: *Obviously* Napoleon *wouldn't permit you to shoot with a small crew and flexible conditions on location. But in the foreseeable future do you see yourself shedding the shell of the studio superstructure and working simply again?*

K: Yes, if I could find a contemporary story susceptible to such an approach which I liked enough to do. But I would certainly enjoy filming primarily on location. If you have the right story, it's a waste of time and energy to re-create conditions in a studio which exist outside. And if you make sensible arrangements, there are no technical difficulties about location shooting. Sound, which once presented problems, really doesn't anymore, since with skirt mikes you get a favorable voice-to-noise ratio. And in any case, background noise just adds to the verisimilitude of the scene. It's only when you're doing a period film that causes difficulties; in *Napoleon*, for example, I'd hardly want a jet to fly overhead in the middle of the battle of Jena.

G: *Your last film was about the twenty-first century. Your next film is about the nineteenth century. Do you think it's significant that you aren't very interested or satisfied with contemporary stories or themes of twentieth-century life?*

K: It's not a question of my own satisfaction or lack of it, but of the basic purpose of a film, which I believe is one of illumination, of showing the viewer something he can't see any other way. And I think at times this can be best accomplished by staying away from his own immediate environment. This is particularly true when you're dealing in a primarily visual experience, and telling a story through the eyes. You don't find reality only in your own back-yard, you know—in fact, sometimes that's the last place you find it. Another asset about dealing with themes that are either futuris-tic or historic is that it enables you to make a statement with which you're not personally blinded; it removes the environmen-tal blinkers, in a sense, and gives you a deeper and more objective perspective.

G: *In your last genuinely contemporary film,* Lolita, *you were frus-trated in your efforts to make the movie as erotic as the novel, and there was some criticism that the girl was too old to play the nymphet of the novel.*

K: She was actually just the right age. Lolita was twelve and a half in the book; Sue Lyon was thirteen. I think some people had a men-tal picture of a nine-year-old. I would fault myself in one area of the film, however; because of all the pressure over the Production Code and the Catholic Legion of Decency at the time, I believe I didn't sufficiently dramatize the erotic aspect of Humbert's rela-tionship with Lolita, and because his sexual obsession was only barely hinted at, many people guessed too quickly that Humbert was in love with Lolita. Whereas in the novel this comes as a dis-covery at the end, when she is no longer a nymphet but a dowdy, pregnant suburban housewife; and it's this encounter, and his sudden realization of his love, that is one of the most poignant elements of the story. If I could do the film over again, I would have stressed the erotic component of their relationship with the same weight Nabokov did. But that is the only major area where I believe the film is susceptible to valid criticism.

G: *At what point did you decide to structure the film so that Humbert is telling the story to the man he's going to shoot?*

K: I discussed this approach with Nabokov at the very outset, and he liked it. One of the basic problems with the book, and with the film even in its modified form, is that the main narrative interest boils down to the question "Will Humbert get Lolita into bed?" And you find in the book that, despite the brilliant writing, the second half has a drop in narrative interest after he does. We wanted to avoid this problem in the film, and Nabokov and I agreed that if we had Humbert shoot Quilty without explanation at the beginning, then throughout the film the audience would wonder what Quilty was up to. Of course, you obviously sacrifice a great ending by opening with Quilty's murder, but I felt it served a worthwhile purpose.

G: *Starting with* Lolita, *you've been making all your films abroad. Why?*

K: Circumstances have just dictated it that way. As I explained earlier, it was necessary to make *Lolita* in England for financial reasons and to mitigate censorship problems, and in the case of *Dr. Strangelove*, Peter Sellers was in the process of getting a divorce and could not leave England for an extended period, so it was necessary to film there. By the time I decided to do *2001* I had gotten so acclimated to working in England that it would have been pointless to tear up roots and move everything to America. And with *Napoleon* we'll be doing a great deal of the shooting on the continent, so London is a convenient base of operations.

G: *Are there any specific advantages to working in London?*

K: Next to Hollywood, London is probably the second best place to make a film, because of the degree of technical expertise and facilities you find in England, and that isn't really a backhanded compliment.

G: *Do you have any reluctance to work in Hollywood while the studio chiefs stand over the director's shoulder?*

K: No, because I'm in the fortunate position where I can make a film without that kind of control. Ten years ago, of course, it would have been an entirely different story.

G: *You don't consider yourself an expatriate then?*

K: Not at all.

G: *Why not? You've lived in England seven years and made your last three films there—even those which were set in America.*

K: Yes, but there's nothing permanent about my working and living in England. Circumstances have kept me there until now, but it's quite possible I'll be making a film in America in the future. And in any case, I commute back and forth several times a year.

G: *But always by ocean liner. You have a pilot's license but you don't like flying anymore. Why?*

K: Call it enlightened cowardice, if you like. Actually, over the years I discovered that I just didn't enjoy flying, and I became aware of compromised safety margins in commercial aviation that are never mentioned in airline advertising. So I decided I'd rather travel by sea, and take my chances with the icebergs.

G: *In your profession isn't it a problem not to fly?*

K: It would be if I had to hop about all the time from spot to spot like many people do. But when I'm working on a film I'm tied down to one geographic area for long periods of time and I travel very little. And when I do, I find boats or railroads adequate and more relaxing.

G: Dr. Strangelove *was a particularly word-oriented film, whereas* 2001 *seemed to be a total breakaway from what you'd done before.*

K: Yes, I feel it was. *Strangelove* was a film where much of its impact hinged on the dialogue, the mode of expression, the euphemisms employed. As a result, it's a picture that is largely destroyed in translation or dubbing. *2001*, on the other hand, is basically a visual, nonverbal experience. It avoids intellectual verbalization and reaches the viewer's subconscious in a way that is essentially poetic and philosophic. The film thus becomes a subjective experience which hits the viewer at an inner level of consciousness, just as music does, or painting.

Actually, film operates on a level much closer to music and to painting than to the printed word, and, of course, movies present the opportunity to convey complex concepts and abstractions without the traditional reliance on words. I think that *2001*, like music, succeeds in short-circuiting the rigid surface cultural blocks that shackle our consciousness to narrowly limited areas of experience and is able to cut directly through to areas of emotional comprehension. In two hours and forty minutes of film there are only forty minutes of dialogue.

I think one of the areas where *2001* succeeds is in stimulating thoughts about man's destiny and role in the universe in the minds of people who in the normal course of their lives would never have considered such matters. Here again, you've got the resemblance to music; an Alabama truck driver, whose views in every other respect would be extremely narrow, is able to listen to a Beatles record on the same level of appreciation and perception as a young Cambridge intellectual, because their emotions and subconscious are far more similar than their intellects. The common bond is their subconscious emotional reaction; and I think that a film which can communicate on this level can have a more profound spectrum of impact than any form of traditional verbal communication.

The problem with movies is that since the talkies the film industry has historically been conservative and word-oriented. The three-act play has been the model. It's time to abandon the conventional view of the movie as an extension of the three-act play. Too many people over thirty are still word-oriented rather than picture-oriented.

For example, at one point in *2001* Dr. Floyd is asked where he's going and he replies, "I'm going to Clavius," which is a lunar crater. Following that statement you have more than fifteen shots of Floyd's spacecraft approaching and landing on the moon, but one critic expressed confusion because she thought Floyd's destination was a planet named Clavius. Young people, on the other hand, who are more visually oriented due to their new television environment, had no such problems. Kids all know he went to the moon. When you ask how they know they say, "Because we *saw* it."

So you have the problem that some people are only listening and not really paying attention with their eyes. Film is *not* theater—and until that basic lesson is learned I'm afraid we're going to be shackled to the past and miss some of the greatest potentialities of the medium.

G: *Did you deliberately try for ambiguity as opposed to a specific meaning for any scene or image?*

K: No, I didn't have to try for ambiguity; it was inevitable. And I think in a film like *2001*, where each viewer brings his own emotions and perceptions to bear on the subject matter, a certain degree of ambiguity is valuable, because it allows the audience to "fill in" the visual experience themselves. In any case, once you're dealing on a nonverbal level, ambiguity is unavoidable. But it's the ambiguity of all art, of a fine piece of music or a painting—you don't need written instructions by the composer or painter accompanying such works to "explain" them. "Explaining" them contributes nothing but a superficial "cultural" value which has no value except for critics and teachers who have to earn a living. Reactions to art are always different because they are always deeply personal.

G: *The final scenes of the film seemed more metaphorical than realistic. Will you discuss them—or would that be part of the "road map" you're trying to avoid?*

K: No, I don't mind discussing it, on the *lowest* level, that is, straightforward explanation of the plot. You begin with an artifact left on earth four million years ago by extraterrestrial explorers who observed the behavior of the man-apes of the time and decided to influence their evolutionary progression. Then you have a second artifact buried on the lunar surface and programmed to signal word of man's first baby steps into the universe—a kind of cosmic burglar alarm. And finally there's a third artifact placed in orbit around Jupiter and waiting for the time when man has reached the outer rim of his own solar system.

When the surviving astronaut, Bowman, ultimately reaches Jupiter, this artifact sweeps him into a force field or star gate that hurls him on a journey through inner and outer space and finally transports him to another part of the galaxy, where he's placed in a human zoo approximating a hospital terrestrial environment drawn out of his own dreams and imagination. In a timeless state, his life passes from middle age to senescence to death. He is reborn, an enhanced being, a star child, an angel, a superman, if you like, and returns to earth prepared for the next leap forward of man's evolutionary destiny.

That is what happens on the film's simplest level. Since an encounter with an advanced interstellar intelligence would be incomprehensible within our present earthbound frames of reference, reactions to it will have elements of philosophy and metaphysics that have nothing to do with the bare plot outline itself.

G: *What are those areas of meaning?*

K: They are the areas I prefer not to discuss because they are highly subjective and will differ from viewer to viewer. In this sense, the film becomes anything the viewer sees in it. If the film stirs the emotions and penetrates the subconscious of the viewer, if it stimulates, however inchoately, his mythological and religious yearnings and impulses, then it has succeeded.

G: *Why does* 2001 *seem so affirmative and religious a film? What has happened to the tough, disillusioned, cynical director of* The Killing, Spartacus, Paths of Glory, *and* Lolita, *and the sardonic black humorist of* Dr. Strangelove?

K: The God concept is at the heart of this film. It's unavoidable that it would be, once you believe that the universe is seething with advanced forms of intelligent life. Just think about it for a moment. There are a hundred billion stars in the galaxy and a hundred billion galaxies in the visible universe. Each star is a sun, like our own, probably with planets around them. The evolution of life, it is widely believed, comes as an inevitable consequence of a certain amount of time on a planet in a stable orbit which is not too hot or too cold. First comes chemical evolution—chance rearrangements of basic matter, then biological evolution.

Think of the kind of life that may have evolved on those planets over the millennia, and think, too, what relatively giant technological strides man has made on earth in the six thousand years of his recorded civilization—a period that is less than a single grain of sand in the cosmic hourglass. At a time when man's distant evolutionary ancestors were just crawling out of the primordial ooze, there must have been civilizations in the universe sending out their starships to explore the farthest reaches of the cosmos and conquering all the secrets of nature. Such cosmic intelligences, growing in knowledge over the aeons, would be as far removed from man as we are from the ants. They could be in instantaneous telepathic communication throughout the universe; they might have achieved total mastery over matter so that they can telekinetically transport themselves instantly across billions of light years of space; in their ultimate form they might shed the corporeal shell entirely and exist as a disembodied immortal consciousness throughout the universe.

Once you begin discussing such possibilities, you realize that the religious implications are inevitable, because all the essential attributes of such extraterrestrial intelligences are the attributes we give to God. What we're really dealing with here is, in fact, a scientific definition of God. And if these beings of pure intelligence ever did intervene in the affairs of man, we could only understand it in terms of God or magic, so far removed would their powers be from our own understanding. How would a sentient ant view the foot that crushes his anthill—as the action of another being on a higher evolutionary scale than itself? Or as the divinely terrible intercession of God?

G: *Although* 2001 *dealt with the first human contact with an alien civilization, we never did actually see an alien, though you communicated through the monoliths an experience of alien beings.*

K: From the very outset of work on the film we all discussed means of photographically depicting an extraterrestrial creature in a manner that would be as mind-boggling as the being itself. And it soon became apparent that you cannot imagine the unimaginable. All you can do is try to represent it in an artistic manner that will convey something of its quality. That's why we settled on the black monolith—which is, of course, in itself something of a Jungian archetype, and also a pretty fair example of "minimal art."

G: *Isn't a basic problem with science fiction films that alien life always looks like some Creature from the Black Lagoon, a plastic rubber monster?*

K: Yes, and that's one of the reasons we stayed away from the depiction of biological entities, aside from the fact that truly advanced beings would probably have shed the chrysalis of a biological form at one stage of their evolution. You cannot design a biological entity that doesn't look either overly humanoid or like the traditional Bug-Eyed Monster of pulp science fiction.

G: *The man-ape costumes in* 2001 *were impressive.*

K: We spent an entire year trying to figure out how to make the ape-heads look convincing, and not just like a conventional makeup job. We finally constructed an entire sub-skull of extremely light and flexible plastic, to which we attached the equivalent of face muscles which pulled the lips back in a normal manner whenever the mouth was opened. The mouth itself took a great deal of work—it had artificial teeth and an artificial tongue which the actors could manipulate with tiny toggles to make the lips snarl in a lifelike fashion. Some of the masks even had built-in devices whereby the artificial muscles in the cheeks and beneath the eyes could be moved. All the apes except for two baby chimps were men, and most of them were dancers or mimes, which enabled them to move a little better than most movie apes.

G: *Was the little girl Dr. Floyd telephoned from the orbital satellite one of your daughters?*

K: Yes, my youngest girl, Vivian. She was six then. We didn't give her any billing, a fact I hope she won't decide to take up with me when she's older.

G: *Why was Martin Balsam's voice as HAL, the computer, redubbed by Douglas Rain the Canadian actor?*

K: Well, we had some difficulty deciding exactly what HAL should sound like, and Marty just sounded a little bit too colloquially American, whereas Rain had the kind of bland mid-Atlantic accent we felt was right for the part.

G: *Some critics have detected in HAL's wheedling voice an undertone of homosexuality. Was that intended?*

K: No. I think it's become something of a parlor game for some people to read that kind of thing into everything they encounter. HAL was a "straight" computer.

G: *Why was the computer more emotional than the human beings?*

K: This was a point that seemed to fascinate some negative critics, who felt that it was a failing of this section of the film that there was more interest in HAL than in the astronauts. In fact, of course, the computer is the central character of this segment of the story. If HAL had been a human being, it would have been obvious to everyone that he had the best part, and was the most interesting character; he took all the initiatives, and all the problems related to and were caused by him.

Some critics seemed to feel that because we were successful in making a voice, a camera lens, and a light come alive as a character this necessarily meant that the human characters failed dramatically. In fact, I believe that Keir Dullea and Gary Lockwood, the astronauts, reacted appropriately and realistically to their circumstances. One of the things we were trying to convey in this part of the film is the reality of a world populated—as ours soon will be—by machine entities who have as much, or more, intelligence as human beings, and who have the same emotional potentialities in their personalities as human beings. We wanted to stimulate people to think what it would be like to share a planet with such creatures.

In the specific case of HAL, he had an acute emotional crisis because he could not accept evidence of his own fallibility. The idea of neurotic computers is not uncommon—most advanced computer theorists believe that once you have a computer which is more intelligent than man and capable of learning by experience, it's inevitable that it will develop an equivalent range of emotional reactions—fear, love, hate, envy, etc. Such a machine could eventually become as incomprehensible as a human being, and could, of course, have a nervous breakdown—as HAL did in the film.

G: *Since* 2001 *is a visual experience, what happened when your collaborator, Arthur C. Clarke, finally put the screenplay down in black and white in the novelization of the film?*

K: It's a totally different kind of experience, of course, and there are a number of differences between the book and the movie. The novel, for example, attempts to explain things much more explicitly than the film does, which is inevitable in a verbal medium. The novel came about after we did a 130-page prose treatment of the film at the very outset. This initial treatment was subsequently changed in the screenplay, and the screenplay in turn was altered during the making of the film. But Arthur took all the existing material, plus an impression of some of the rushes, and wrote the novel. As a result, there's a difference between the novel and the film.

G: *To take one specific, in the novel the black monolith found by curious man-apes three million years ago does explicit things which it doesn't do in the film. In the movie, it has an apparent catalytic effect which enables the ape to discover how to use a bone as a weapon-tool. In the novel, the slab becomes milky and luminous and we're told it's a testing and teaching device used by higher intelligences to determine if the apes are worth helping. Was that in the original screenplay? When was it cut out of the film?*

K: Yes, it was in the original treatment but I eventually decided that to depict the monolith in such an explicit manner would be to run the risk of making it appear no more than an advanced television teaching machine. You can get away with something so literal in print, but I felt that we could create a far more powerful and magical effect by representing it as we did in the film.

G: *Do you feel that the novel, written so explicity, in some way diminishes the mysterious aspect of the film?*

K: I think it gives you the opportunity of seeing two attempts in two different mediums, print and film, to express the same basic concept and story. In both cases, of course, the treatment must accommodate to the necessities of the medium. I think that the divergencies between the two works are interesting. Actually, it was an unprecedented situation for someone to do an essentially original literary work based on glimpses and segments of a film he had not yet seen in its entirety. In fact, *nobody* saw the film in its final form until eight days before we held the first press screening in April 1968, and the first time I saw the film completed with a proper soundtrack was one week before it opened. I completed the portion of the film in which we used actors in June 1966 and from then until the first week of March 1968 I spent most of my time working on the 205 special effects shots. The final shot was actually cut into the negative at M-G-M's Hollywood studios only days before the film was ready to open. There was nothing intentional about the fact that the film wasn't shown until the last minute. It just wasn't finished.

G: *Why did you cut scenes from the film after it opened?*

K: I always try to look at a completed film as if I had never seen it before. I usually have several weeks to run the film, alone and with audiences. Only in this way can you judge length. I've always done precisely that with my previous films; for example, after a screening of *Dr. Strangelove* I cut out a final scene in which the Russians and Americans in the War Room engage in a free-for-all fight with custard pies. I decided it was farce and not consistent with the satiric tone of the rest of the film. So there was nothing unusual about the cutting I did on *2001*, except for the eleventh-hour way in which I had to do it.

G: Strangelove *was based on a serious book,* Red Alert. *At what point did you decide to make it a comedy?*

K: I started work on the screenplay with every intention of making the film a serious treatment of the problem of accidental nuclear war. As I kept trying to imagine the way in which things would really happen, ideas kept coming to me which I would discard because they were so ludicrous. I kept saying to myself: "I can't do this. People will laugh." But after a month or so I began to realize that all the things I was throwing out were the things which were most truthful. After all, what could be more absurd than the very idea of two mega-powers willing to wipe out all human life because of an accident, spiced up by political differences that will seem as meaningless to people a hundred years from now as the theological conflicts of the Middle Ages appear to us today?

So it occurred to me that I was approaching the project in the wrong way. The only way to tell the story was as a black comedy or, better, a nightmare comedy, where the things you laugh at most are really the heart of the paradoxical postures that make a nuclear war possible.

Most of the humor in *Strangelove* arises from the depiction of everyday human behavior in a nightmarish situation, like the Russian premier on the hot line who forgets the telephone number of his general staff headquarters and suggests the American President try Omsk information, or the reluctance of a U.S. officer to let a British officer smash open a Coca-Cola machine for change to phone the President about a crisis on the SAC base because of his conditioning about the sanctity of private property.

G: *When you read a book like* Red Alert *which you're interested in turning into a film, do you right away say to yourself, this character should be played by such and such an actor?*

K: Not usually. I first try to define the character fully as he will appear in the film and then try to think of the proper actor to play the role. When I'm in the process of casting a part I sit down with a list of actors I know. Of course, once you've narrowed the list down to several possibilities for each part then it becomes a question of who's currently available, and how the actor you choose to play one part will affect the people you're considering for other parts.

G: *How do you get a good performance from your actors?*

K: The director's job is to know what emotional statement he wants a character to convey in his scene or his line, and to exercise taste and judgment in helping the actor give his best possible performance. By knowing the actor's personality and gauging his strengths and weaknesses a director can help him to overcome specific problems and realize his potential. But I think this aspect of directing is generally overemphasized. The director's taste and imagination play a much more crucial role in the making of a film. Is it meaningful? Is it believable? Is it interesting? Those are the questions that have to be answered several hundred times a day.

It's rare for a bad performance to result from an actor ignoring everything a director tells him. In fact it's very often just the opposite. After all, the director is the actor's sole audience for the months it takes to shoot a film, and an actor would have to possess supreme self-confidence and supreme contempt for the director to consistently defy his wishes. I think you'll find that most disappointing performances are the mutual fault of both the actor and the director.

G: *Some directors don't let their actors see the daily rushes. Do you?*

K: Yes. I've encountered very few actors who are so insecure or self-destructive that they're upset by the rushes or find their self-confidence undermined. Actually, most actors profit by seeing their rushes and examining them self-critically. In any case, a professional actor who's bothered by his own rushes just won't turn up to see them—particularly in my films, since we run the rushes at lunch time and unless an actor is really interested, he won't cut his lunch to half an hour.

G: *On the first day of shooting on the set, how do you establish that rapport or fear or whatever relationship you want with your actors to keep them in the right frame of mind for the three months you'll be working with them?*

K: Certainly not through fear. To establish a good working relationship I think all the actor has to know is that you respect his talent enough to want him in your film. He's obviously aware of that as long as *you've* hired him and he hasn't been foisted on you by the studio or the producer.

G: *Do you rehearse at all?*

K: There's really a limit to what you can do with rehearsals. They're very useful, of course, but I find that you can't rehearse effectively unless you have the physical reality of the set to work with. Unfortunately, sets are practically never ready until the last moment before you start shooting, and this significantly cuts down on your rehearsal time. Some actors, of course, need rehearsals more than others. Actors are essentially emotion-producing instruments, and some are always tuned and ready while others will reach a fantastic pitch on one take and never equal it again, no matter how hard they try. In *Strangelove*, for example, George Scott could do his scenes equally well take after take, whereas Peter Sellers was always incredibly good on one take, which was never equaled.

G: *At what point do you know what take you're going to use?*

K: On some occasions the take is so obviously superior you can tell immediately. But particularly when you're dealing with dialogue scenes, you have to look them over again and again and select portions of different takes and make the best use of them. The greatest amount of time in editing is this process of studying the takes and making notes and struggling to decide which segments you want to use; this takes ten times more time and effort than the actual cutting, which is a very quick process. Purely visual action scenes, of course, present far less of a problem; it's generally the dialogue scenes, where you've got several long takes printed on each angle on different actors, that are the most time-consuming to cut.

G: *How much cutting are you responsible for, and how much is done by somebody you trust as an editor?*

K: Nothing is cut without me. I'm in there every second, and for all practical purposes I cut my own film; I mark every frame, select each segment, and have everything done exactly the way I want it. Writing, shooting, *and* editing are what you have to do to make a film.

G: *Where did you learn film editing? You started out as a still photographer.*

K: Yes, but after I quit *Look* in 1950—where I had been a staff photographer for five years, ever since I left high school—I took a crack at films and made two documentaries, *Day of the Fight*, about prize fighter Walter Cartier, and *The Flying Padre*, a silly thing about a priest in the Southwest who flew to his isolated parishes in a small airplane. I did all the work on those two films, and all the work on my first two feature films, *Fear and Desire* and *Killer's Kiss*. I was cameraman, director, editor, assistant editor, sound effects man—you name it, I did it. And it was invaluable experience, because being forced to do everything myself I gained a sound and comprehensive grasp of all the technical aspects of filmmaking.

G: *How old were you when you decided to make movies?*

K: I was around twenty-one. I'd had my job with *Look* since I was seventeen, and I'd always been interested in films, but it never actually occurred to me to make a film on my own until I had a talk with a friend from high school, Alex Singer, who wanted to be a director himself (and has subsequently become one) and had plans for a film version of the *Iliad*. Alex was working as an office boy for "The March of Time" in those days, and he told me they spent forty thousand dollars making a one-reel documentary. A bit of simple calculation indicated that I could make a one-reel documentary for about fifteen hundred. That's what gave me the financial confidence to make *Day of the Fight*.

I was rather optimistic about expenses; the film cost me thirty-nine hundred. I sold it to RKO-Pathé for four thousand dollars, a hundred-dollar profit. They told me that was the most they'd ever paid for a short. I then discovered that "The March of Time" itself was going out of business. I made one more short for RKO, *The Flying Padre*, on which I just barely broke even. It was at this point that I formally quit my job at *Look* to work full time on filmmaking. I then managed to raise ten thousand dollars, and shot my first feature film, *Fear and Desire*.

G: *What was your own experience making your first feature film?*

K: *Fear and Desire* was made in the San Gabriel Mountains outside Los Angeles. I was the camera operator and director and just about everything else. Our "crew" consisted of three Mexican laborers who carried all the equipment. The film was shot in 35 mm without a soundtrack and then dubbed by a post-synchronized technique. The dubbing was a big mistake on my part; the actual shooting cost of the film was nine thousand dollars but because I didn't know what I was doing with the soundtrack it cost me another thirty thousand. There were other things I did expensively and foolishly, because I just didn't have enough experience to know the proper and economical approach. *Fear and Desire* played the art house circuits and some of the reviews were amazingly good, but it's not a film I remember with any pride, except for the fact it was finished.

G: *After* Fear and Desire *failed to pay back the investors, how did you get the money to make your next film,* Killer's Kiss?

K: *Fear and Desire* was financed mainly by my friends and relatives, whom I've since paid back, needless to say. Different people gave me backing for *Killer's Kiss*, which also lost half of its forty-thousand-dollar budget. I've subsequently repaid those backers also. After *Killer's Kiss* I met Jim Harris, who was interested in getting into films, and we formed a production company together. Our first property was *The Killing*, based on Lionel White's story "The Clean Break." This time we could afford good actors, such as Sterling Hayden, and a professional crew. The budget was larger than the earlier films—$320,000—but still very low for a Hollywood production. Our next film was *Paths of Glory*, which nobody in Hollywood wanted to do at all, even though we had a very low budget. Finally Kirk Douglas saw the script and liked it. Once he agreed to appear in the film United Artists was willing to make it.

G: *How'd you get that great performance out of Douglas?*

K: A director can't get anything out of an actor that he doesn't already have. You can't start an acting school in the middle of making a film. Kirk is a good actor.

G: *What did you do after* Paths of Glory?

K: I did two scripts that no one wanted. A year went by and my finances were rather rocky. I received no salary for *The Killing* or *Paths of Glory* but had worked on 100 per cent deferred salary— and since the films didn't make any money, I had received nothing from either of them. I subsisted on loans from my partner, Jim Harris. Next I spent six months working on a screenplay for a Western, *One-Eyed Jacks*, with Marlon Brando and Calder Willingham. Our relationship ended amicably a few weeks before Marlon began directing the film himself. By the time I had left Brando I had spent two years doing nothing. At this point, I was hired to direct *Spartacus* with Kirk Douglas. It was the only one of my films over which I did not have complete control; although I was the director, mine was only one of many voices to which Kirk listened. I am disappointed in the film. It had everything but a good story.

G: *What do you consider the director's role?*

K: A director is a kind of idea and taste machine; a movie is a series of creative and technical decisions, and it's the director's job to make the right decisions as frequently as possible. Shooting a movie is the worst milieu for creative work ever devised by man. It is a noisy, physical apparatus; it is difficult to concentrate—and you have to do it from eight-thirty to six-thirty, five days a week. It's not an environment an artist would ever choose to work in. The only advantage it has is that you must do it, and you can't procrastinate.

G: *How did you learn to actually* make *the films, since you'd had no experience?*

K: Well, my experience in photography was very helpful. For my two documentaries I'd used a small 35-mm hand camera called an Eyemo, a daylight loading camera which was very simple to operate. The first time I used a Mitchell camera was on *Fear and Desire*. I went to the Camera Equipment Company, at 1600 Broadway, and the owner, Bert Zucker, spent a Saturday morning showing me how to load and operate it. So that was the extent of my formal training in movie camera technique.

G: *As a beginner, you mean you just walked cold into a rental outfit and had them give you a cram course in using movie equipment?*

K: Bert Zucker, who has subsequently been killed in an airline crash, was a young man, in his early thirties, and he was very sympathetic. Anyway, it was a sensible thing for them to do. I was paying for the equipment. At that time I also learned how to do cutting. Once somebody showed me how to use a Movieola and synchronizer and how to make a splice I had no trouble at all. The technical fundamentals of moviemaking are not difficult.

G: *What kind of movies did you go to in those days?*

K: I used to want to see almost anything. In fact, the bad films were what really encouraged me to start out on my own. I'd keep seeing lousy films and saying to myself, "I don't know anything about moviemaking but I *couldn't* do anything worse than this."

G: *You had technical skills and audacity, but what made you think you could get a good performance out of an actor?*

K: Well, in the beginning I really didn't get especially good performances, either in *Fear and Desire* or *Killer's Kiss*. They were both amateurish films. But I did learn a great deal from making them, experience which helped me greatly in my subsequent films. The best way to learn is to do—and this is something few people manage to get the opportunity to try. I was also helped a great deal by studying Stanislavski's books, as well as an excellent book about him, *Stanislavski Directs*, which contains a great deal of highly illustrative material on how he worked with actors. Between those books and the painful lessons I learned from my own mistakes I accumulated the basic experience needed to start to do good work.

G: *Did you also read film theory books?*

K: I read Eisenstein's books at the time, and to this day I still don't really understand them. The most instructive book on film aesthetics I came across was Pudovkin's *Film Technique*, which simply explained that editing was the aspect of the film art form which was completely unique, and which separated it from all other art forms. The ability to show a simple action like a man cutting wheat from a number of angles in a brief moment, to be able to see it in a special way not possible except through film—that this is what it was all about. This is obvious, of course, but it's so important it cannot be too strongly stressed. Pudovkin gives many clear examples of how good film editing enhances a scene, and I would recommend his book to anyone seriously interested in film technique.

G: *But you weren't impressed by Eisenstein's books. What do you think of his films?*

K: Well, I have a mixed opinion. Eisenstein's greatest achievement is the beautiful visual composition of his shots, and his editing. But as far as content is concerned, his films are silly, his actors are wooden and operatic. I sometimes suspect that Eisenstein's acting style derives from his desire to keep the actors framed within his compositions for as long as possible; they move very slowly, as if under water. Interesting to note, a lot of his work was being done concurrently with Stanislavski's work. Actually, anyone seriously interested in comparative film techniques should study the differences in approach of two directors, Eisenstein and Chaplin. Eisenstein is all form and no content, whereas Chaplin is content and no form. Of course, a director's style is partly the result of the manner in which he imposes his mind on the semicontrollable conditions that exist on any given day—the responsiveness and talent of actors, the realism of the set, time factors, even weather.

G: *You've been quoted as saying that Max Ophuls' films fascinated you when you were starting out as a director.*

K: Yes, he did some brilliant work. I particularly admired his fluid camera techniques. I saw a great many films at that time at the Museum of Modern Art and in movie theaters, and I learned far more by seeing films than from reading heavy tomes on film aesthetics.

G: *If you were nineteen and starting out again, would you go to film school?*

K: The best education in film is to make one. I would advise any neo-phyte director to try to make a film by himself. A three-minute short will teach him a lot. I know that all the things I did at the beginning were, in microcosm, the things I'm doing now as a director and producer. There are a lot of noncreative aspects to filmmaking which have to be overcome, and you will experience them all when you make even the simplest film: business, organi-zation, taxes, etc., etc. It is rare to be able to have uncluttered, artistic environment when you make a film, and being able to accept this is essential.

The point to stress is that anyone seriously interested in making a film should find as much money as he can as quickly as he can and go out and do it. And this is no longer as difficult as it once was. When I began making movies as an independent in the early 1950s I received a fair amount of publicity because I was some-thing of a freak in an industry dominated by a handful of huge stu-dios. Everyone was amazed that it could be done at all. But anyone can make a movie who has a little knowledge of cameras and tape recorders, a lot of ambition and—hopefully—talent. It's gotten down to the pencil and paper level. We're really on the threshold of a revolutionary new era in film.

Playboy Interview: Stanley Kubrick

ERIC NORDERN

PLAYBOY: *Much of the controversy surrounding* 2001 *deals with the meaning of the metaphysical symbols that abound in the film— the polished black monoliths, the orbital conjunction of Earth, Moon and sun at each stage of the monoliths' intervention in human destiny, the stunning final kaleidoscopic maelstrom of time and space that engulfs the surviving astronaut and sets the stage for his rebirth as a "star child" drifting toward Earth in a translucent placenta. One critic even called* 2001 *"the first Nietzschean film," contending that its essential theme is Nietzsche's concept of man's evolution from ape to human to superman. What* was *the metaphysical message of* 2001?

KUBRICK: It's not a message that I ever intend to convey in words. *2001* is a nonverbal experience; out of two hours and 19 minutes of film, there are only a little less than 40 minutes of dialog. I tried to create a *visual* experience, one that bypasses verbalized pigeon-holing and directly penetrates the subconscious with an emotional and philosophic content. To convolute McLuhan, in *2001* the message is the medium. I intended the film to be an intensely subjective experience that reaches the viewer at an inner level of consciousness, just as music does; to "explain" a Beethoven symphony would be to emasculate it by erecting an artificial barrier between conception and appreciation. You're free to speculate as you wish about the philosophical and allegorical meaning of the film—and such speculation is one indication that it has succeeded in gripping the audience at a deep level—but I don't want to spell out a verbal road map for *2001* that every viewer will feel obligated to pursue or else fear he's missed the point. I think that if *2001* succeeds at all, it is in reaching a wide spectrum of people who would not often give a thought to man's destiny, his role in the cosmos and his relationship to higher forms of life. But even in the case of someone who is highly intelligent, certain ideas found in *2001* would, if presented as abstractions, fall rather lifelessly and be automatically assigned to pat intellectual categories; experienced in a moving visual and emotional context, however, they can resonate within the deepest fibers of one's being.

PLAYBOY: *Without laying out a philosophical road map for the viewer, can you tell us your own interpretation of the meaning of the film?*

KUBRICK: No, for the reasons I've already given. How much would we appreciate *La Gioconda* today if Leonardo had written at the bottom of the canvas: "This lady is smiling slightly because she has rotten teeth"—or "because she's hiding a secret from her lover"? It would shut off the viewer's appreciation and shackle him to a "reality" other than his own. I don't want that to happen to *2001*.

PLAYBOY: *Arthur Clarke has said of the film, "If anyone understands it on the first viewing, we've failed in our intention." Why should the viewer have to see a film twice to get its message?*

KUBRICK: I don't agree with that statement of Arthur's, and I believe he made it facetiously. The very nature of the visual experience in *2001* is to give the viewer an instantaneous, visceral reaction that does not—and should not—require further amplification. Just speaking generally, however, I would say that there are elements in any good film that would increase the viewer's interest and appreciation on a second viewing; the momentum of a movie often prevents every stimulating detail or nuance from having a full impact the first time it's seen. The whole idea that a movie should be seen only once is an extension of our traditional conception of the film as an ephemeral entertainment rather than as a visual work of art. We don't believe that we should hear a great piece of music only once, or see a great painting once, or even read a great book just once. But the film has until recent years been exempted from the category of art—a situation I'm glad is finally changing.

PLAYBOY: *Some prominent critics—including Renata Adler of* The New York Times, *John Simon of* The New Leader, *Judith Crist of* New York *magazine and Andrew Sarris of the* Village Voice— *apparently felt that* 2001 *should be among those films still exempted from the category of art; all four castigated it as dull, pretentious and overlong. How do you account for their hostility?*

KUBRICK: The four critics you mention all work for New York publications. The reviews across America and around the world have been 95 percent enthusiastic. Some were more perceptive than others, of course, but even those who praised the film on relatively superficial grounds were able to get something of its message. New York was the only really hostile city. Perhaps there is a certain element of the lumpen literati that is so dogmatically atheist and materialist and Earth-bound that it finds the grandeur of space and the myriad mysteries of cosmic intelligence anathema. But film critics, fortunately, rarely have any effect on the general public; houses everywhere are packed and the film is well on its way to becoming the greatest money-maker in M-G-M's history. Perhaps this sounds like a crass way to evaluate one's work, but I think that, especially with a film that is so obviously *different*, record audience attendance means people are saying the right things to one another after they see it—and isn't this really what it's all about?

PLAYBOY: *Speaking of what it's all about—if you'll allow us to return to the philosophical interpretation of 2001—would you agree with those critics who call it a profoundly religious film?*

KUBRICK: I will say that the God concept is at the heart of *2001*—but not any traditional, anthropomorphic image of God. I don't believe in any of Earth's monotheistic religions, but I do believe that one can construct an intriguing *scientific* definition of God, once you accept the fact that there are approximately 100 billion stars in our galaxy alone, that each star is a life-giving sun and that there are approximately 100 billion galaxies in just the *visible* universe. Given a planet in a stable orbit, not too hot and not too cold, and given a few billion years of chance chemical reactions created by the interaction of a sun's energy on the planet's chemicals, it's fairly certain that life in one form or another will eventually emerge. It's reasonable to assume that there must be, in fact, countless *billions* of such planets where biological life has arisen, and the odds of some proportion of such life developing intelligence are high. Now, the sun is by no means an old star, and its planets are mere children in cosmic age, so it seems likely that there are billions of planets in the universe not only where intelligent life is on a lower scale than man but other billions where it is approximately equal and others still where it is hundreds of thousands of millions of years in advance of us. When you think of the giant technological strides that man has made in a few millennia—less than a microsecond in the chronology of the universe—can you imagine the evolutionary development that much older life forms have taken? They may have progressed from biological species, which are fragile shells for the mind at best, into immortal machine entities—and then, over innumerable, eons, they could emerge from the chrysalis of matter transformed into beings of pure energy and spirit. Their potentialities would be limitless and their intelligence ungraspable by humans.

PLAYBOY: *Even assuming the cosmic evolutionary path you suggest, what has this to do with the nature of God?*

KUBRICK: Everything—because these beings would *be* gods to the billions of less advanced races in the universe, just as man would appear a god to an ant that somehow comprehended man's existence. They would possess the twin attributes of all deities—omniscience and omnipotence. These entities might be in telepathic communication throughout the cosmos and ⁺hus be aware of everything that occurs, tapping every intelligent mind as effortlessly as we switch on the radio; they might not be limited by the speed of light and their presence could penetrate to the farthest corners of the universe; they might possess complete mastery over matter and energy; and in their final evolutionary stage, they might develop into an integrated collective immortal consciousness. They would be incomprehensible to us except as gods; and if the tendrils of their consciousness ever brushed men's minds, it is only the hand of God we could grasp as an explanation.

PLAYBOY: *If such creatures do exist, why should they be interested in man?*

KUBRICK: They may not be. But why should man be interested in microbes? The motives of such beings would be as alien to us as their intelligence.

PLAYBOY: *In 2001, such incorporeal creatures seem to manipulate our destinies and control our evolution, though whether for good or evil—or both, or neither—remains unclear. Do you really believe it's possible that man is a cosmic plaything of such entities?*

KUBRICK: I don't really *believe* anything about them; how can I? Mere speculation on the possibility of their existence is sufficiently overwhelming, without attempting to decipher their motives. The important point is that all the standard attributes assigned to God in our history could equally well be the characteristics of biological entities who billions of years ago were at a stage of development similar to man's own and evolved into something as remote from man as man is remote from the primordial ooze from which he first emerged.

PLAYBOY: *In this cosmic phylogeny you've described, isn't it possible that there might be forms of intelligent life on an even higher scale than these entities of pure energy—perhaps as far removed from them as they are from us?*

KUBRICK: Of course there could be; in an infinite, eternal universe, the point is that *anything* is possible, and it's unlikely that we can even begin to scratch the surface of the full range of possibilities. But at a time [1968] when man is preparing to set foot on the Moon, I think it's necessary to open up our Earth bound minds to such speculation. No one knows what's waiting for us in the universe. I think it was a prominent astronomer who wrote recently, "Sometimes I think we are alone, and sometimes I think we're not. In either case, the idea is quite staggering."

PLAYBOY: *You said there must be billions of planets sustaining life that is considerably more advanced than man but has not yet evolved into non- or suprabiological forms. What do you believe would be the effect on humanity if the Earth were contacted by a race of such ungodlike but technologically superior beings?*

KUBRICK: There's a considerable difference of opinion on this subject among scientists and philosophers. Some contend that encountering a highly advanced civilization—even one whose technology is essentially comprehensible to us—would produce a traumatic cultural shock effect on man by divesting him of his smug ethnocentrism and shattering the delusion that he is the center of the universe. Carl Jung summed up this position when he wrote of contact with advanced extraterrestrial life that the "reins would be torn from our hands and we would, as a tearful old medicine man once said to me, find ourselves 'without dreams' . . . we would find our intellectual and spiritual aspirations so outmoded as to leave us completely paralyzed." I personally don't accept this position, but it's one that's widely held and can't be summarily dismissed.

In 1960, for example, the Committee for Long Range Studies of the Brookings Institution prepared a report for the National Aeronautics and Space Administration warning that even indirect contact—i.e., alien artifacts that might possibly be discovered through our space activities on the Moon, Mars or Venus or via radio contact with an interstellar civilization—could cause severe psychological dislocations. The study cautioned that "Anthropological files contain many examples of societies, sure of their place in the universe, which have disintegrated when they have had to associate with previously unfamiliar societies espousing different ideas and different life ways; others that survived such an experience usually did so by paying the price of changes in values and attitudes and behavior." It concluded that since intelligent life might be discovered at any time, and that since the consequences of such a discovery are "presently unpredictable," it was advisable that the Government initiate continuing studies on the psychological and intellectual impact of confrontation with extraterrestrial life. What action was taken on this report I don't know, but I assume that such studies are now under way. However, while not discounting the possible adverse emotional impact on some people, I would personally tend to view such contact with a tremendous amount of excitement and enthusiasm. Rather than shattering our society, I think it could immeasurably enrich it.

Another positive point is that it's a virtual certainty that all intelligent life at one stage in its technological development must have discovered nuclear energy. This is obviously the watershed of any civilization; does it find a way to use nuclear power without destruction and harness it for peaceful purposes, or does it annihilate itself? I would guess that any civilization that has existed for 1000 years after its discovery of atomic energy has devised a means of accommodating itself to the bomb, and this could prove tremendously reassuring to us—as well as give us specific guidelines for our own survival. In any case, as far as cultural shock is concerned, my impression is that the attention span of most people is quite brief; after a week or two of great excitement and over-saturation in newspapers and on television, the public's interest would drop off and the United Nations, or whatever world body we then had, would settle down to discussions with the aliens.

PLAYBOY: *You're assuming that extraterrestrials would be benevolent. Why?*

KUBRICK: Why should a vastly superior race *bother* to harm or destroy us? If an intelligent ant suddenly traced a message in the sand at my feet reading, "I am sentient; let's talk things over," I doubt very much that I would rush to grind him under my heel. Even if they weren't superintelligent, though, but merely more advanced than mankind, I would tend to lean more toward the benevolence, or at least indifference, theory. Since it's most unlikely that we would be visited from within our own solar system, any society capable of traversing light-years of space would have to have an extremely high degree of control over matter and energy. Therefore, what possible motivation for hostility would they have? To steal our gold or oil or coal? It's hard to think of any nasty intention that would justify the long and arduous journey from another star.

PLAYBOY: *You'll admit, though, that extraterrestrials are commonly portrayed in comic strips and cheap science-fiction films as bug-eyed monsters scuttling hungrily after curvaceous Earth maidens.*

KUBRICK: This probably dates back to the pulp science-fiction magazines of the Twenties and Thirties and perhaps even to the Orson Welles Martian-invasion broadcast in 1938 and the resultant mass hysteria, which is always advanced in support of the hypothesis that contact would cause severe cultural shock. In a sense, the lines with which Welles opened that broadcast set the tone for public consideration of extraterrestrial life for years to come. I've memorized them: "Across an immense ethereal gulf, minds that are to our minds as ours are to the beasts in the jungle—intellects vast, cool and unsympathetic—regarded this Earth with envious eyes and slowly and surely drew their plans against us. . . ." Anything we can imagine about such other life forms is possible, of course. You could have psychotic civilizations, or decadent civilizations that have elevated pain to an aesthetic and might covet humans as gladiators or torture objects, or civilizations that might want us for zoos, or scientific experimentation, or slaves or even for food. While I am appreciably more optimistic, we just can't be sure *what* their motivations will be.

I'm interested in the argument of Professor Freeman Dyson of Princeton's Institute for Advanced Study, who contends that it would be a mistake to expect that all potential space visitors will be altruistic, or to believe that they would have *any* ethical or moral concepts comparable to mankind's. Dyson writes, if I remember him correctly, that "Intelligence may indeed be a benign influence creating isolated groups of philosopher kings far apart in the heavens," but it's just as likely that "Intelligence may be a cancer of purposeless technological exploitation, sweeping across a galaxy as irresistibly as it has swept across our own planet." Dyson concludes that it's "just as unscientific to impute to remote intelligence wisdom and serenity as it is to impute to them irrational and murderous impulses. We must be prepared for either possibility and conduct our searches accordingly."

This is why some scientists caution, now that we're attempting to intercept radio signals from other solar systems, that if we do receive a message we should wait awhile before answering it. But we've been transmitting radio and television signals for so many years that any advanced civilization could have received the emissions long ago. So in the final analysis, we really don't have much choice in this matter; they're either going to contact us or they're not, and if they do we'll have nothing to say about their benevolence or malevolence.

Even if they prove to be malevolent, their arrival would have at least one useful by-product in that the nations of the Earth would stop squabbling among themselves and forge a common front to defend the planet. I think it was André Maurois who suggested many years ago that the best way to realize world peace would be to stage a false threat from outer space; it's not a bad idea. But I certainly don't believe we should view contact with extraterrestrial life forms with foreboding, or hesitate to visit other planets for fear of what we may find there. If others don't contact us, we must contact them; it's our destiny.

PLAYBOY: *You indicated earlier that intelligent life is extremely unlikely elsewhere within our solar system. Why?*

KUBRICK: From what we know of the other planets in this system, it appears improbable that intelligence exists, because of surface temperatures and atmospheres that are inhospitable to higher life forms. Improbable, but not impossible. I will admit that there are certain tantalizing clues pointing in the other direction. For example, while the consensus of scientific opinion dismisses the possibility of intelligent life on Mars—as opposed to plant or low orders of organic life—there are some eminently respectable dissenters. Dr. Frank B. Salisbury, professor of plant physiology at Utah State University, has contended in a study in *Science* magazine that if vegetation exists on a planet, then it is logical that there will be higher orders of life to feed on it. "From there," he writes, "it is but one more step—granted, a big one—to intelligent beings."

Salisbury also points out that a number of astronomers have observed strange flashes of light, possibly explosions of great magnitude, on Mars' surface, some of which emit clouds; and he suggests that these could actually be nuclear explosions. Another intriguing facet of Mars is the peculiar orbits of its twin satellites,

Phobos and Deimos, first discovered in 1877—the same year, incidentally, that Schiaparelli discovered his famous but still elusive Martian "canals." One eminent astronomer, Dr. Josif Shklovsky, chairman of the department of radio astronomy at the Shternberg Astronomical Institute in Moscow, has propounded the theory that both moons are artificial space satellites launched by the Martians thousands of years ago in an effort to escape the dying surface of their planet. He bases this theory on the unique orbits of the two moons, which, unlike the 31 other satellites in our solar system, orbit *faster* than the revolution of their host planet. The orbit of Phobos is also deteriorating in an inexplicable manner and dragging the satellite progressively closer to Mars' surface. Both of these circumstances, Shklovsky contends, make sense only if the two moons are *hollow*.

Shklovsky believes that the satellites are the last remnants of an extinct ancient Martian civilization; but Professor Salisbury goes a step further and suggests that they were launched within the past hundred years. Noting that the moons were discovered by a relatively small power telescope in 1877 and not detected by a much more powerful telescope observing Mars in 1862—when the planet was appreciably nearer Earth—he asks: "Should we attribute the failure of 1862 to imperfections in the existing telescope, or may we imagine that the satellites were launched into orbit between 1862 and 1877?" There are no answers here, of course, only questions, but it is fascinating speculation. On balance, however, I would have to say that the weight of available evidence dictates against intelligent life on Mars.

PLAYBOY: *How about possibilities, if not the probabilities, of intelligent life on the other planets?*

KUBRICK: Most scientists and astronomers rule out life on the outer planets since their surface temperatures are thousands of degrees either above or below zero and their atmospheres would be poisonous. I suppose it's possible that life could evolve on such planets with, say, a liquid ammonia or methane base, but it doesn't appear too likely. As far as Venus goes, the Mariner probes indicate that the surface temperature of the planet is approximately 800 degrees Fahrenheit, which would deny the chemical basis for molecular development of life. And there could be no indigenous intelligent life on the Moon, because of the total lack of atmosphere—no life as we know it, in any case; though I suppose that intelligent rocks or crystals, or statues, with a silicone life base are not really impossible, or even conscious gaseous matter or swarms of sentient electric particles. You'd get no technology from such creatures, but if their intelligence could control matter, why would they need it? There could be nothing about them, however, even remotely humanoid—a form that would appear to be an eminently practicable universal life prototype.

PLAYBOY: *What do you think we'll find on the Moon?*

KUBRICK: I think the most exciting prospect about the Moon is that if alien races have ever visited Earth in the remote past and left artifacts for man to discover in the future, they probably chose the arid, airless lunar vacuum, where no deterioration would take place and an object could exist for millennia. It would be inevitable that as man evolved technologically, he would reach his nearest satellite and the aliens would then expect him to find their calling card—perhaps a message of greeting, a cache of knowledge or simply a cosmic burglar alarm signaling that another race had mastered space flight. This, of course, was the central situation of *2001*.

But an equally fascinating question is whether there could be another race of intelligent life on Earth. Dr. John Lilly, whose research into dolphins has been funded by the National Aeronautics and Space Administration, has amassed considerable evidence pointing to the possibility that the bottle-nosed dolphin may be as intelligent as or more intelligent than man. [See *Deep Thinkers* in PLAYBOY, August 1968—*Ed.*] He bases this not only on its brain size—which is larger than man's and with a more complex cortex—but on the fact that dolphins have evolved an extensive language. Lilly is currently attempting, with some initial success, to decipher this language and establish communication with the dolphins. NASA's interest in this is obvious, because learning to communicate with dolphins would be a highly instructive precedent for learning to communicate with alien races on other planets. Of course, if the dolphins are really intelligent, theirs is obviously a nontechnological culture, since without an opposable thumb, they could never create artifacts. Their intelligence might also be on a totally different order than man's, which could make communication additionally difficult. Dr. Lilly has written that, "It is probable that their intelligence is comparable to ours, though in a very strange fashion . . . they may have a new class of large brain so dissimilar to ours that we cannot within our lifetime possibly understand its mental processes." Their culture may be totally devoted to creating works of poetry or devising abstract mathematical concepts, and they could conceivably share a telepathic communication to supplement their high-frequency underwater language.

What is particularly interesting is that dolphins appear to have developed a concept of altruism; the stories of shipwrecked sailors rescued by dolphins and carried to shore, or protected by them against sharks, are by no means all old wives' tales. But I'm rather disturbed by some recent developments that indicate not only how we may treat dolphins but also how we may treat intelligent races on other planets. The Navy, impressed by the dolphin's apparent intelligence, is reported to have been engaging in underwater-demolition experiments in which a live torpedo is strapped to a dolphin and detonated by radio when it nears a prototype enemy submarine. These experiments have been officially denied; but if they're true, I'm afraid we may learn more about man through dolphins than the other way around. The Russians, paradoxically, seem to be one step ahead of us in this area; they recently banned all catching of dolphins in Russian waters on the grounds that "Comrade Dolphin" is a fellow sentient being and killing him would be morally equivalent to murder.

PLAYBOY: *Although flying saucers are frequently an object of public derision, there has been a good deal of serious discussion in the scientific community about the possibility that UFOs could be alien spacecraft. What's your opinion?*

KUBRICK: The most significant analysis of UFOs I've seen recently was written by L. M. Chassin, a French Air Force general who had been a high ranking NATO officer. He argues that by any legal rules of evidence, there is now sufficient sighting data amassed from reputable sources—astronomers, pilots, radar operators and the like—to initiate a serious and thorough worldwide investigation of UFO phenomena. Actually, if you examine even a fraction of the extant testimony you will find that people have been sent to the gas chamber on far less substantial evidence. Of course, it's possible that all the governments in the world really *do* take UFOs seriously and perhaps are already engaging in secret study projects to determine their origin, nature and intentions. If so, they may not be disclosing their findings for fear that the public would be alarmed—the danger of cultural shock deriving from confrontation with the unknown which we discussed earlier, and which is an element of *2001*, when news of the monolith's discovery on the Moon is suppressed. But I think even the two percent of sightings that the Air Force's Project Blue Book admits is unexplainable by conventional means should dictate a serious, searching probe. From all indications, the current Government-authorized investigation at the University of Colorado is neither serious nor searching.

One hopeful sign that this subject may at last be accorded the serious discussion it deserves, however, is the belated but exemplary conversion of Dr. J. Allen Hynek, since 1948 the Air Force's consultant on UFOs and currently chairman of the astronomy department at Northwestern University. Hynek, who in his official capacity pooh-poohed UFO sightings, now believes that UFOs deserve top priority attention—as he wrote in PLAYBOY [December 1967]—and even concedes that the existing evidence may indicate a possible connection with extraterrestrial life. He predicts: "I will be surprised if an intensive study yields nothing. To the contrary, I think that mankind may be in for the greatest adventure since dawning human intelligence turned outward to contemplate the universe." I agree with him.

PLAYBOY: *If flying saucers are real, who or what do you think they might be?*

KUBRICK: I don't know. The evidence proves they're up there, but it gives us very little clue as to what they are. Some science-fiction writers theorize half-seriously that they could be time shuttles flicking back and forth between eons to a future age when man has mastered temporal travel; and I understand that biologist Ivan Sanderson has even advanced a theory that they may be some kind of living space animal inhabiting the upper stratosphere—though I can't give much credence to that suggestion. It's also possible that they are perfectly natural phenomena, perhaps chain lightning, as one American science writer has suggested; although this, again, does not explain some of the photographs taken by reputable sources, such as the Argentine navy, which clearly show spherical metallic objects hovering in the sky. As you've probably deduced, I'm really fascinated by UFOs and I only regret that this field of investigation has to a considerable extent been pre-empted by a crackpot fringe that claims to have soared to Mars on flying saucers piloted by three-foot-tall green humanoids with pointy heads. That kind of kook approach makes it very easy to dismiss the whole phenomenon which we do at our own risk.

I think another problem here—and one of the reasons that, despite the overwhelming evidence, there has been remarkably little public interest—is that most people don't really *want* to think about extraterrestrial beings patrolling our skies and perhaps observing us like bugs on a slide. The thought is too disturbing; it upsets our tidy, soothing, sanitized suburban *Weltanschauung*; the cosmos is more than light-years away from Scarsdale. This could be a survival mechanism, but it could also blind us to what may be the most dramatic and important moment in man's history—contact with another civilization.

PLAYBOY: *Among the reasons adduced by those who doubt the interstellar origin of UFOs is Einstein's special theory of relativity, which states that the speed of light is absolute and that nothing can exceed it. A journey from even the nearest star to Earth would consequently take thousands of years. They claim this virtually rules out interstellar travel—at least for sentient beings with life spans as short as the longest known to man. Do you find this argument valid?*

KUBRICK: I find it difficult to believe that we have penetrated to the ultimate depths of knowledge about the physical laws of the universe. It seems rather presumptuous to believe that in the space of a few hundred years, we've figured out most of what there is to know. So I don't think it's right to declaim with unshakable certitude that light is the absolute speed limit of the universe. I'm suspicious of dogmatic scientific rules; they tend to have a rather short life span. The most eminent European scientists of the early 19th Century scoffed at meteorites, on the grounds that "stones can't fall from the sky"; and just a year before Sputnik, one of the world's leading astrophysicists stated flatly that "space flight is bunk." Actually, there are already some extremely interesting theoretical studies underway—one by Dr. Gerald Feinberg at Columbia University—which indicate that short cuts could be found that would enable some things under certain conditions to exceed the speed of light.

In addition, there's always the possibility that the speed-of-light limitation, even if it's rigid, could be circumvented via a space-time warp, as Arthur Clarke has proposed. But let's take another, slightly more conservative, means of evading the speed of light's restrictions: If radio contact is developed between ourselves and another civilization, within 200 years we will have reached a stage in genetic engineering where the other race could transmit its genetic code to us by radio and we could then re-create their DNA pattern and artificially duplicate one of their species in our laboratories—and vice versa. This sounds fantastic only to those who haven't followed the tremendous breakthroughs being made in genetic engineering.

But actual interstellar travel wouldn't be impossible even if light speed *can't* be achieved. Whenever we dismiss space flight beyond our solar system on the grounds that it would take thousands of years, we are thinking of beings with life spans similar to ours. Fruit flies, I understand, live out their entire existence—birth, reproduction and death—within 24 hours; well, man may be to other creatures in the universe as the fruit fly is to man. There may be countless races in the universe with life spans of hundreds of thousands or even millions of years, to whom a 10,000–year journey to Earth would be about as intimidating as an afternoon outing in the park. But even in terms of our own time scale, within a few years it should be possible to freeze astronauts or induce a hibernatory suspension of life functions for the duration of an interstellar journey. They could spend 300 or 1000 years in space and be awakened automatically, feeling no different than if they had had a hearty eight hours' sleep.

The speed-of-light theory, too, could work in favor of long journeys; the peculiar "time dilation" factor in Einstein's relativity theory means that as an object accelerates toward the speed of light, time slows down. Everything would appear normal to those on board; but if they had been away from Earth for, say, 56 years, upon their return they would be merely 20 years older than when they departed. So, taking all these factors into consideration, I'm not unduly impressed by the claims of some scientists that the speed-of-light limitation renders interstellar travel impossible.

PLAYBOY: *You mentioned freezing astronauts for lengthy space journeys, as in the "hibernacula" of 2001. As you know, physicist Robert Ettinger and others have proposed freezing dead bodies in liquid nitrogen until a future time when they can be revived. What do you think of this proposal?*

KUBRICK: I've been interested in it for many years, and I consider it eminently feasible. Within ten years, in fact, I believe that freezing of the
dead will be a major industry in the United States and throughout
the world; I would recommend it as a field of investment for imaginative speculators. Dr. Ettinger's thesis is quite simple: If a body is
frozen cryogenically in liquid nitrogen at a temperature near
absolute zero—minus 459.6 degrees Fahrenheit—and stored in adequate facilities, it may very well be possible at some as-yet-indeter-
minate date in the future to thaw and revive the corpse and then
cure the disease or repair the physical damage that was the original
cause of death. This would, of course, entail a considerable gamble;
we have no way of knowing that future science will be sufficiently
advanced to cure, say; terminal cancer, or even successfully revive a
frozen body. In addition, the dead body undergoes damage in the
course of the freezing process itself; ice crystallizes within the blood
stream. And unless a body is frozen at the precise moment of death,
progressive brain-cell deterioration also occurs. But what do we
have to lose? Nothing—and we have immortality to gain. Let me
read you what Dr. Ettinger has written: "It used to be thought that
the distinction between life and death was simple and obvious. A living man breathes, sweats and makes stupid remarks; a dead one
just lies there, pays no attention, and after a while gets putrid. But
nowadays nothing is that simple."

Actually, when you really examine the concept of freezing the
dead, it's nowhere nearly as fantastic—though every bit as revolutionary—as it appears at first. After all, countless thousands of
patients "die" on the operating table and are revived by artificial
stimulation of the heart after a few seconds or even a few minutes—and there is really little substantive difference between
bringing a patient back to life after three minutes of clinical death
or after an "intermezzo" stage of 300 years. Fortunately, the freezing concept is now gaining an increasing amount of attention
within the scientific community. France's Dr. Jean Rostand, an
internationally respected biologist, has proposed that every nation
begin a freezer program immediately, funded by government
money and utilizing the top scientific minds in each country. "For
every day that we delay," he says, "untold thousands are going to
an unnecessary grave."

PLAYBOY: *Are you interested in being frozen yourself?*

KUBRICK: I would be if there were adequate facilities available at the
present time—which, unfortunately, there are not. A number of
organizations are attempting to disseminate information and raise
funds to implement an effective freezing program—the Life
Extension Society of Washington, the Cryonics Society of New
York, etc.—but we are still in the infancy of cryobiology. Right
now, all existing freezer facilities—and there are only a handful—
aren't sufficiently sophisticated to offer any realistic hope. But

that could and probably will change far more rapidly than we imagine.

A key point to remember, particularly by those ready to dismiss this whole concept as preposterous, is that science has made fantastic strides in just the past 40 years; within this brief period of time, a wide range of killer diseases that once were the scourge of mankind, from smallpox to diphtheria, have been virtually eliminated through vaccines and antibiotics, while others, such as diabetes, have been brought under control—though not yet completely eliminated—by drugs such as insulin. Already, heart transplants are almost a viable proposition and organ banks are being prepared to stock supplies of spleens, kidneys, lungs and hearts for future transplant surgery.

Dr. Ettinger predicts that a "freezee" who died after a severe accident or massive internal damage would emerge resuscitated from a hospital of the future a "crazy quilt of patchwork." His internal organs—heart, lungs, liver, kidneys, stomach and the rest—may be grafts, implanted after being grown in the laboratory from someone's donor cells. His arms and legs may be "bloodless artifacts of fabric, metal and plastic, directed by tiny motors." His brain cells, writes Ettinger, "may be mostly new, regenerated from the few which would be saved, and some of his memories and personality traits may have had to be imprinted onto the new cells by micro-techniques of chemistry and physics." The main challenge to the scientist of the future will not be revival but eliminating the original cause of death; and in this area, we have every reason for optimism as a result of recent experience. So before anyone dismisses the idea of freezing, he should take a searching look at what we have accomplished in a few decades—and ponder what we're capable of accomplishing over the next few centuries.

PLAYBOY: *If such a program does succeed, the person who is frozen will have no way of knowing, of course, if he will ever be successfully revived. Do you think future scientists will be willing, even if they're able, to bring their ancestors back to life?*

KUBRICK: Well, 20th-Century man may not be quite the cup of tea for a more advanced civilization of even 100 years in the future; but unless the future culture has achieved immortality—which is scientifically quite possible—they themselves would be frozen at death, and every generation would have a vested interest in the preservation of the preceding frozen generation in order to be, in turn, preserved by its own descendants. Of course, it would be something of a letdown if, 300 years from now, somebody just pulled the plug on us all, wouldn't it?

Another problem here, quite obviously, is the population explosion; what will be the demographic effect on the Earth of billions of frozen bodies suddenly revived and taking their places in society? But by the time future scientists have mastered the techniques to revive their frozen ancestors, space flight will doubtless be a reality and other planets will be open for colonization. In addition, vast freezer facilities could possibly be constructed on the dark side of the Moon to store millions of bodies. The problems are legion, of course, but so are the potentialities.

PLAYBOY: *Opponents of cryogenic freezing argue that death is the natural and inevitable culmination of life and that we shouldn't tamper with it—even if we're able to do so. How would you answer them?*

KUBRICK: Death is no more natural or inevitable than smallpox or diphtheria. Death is a disease and as susceptible to cure as any other disease. Over the eons, man's powerlessness to prevent death has led him to force it from the forefront of his mind, for his own psychological health, and to accept it unquestioningly as the unavoidable termination. But with the advance of science, this is no longer necessary—or desirable. Freezing is only one possible means of conquering death, and it certainly would not be binding on everyone; those who desire a "natural" death can go ahead and die, just as those in the 19th Century who desired "God-ordained" suffering resisted anesthesia. As Dr. Ettinger has written, "To each his own, and to those who choose not to be frozen, all I can say is—rot in good health."

PLAYBOY: *Freezing and resuscitation of the dead is just one revolutionary scientific technique that could transform our society. Looking ahead to the year of your film, 2001, what major social and scientific changes do you foresee?*

KUBRICK: Perhaps the greatest breakthrough we may have made by 2001 is the possibility that man may be able to eliminate old age. We've just discussed the steady scientific conquest of disease; even when this is accomplished, however, the scourge of old age will remain. But too many people view senile decay, like death itself, as inevitable. It's nothing of the sort. The highly respected Russian scientist V. F. Kuprevich has written, "I am sure we can find means for switching off the mechanisms which make cells age." Dr. Bernard Strehler, an eminent gerontology expert, contends that there is no inherent contradiction, no inherent property of cells or of Metazoa that precludes their organization into perpetually functioning and self-replenishing individuals.

One encouraging indication that we may already be on this road is the work of Dr. Hans Selye, who in his book *Calciphylaxis* presents an intriguing and well-buttressed argument that old age is caused by the transfer of calcium within the body—a transfer that can be arrested by circulating throughout the system specific iron compounds that flush out the calcium, absorb it and prevent it from permeating the tissue. Dr. Selye predicts that we may soon be able to prevent the man of 60 from progressing to the condition of the man of 90. This is something of an understatement; Selye could have added that the man of 60 could *stay* 60 for hundreds or even thousands of years if all other diseases have been eradicated. Even accidents would not necessarily impair his relative immortality; even if a man is run over by a steam-roller, his mind and body will be completely re-creatable from the tiniest fragment of his tissue, if genetic engineering continues its rapid progress.

PLAYBOY: *What impact do you think such dramatic scientific breakthroughs will have on the life style of society at the turn of the century?*

KUBRICK: That's almost impossible to say. Who could have predicted in 1900 what life in 1968 would be like? Technology is, in many ways, more predictable than human behavior. Politics and world affairs change so quickly that it's difficult to predict the future of social institutions for even ten years with a modicum of accuracy. By 2001, we could be living in a Gandhiesque paradise where all men are brothers, or in a neofascist dictatorship, or just be muddling along about the way we are today. As technology evolves, however, there's little doubt that the whole concept of leisure will be both quantitatively and qualitatively improved.

PLAYBOY: *What about the field of entertainment?*

KUBRICK: I'm sure we'll have sophisticated 3–D holographic television and films, and it's possible that completely new forms of entertainment and education will be devised. You might have a machine that taps the brain and ushers you into a vivid dream experience in which you are the protagonist in a romance or an adventure. On a more serious level, a similar machine could directly program you with knowledge; in this way, you might, for example, easily be able to learn fluent German in 20 minutes. Currently, the learning processes are so laborious and time-consuming that a breakthrough is really needed.

On the other hand, there are some risks in this kind of thing; I understand that at Yale they've been engaging in experiments in which the pleasure center of a mouse's brain has been localized and stimulated by electrodes; the result is that the mouse undergoes an eight-hour orgasm. If pleasure that intense were readily available to all of us, we might well become a race of sensually stultified zombies plugged into pleasure stimulators while machines do our work and our bodies and minds atrophy. We could also have this same problem with psychedelic drugs; they offer great promise of unleashing perceptions, but they also hold commensurate dangers of causing withdrawal and disengagement from life into a totally inner-directed kind of Soma world. At the present time, there are no ideal drugs; but I believe by 2001 we will have devised chemicals with no adverse physical, mental or genetic results that can give wings to the mind and enlarge perception beyond its present evolutionary capacities.

Actually, up to now, perception on the deepest level has really, from an evolutionary point of view, been detrimental to survival; if primitive man had been content to sit on a ledge by his cave absorbed in a beautiful sunset or a complex cloud configuration, he might never have exterminated his rival species—but neither would he have achieved mastery of the planet. Now, however, man is faced with the unprecedented situation of potentially unlimited material and technological resources at his disposal and a tremendous amount of leisure time. At last, he has the opportunity to look both within and beyond himself with a new perspective—without endangering or impeding the progress of the species. Drugs, intelligently used, can be a valuable guide to this new expansion of our consciousness. But if employed just for kicks, or to dull rather than to expand perception, they can be a highly negative influence. There should be fascinating drugs available by 2001; what *use* we make of them will be the crucial question.

PLAYBOY: *Have you ever used LSD or other so-called consciousness-expanding drugs?*

KUBRICK: No. I believe that drugs are basically of more use to the audience than to the artist. I think that the illusion of oneness with the universe, and absorption with the significance of every object in your environment, and the pervasive aura of peace and contentment is not the ideal state for an artist. It tranquilizes the creative personality, which thrives on conflict and on the clash and ferment of ideas. The artist's transcendence must be within his own work; he should not impose any artificial barriers between himself and the mainspring of his subconscious. One of the things that's turned me against LSD is that all the people I know who use it have a peculiar inability to distinguish between things that are really interesting and stimulating and things that *appear* so in the state of universal bliss the drug induces on a "good" trip. They seem to completely lose their critical faculties and disengage themselves from some of the most stimulating areas of life. Perhaps when *everything* is beautiful, nothing is beautiful.

PLAYBOY: *What stage do you believe today's sexual revolution will have reached by 2001?*

KUBRICK: Here again, it's pure speculation. Perhaps there will have been a reaction against present trends, and the pendulum will swing back to a kind of neo-puritanism. But it's more likely that the so-called sexual revolution, midwifed by the pill, will be extended. Through drugs, or perhaps via the sharpening or even mechanical amplification of latent ESP functions, it may be possible for each partner to simultaneously experience the sensations of the other; or we may eventually emerge into polymorphous sexual beings, with the male and female components blurring, merging and interchanging. The potentialities for exploring new areas of sexual experience are virtually boundless.

PLAYBOY: *In view of these trends, do you think romantic love may have become unfashionable by 2001?*

KUBRICK: Obviously, people are finding it increasingly easy to have intimate and fulfilling relationships outside the concept of romantic love—which, in its present form, is a relatively recent acquisition, developed at the court of Eleanor of Aquitaine in the 12th Century—but the basic love relationship, even at its most obsessional, is too deeply ingrained in man's psyche not to endure in one form or another. It's not going to be easy to circumvent our primitive emotional programming. Man still has essentially the same set of pair-bonding instincts—love, jealousy, possessiveness—imprinted for individual and tribal survival millions of years ago, and these still lie quite close to the surface, even in these allegedly enlightened and liberated times.

PLAYBOY: *Do you think that by 2001 the institution of the family, which some social scientists have characterized as moribund, may have evolved into something quite different from what it is today?*

KUBRICK: One can offer all kinds of impressive intellectual arguments against the family as an institution—its inherent authoritarianism, etc.; but when you get right down to it, the family is the most primitive and visceral and vital unit in society. You may stand outside your wife's hospital room during childbirth muttering, "My God, what a responsibility! Is it right to take on this terrible obligation? What am I really doing here?"; and then you go in and look down at the face of your child and—zap!—that ancient programming takes over and your response is one of wonder and joy and pride. It's a classic case of genetically imprinted social patterns. There are very few things in this world that have an unquestionable importance in and of themselves and are not susceptible to debate or rational argument, but the family is one of them. Perhaps man has been too "liberated" by science and evolutionary social trends. He has been turned loose from religion and has hailed the death of his gods; the imperative loyalties of the old nation-state are dissolving and all the old social and ethical values, however reactionary and narrow they often were, are disappearing. Man in the 20th Century has been cut adrift in a rudderless boat on an uncharted sea; if he is going to stay sane throughout the voyage, he must have someone to care about, something that is more important than himself.

PLAYBOY: *Some critics have detected not only a deep pessimism but also a kind of misanthropy in much of your work. In* Dr. Strangelove, *for example, one reviewer commented that your directorial attitude, despite the film's antiwar message, seemed curiously aloof and detached and unmoved by the annihilation of mankind, almost as if the Earth were being cleansed of an infection. Is there any truth to that?*

KUBRICK: Good God, no. You don't stop being concerned with man because you recognize his essential absurdities and frailties and pretensions. To me, the only real immorality is that which endangers the species; and the only absolute evil, that which threatens its annihilation. In the deepest sense, I believe in man's potential and in his capacity for progress. In *Strangelove*, I was dealing with the inherent irrationality in man that threatens to destroy him; that irrationality is with us as strongly today, and must be conquered. But a recognition of insanity doesn't imply a celebration of it—nor a sense of despair and futility about the possibility of curing it.

PLAYBOY: *In the five years since* Dr. Strangelove *was released, the two major nuclear powers, the U.S. and the U.S.S.R., have reached substantial accommodation with each other. Do you think this has reduced the danger of nuclear war?*

KUBRICK: No. If anything, the overconfident Soviet-American *détente increases* the threat of accidental war through carelessness; this has always been the greatest menace and the one most difficult to cope with. The danger that nuclear weapons may be used—perhaps by a secondary power—is as great if not greater than it has ever been, and it is really quite amazing that the world has been able to adjust to it psychologically with so little apparent dislocation.

Particularly acute is the possibility of war breaking out as the result of a sudden unanticipated flare-up in some part of the world, triggering a panic reaction and catapulting confused and frightened men into decisions they are incapable of making rationally. In addition, the serious threat remains that a psychotic figure somewhere in the modern command structure could start a war, or at the very least a limited exchange of nuclear weapons that could devastate wide areas and cause innumerable casualties. This, of course, was the theme of *Dr. Strangelove*; and I'm not entirely assured that somewhere in the Pentagon or the Red army upper echelons there does not exist the real-life prototype of General Jack D. Ripper.

PLAYBOY: *Fail-safe strategists have suggested that one way to obviate the danger that a screwball might spark a war would be to administer psychological-fitness tests to all key personnel in the nuclear command structure. Would that be an effective safeguard?*

KUBRICK: No, because any seriously disturbed individual who rose high within the system would have to possess considerable self-discipline and be able to effectively mask his fixations. Such tests already do exist to a limited degree, but you'd really have to be pretty far gone to betray yourself in them, and the type of individual we're discussing would have to be a highly controlled psychopathic personality not to have given himself away long ago. But beyond those tests, how are you going to objectively assess the sanity of the President, in whom, as Commander-in-Chief, the ultimate responsibility for the use of nuclear weapons resides? It's improbable but not impossible that we could someday have a psychopathic President, or a President who suffers a nervous breakdown, or an alcoholic President who, in the course of some stupefying binge, starts a war. You could say that such a man would be detected and restrained by his aides—but with the powers of the Presidency what they are today, who really knows? Less farfetched and even more terrifying is the possibility that a psychopathic individual could work his way into the lower echelons of the White House staff. Can you imagine what might have happened at the height of the Cuban Missile Crisis if some deranged waiter had slipped LSD into Kennedy's coffee—or, on the other side of the fence, into Khrushchev's vodka? The possibilities are chilling.

PLAYBOY: *Do you share the belief of some psychiatrists that our continued reliance on the balance of nuclear power, with all its attendant risks of global catastrophe, could reflect a kind of collective death wish?*

KUBRICK: No, but I think the *fear* of death helps explain why people accept this Damoclean sword over their heads with such bland equanimity. Man is the only creature aware of his own mortality and is at the same time generally incapable of coming to grips with this awareness and all its implications. Millions of people thus, to a greater or lesser degree, experience emotional anxieties, tensions and unresolved conflicts that frequently express themselves in the form of neuroses and a general joylessness that permeates their lives with frustration and bitterness and increases as they grow older and see the grave yawning before them. As fewer and fewer people find solace in religion as a buffer between themselves and the terminal moment, I actually believe that they unconsciously derive a kind of perverse solace from the idea that in the event of nuclear war, the world dies with them. God is dead, but the bomb endures; thus, they are no longer alone in the terrible vulnerability of their mortality. Sartre once wrote that if there was one thing you could tell a man about to be executed that would make him happy, it was that a comet would strike the earth the next day and destroy every living human being. This is not so much a collective death wish or self-destructive urge as a reflection of the awesome and agonizing loneliness of death. This is extremely pernicious, of course, because it aborts the kind of fury and indignation that should galvanize the world into defusing a situation where a few political leaders on both sides are seriously prepared to incinerate millions of people out of some misguided sense of national interest.

PLAYBOY: *Are you a pacifist?*

KUBRICK: I'm not sure what pacifism really means. Would it have been an act of superior morality to have submitted to Hitler in order to avoid war? I don't think so. But there have also been tragically senseless wars such as World War One and the current mess in Vietnam and the plethora of religious wars that pockmark history. What makes today's situation so radically different from anything that has gone before, however, is that, for the first time in history, man has the means to destroy the entire species—and possibly the planet as well. The problem of dramatizing this to the public is that it all seems so abstract and unreal; it's rather like saying, "The sun is going to die in a billion years." What is required as a minimal first corrective step is a concrete alternative to the present balance of terror—one that people can understand and support.

PLAYBOY: *Do you believe that some form of all-powerful world government, or some radically new social, political and economic system, could deal intelligently and farsightedly with such problems as nuclear war?*

KUBRICK: Well, none of the present systems has worked very well, but I don't know what we'd replace them with. The idea of a group of philosopher kings running everything with benign and omniscient paternalism is always attractive, but where do we find the philosopher kings? And if we do find them, how do we provide for their successors? No, it has to be conceded that democratic society, with all its inherent strains and contradictions, is unquestionably the best system anyone ever worked out. I believe it was Churchill who once remarked that democracy is the worst social system in the world, except for all the others.

PLAYBOY: *You've been accused of revealing, in your films, a strong hostility to the modern industrialized society of the democratic West, and a particular antagonism—ambivalently laced with a kind of morbid fascination—toward automation. Your critics claim this was especially evident in 2001, where the archvillain of the film, the computer HAL 9000, was in a sense the only human being. Do you believe that machines are becoming more like men and men more like machines—and do you detect an eventual struggle for dominance between the two?*

KUBRICK: First of all, I'm not hostile toward machines at all; just the opposite, in fact. There's no doubt that we're entering a mechanarchy, however, and that our already complex relationship with our machinery will become even more complex as the machines become more and more intelligent. Eventually, we will have to share this planet with machines whose intelligence and abilities far surpass our own. But the interrelationship—if intelligently managed by man—could have an immeasurably enriching effect on society.

Looking into the distant future, I suppose it's not inconceivable that a semisentient robot-computer subculture could evolve that might one day decide it no longer needed man. You've probably heard the story about the ultimate computer of the future: For months scientists think of the first question to pose to it, and finally they hit on the right one: "Is there a God?" After a moment of whirring and flashing lights, a card comes out, punched with the words: THERE IS NOW. But this problem is a distant one and I'm not staying up nights worrying about it; I'm convinced that our toasters and TVs are fully domesticated, though I'm not so sure about integrated telephone circuits, which sometimes strike me as possessing a malevolent life all their own.

PLAYBOY: *Speaking of futuristic electronics and mechanics,* 2001's *incredibly elaborate gadgetry and scenes of space flight have been hailed—even by hostile critics—as a major cinematic breakthrough. How were you able to achieve such remarkable special effects?*

KUBRICK: I can't answer that question technically in the time we have available, but I can say that it was necessary to conceive, design and engineer completely new techniques in order to produce the special effects. This took 18 months and $6,500,000 out of a $10,500,000 budget. I think an extraordinary amount of credit must go to Robert H. O'Brien, the president of M-G-M, who had sufficient faith to allow me to persevere at what must have at times appeared to be a task without end. But I felt it was necessary to make this film in such a way that every special-effects shot in it would be completely convincing—something that had never before been accomplished in a motion picture.

PLAYBOY: *Thanks to those special effects,* 2001 *is undoubtedly the most graphic depiction of space flight in the history of films—and yet you have admitted that you yourself refuse to fly, even in a commercial jet liner. Why?*

KUBRICK: I suppose it comes down to a rather awesome awareness of mortality. Our ability, unlike the other animals, to conceptualize our own end creates tremendous psychic strains within us; whether we like to admit it or not, in each man's chest a tiny ferret of fear at this ultimate knowledge gnaws away at his ego and his sense of purpose. We're fortunate, in a way, that our body, and the fulfillment of its needs and functions, plays such an imperative role in our lives; this physical shell creates a buffer between us

and the mind-paralyzing realization that only a few years of existence separate birth from death. If man really sat back and thought
about his impending termination and his terrifying insignificance
and aloneness in the cosmos, he would surely go mad, or suc-
cumb to a numbing sense of futility. Why, he might ask himself,
should he bother to write a great symphony, or strive to make a
living, or even to love another, when he is no more than a
momentary microbe on a dust mote whirling through the unimaginable immensity of space.

Those of us who are forced by their own sensibilities to view
their lives in this perspective—who recognize that there is no purpose they can comprehend and that amidst a countless myriad of
stars their existence goes unknown and unchronicled—can fall
prey all too easily to the ultimate *anomie*. I can well understand
how life became for Matthew Arnold "a darkling plain . . . where
ignorant armies clash by night . . . and there is neither love nor
hope nor certitude nor faith nor surcease from pain." But even for
those who lack the sensitivity to more than vaguely comprehend
their transience and their triviality, this inchoate awareness robs
life of meaning and purpose; it's why "the mass of men lead lives
of quiet desperation," why so many of us find our lives as absent
of meaning as our deaths.

The world's religions, for all their parochialism, did supply a
kind of consolation for this great ache; but as clergymen now pro-
nounce the death of God and, to quote Arnold again, "the sea of
faith" recedes around the world with a "melancholy, long, with-
drawing roar," man has no crutch left on which to lean—and no
hope, however irrational, to give purpose to his existence. This
shattering recognition of our mortality is at the root of far more
mental illness than I suspect even psychiatrists are aware.

PLAYBOY: *If life is so purposeless, do you feel that it's worth living?*

KUBRICK: Yes, for those of us who manage somehow to cope with our
mortality. The very meaninglessness of life forces man to create
his own meaning. Children, of course, begin life with an untar-
nished sense of wonder, a capacity to experience total joy at something as simple as the greenness of a leaf; but as they grow older,
the awareness of death and decay begins to impinge on their consciousness and subtly erode their *joie de vivre*, their idealism—
and their assumption of immortality. As a child matures, he sees
death and pain everywhere about him, and begins to lose faith in
the ultimate goodness of man. But if he's reasonably strong—and
lucky—he can emerge from this twilight of the soul into a rebirth
of life's *élan*. Both because of and in spite of his awareness of the
meaninglessness of life, he can forge a fresh sense of purpose and
affirmation. He may not recapture the same pure sense of wonder
he was born with, but he can shape something far more enduring
and sustaining. The most terrifying fact about the universe is not

that it is hostile but that it is indifferent; but if we can come to terms with this indifference and accept the challenges of life within the boundaries of death—however mutable man may be able to make them—our existence as a species can have genuine meaning and fulfillment. However vast the darkness, we must supply our own light.

PLAYBOY: *Will we be able to find any deep meaning or fulfillment, either as individuals or as a species, as long as we continue to live with the knowledge that all human life could be snuffed out at any moment in a nuclear catastrophe?*

KUBRICK: We *must*, for in the final analysis, there may be no sound way to eliminate the threat of self-extinction without changing human nature; even if you managed to get every country disarmed down to the bow and arrow, you would still be unable to lobotomize either the knowledge of how to build nuclear warheads or the perversity that allows us to rationalize their use. Given these two categorical imperatives in a disarmed world, the first country to amass even a few weapons would have a great incentive to use them quickly. So an argument might be made that there is a greater chance for *some* use of nuclear weapons in a totally disarmed world, though less chance of global extinction; while in a world armed to the teeth you have less chance for *some* use—but a great chance of extinction if they're used.

If you try to remove yourself from an Earthly perspective and look at this tragic paradox with the detachment of an extraterrestrial, the whole thing is totally irrational. Man now has the power in one mad, incandescent moment, as you point out, to exterminate the entire species; our own generation could be the last on Earth. One miscalculation and all the achievements of history could vanish in a mushroom cloud; one misstep and all of man's aspirations and strivings over the millennia could be terminated. One short circuit in a computer, one lunatic in a command structure and we could negate the heritage of the billions who have died since the dawn of man and abort the promise of the billions yet unborn—the ultimate genocide. What an irony that the discovery of nuclear power, with its potential for annihilation, also constitutes the first tottering step into the universe that must be taken by all intelligent worlds. Unhappily, the infant-mortality rate among emerging civilizations in the cosmos may be very high. Not that it will matter except to us; the destruction of this planet would have no significance on a cosmic scale; to an observer in the Andromeda nebulae, the sign of our extinction would be no more than a match flaring for a second in the heavens; and if that match does blaze in the darkness, there will be none to mourn a race that used a power that could have lit a beacon in the stars to light its funeral pyre. The choice is ours.

The *Rolling Stone* Interview: Stanley Kubrick

TIM CAHILL

He didn't bustle into the room, and he didn't wander in. Truth, as he would reiterate several times, is multifaceted, and it would be fair to say that Stanley Kubrick entered the executive suite at Pinewood Studios, outside London, in a multifaceted manner. He was at once happy to have found the place after a twenty-minute search, apologetic about being late and apprehensive about the torture he might be about to endure. Stanley Kubrick, I had been told, hates interviews.

It's hard to know what to expect of the man if you've only seen his films. One senses in those films painstaking craftsmanship, a furious intellect at work, a single-minded devotion. His movies don't lend themselves to easy analysis; this may account for the turgid nature of some of the books that have been written about his art. Take this example: "And while Kubrick feels strongly that the visual powers of film make ambiguity an inevitability as well as a virtue, he would not share Bazin's mystical belief that the better film makers are those who sacrifice their personal perspectives to a 'fleeting crystallization of a reality [of] whose environing presence one is ceaselessly aware.'"

One feels that an interview conducted on this level would be pretentious bullshit. Kubrick, however, seemed entirely unpretentious. He was wearing running shoes and an old corduroy jacket. There was an ink stain just below the pocket where some ball point pen had bled to death.

"What is this place?" Kubrick asked.

"It's called the executive suite," I said. "I think they put big shots up here."

Kubrick looked around at the dark wood-paneled walls, the chandeliers, the leather couches and chairs. "Is there a bathroom?" he asked, with some urgency.

"Across the hall," I said.

The director excused himself and went looking for the facility. I reviewed my notes. Kubrick was born in the Bronx in 1928. He was an undistinguished student whose passions were tournament-level chess and photography. After graduation from Taft High School at the age of seventeen, he landed a prestigious job as a photographer for *Look* magazine, which he quit after four years in order to make his first film. *Day of the Fight* (1950) was a documentary about the middleweight boxer Walter Cartier. After a second documentary, *Flying Padre* (1951), Kubrick borrowed $10,000 from relatives to make *Fear and Desire* (1953), his first feature, an arty film that he now finds "embarrassing." Kubrick, his first wife and two friends were the entire crew for the film. By necessity, Kubrick was director, cameraman, lighting engineer, makeup man, administrator, propman and unit chauffeur. Later in his career, he would take on some of these duties again, for reasons other than necessity.

Kubrick's breakthrough film was *Paths of Glory* (1957). During the filming, he met an actress, Christiane Harlan, whom he eventually married. Christiane sings a song at the end of the film in a scene that, on four separate viewings, has brought tears to my eyes.

Kubrick's next film was *Spartacus* (1960), a work he finds disappointing. He was brought in to direct after the star, Kirk Douglas, had a falling-out with the original director, Anthony Mann. Kubrick was not given control of the script, which he felt was full of easy moralizing. He was used to making his own films his own way, and the experience chafed. He has never again relinquished control over any aspect of his films.

And he has taken some extraordinary and audacious chances with those works. The mere decision to film Vladimir Nabokov's *Lolita* (1961) was enough to send some censorious sorts into a spittle-spewing rage. *Dr. Strangelove* (1963), based on the novel *Red Alert*, was conceived as a tense thriller about the possibility of accidental nuclear war. As Kubrick worked on the script, however, he kept bumping up against the realization that the scenes he was writing were funny in the darkest possible way. It was a matter of slipping on a banana peel and annihilating the human race. Stanley Kubrick went with his gut feeling: he directed *Dr. Strangelove* as a black comedy. The film is routinely described as a masterpiece.

Most critics also use that word to describe the two features that followed, *2001: A Space Odyssey* (1968) and *A Clockwork Orange* (1971). Some reviewers see a subtle falling off of quality in his *Barry Lyndon* (1975) and *The Shining* (1980), though there is a critical reevaluation of the two films in process. This seems to be typical of his critical reception.

Kubrick moved to England in 1961. He lives outside of London with Christiane (now a successful painter), three golden retrievers and a mutt he found wandering forlornly along the road. He has three grown daughters. Some who know him say he can be "difficult" and "exacting."

He had agreed to meet and talk about his latest movie, *Full Metal Jacket*, a film about the Vietnam War that he produced and directed. He also co-wrote the screenplay with Michael Herr, the author of *Dispatches*, and Gustav Hasford, who wrote *The Short-Timers*, the novel on which the film is based. *Full Metal Jacket* is Kubrick's first feature in seven years.

The difficult and exacting director returned from the bathroom looking a little perplexed. "I think you're right," he said. "I think this is a place where people stay. I looked around a little, opened a door, and there was this guy sitting on the edge of a bed."

"Who was he?" I asked.

"I don't know," he replied.

"What did he say?"

"Nothing. He just looked at me, and I left."

There was a long silence while we pondered the inevitable ambiguity of reality, specifically in relation to some guy sitting on a bed across the hall. Then Stanley Kubrick began the interview:

I'm not going to be asked any conceptualizing questions, right?

All the books, most of the articles I read about you—It's all conceptualizing.

Yeah, but not by me.

I thought I had to ask those kinds of questions.

No. Hell, no. That's my . . . [*He shudders.*] It's the thing I hate the worst.

Really? I've got all these questions written down in a form I thought you might require. They all sound like essay questions for the finals in a graduate philosophy seminar.

The truth is that I've always felt trapped and pinned down and harried by those questions.

Questions like [reading from notes] *"Your first feature,* Fear and Desire, *in 1953, concerned a group of soldiers lost behind enemy lines in an unnamed war;* Spartacus *contained some battle scenes;* Paths of Glory *was an indictment of war and, more specifically, of the generals who wage it; and* Dr. Strangelove *was the blackest of comedies about accidental nuclear war. How does* Full Metal Jacket *complete your examination of the subject of war? Or does it?"*

Those kinds of questions.

You feel the real question lurking behind all the verbiage is "What does this new movie mean?"

Exactly. And that's almost impossible to answer, especially when you've been so deeply inside the film for so long. Some people demand a five-line capsule summary. Something you'd read in a magazine. They want you to say, "This is the story of the duality of man and the duplicity of governments." [A pretty good description of the subtext that informs *Full Metal Jacket*, actually.] I hear people try to do it—give the five-line summary—but if a film has any substance or subtlety, whatever you say is never complete, it's usually wrong, and it's necessarily simplistic: truth is too multifaceted to be contained in a five-line summary. If the work is good, what you say about it is usually irrelevant.

I don't know. Perhaps it's vanity, this idea that the work is bigger than one's capacity to describe it. Some people can do interviews. They're very slick, and they neatly evade this hateful conceptualizing. Fellini is good; his interviews are very amusing. He just makes jokes and says preposterous things that you know he can't possibly mean.

I mean, I'm doing interviews to help the film, and I think they do help the film, so I can't complain. But it isn't . . . it's . . . it's difficult.

So let's talk about the music in Full Metal Jacket. *I was surprised by some of the choices, stuff like "These Boots Are Made for Walkin'," by Nancy Sinatra. What does that song mean?*

It was the music of the period. The Tet offensive was in '68. Unless we were careless, none of the music is post-'68.

I'm not saying it's anachronistic. It's just that the music that occurs to me in that context is more, oh, Jimi Hendrix, Jim Morrison.

The music really depended on the scene. We checked through *Billboard's* list of Top 100 hits for each year from 1962 to 1968. We were looking for interesting material that played well with a scene. We tried a lot of songs. Sometimes the dynamic range of the music was too great, and we couldn't work in dialogue. The music has to come up under speech at some point, and if all you hear is the bass, it's not going to work in the context of the movie.

Why? Don't you like "These Boots Are Made for Walkin'"?

Of the music in the film, I'd have to say I'm more partial to Sam the Sham's "Wooly Bully," which is one of the great party records of all time. And "Surfin' Bird."

An amazing piece, isn't it?

"Surfin', Bird" comes in during the aftermath of a battle, as the marines are passing a medevac helicopter. The scene reminded me of Dr. Strangelove, where the plane is being refueled in midair with that long, suggestive tube, and the music in the background is "Try a Little Tenderness." Or the cosmic waltz in 2001, where the spacecraft is slowly cartwheeling through space in time to "The Blue Danube." And now you have the chopper and the "Bird."

What I love about the music in that scene is that it suggests postcombat euphoria—which you see in the marine's face when he fires at the men running out of the building: he misses the first four, waits a beat, then hits the next two. And that great look on his face, that look of euphoric pleasure, the pleasure one has read described in so many accounts of combat. So he's got this look on his face, and suddenly the music starts and the tanks are rolling and the marines are mopping up. The choices weren't arbitrary.

You seem to have skirted the issue of drugs in Full Metal Jacket.

It didn't seem relevant. Undoubtedly, marines took drugs in Vietnam. But this drug thing, it seems to suggest that all marines were out of control, when in fact they weren't. It's a little thing, but check out the pictures taken during the battle of Hue: you see marines in fully fastened flak jackets. Well, people hated wearing them. They were heavy and hot, and sometimes people wore them but didn't fasten them. Disciplined troops wore them, and they wore them fastened.

People always look at directors, and you in particular, in the context of a body of work. I couldn't help but notice some resonance with Paths of Glory *at the end of* Full Metal Jacket: *a woman surrounded by enemy soldiers, the odd, ambiguous gesture that ties these people together. . . .*

That resonance is an accident. The scene comes straight out of Gustav Hasford's book.

So your purpose wasn't to poke the viewer in the ribs, point out certain similarities . . .

Oh, God, no. I'm trying to be true to the material. You know, there's another extraordinary accident. Cowboy is dying, and in the background there's something that looks very much like the monolith in *2001*. And it just happened to be there.

The whole area of combat was one complete area—it actually exists. One of the things I tried to do was give you a sense of where you were, where everything else was. Which, in war movies, is something you frequently don't get. The terrain of small-unit action is really the story of the action. And this is something we tried to make beautifully clear: there's a low wall, there's the building space. And once you get in there, everything is exactly where it actually was. No cutting away, no cheating. So it came down to where the sniper would be and where the marines were. When Cowboy is shot, they carry him around the corner—to the very most logical shelter. And there, in the background was this thing, this monolith. I'm sure some people will think that there was some calculated reference to *2001*, but honestly, it was just there.

You don't think you're going to get away with that, do you?

[*Laughs*] I know it's an amazing coincidence.

Where were those scenes filmed?

We worked from still photographs of Hue in 1968. And we found an area that had the same 1930s functionalist architecture. Now, not every bit of it was right, but some of the buildings were absolute carbon copies of the outer industrial areas of Hue.

Where was it?

Here. Near London. It had been owned by British Gas, and it was scheduled to be demolished. So they allowed us to blow up the buildings. We had demolition guys in there for a week, laying charges. One Sunday, all the executives from British Gas brought their families down to watch us blow the place up. It was spectacular. Then we had a wrecking ball there for two months, with the art director telling the operator which hole to knock in which building.

Art direction with a wrecking ball.

I don't think anybody's ever had a set like that. It's beyond any kind of economic possibility. To make that kind of three-dimensional rubble, you'd have to have everything done by plasterers, modeled, and you couldn't build that if you spent $80 million and had five years to do it. You couldn't duplicate, oh, all those twisted bits of reinforcement. And to make rubble, you'd have to go find some real rubble and copy it. It's the only way. If you're going to make a tree, for instance, you have to copy a real tree. No one can "make up" a tree, because every tree has an inherent logic in the way it branches. And I've discovered that no one can make up a rock. I found that out in *Paths of Glory*. We had to copy rocks, but every rock also has an inherent logic you're not aware of until you see a fake rock. Every detail looks right, but something's wrong.

So we had real rubble. We brought in palm trees from Spain and a hundred thousand plastic tropical plants from Hong Kong. We did little things, details-people don't notice right away, that add to the illusion. All in all, a tremendous set dressing and rubble job.

How do you choose your material?

I read. I order books from the States. I literally go into bookstores, close my eyes and take things off the shelf. If I don't like the book after a bit, I don't finish it. But I like to be surprised.

Full Metal Jacket *is based on Gustav Hasford's book* The Short-Timers.

It's a very short, very beautifully and economically written book, which, like the film, leaves out all the mandatory scenes of character development: the scene where the guy talks about his father, who's an alcoholic, his girlfriend—all that stuff that bogs down and seems so arbitrarily inserted into every war story.

What I like about not writing original material—which I'm not even certain I could do—is that you have this tremendous advantage of reading something for the first time. You never have this experience again with the story. You have a reaction to it: it's a kind of falling-in-love reaction.

That's the first thing. Then it becomes almost a matter of code breaking, of breaking the work down into a structure that is truthful, that doesn't lose the ideas or the content or the feeling of the book. And fitting it all into the much more limited time frame of a movie.

And as long as you possibly can, you retain your emotional attitude, whatever it was that made you fall in love in the first place. You judge a scene by asking yourself, "Am I still responding to what's there?" The process is both analytical and emotional. You're trying to balance calculating analysis against feeling. And it's almost never a question of "What does this scene mean?" It's "Is this truthful, or does something about it feel false?" It's "Is this scene interesting? Will it make me feel the way I felt when I first fell in love with the material?" It's an intuitive process, the way I imagine writing music is intuitive. It's not a matter of structuring an argument.

You said something almost exactly the opposite once.

Did I?

Someone had asked you if there was any analogy between chess and filmmaking. You said that the process of making decisions was very analytical in both cases. You said that depending on intuition was a losing proposition.

I suspect I might have said that in another context. The part of the film that involves telling the story works pretty much the way I said. In the actual making of the movie, the chess analogy becomes more valid. It has to do with tournament chess, where you have a clock and you have to make a certain number of moves in a certain time. If you don't, you forfeit, even if you're a queen ahead. You'll see a grandmaster, the guy has three minutes on the clock and ten moves left. And he'll spend two minutes on one move, because he knows that if he doesn't get that one right, the game will be lost. And then he makes the last nine moves in a minute. And he may have done the right thing.

Well, in filmmaking, you always have decisions like that. You are always pitting time and resources against quality and ideas.

You have a reputation for having your finger on every aspect of each film you make, from inception right on down to the première and beyond. How is it that you're allowed such an extraordinary amount of control over your films?

I'd like to think it's because my films have a quality that holds up on second, third and fourth viewing. Realistically, it's because my budgets are within reasonable limits and the films do well. The only one that did poorly from the studio's point of view was *Barry Lyndon*. So, since my films don't cost that much, I find a way to spend a little extra time in order to get the quality on the screen.

Full Metal Jacket *seemed a long time in the making.*

Well, we had a couple of severe accidents. The guy who plays the drill instructor, Lee Ermey, had an auto accident in the middle of shooting. It was about 1:00 in the morning, and his car skidded off the road. He broke all his ribs on one side, just tremendous injuries, and he probably would have died, except he was conscious and kept flashing his lights. A motorist stopped. It was in a place called Epping Forest, where the police are always finding bodies. Not the sort of place you get out of your car at 1:30 in the morning and go see why someone's flashing their lights. Anyway, Lee was out for four and a half months.

He had actually been a marine drill instructor?

Parris Island.

How much of his part comes out of that experience?

I'd say fifty percent of Lee's dialogue, specifically the insult stuff, came from Lee. You see, in the course of hiring the marine recruits, we interviewed hundreds of guys. We lined them all up and did an improvisation of the first meeting with the drill instructor. They didn't know what he was going to say, and we could see how they reacted. Lee came up with, I don't know, 150 pages of insults. Off the wall stuff: "I don't like the name Lawrence. Lawrence is for faggots and sailors."

Aside from the insults, though, virtually every serious thing he says is basically true. When he says, "A rifle is only a tool, it's a hard heart that kills," you know it's true. Unless you're living in a world that doesn't need fighting men, you can't fault him. Except maybe for a certain lack of subtlety in his behavior. And I don't think the United States Marine Corps is in the market for subtle drill instructors.

This is a different drill instructor than the one Lou Gosset played in An Officer and a Gentlemen.

I think Lou Gosset's performance was wonderful, but he had to do what he was given in the story. The film clearly wants to ingratiate itself with the audience. So many films do that. You show the drill instructor really has a heart of gold—the mandatory scene where he sits in his office, eyes swimming with pride about the boys and so forth. I suppose he actually is proud, but there's a danger of falling into what amounts to so much sentimental bullshit.

So you distrust sentimentality.

I don't mistrust sentiment and emotion, no. The question becomes, are you giving them something to make them a little happier, or are you putting in something that is inherently true to the material? Are people behaving the way we all really behave, or are they behaving the way we would like them to behave? I mean, the world is not as it's presented in Frank Capra films. People love those films—which are beautifully made— but I wouldn't describe them as a true picture of life.

The questions are always, is it true? Is it interesting? To worry about those mandatory scenes that some people think make a picture is often just pandering to some conception of an audience. Some films try to outguess an audience. They try to ingratiate themselves, and it's not something you really have to do. Certainly audiences have flocked to see films that are not essentially true, but I don't think this prevents them from responding to the truth.

Books I've read on you seem to suggest that you consider editing the most important aspect of the filmmaker's art.

There are three equal things: the writing, slogging through the actual shooting and the editing.

You've quoted Pudovkin to the effect that editing is the only original and unique art form in film.

I think so. Everything else comes from something else. Writing, of course, is writing, acting comes from the theater, and cinematography comes from photography. Editing is unique to film. You can see something from different points of view almost simultaneously, and it creates a new experience.

Pudovkin gives an example: You see a guy hanging a picture on the wall. Suddenly you see his feet slip; you see the chair move; you see his hand go down and the picture fall off the wall. In that split second, a guy falls off a chair, and you see it in a way that you could not see it any other way except through editing.

TV commercials have figured that out. Leave content out of it, and some of the most spectacular examples of film art are in the best TV commercials.

Give me an example.

The Michelob commercials. I'm a pro-football fan, and I have videotapes of the games sent over to me, commercials and all. Last year Michelob did a series, just impressions of people having a good time—

The big city at night—

And the editing, the photography, was some of the most brilliant work I've ever seen. Forget what they're doing—selling beer—and it's visual poetry. Incredible eight-frame cuts. And you realize that in thirty seconds they've created an impression of something rather complex. If you could ever tell a story, something with some content, using that kind of visual poetry, you could handle vastly more complex and subtle material.

People spend millions of dollars and months' worth of work on these thirty seconds.

So it's a bit impractical. And I suppose there's really nothing that would substitute for the great dramatic moment, fully played out. Still, the stories we do on film are basically rooted in the theater. Even Woody Allen's movies, which are wonderful, are very traditional in their structure. Did I get the year right on those Michelob ads?

I think so.

Because occasionally I'll find myself watching a game from 1984.

It amazes me that you're a pro-football fan.

Why?

It doesn't fit my image of you.

Which is . . .

Stanley Kubrick is a monk, a man who lives for his work and virtually nothing else, certainly not pro football. And then there are those rumors—

I know what's coming.

You want both barrels?

Fire.

Stanley Kubrick is a perfectionist. He is consumed by mindless anxiety over every aspect of every film he makes. Kubrick is a hermit, an expatriate, a neurotic who is terrified of automobiles and who won't let his chauffeur drive more than thirty miles an hour.

Part of my problem is that I cannot dispel the myths that have somehow accumulated over the years. Somebody writes something, it's completely off the wall, but it gets filed and repeated until everyone believes it. For instance, I've read that I wear a football helmet in the car.

You won't let your driver go more than thirty miles an hour, and you wear a football helmet, just in case.

In fact, I don't have a chauffeur. I drive a Porsche 928 S, and I sometimes drive it at eighty or ninety miles an hour on the motorway.

Your film editor says you still work on your old films. Isn't that neurotic perfectionism?

I'll tell you what he means. We discovered that the studio had lost the picture negative of *Dr. Strangelove*. And they also lost the magnetic master soundtrack. All the printing negatives were badly ripped dupes. The search went on for a year and a half. Finally, I had to try to reconstruct the picture from two not-too-good fine-grain positives, both of which were damaged already. If those fine-grains were ever torn, you could never make any more negatives.

Do you consider yourself an expatriate?

Because I direct films, I have to live in a major English-speaking production center. That narrows it down to three places: Los Angeles, New York and London. I like New York, but it's inferior to London as a production center. Hollywood is best, but I don't like living there.

You read books or see films that depict people being corrupted by Hollywood, but it isn't that. It's this tremendous sense of insecurity. A lot of destructive competitiveness. In comparison, England seems very remote. I try to keep up, read the trade papers, but it's good to get it on paper and not have to hear it every place you go. I think it's good to just do the work and insulate yourself from that undercurrent of low-level malevolence.

I've heard rumors that you'll do a hundred takes for one scene.

It happens when actors are unprepared. You cannot act without knowing dialogue. If actors have to think about the words, they can't work on the emotion. So you end up doing thirty takes of something. And still you can see the concentration in their eyes; they don't know their lines. So you just shoot it and shoot it and hope you can get something out of it in pieces.

Now, if the actor is a nice guy, he goes home, he says, "Stanley's such a perfectionist, he does a hundred takes on every scene." So my thirty takes become a hundred. And I get this reputation.

If I did a hundred takes on every scene, I'd never finish a film. Lee Ermey, for instance, would spend every spare second with the dialogue coach, and he always knew his lines. I suppose Lee averaged eight or nine takes. He sometimes did it in three. Because he was prepared.

There's a rumor that you actually wanted to approve the theaters that show Full Metal Jacket. *Isn't that an example of mindless anxiety?*

Some people are amazed, but I worry about the theaters where the picture is being shown. They think that's some form of demented anxiety. But Lucas films has a Theater Alignment Program. They went around and checked a lot of theaters and published the results in a [1985] report that virtually confirms all your worst suspicions. For instance, within one day, fifty percent of the prints are scratched. Something is usually broken. The amplifiers are no good, and the sound is bad. The lights are uneven. . . .

Is that why so many films I've seen lately seem too dark? Why you don't really see people in the shadows when clearly the director wants you to see them?

Well, theaters try to put in a screen that's larger than the light source they paid for. If you buy a 2000–watt projector, it may give you a decent picture twenty feet wide. And let's say that theater makes the picture forty feet wide by putting it in a wider-angle projector. In fact, then you're getting 200 percent less light. It's an inverse law of squares. But they want a biggest picture, so it's dark.

Many exhibitors are terribly guilty of ignoring minimum standards of picture quality. For instance, you now have theaters where all the reels are run in one continuous string. And they never clean the aperture gate. You get one little piece of gritty dust in there, and every time the film runs, it gets bigger. After a couple of days, it starts to put a scratch on the film. The scratch goes from one end of the film to the other. You've seen it, I'm sure.

That thing you see, it looks like a hair dangling down from the top of the frame, sort of wiggling there through the whole film?

That's one manifestation, yeah. The Lucas report found that after fifteen days, most films should be junked. [The report says that after seventeen days, most films are damaged.] Now, is it an unreal concern if I want to make sure that on the press shows or on key city openings, everything in the theater is going to run smoothly? You just send someone to check the place out three or four days ahead of time. Make sure nothing's broken. It's really only a phone call or two, pressuring some people to fix things. I mean, is this a legitimate concern, or is this mindless anxiety?

Initial reviews of most of your films are sometimes inexplicably hostile. Then there's a reevaluation. Critics seem to like you better in retrospect.

That's true. The first reviews of *2001* were insulting, let alone bad. An important Los Angeles critic faulted Paths of Glory because the actors didn't speak with French accents. When Dr. Strangelove came out, a New York paper ran a review under the head MOSCOW COULD NOT BUY MORE HARM TO AMERICA. Something like that. But critical opinion on my films has always been salvaged by what I would call subsequent critical opinion. Which is why I think audiences are more reliable than critics, at least initially.

Audiences tend not to bring all that critical baggage with them to each film.

And I really think that a few critics come to my films expecting to see the last film. They're waiting to see something that never happens. I imagine it must be something like standing in the batter's box waiting for a fast ball, and the pitcher throws a change-up. The batter swings and misses. He thinks, "Shit, he threw me the wrong pitch." I think this accounts for some of the initial hostility.

Well, you don't make it easy on viewers or critics. You've said you want an audience to react emotionally. You create strong feelings, but you won't give us any easy answers.

That's because I don't have any easy answers.

ARTICLES AND ESSAYS ON STANLEY KUBRICK

The Early Films: Killer's Kiss *to* Lolita

Materiality and Sociality in *Killer's Kiss*

DANA POLAN

Before the first image of *Killer's Kiss* comes up on the screen, we hear the noise of a train. The fade-in to the first image reveals that we are in a train station where the hero, Davey, waits wondering if Gloria, his newfound love, will be showing up to meet him. The images thus clarify and lend logic to the first sounds. The initial separation of sound and image, however, creates a conflict: already in this early film of Kubrick, we find the opposition of machine and Man that will run through many of his films. (At points in this essay, I will refer to the Kubrick protagonist as "Man," not out of some misguided attempt to use supposedly generic language, but to reiterate how Kubrick's cinema itself figures that attempt: even as it appears to be dealing with a broadly "human" condition—as in the mythic world of *2001*—Kubrick's cinema remains a masculinist one, women reduced to exchangeable objects in its world.)

In Kubrick's films, material objects are not passive tools or prosthetic utensils that people can manipulate to whatever end they desire. Materiality is instead resistant to the human project, to the desire of human beings to imprint their subjectivity on the world and bend it to their will. Instead of serving as instruments to extend the power of humans, the world and its materials fatalistically overcome human domi-

This essay was written specifically for this volume and is published here for the first time by permission of the author.

nation and frequently even become narrative agents in their own right. Humans create technology, but that technology often seems to take on a life, or a will, of its own (the paradigmatic case, of course, being HAL in *2001*).

And the relative independence of technology from human control is only a subset of a widespread refusal of objects per se—not just machines, not just technologies, but all material things—to conform to the needs of humans who would use them for their own purposes. As a disembodied sound that precedes the film's entrance into narrative, the train is at first a pure thing, a non-anthropomorphized materiality. It serves the same purpose as the zooms in *Barry Lyndon* that depict human actions against the backdrop of an ongoing Nature which takes no heed of human history (as in the first scene in which Barry's father dies in a duel), or the cut in *2001* from bone to spaceship that renders the adventure of "manly" space exploration little more than a step in evolution. It is similar, as well, to the narrative progression in *Dr. Strangelove* from copulating planes to men reading *Playboy* in which airmen are portrayed as merely secondary extensions of their aircraft. *Killer's Kiss* portrays human narrative as a derivative of materiality, the stories of humanity as mere blips in time, mere trivialities against the background of a material world that seems unchanging and that threatens to surpass or outlast its human inhabitants. (The very development of *Killer's Kiss* as a low-budget movie would seem appropriate; for all his later big-budget artsy films, Kubrick is a director of trivial human stories, of squalid little tales of pitiful, anonymous, forgettable beings.)

Against its material backdrop, Kubrick's human world is an inadequate one. In *Killer's Kiss*, for example, people are endlessly tripping over small objects or handling them clumsily and inefficiently, finding them impossible to deal with. Take, for instance, the entire section of the film dealing with Davey's rescue of Gloria: despite the overall heroism of Davey's action, the rescue includes a man beaten into unconsciousness (after being overcome by a deck of cards flung in his face), another knocked over who flops to the ground, one who is stunned by his crash through a window, one who falls down twice during a rooftop chase (spraining his ankle during the second fall), and two men who fall over during a chaotic fight. Additionally, in anticipation of *A Clockwork Orange* with its mannequins and battles between human and sculpture (Alex with the plaster phallus against the Cat Woman), *Killer's Kiss* offers images of objects that mime human form, creating a sardonic commentary on human existence. Most obviously, there is the surrealism of the battle in the mannequin factory in which two men hammer away at statuesque body parts and even use those body parts as projectiles themselves. In this battle, there is a clear visual contrast between the impassivity of the mannequins and the physical passivity of the humans: we might refer to the efforts of the men in this combat as intensely physical, but only if by such physicality we speak not of a muscular vibrancy but of the physical fatigue of tired, sweaty, clumsy men who reveal themselves to be awkward and inadequate.

And there are other instances in the film of such mimicking and even mocking of humans by human-like objects: Gloria, for example, has a little doll hanging from her bedframe that, shown in quiet close-up several times, seems a reflection of her own drive for innocence in a corrupt world. There are also numerous references to and imagings of photos and drawings: some are family photos that remind the characters of how far they've drifted from the nice world of small-town life; some are caricatures that seem to make fun of the characters' pretensions and their inevitable failures and failings (when Gloria walks out on her love-crazed manager, Rapallo, he is left alone looking at drawings that seem to laugh at him; the camera takes the position of these drawings as the enraged Rapallo throws a glass toward them and actually cracks the lens of the film camera).

Moreover, the resistance of objects in Kubrick's films to usage by humans is operational at all levels of materiality, from the micro- to the macroscopic. In the Kubrickian universe, things are out of kilter for humans both in the little details of everyday life (the gun that jams in *Full Metal Jacket*, the suitcase the flies open in *The Killing*, the electronic circuitry that breaks down in *Dr. Strangelove*, the elevator that doesn't work in *A Clockwork Orange*) and in the broad spaces of surrounding environment as figured in the vast chasms that in film after film swallow up humans and render trivial their aspirations (the cavernous rooms of *Paths of Glory* or *The Shining*, for example). *2001*'s temporal evolutionism—in which Man is pictured as a banal step between Ape and God—is matched throughout Kubrick's films by a spatial relativism—that is to say, a rendering of Man as only one element among others which has as its consequence that Man is undone both by the objects he clumsily seeks to manipulate and by the surrounding environment that turns Man himself into an object for manipulation. In this respect, there is an intriguing anticipation in *Killer's Kiss* of a later and famous shift of spatial scale in *The Shining* where a zoom on Wendy and Danny on their own and away from Jack suddenly reveals them to be little more than laboratory rats in a miniature maze lorded over by Jack. Early in *Killer's Kiss*, Davey feeds his fish in their tank and the camera films him through the glass; this weird angle distorts his face and makes him loom gigantically and grotesquely over the minature and tightly enclosed aquatic world. Most immediately, this overstated shot would appear to be the mark of a young director trying to be flashy by being artsy (a pretension all too indulged in in his first feature, *Fear and Desire*). But it can also fit in with the central thematics of the film in which human grandeur ultimately reveals how puny it really is. Davey may seem to lord over the little world of his apartment, but he himself is ruled by the vast spaces around him, his apartment building revealed in subsequent scenes to be a virtual maze or labyrinth that his little story is played out in.

Perhaps the most explicit use of objects to comment on the failures of human aspiration show up in a little montage early in the film. We cut from a wind-up toy of a swimmer paddling furiously but ineffectively in a little bucket of water to a close-up of a record spinning round and round on a phonograph; from this we move to dancers moving round and round on the dance floor of Rapallo's sleazy dance hall. In the three shots, we are introduced to a world of aimless repetition, culminating in the image of Gloria stuck in her boring, dead-end job as a dance hostess.

The repetition of this image of spinning has an echo in the overall structure of the film which returns cyclically to a very few locations. Like so many other low-budget film noirs (for example, *Detour*), *Killer's Kiss* has a *huis clos* ambiance to it, a "no exit" claustrophobia in which a few ill-fated losers endlessly confront one another in miserable little bouts of aggression. Again, this repetition within a limited number of environments is something that will recur frequently in Kubrick's film career, both in flashback structures (the replay of scenes in *The Killing* and *Lolita*) and in plot twists that bring characters back to places they thought they had progressed beyond (as in Alex's accidental return in *A Clockwork Orange* to Home with all its dangers). Such repetitions of locale become ironic deflations of the aspiration of human figures caught in that space. Through these repetitions, characters are regressed, brought back to starting points: they are in thrall to a past they can never fully leave behind. Here, again, Gloria's little doll has its significance: however wise she would seem to the ways of the world, this dance hall hostess is far from grown up, far from a maturity that would let her control her fate. The invocation of childhood in Kubrick's films is rarely, if ever, the capturing of an innocence and authenticity. At best, in *Barry Lyndon*'s image of the protagonist's son, childhood represents a purity that is impossible to attain, destined as it is to fall, to give into a physicality that brings it fatally crashing down. Adults-become-children are immature victims, and inversely, children-become-adults are precocious oddities (the bellicose brat in *The Flying Padre*, the femme-fatale nymphet Lolita, the weird star-child of *2001*). There is no pristine and attainable space of childhood in this cinema. Rather, it involves a regressiveness, a bursting forth of immaturity. Sidney in *Fear and Desire* goes mad and turns into a giggly mass of sexual immaturity. Alex in *A Clockwork Orange* becomes more vulnerable and less haughty as he undergoes the punitions of the State. Gomer Pyle in *Full Metal Jacket* is forced to suck his thumb and to screw up ever more as Hartman tries to make a Marine of him. The Cold Warriors of *Dr. Strangelove* are turned into petulant little brats (especially in the first cut of the film with its infamous War Room pie fight). Perhaps most striking in this respect is *The Shining*. On the one hand, Danny is one more example (with Lolita and the star-child) of a weird and precocious childhood (and in any case, as Fredric Jameson points out in his essay on the film, Danny and the entire theme of "shining" are red herrings in the story). On the other hand, Danny becomes secondary to the real petulant child of the film, Jack, who regresses (literally so in the film's final images) and lives out adulthood as a series of immature tantrums, suspicions, and outbursts of gawkish violence.

Beyond its image of the future as really no more than another cycle in the repetitions of the past, *Killer's Kiss* offers yet another image of space as an inescapable constraint on freedom. Here, we need to note the recurrence in numerous Kubrick films of an image of forward movement. The typical version of this common shot—which we can see in its purest form in Alex's promenade through the shopping arcade in *A Clockwork Orange*, in Hartman's various marches through the barracks in *Full Metal Jacket*, and in General Mireau's stroll through the trenches in *Paths of Glory*, to name only a few examples—shows a character (generally an upright male) who strides either from foreground to background or vice versa through a corridor that is shot frontally so that it recedes into the distance forming a perfect vanishing point. This shot—which I call "the corridor shot"—is an apt emblem of human pretension in Kubrick films: in the world, humans strive to see themselves as more than the world, moving through it with a purpose and air of high superiority.

If the forward rush through a corridor figures a myth of possible progress, the inverse of such corridors extending dramatically into the future are the numerous mazes and labyrinths in Kubrick's films. And even in this early film, space is often rendered as a confused and tangled weave of folds and furrows. From the arrangement of hallways and object-laden rooftops between Davey's and Gloria's apartments to the rooftop obstacle courses through which Rapallo and his men chase Davey to the mannequin-filled factory turned into a maze by an overflow of bodies and body parts, *Killer's Kiss* offers an unclear space with no clear directions. If Davey dreams (but as a nightmare) of breathless motion down city streets imaged as corridors, his lived reality of city streets finds them not easy spaces for facile motion but mazes within mazes—clumsy routes for abortive escapes which end in dead ends (just as Davey's manager is trapped in a cluttered dead end where Rapallo's boys will murder him). If later Kubrick films narrate a deflation of human aspiration through punch lines that ironically undo forward motion—for example, General Mireau's stroll through the trenches ends with his confrontation with a shell-shocked soldier and is followed later by Dax's own much less glorious walk through the same trenches—*Killer's Kiss*'s rendition of corridors as either nightmarish inversions or as confused labyrinths implies that human dreams are tarnished from the start, corrupt from within. Interestingly, Davey may dream in images of perfectly symmetrical corri-

dor movement, and later films may perfect the corridor shot as a compositional and thematic schema, yet when Davey comes driving up to the rescue (his taxi pulls up alongside Rapallo, and then he drives up to the
warehouse with Rapallo), the scene is filmed slightly off its symmetrical
center. Drawing no special visual attention (as opposed, say, to the com-
positionally striking corridor movement of *A Clockwork Orange* or the
stargate voyage of *2001*), Davey's forward rush to the rescue is handled
ordinarily, given no grandeur, no mythos (and in any case, as a Kubrick
hero, he comes close, in the next scene, to bungling the rescue). For all its
violence, its chases, its murders, its amours, *Killer's Kiss*'s story is offered
up as one more arbitrary and ordinary tale of life in the big city.

In his book, *Stanley Kubrick Directs*, Alexander Walker aptly points out
the fairy-tale-like nature of *Killer's Kiss*: Davey is the "knight in shining
armour" who moves through a dream-like space to rescue the blonde from
the high tower in which the evil and ugly ogre has trapped her. But it is
necessary to note the film's all too material deflation of fairy-tale sweetness
and lightness: Davey is no knight but an ordinary schnook; Gloria is no
princess but a working-class woman. Their universe is not one of castles
and pastoral green spaces, but of sordid city streets and sites of banality
and crassness. Even the seemingly happy ending of the film—Gloria finally
does show up at the train station to go off with Davey to Seattle—has little
of the optimism or perfection that characterizes the "they lived happily
ever after" eternal ending of the fairy tale. Doubts have already been raised
about the strength of the commitment in this relationship of two people
who have known each other for only two days: Davey has wondered if
Gloria's last play at Rapallo was really a put-on: Gloria may have wondered
why her knight fled rather than fought. The sheer flatness of the characters
and their meager aspirations minimizes the triumph of the ending.

But it is not only things and spaces that show up the limits and limitations of people in *Killer's Kiss*. Most immediately, people are betrayed by
their own selves—selves that are bundles of misunderstood desire rather
than good sense, clumsy frames of inefficiency rather than bodies perfected to accomplish important tasks with ease and grace. Almost everyone we
come across is limited, especially in the physical realm. Obviously, for
example, Davey, the hero, is a failure at his career in boxing. A cut from
the black undergarments on Gloria as she undresses to an extreme close-
up of Davey's naked chest as he is being rubbed down in preparation for
his fight suggests that the shot of Davey might be treated with the same
voyeurism with which the film treats the woman. But the plot implies that
his is a body less of libidinal desire than of violence and especially of vulnerability to violence: he falls down in the boxing match; he is beaten up
in fights; he is often falling into dopey sleep; he becomes a passive zombie
on his subway ride through town; he nearly falls unconscious after his leap
from a window to escape Rapallo and his henchmen. Critics have endlessly

attacked the bad acting or non-acting of Jamie Smith in the role of Davey, but the lifeless performance seems appropriate to the characterization of this central figure as a loser, a passive absorber of the worst that life can dish out. (Indeed, the acting in *Killer's Kiss* is generally inadequate, either flat or awkwardly and overly histrionic, and this, plus the distancing provided by a quite disembodied tone in the clumsy post-synchronization, serves to make all the characters somewhat flat, dull, unengaging, and disengaging.)

Davey is not the only loser. Rapallo does no better in running a cheap dance hall and is fully consumed by a love he can't consummate. Soon after the fade-out of him kissing Gloria passionately and her evidently responding to him, he comes to her apartment to apologize, but what he is guilty of is never made clear. Did he force himself on her? Was he inadequate? Here is a man totally trapped by his awkward physicality: as Gloria says, he is an old man who smells bad. Like Barry Lyndon in a later Kubrick film, Rapallo is caught in an irreversible process of aging that makes him inappropriate for a vibrant, modern age. (In the woeful gay man of *The Killing*, the blubbery Gracchus in *Spartacus*, the homeless in *A Clockwork Orange*, the beauty-turned-hag in *The Shining*, Kubrick renders old age as a realm apart, a realm of decay, inadequacy, inhumanity.) Rapallo's very being is taken over by his obsession, and each step he takes to get Gloria back only makes things worse for him. One might call Rapallo's obsession an all-consuming "passion" but for the fact that, again, a strangely emotionless performance robs the character of any depth or psychology. It is as if Rapallo's desire has as its consequence a deadening of the body, a shutting down of affect as the self is taken over by lethargy.

In this early film, then, there is a representation of the limits to human aspiration posed not only by the resistance of external objects to that aspiration but also by the resistance of the human body itself. If people have goals in Kubrick films—and if their aspiration and ambition to achieve their goals is positively figured in the image of their bodies advancing brusquely and confidently through a space that they assume to be under their control—it is their very bodies that often resist being used in a purely effective and instrumental way. For instance, Kubrick films emphasize human corporeality as a visceral materiality that can corrode and give way (the gooey brains of Gomer Pyle splattered across the wall of the lavatory in *Full Metal Jacket*; men shot in the kneecaps and brought crashing to the ground in *Barry Lyndon* or *Full Metal Jacket*; Bowman growing old in *2001*). Humans are often little more than meat, a conceit hinted at in *Spartacus* which moves from slaves as shells onto which "kill zones" can be painted to slaves as carcasses hanging horribly from crucifixes. One wonders if it was the movie morality of the early 1960s that led the filmmakers not to include the suggestion from Howard Fast's novel that the bodies of the slaves were bought up as fodder by a sausagemaker.

Davey and Rapallo are both losers of the flesh in their own fashion. Gloria seems less defined than the two men (although she also is acted with the same listlessness as the two men). But this in itself is significant: like the woman pulled back and forth by Billy Boy's gang in *A Clockwork Orange*, like the prostitute argued over by the soldiers in *Full Metal Jacket*, like the wife in *The Shining* whose fate is planned out by malevolent men around her (Jack and Grady), the woman in this early film is a stake fought over by men, negotiated for by them. Kubrick is simultaneously a sexist director and one of the most interesting depicters of a fundamental sexism in men's treatment of women. The films present the ways in which men treat women as a bounty to be exchanged in an effort towards masculine solidarity, rarely imparting any willful identity to women outside the system of masculine exchange. (*The Shining* is most curious in this respect, showing up all the machismo that feeds into Jack's desire to take Grady's advice and triumph over the woman, but at the same time never representing that woman as more than a ditz and a bundle of corny clichés poured into her by the popular culture she seems to have voraciously consumed.)

Killer's Kiss's Gloria is most immediately a typical Kubrick woman, something for men to battle over thereby discovering that the fundamental relationship for a man is one with other men (whether in relationships of competition, solidarity, or the two blended together). At the same time, the film goes farther with Gloria than with the men in suggesting reasons for her current deplorable place in the world. Where, say, the "girl" (as she is named) in *Fear and Desire* is so much a function of what aggressive men do to her that she has little identity and doesn't even speak. Gloria is rare among Kubrick women in being given a voice and accorded the attributes of will and desire. Gloria is even given point-of-view shots in which she voyeuristically stares in on Davey in his apartment. And, more than other women in Kubrick films, Gloria is given a biography: in a long flashback (within the overall flashback of the film) she explains how the death of her father from illness and the suicide of her sister were the factors that led to her coming to New York.

And yet for all the biographical definition given her that is lacking in other women in Kubrick films, Gloria is no more a winner at life than those women. She is a flat, trivial character in a flat, trivial world, her aspirations seeming to rise no higher than a dance hall manager and a has-been boxer. Even the flashback does little to make her seem the master of an admirable fate: much of the narration in the flashback and all of its imagery are devoted to Gloria's sister, and the moral of the flashback has to do not with Gloria's freedom in the future but with her subjection to the past.

If directly physical things like environment, objects, and one's own corporeality are forms of resistance to human desires and goals in Kubrick films, it is also the case that all of these coalesce in another manifestation of defeat—namely, of the social world itself.

With *2001*'s evolutionary conception of humanity, it is easy to imagine that Kubrick is not a sociologically oriented director but one whose investigations of humankind have to do with ontological definitions—humanity, for instance, as a life-form that by nature is destined to behave a certain way, to be in a certain way. Above all, we are often inclined to think of Kubrick as a metaphysician, a dealer in big eternal themes, heavy concepts that float free from historical specificity and offer up overarching ideas on ostensibly grand issues.

But even in *2001*, the evolution from ape to human is not a progression to just any humankind, but to a humankind quite precisely located and defined (to a large degree by the intense specificity of gadgets and gizmos that surround the humans and date them in time). Not for nothing is the title of the film an exact date (just as *Barry Lyndon* ends with an account of the moment of Revolution, 1789, and *The Shining* ends with an invocation of an important American date, the Fourth of July, in the high-society days of the 1920s). *2001* is not just about Man in space but American men in space (it is clear that they are excluding the Soviets from their discovery of the monolith), still battling out the cold war and luxuriating in the happy-go-lucky matter-of-factness of American technophilic professionals (in this respect, they are the inheritors of the New Frontier politics of the 1960s, so aptly parodied in *Dr. Strangelove.*)

Americanness is indeed a recurrent concern of Kubrick films (with the exception of *A Clockwork Orange*). Although set in foreign cultures, *Paths of Glory*, *Spartacus*, and *Barry Lyndon* all seem to play on a vague Americanist populism that operates by contrasting corrupt or decadent officials—snobby officers, backstabbing politicians, continental wags—with down-to-earth, ordinary guys whose honesty is invoked in the quality of their voice and accents, as much as their actions. *Spartacus*, for example, juxtaposes Tony Curtis's Brooklynisms with the Englishness of Laurence Olivier's uppercrust eloquence and plays out the attempted seduction as a conflict between two ways of life, while *Barry Lyndon* puts former *Peyton Place* and *Love Story* loverboy Ryan O'Neal into the role of a rough-cut Irish lad who will never really assimilate into the aristocracy and whose very un-English accent signals his inability to cross rigorously drawn social lines. The earlier of these films pits the purity of the people's voice against the corruption and decadence of high power (it is perhaps significant that in Kubrick's two most populist films, *Spartacus* and *Paths of Glory*, Kirk Douglas had major control; these films seem as much projects to show off the humanism of the producer-star as they are films within the Kubrick corpus).

More generally, Americanness is a burden, one more of the resistant forces that drag people down and ruin their ambition. If Kubrick is a director of fatalism, one thing fatal for his characters is their national belonging. I've already suggested that Kubrick's characters find the potential for pure freedom limited—limited by their surrounding environment, by the reversibility and cyclical nature of repetitive time, by their own bodies as materialities that resist expression and accomplishment. In addition, they are also limited by their roles, by the identities they assume or are given within a social structure.

Full Metal Jacket is most explicit in this respect: much of the way in which Sergeant Hartman makes the young men into marines has to do with an assigning to them of generic identities that he draws from a pool of available choices. It is tempting to read the opening sequence of head-shaving as a robbing of the men's prior identities in order to prepare them for ones arbitrarily decided upon by a mechanical system of power and control. But to read the military training as a deindividualization is, I think, to opt for a humanist interpretation. First of all, we learn nothing about these men before their military training. Second, and quite ironically, there is the implication that Hartman's assignation of identities is not so arbitrary after all and simply provides new names to describe the men as they are (Joker is, indeed, a joker; Pyle is a misfit; Cowboy laments the lack of horses in Vietnam). These men have no pasts that would be more authentically human than the social identities given to them by their country's military. Much of the moral ambiguity that spectators find in *Full Metal Jacket*—is it antiwar? does it promote masculine courage?—comes from the contradictory nature of the film's ending in which Joker's voice-over announces that he is no longer afraid as the visuals show us the men marching in unison to the Mickey Mouse song. On the one hand, the Kubrick character seems to have progressed within the story: his new identity is that of a courageous man. On the other hand, this "progress" seems to entail no advance at all in social terms: American boys have always been socialized to be fighters and Joker seems finally to be growing into an identity fully provided for him by his social world. Indeed, whatever past the soldiers have is an exclusively collective rather than an individual one, made up of eccentric bits of American history (they all know who Lee Harvey Oswald was), banalities of American popular culture (the Mickey Mouse song), and American "masculine" fantasies (Joker's only reference to the past is an expression of longing for "Mary Jane Rottencrotch and the Great Homecoming Fuck Fantasy," a fantasy offered to him by Hartman). The function of the disciplinary apparatus that we frequently encounter in Kubrick films—authority figures, training sessions, laboratories and institutes, the enunciation of rules—seems not so much to be the assignment of new identities but the reclamation of old ones from a position of deviation, social perversity, marginality. The opening of *The Shining*—"The Interview"—is typical in this respect: in a symmetrical space, marked by the American flag, Jack submits to an interrogation that seeks to investigate his ability to take up his role as model employee, model father, model American writer.

Michel Ciment in his book on Kubrick astutely points out the director's propensity for caricature, for his reduction or exaggeration of personages to fixed types. And indeed, one could certainly cite the ways in which Kubrick intervenes explicitly to dehumanize his characters and render them according to comical modes: one thinks, for instance, of his carica-tural style for the filming of faces, a fish-eye lens or an extreme close-up elongating or accentuating the faces of actors chosen, so it would seem, for cranial structures in which eyeballs retreat behind overbearing brows (see, for instance, the first shot of Alex in *A Clockwork Orange* or the writer's moment of recognition in the same film; the madness of Pyle in *Full Metal Jacket*; the skully skulkiness of Jack in *The Shining*; the apes in *2001*; the simian stupidity of Buck Turgidson in *Dr. Strangelove*).

And yet, as much as he is a director of clearly stated, obvious, broad-stroke effects, Kubrick is also a director whose films frequently refuse direct commentary, full judgment, or editorial intervention. The camera is frequently pulled back from an action, impassively regarding the foibles of humans but taking up no angle from which one could derive an unam-biguous attitude. Take, for instance, the general lack of reaction shots in *Full Metal Jacket*. When, for example, Hartman violently slaps Pyle in an effort to teach him "right" and "left," a reaction shot shows Cowboy regarding the action with complete impassivity. Nothing in the way the shot is set up, nothing in the arrangement of the narrative world within the shot, allows us to draw an attitude from the shot or from Cowboy's look within the shot.

Kubrick began filmmaking in the area of documentary, and even in his most interventional moments in his later films, there is frequently the impression of a dispassionate, even antiseptic study of a found world. Some of this impression comes from filmic technique: the straight-on shooting, the gradual zooms that reveal a preexisting space, the long shots that appear to respect the spatial-temporal integrity of the found narrative universe. But it also has to do with the representation in the films of the found world as finished and preformed. Characters, as I've already hinted, rarely possess defined pasts in Kubrick films. Or, at best, their past is merely an earlier form of what they are in the present. From the first moment—the birth of the narrative which coincides with the birth of the character—characters have their identities, their fixed meaning within a fixed universe. And these identities, these meanings, are less personal pos-sessions, particularities that fully distinguish one personage from another, than social roles, so that even in their particularity characters take on the impression of types. Kubrick's narrative universe is not so much "peopled" with characters as filled with human stereotypes: the mad or corrupt gen-erals, the overbearing guards or trainers, the astronaut, the delinquent, the upstart, the prostitute, the mistress, the wife. The fact that the pressure on the human subject is not for him/her to be an individual but to assume his/her defined role in society is brought out most ironically perhaps in *The Shining*. As Fredric Jameson nicely points out in his essay on the film, a great part of Jack's problems comes from his misunderstanding of the role available to him by the end of the 1970s. Jack believes himself to be a great American writer, but that role is already over and done with in American cultural history: in the post-modern moment, Jack can only be an ersatz, second-hand Hemingway or Fitzgerald. If Jack Nicholson's performance in the film is an excess of caricatural monstrosity, this is so because the character of Jack Torrance can only be a caricature of the American writer, of the American male. With his lumberman shirts (now the virtual uniform of so many would-be writers), Jack is a walking cliché.

But already in *Killer's Kiss*, the social world is made up of fixed types: the down-on-his-luck boxer, the jaded dance hall hostess, the crummy old club owner, the henchman, the ineffective cops. This world goes around and around and never progresses because its actors stay the same, unable to break out of the mold in which their roles have enclosed them.

To be sure, by the end of *Killer's Kiss*—as Davey's own narration tells us—changes have been made in the narrative universe of the film. Rapallo has been killed, the henchmen have been rounded up, and the final image shows us a Davey and Gloria ready to move on and attempt to start a new life. Yet it is possible to wonder if the ending really represents much of progress. On the one hand, there is little to suggest that Davey and Gloria have developed, have gained a new ability to take control of life and make it their own. They will still be types; they will still coincide with their roles.

On the other hand, the few glimpses we are granted of the world to which Davey and Gloria intend to escape suggests that this world is no utopia, but simply another bundle of stereotypes, roles, social fixities. In a semantic overlap, the word in French for a photograph is *cliché* and so is the word for stereotype. I would suggest that the photos we see in Davey's apartment of life back in Seattle are doubly *clichés*—images of country living, that render that existence as little more than a few easy stereotypes. There is a patness, an ordinariness, a social obviousness to the photos, just as there is a stereotypicality to the New York world in which Davey and Gloria have thus far operated. This sense of cliché—of the reduction of a world to a limited type—seems confirmed by the scene in which Davey takes a subway ride and reads his uncle's letter. In a voice-over that adds a yokelish quality to the self-parodic blandness or matter-of-factness of so many Kubrick voice-overs (as in *The Killing, Dr. Strangelove*, and *Full Metal Jacket*), the uncle's letter renders farm life a meager set of banal homilies ("things are about the same") and minor nonevents (the buying of a farm animal, someone trying to get over minor arthritis).

Only perhaps in *2001* is there a hint of the possibility of a space beyond the social nature of humanity, but even in that "visionary" film, the vision is ambiguous, incomplete. Just as Kubrick characters have no irremediably different past that they grow out of, so too is there no defined future that they grow into (*2001* stops significantly before we know anything about what it is like to be a star-child). In a curious fashion, *2001* seems most in continuity with Kubrick's first feature film, *Fear and Desire*: the soldiers do manage to escape the horrors of the war zone by rafting down a river, but this escape appears to be leading them to a zone of indefinition, not so much a utopia as an "a-topia."

In contrast, in spite of the very meagerness of its means of production—an example of 1950s low-budget cinema—*Killer's Kiss* seems in direct continuity with the major body of Kubrick's filmmaking. Indeed, one might argue that it is because of its meagerness that the film fits so well. In its reduction of narrative spaces to a few claustrophobic sites, in its reduction of narrative to a bare outline of conflictual interaction, in its confining of character within a few social types, *Killer's Kiss* sets out as a virtual matrix many of the stereotypes, images, and social fixities that Kubrick's cinema will return to again and again.

Ciment, Michel. *Stanley Kubrick*. Paris: Calmann Lévy, 1982.

Jameson, Fredric. *"The Shining," Signatures of the Visible*. New York: Routledge, 1992.

Walker, Alexander. *Stanley Kubrick Directs*. New York: Harcourt Brace Jovanovich, 1972.

Patterns of Filmic Narration in
The Killing and *Lolita*

MARIO FALSETTO

The following analysis examines several narrational strategies that help structure Stanley Kubrick's *The Killing* (1956) and *Lolita* (1962). Although *The Killing*, adapted from Lionel White's novel *Clean Break*, was only the third feature-length film directed by Kubrick, it represents his most radical experiment in constructing a nonlinear time structure. This discussion will focus on the film's nonlinearity and the use of a third-person, voice-over commentary. It will also explore the film's characterizations and their relation to narrational patterns and subtextual meaning.

Lolita, Kubrick's adaptation of Vladimir Nabokov's novel, is one of the director's most accomplished films, yet it has received little critical attention. This is surprising since its ironic playfulness and fine performances make it an immensely enjoyable film, as well as a richly complicated one in terms of narrative strategies. I will examine some of the more intricate aspects of the film, including its complex scene construction, the narrative gaps associated with the character of Clare Quilty (Peter Sellers), the voice-over commentary, and, again, the issue of sub-textual meaning.

THE KILLING: A FRAGMENTED UNIVERSE

The notion of anchoring a film's narrative progression to several relations or arrangements of narrative material is not unique to Stanley Kubrick. Yet, it is an important aspect of the director's work, especially in *The Killing*. Narrational patterning illuminates many features of scene construction and other concerns that can potentially elude even close, shot-by-shot analysis. To facilitate our discussions, we will break down the film's narrative action into units. As Todorov has stated, "to study the structure of a narrative's plot, we must first present this plot in summary form in which each distinct action of the story has a corresponding proposition."[1]

In my analysis, I have determined that *The Killing* can be segmented into thirty-five separate, narrative actions or units (See Appendix). A narrative unit, for our purpose, will involve a character or characters performing an action in one location, or it will follow one character to the conclusion of a particular action over several locations. Thus, a narrative sequence is not

This essay is adapted from Mario Falsetto, *Stanley Kubrick: A Narrative and Stylistic Analysis* (Westport, Conn.: Greenwood Press, 1994) by permission of the author.

strictly defined in terms of one cinematic space, but in terms of an individual narrative action.

The first few sequences of *The Killing* are particularly illuminating in terms of the film's structure. Not only do they serve to introduce the main characters, but we are quickly made aware of the film's nonlinear temporal structure. The device of the off-screen, omniscient, voice-over commentary is immediately emphasized. Kubrick also introduces many elements of character motivation in the first fifteen minutes of screen time. The gang members are presented as somewhat atypical criminals. As Johnny Clay (Sterling Hayden) mentions in his scene with Fay (Coleen Gray), they are not criminals in the ordinary sense of the word. We learn of Mike's (Joe Sawyer) devotion to his bedridden wife, Officer Kennan's (Ted de Corsia) money problems, George's (Elisha Cook) subservient relationship to his wife, Sherry (Marie Windsor), and Johnny's history as a smalltime crook and his five-year prison stretch. And, in a typical "film noir" opposition, we are presented with Fay's intense devotion to Johnny, in stark contrast to Sherry's *femme fatale*. The character who remains least defined is Marv Unger (Jay C. Flippen), due, in part, to the delicacy of the homosexual subtext in his unrequited relationship with Johnny.

The idea of presenting the main characters' motivations in the first fifteen or twenty minutes of screen time is a convention of the (late) classical Hollywood model of the time (mid-1950s). Where *The Killing* is unusual is in the way it organizes its presentation. It is in the precise nature of its discourse that the film breaks with convention.

The opening scenes incorporate an omniscient commentary that specifies the exact time of the actions. The use of a voice-over in itself was obviously not radical in Hollywood fiction film, but its use in *The Killing* is somewhat atypical and represents the reworking of a well-worn, narrative convention. The "voice of God" commentary is used primarily to organize the film's nonlinear temporal structure. Using a conventional device in an unconventional way has remained a consistent and coherent strategy throughout Kubrick's work. One finds many instances in the director's career of such formal reworkings.

The specific characteristics of the voice in *The Killing* would have been familiar to audiences of the mid-1950s from numerous other filmic sources, such as the Louis de Rochemont productions of the 1940s and the March of Time documentaries. The voice in *The Killing* is not necessarily the same voice, but it has similar expressive qualities, particularly its masculine, authoritative tone.

In *The Killing*, the voice-over performs several functions. Most obviously, it transmits narrative information and organizes the complicated time structure of the film. It also functions as a distancing device, putting the audience at a remove from the film's drama. The voice-over in *The Killing* is an impersonal voice that is masculine, deeply resonant, and seemingly authoritative. It prefigures the kind of emotional distance found in Kubrick's later work.

Thus, while the voice-over operates in a somewhat distancing way, it is familiar and reassuring as a result of its frequent use in other films. Although its primary function is to pinpoint the exact time of each action, viewers are also reminded of those other, often nameless films. Through its familiarity, while the voice carries with it an element of its own cinematic history, it bears traces of those other films.

The film's narrative events are arranged in nonchronological order. The unusual arrangement of the narrative action is a key characteristic of *The Killing* and sets it apart from most other narrative films. To use Seymour Chatman's terminology, the film's story time is substantially different from its discourse time.[2] The film exhibits its most unconventional strategy in the radicalness of its ordering of narrative events.

The complete scene breakdown of the film indicates that the pattern of the first few narrative units is sustained throughout. Each time the voice-over is heard, it informs the audience of the precise time of the action. When the voice is not heard, the time is unclear. In some sequences without voice-over, it is possible to have a general idea of the time of the action. For example, viewers do not know the exact time of the final sequence at the airport, but they know that it is the same evening as the robbery and massacre. Likewise in unit 29, when they see Johnny throw the bag of money out the window, the time is not given and there is no voice-over. Still, it should be clear from the preceding sequences (the time of the start of the seventh race is announced, as is the time of the two diversions), that the approximate time of the robbery is between 4:00 and 4:30 P.M.

At times, the ambiguity is more pronounced, however, as in unit 10, when Johnny meets Nikki (Timothy Carey), who is to shoot the horse at the racetrack in one of two planned diversions. In unit 11, when Johnny rents a cabin, the audience has no way of knowing on which day these events occur, let alone the exact time. All we can ascertain is that they occur sometime during the week before Saturday, the day of the robbery, since the fictional time of the film comprises one week (Saturday to the following Saturday).

An important issue involving the use of voice-over in *The Killing* is the extent to which viewers consider the voice reliable. There are two instances in the film's temporal sequencing that lead one to believe that the voice-over has made an "error," which somewhat undercuts its generally reliable use in the film. One error occurs at units 14 and 15. The commentary announces that "at 7:00 A.M. that morning, Johnny began what might be the last day of his life." A scene takes place between Johnny and Marv in which Marv's feelings for Johnny are made relatively clear. In a typical 1950s display of machismo, Johnny treats Marv's show of affection as something of a good-natured joke. Johnny's rebuff leads directly to Marv's drunken condition later at the robbery. Although Marv's role in the heist is not crucial, his drunkenness signals that all will not go well with the robbery.

The scene between Johnny and Marv is followed by a scene showing Johnny arriving at the airport as the narrator announces, "it was exactly 7:00 A.M. when he got to the airport." Either there is an error in the film's temporal sequencing, or the voice-over (and, by implication, the film's narration) does not account for the scene between Johnny and Marv that occurs before Johnny reaches the airport. The second explanation does not seem probable. If the audience accepts the first explanation, that there is an error in the film's time structure, is there any way to determine if the error is intentional or merely an oversight?

The second "error" occurs at units 30 through 32. George Peatty announces the time as 7:15 P.M., and he declares that Johnny is fifteen minutes late. If George is to be believed (and generally characters do not openly lie in films such as this, unless motivated by their character or a circumstance within the fiction), viewers must assume that Johnny's original arrival time was 7:00 P.M. In unit 31, the voice-over announces that Johnny arrived at the meeting place at 7:29 P.M. and that made him "still fifteen minutes late." If viewers take this narrative moment to be of some significance, either George is mistaken about Johnny's projected arrival time or the voice-over has made an error. If this is a simple oversight/error of the film's narration, then neither "character" is wrong. But, as in the previous example, this seems the least satisfactory explanation, since elaborating the precise time of almost every sequence has been a critical strategy of the film.

These two temporal errors indicate that a discrepancy exists between the action (or what a character says) and the "voice of God" commentary. There seem to be two conceivable explanations for this discrepancy. Either these two instances in the film's temporal structuring are so minor as to be of no consequence—and the fact that I am even pointing them out is an act of "over-reading"—or they have some meaning. If they have meaning, what is the nature of that meaning?

I believe that both errors are meaningful and that perhaps Kubrick is making an "authorial" comment through them. Both sequences present viewers with something of a dilemma. There is conflicting narrative information in each instance but no way of knowing which is the more truthful presentation. Whom are viewers to believe? If they assume that, within the fictional world of *The Killing*, the omniscient voice-over and the fictional characters have equal status (that is, there is no reason to believe that one has more of a claim to the truth than the other), then there is no clear way to resolve the dilemma. The audience is given no further narrative cues to help resolve this dilemma, since the discrepancies are not referred to in any other part of the film.

In general, the use of an omniscient, voice-over commentary is associated with a certain kind of filmic authority. The type of impersonal voice we hear in *The Killing* is reminiscent of film noir, certain types of documentary film, and documentary-style fiction. This kind of voice-over is generally considered reliable, in the sense that it is not known to lie openly. If the two errors that I have pointed out are indeed deliberate, they may constitute an attempt to undercut the conventional faith in the authority of the voice-over.

A central theme of *The Killing*, and of Kubrick's work as a whole, is the fallibility of the individual. No matter how precisely an action or event is planned, it is always impossible to predict its outcome since one cannot entirely account for the human element. In his meticulous planning of the heist, Johnny is unaware of the subplot involving Sherry and Val that leads directly to the massacre. Moreover, Johnny has no way of knowing that his rebuff of Marv's show of affection will result in Marv's drunken condition during the heist (since Johnny does not indicate that he is aware of the sexual subtext of Marv's behavior toward him). No matter how predictable or rational the world, there are always unforeseen elements that can potentially disrupt this orderliness. The errors involving the voice-over and the film's time structure may be connected to this Kubrickian theme.

Kubrick's work often invokes the idea that nothing concerning human behavior can ever be entirely predictable. Human fallibility is a key element of our humanity—a point Kubrick explores in greater depth in such films as *2001: A Space Odyssey*, *A Clockwork Orange*, and *Barry Lyndon*. The beginnings of this exploration can be seen in *The Killing*.

Returning to the film's time structure, we can see that in units 14 through 18, as the narrative follows Johnny, the time structure is chronological. It is also sequential in units 19 through 22, when the film shifts its attention to Mike O'Reilly's character. It continues in this linear fashion as viewers follow Randy Kennan up to the start of the crucial seventh race and the robbery itself, in unit 24. In unit 25, there is a backward shift in time as viewers follow Maurice's actions. The film stays with his character until the start of the seventh race, in unit 26. As the film switches to Nikki, there is again a backward movement in time. It stays with Nikki until he is gunned down. When the film returns to Johnny in unit 28, it has again shifted back in time. Viewers then follow the robbery completely through for the first and only time, in unit 29.

Thus, within the overall, dominant framework of the film's nonlinear time structure, there are sections of chronological presentation. In terms of Hollywood convention, it is entirely appropriate to focus on Johnny's character as he carries out the robbery. He is the film's leading character (and star), as well as the only character to go into the money room to execute the heist, a key dramatic moment. What is unusual is to structure the narrative to follow each character essentially up to the same point in the narrative (the start of the seventh race, which is the moment of the actual robbery) but then to follow the robbery through only when Johnny is involved. This method of structuring the narrative might have resulted in viewer frustration in the hands of a less capable director. As it is, the film is not difficult to follow even though it has an intricate structure.

The narrative action proceeds swiftly and is made more interesting and complex because of this jigsaw-puzzle structure. Some pieces of the puzzle are left unexplained when we finally see the robbery carried through in unit 29. It is not until unit 30 that all is explained. It is here that we learn how the moneybag was removed from the track and the precise role played by Officer Randy Kennan. The shifting points of view contribute to the effectiveness of the jigsaw narrative structure, and they work in tandem with the nonlinear time structure to create a coherence and complexity that the film would otherwise not have.

The complicated, nonlinear time structure is also related to the film's reworking of various genre conventions. Two key elements of the robbery or heist film are the temporal construction and the revelation of the mechanics of planning and executing the crime. Every robbery, usually the central narrative event in such films, depends on precise timing. This aspect is usually prominent in models of the genre such as *The Asphalt Jungle* (John Huston, 1950), *The Killers* (Robert Siodmak, 1946) and *Rififi* (Jules Dassin, 1954). Often these films present an array of details that implicate the viewer in the planning process of the robbery. Viewers frequently share a character's point of view as the films follow the crime to its conclusion. The genre seems to have peaked in the 1960s with films such as *Topkapi* (Jules Dassin, 1964), *Robbery* (Peter Yates, 1967), *Ocean's Eleven* (Lewis Milestone, 1960), and *Seven Thieves* (Henry Hathaway, 1960). To my knowledge, no film elaborates as complicated a time structure as *The Killing*.

The conventions of the heist genre that stress the precise time element and that foreground planning and execution of the robbery are the starting points from which *The Killing* elaborates its complex time structure and shifting-point-of-view strategy. Although *The Killing* may appear to have a rather distanced presentation because of this complicating of narrative convention, the viewer is always involved in the narrative action. The material is compelling to watch, and we as viewers never lose interest in the central narrative action. Perhaps our understanding of narrative distance needs revision, for it does not always follow that the viewer is uninvolved in the proceedings when distancing devices, such as those found in *The Killing*, are used.

The device of allowing Johnny the most sustained point of view is, of course, not unexpected since Sterling Hayden, who plays the gang leader, is the film's star. The character of Johnny Clay is also interesting because he is the most knowledgeable character in the film. Johnny deliberately conceals details of the robbery from other gang members and from the audience at various points in the film. This heightens viewer curiosity about how certain narrative actions will be carried out.

But no character in the film, including the "omniscient" commentary, is privileged with all the information. Sections of the film do not involve the voice-over, and there are elements of which Johnny is seemingly unaware. For example, Johnny does not see Nikki shoot Red Lightning. He does not see Randy drive away with the money, nor does he see Sherry and Vince in their intimate moments as they discuss details of the heist. Most significantly, Johnny is excluded from the film's climactic massacre, although he does see its partial result as George Peatty, covered in blood, stumbles out of the building. The viewer, by contrast, does see these actions. In fact, it is the viewer who is placed in the most privileged position in terms of the film's narrative action. Viewers see every aspect of the robbery, although it is only over the course of the film that they make sense of the details. The film's presentation of narrative information may be fragmented, but the audience ultimately possesses more information than any of the film's characters. It shares a kind of complicity with the film's narration (and the makers of the film), that places it in a special position.

The unusual structure of the film contributes to the notion of combining familiar, reassuring elements with unfamiliar ones. Many generic elements would have been familiar to a 1950s audience: the archetypal characters; the omniscient voice-over; the stress on time; the emphasis on the planning and execution of the robbery; visual and thematic aspects of film noir, and so on. But it is the way that these familiar ingredients are combined and elaborated on that make the film interesting and successful. The story may be familiar, but its discourse is unique. The nonlinear time structure and the shifting-point-of-view strategy are ways in which the film plays on familiar genre conventions. The unfamiliar elements of its discourse contribute to the film's distanced presentation and reflexiveness, and they partly explain why viewers have little emotional involvement with the characters.

Another issue of great interest in *The Killing* is the relationship of characterization to narrative structure and subtextual meaning. It could be argued, for example, that the characters of Johnny Clay and Maurice have very specific functions that are not always related to the film's plot. Apart from their more obvious function within the narrative, there is a philosophizing tone in much of their dialogue. I would argue that, in certain select moments, primarily through the creation of particular subtexts, Kubrick is making a specific intervention to communicate his personal point of view. Here is Maurice talking to Johnny in a scene at a chess club:

You have not heard that in this life you have to be like everyone else, the perfect mediocrity, no better, no worse. Individuality is a monster and it must be strangled in its cradle to make our friends feel comfortable. You know, I often thought that the gangster and the artist are the same in the eyes of the masses. They are admired and hero-worshipped. But there is always present an underlying wish to see them destroyed at the peak of their glory.

This crucial dialogue begins ironically, but one senses the filmmaker's voice at the center of Maurice's argument. The dialogue is delivered casually, in an offhand way. The speech is not critical to the main narrative but functions as a kind of philosophical subtext. Maurice is not only a relatively minor character, but his lines are difficult to understand, due to the actor's speech patterns. If Kubrick is using this minor character to communicate his personal view about the role of the artist in contemporary society, why state it in a half-hidden voice? Why not have it resound through a major character in a pivotal scene?

It may be that the director is experimenting with the possible ways in which he can speak through his characters. Kubrick's early development as a filmmaker contains numerous instances of such experimentation. It is a consistent feature of his work, but here it sounds like the effort of a youthful director still learning how to construct an intricate narrative. Maurice's dialogue, in fact, sounds a little out of place, though not necessarily out of character since this scene is the viewer's only real exposure to him. His only other scene involves the diversionary brawl staged at the racetrack during the heist. Maurice's character is opaque, and his real function in the film seems to be to deliver this piece of philosophizing.

The manner in which Johnny Clay's character allows the audience to hear the director's voice is a little more complicated. It is not so much *what* Johnny says that is important but rather his role in the fragmented narrative process in which Kubrick's views may be located. I argued earlier that the impersonal narrator in *The Killing* could reasonably be described as fallible, if the errors in the film's time structure were significant. The one character in the film who possesses the most knowledge is, in fact, not the commentator but Johnny Clay. He organizes every detail of the heist and tells each gang member only the necessary minimum to successfully carry out each assigned task. Johnny deliberately fragments the information he gives to each character (and to the viewer). He tells some more than others but never tells any single character all the details of the robbery. This fragmentation includes Johnny's relationship with Fay, who seems particularly in the dark about Johnny's world and never seems to question any of his actions.

The fragmentation of information involving Johnny and the other characters is related to the fragmented time structure of the film. The viewer's attention is continually shifted from one detail or character to the next, and from one time frame to the next. The audience never sees any action carried out to completion. Thus, two very deliberate strategies of fragmentation seem to be operating parallel to one another.

Both the process of fragmenting information and the film's nonlinear time structure reflexively comment on the process of filmmaking. The complicated structure makes viewers more aware of the importance of temporal ordering in film, forcing them to reflect on the organizing function of the filmmaker and the manipulation that goes into creating a film's narrative. By continually shifting the viewer's attention from one action to another and by frustrating conventional expectations of closure, Kubrick has constructed a more modernist narrative.

In some ways, I take the character of Johnny Clay as a stand-in for the filmmaker. The director organizes the act of making a film as Johnny organizes the heist. Each member of the crew has an assigned task; no one person has all the information. A director such as Kubrick is the only individual involved in the entire process from beginning to end. He is privileged with the most knowledge in the process of making the film. Johnny's organization and manipulation of the heist can be viewed as analogous to the act of film directing. Both procedures involve crews, fragmentation of information, organization, and precise timing in many different areas. Thought of this way, the film's subtext of reflexiveness is more apparent and intriguing. It becomes a way for Kubrick not only to speak through a character but also to insert himself, somewhat obliquely, into the film.

Maurice's comments about the analogous social roles of the artist and the gangster also make more sense. His remarks help articulate the reflexive subtext of the film. If one takes Maurice's comments and applies them to the role of the narrative filmmaker who is engaged in making what she or he considers to be art, the speech becomes revelatory. The pressures of satisfying a mass audience, the expectations engendered by genre and other aesthetic or historical considerations, and the economic exigencies of making a commercial feature film are all sharply felt by most filmmakers. The artist who tries to be audacious and original will often be consumed by the monster of mediocrity that a mass audience invariably becomes. It is not inconceivable to argue that Kubrick's voice is speaking through Maurice's dialogue. Every Kubrick film, on some level, contains an internal tension between familiar and unfamiliar filmic rhetoric, between classical storytelling and a less classical narrative mode.

In *The Killing*, Kubrick's experiments with temporal structure, voice-over commentary, and the inclusion of subtexts are clear attempts to insert an original voice into his filmic discourse. Even as a young man, Kubrick no doubt keenly felt the pressures of creating a more original film while satisfying the Hollywood system and his financial backers. Maurice's dialogue and Johnny's role are both ways in which the director speaks directly (and not so directly) to the audience. They have less to do with the film's plot and everything to do with its creator.

LOLITA

Narrative Gaps: Absence and Presence

There are several noteworthy aspects to the scene construction of *Lolita*. The scene breakdown of the film (see Appendix) reveals that it too is constructed of thirty-five narrative units. Also, *Lolita* begins with an unusual structuring strategy. The opening sequence sets up the central narrative event that the remainder of the film will attempt to illuminate. Humbert Humbert's (James Mason) subjective voice-over begins at the end of this opening sequence, the only scene in the film not included in the overall framework of the character's story. The fact that the audience is made aware of Humbert's crime, though not the reasons for it or its eventual consequences, makes for a surprising and (retroactively) ironic beginning. The positioning of Clare Quilty's murder here does not dissipate suspense, for it is not the *fact* of Quilty's murder that is important but how and why Humbert has been driven to such extreme behavior.

Additionally, the opening scene echoes other Kubrick films in several interesting ways. For example, the opening shot of Humbert's car driving through a thick fog suggests an actual dream or dreamlike state, perhaps a fairy tale. Kubrick's fondness for the fairy tale can be found in *Killer's Kiss* and *The Shining*. The opening sequence is also similar to later Kubrick films that begin with rather unexpected or overloaded opening sequences or shots. *A Clockwork Orange* is the key example of this informationally loaded opening.

Quilty's first appearance is typical of how the character will be encountered throughout the film. Humbert explores the mansion without noticing that his nemesis is seated on a chair, hidden under a sheet. Humbert is unaware of Quilty's presence until Quilty stirs himself to life beneath the sheet. The encounter foreshadows the elusive relationship the two characters will have throughout the film. The sequence illustrates their adversarial relationship with such verbal, joking allusions as Quilty's reference to "Spartacus," an obvious reference to an earlier Kubrick film. The white sheets draped around Quilty's body visually amplify the references to ancient Rome implied by the remark.

Quilty engages a reluctant Humbert in a game of ping-pong, a game that, as Alexander Walker has pointed out, the director often plays with his guests in real life.[3] The ping-pong match also carries metaphoric connotations of the "game" between Quilty and Humbert for Lolita's (Sue Lyon) affections. Another example of the film's preoccupation with playing games involves Quilty's impersonations, a sample of which viewers see in this opening scene when he reads Humbert's poem with a Western "twang." The fact that Quilty wants to engage a reluctant opponent in this game again foreshadows their relationship in the rest of the film.

The opening of *Lolita* is structurally and narratively important, but it involves an essentially neutral kind of presentation. There is no evidence that the scene is told from any character's point of view. The voice-over does not begin until the end of the sequence. Specifying the precise nature of Humbert's voice-over commentary becomes important because the narrative device of a written diary is introduced in unit 7; a viewer could be tempted to interpret all the instances of voice-over as diary excerpts. In fact, only one voice-over sequence clearly represents an extract from this journal, and this coincides with a visual of Humbert making the written entry. The other four instances of voice-over give no evidence of being journal extracts. They seem to be occurring simultaneously with their visual presentation. Furthermore, there is no indication that Humbert is telling his story after the fact, perhaps from the prison cell that the audience is informed he inhabits at the film's conclusion. Of the thirty-five narrative units in the film, only five involve Humbert's voice-over. Apart from the one particular journal extract (unit 8), the other four instances are examples of direct address to the viewer.

Though Humbert supplies the voice-over, the film does not restrict viewer information to this character's range of knowledge. An example of this occurs in unit 11 after Lolita leaves for Camp Climax, as Humbert lies sobbing on the girl's bed. The camera moves in on a big close-up of a framed picture of Quilty on the bedroom wall. The framing points to an important clue in the relationship between Lolita and Quilty; indeed, the camera movement is highlighted so as to emphasize that Humbert is specifically excluded from this piece of information. One is reminded of a similar moment in *Rear Window* (Alfred Hitchcock, 1954) when the descriptive camera reveals Thorwald (Raymond Burr) leaving the apartment as Jeff (James Stewart) sleeps. In both films, the camera excludes the protagonist from a crucial piece of narrative information meant exclusively for the viewer.

A key structuring component of *Lolita* involves the various ways in which the film makes reference to the character of Quilty. His presence can be detected, either implicitly or overtly, in sixteen of the film's thirty-five narrative units, with significantly more references in the later stages of the film. If the film is divided structurally into two parts, part one ending with Charlotte's death (unit 12), then there are four references to Quilty in this first part and twelve in the second.

The exact nature of these appearances is an intriguing aspect of the film. Almost all of Quilty's scenes in the second part either involve impersonations (such as Dr. Zempf, the school psychologist, or a policeman attending a convention at the hotel) or contain mere traces of his presence (in the form of the sunglasses, a mysterious phone call to Humbert, or the ever-present car that follows Humbert and Lolita after they leave

Beardsley, Ohio). The elusiveness and the involvement of the viewer in trying to solve the puzzle of Quilty's appearances is a great pleasure of the film. It contributes to the game-playing strategy discussed above and involves viewers in testing their knowledge against that of the film's protagonist. It quickly becomes apparent, however, that this game will almost always exclude Humbert, who never seems aware of Quilty's presence. Humbert's murder of Quilty in the opening scene seems rooted in the inability of Humbert's character to accept the "impure" relationship that he perceives to have existed between Quilty and the young Lolita. The murder may also be related to the fact that Quilty (and the film's narration) has made Humbert appear ridiculous for most of the film by excluding him from any awareness of Quilty's presence.

The pattern of Quilty's appearances also merits some comment. The film proceeds from Quilty's actual physical appearances in early scenes (such as the sequence at the school dance) to impersonations that disguise his identity to evidence or traces of his existence (the sunglasses). Viewers are then presented with the mysterious, almost uncanny presence of the car that follows Humbert and Lolita for three days of story time. Quilty is never seen in these sequences, but the observant viewer understands that he is there. The "appearance" of Quilty in these car scenes is emblematic of the character's earlier appearances in the film. He is there for the viewer but not there for Humbert. Quilty then becomes a disembodied voice at the end of a phone line, followed by second-hand reports of his existence from hospital staff members when Lolita is checked out by a mysterious "uncle." In unit 34, Lolita sums up and fills in most of the details about Quilty for Humbert, confirming all of the audience's suspicions. Everything seems a revelation for Humbert. Finally, Quilty is reduced to the flimsiest of references—he becomes a name on the lips of our protagonist and a memory for the viewer. Humbert alludes to the opening scene when he shouts, "Quilty, Quilty." The film comes full circle, although the shooting scene is not repeated.

The character of Quilty is a major presence in *Lolita*, perhaps *the* presence, and more often than not viewers feel his presence by his absence. That is, they are most aware of the character when he is not there. *Lolita*'s narrative construction depends on the ways in which this presence is alluded to throughout the film, especially the strategy of excluding Humbert from much of the film's narrative information.

An example of this exclusion is the scene of Charlotte Haze's (Shelley Winters) death. This is a crucial sequence in narrative terms, but it is played entirely off-screen. Humbert is unaware of the event until after it has occurred. Likewise, much of the film's narrative takes place off-screen or simply outside the main character's field of vision. Humbert's exclusion from much of the narrative information, particularly in contrast with the viewer's privileged position toward this same information, contributes to another important speculation—that, despite the film's subjective voice-over commentary, Humbert does not control the fictional presentation. He does not really tell the film's story. The controlling point of view is more properly supplied by the film's overall narrating function. The voice-over is just one more element in that overall narration.

Another major gap in the film is the absence of any overt sexual component to the representation of Humbert and Lolita's relationship. While it is true that censorship constraints at the time may partially account for the absence of any visual evidence of their sexual relationship, it does not entirely account for its nearly complete exclusion. The dialogue only hints at their illicit relationship with such cryptic lines as "Let's tell mother" or "The neighbors are beginning to talk." Alternatively, we get Quilty's vulgar interpretation of the affair when he calls Humbert in the middle of the night (off-screen) and presumably accuses him of licentious behavior. The lack of overt sexual content is more adequately explained in terms of Humbert's characterization. For Humbert, there is simply no appropriate way to illustrate the pure and ideal relationship he imagines exists with Lolita.

The allusions to their illicit relationship point to another major absence or gap in the film: the discrepancy between how Humbert describes Lolita (in voice-over and in his obsessive behavior) and the film's presentation of her to the viewer. Lolita is nothing like what Humbert imagines her to be. On the evidence of Lolita's behavior in many scenes, most viewers would rightly view her as a vulgar, spoiled, and sexually experienced teenager who manipulates Humbert throughout the film. Certainly audiences in the early 1960s were not used to seeing teenage girls in such manipulating, controlling positions. Although by the end of the film viewers sense Lolita's victimization at the hands of Quilty, there is little in her character itself that is out of the ordinary and little, it seems, that could inspire Humbert's obsessive behavior. Lolita does not seem to merit anywhere near the passion and attention Humbert lavishes on her. Although Humbert is not without his cruel side, especially in his treatment of Charlotte Haze, he is portrayed as the real victim in the film. Obsessive behavior is not rational or logical, and the film's characterization of Lolita as merely banal may be one way of reinforcing this idea.

The difference between how Lolita is presented to the viewer and how Humbert imagines her is an interesting disjunction in the film. It is another example of the way Humbert's view of the world is at odds with the omniscient perspective of the film. The information the viewer receives, particularly about Lolita and Quilty, is tangibly different from Humbert's perception of it. There is a clear difference between how the viewer and Humbert interpret many events depicted in the film, and this difference of interpretation is tied specifically to many of its narrative patterns.

Voice-over Commentary

Lolita's first-person commentary is not as pervasive as some other Kubrick voice-overs, such as Alex in *A Clockwork Orange*. It is noteworthy in many respects, especially as it relates to a key narrative decision: the disparity between Humbert's view of the world and the spectator's. Although Humbert is the audience's narrator and guide, there are many instances in which the narrative and Kubrick's descriptive camera point to some piece of information of which Humbert is not aware (most particularly in references to Quilty).

Humbert Humbert's voice-over is only associated with five of the film's thirty-five narrative segments. Apart from these five instances of voice-over, there is little evidence that the film represents the subjective presentation of its main character. In fact, the major narrative and visual structures point insistently to an objective presentation. The ironic distance between Humbert's view of the world and the presentation of narrative information is what gives the film much of its resonance and pleasure.

As we have discussed, *Lolita* begins with the sequence in which Humbert Humbert confronts and shoots Clare Quilty. If viewers take this unexpected beginning to be the temporal present of the film's narrative, then the temporal movement "Four years earlier" immediately after this first scene marks the rest of the narrative as one long flashback. But whose flashback? A final end credit informs the audience that Humbert died in jail awaiting trial for the murder of Quilty, making the film not only one long flashback but apparently the flashback of a dead man. In fact, the beginning and end of the film put into question the conjecture that the film represents a flashback originating with a particular character. Although *Lolita* appears to be narrated from the perspective of its main character, the temporal shift in the film's narrative structure is merely one aspect of its overall narrating function.

Humbert's first commentary is relatively informational and comes over a montage sequence of shots of travel immediately following the initial murder scene. Humbert describes the circumstances of his arrival in America: "Having recently arrived in America, where so many Europeans had found a haven before, I decided to spend a peaceful summer in the attractive resort town of Ramsdale, New Hampshire. Some English translations I had made of French poetry had enjoyed some popularity."

The tone is straightforward, informational, almost cheery—not the kind of writing one would do in a diary. There is no intimacy about the entry, no observation of people or the world, only expository information meant exclusively for the viewer. The extract hints that the film's protagonist is literate and cultured, a view that will be confirmed in later extracts and the dramatized body of the film. The question of locating the film's "present" in the previous scene is important because there is no indication that this voice is aware of the event that has just occurred on the screen (four years later in story time) or that it knows its possessor's eventual fate. This first extract is in the nature of a direct address that coincides with the time frame of the visual presentation. This coincidence of the commentary with the visual dramatization is important if one is to argue against the notion of character flashback. This is the audience's first introduction to Humbert's voice-over, and, coming as it does immediately after the previous scene of a distraught murderer, the audience is taken aback and more than a little intrigued by its vocal inflection. From what position does the voice narrate? What is its relationship to the narrated events?

After this initial introduction to Humbert's "voice," the second encounter takes the form of a journal entry. This is apparent not only because viewers see Humbert writing as they hear the words on the soundtrack but also because Humbert's language has a literary, intimate quality. Humbert describes his infatuation with Lolita and refers to his role as a secret writer of his thoughts:

> What drives me insane is the twofold nature of this nymphet, of every nymphet perhaps—this mixture in my Lolita of tender, dreamy childishness and a kind of eerie vulgarity. I know it is madness to keep this journal but it gives me a strange thrill to do so. And only a loving wife could decipher my microscopic script.

This extract comes just before Humbert's marriage to Charlotte Haze and ironically predicts her discovery of the diary. It also points to a clarity of thought about his obsession that is not always apparent in Humbert's actions. Humbert's references to madness and insanity interestingly foreshadow the character's mental deterioration in later stages of the film.

Humbert's third voice-over reverts to direct address and is clearly not a journal entry. On the soundtrack, the audience hears Humbert's contemplation of the murder of Charlotte over visuals of him loading bullets into a gun. The sound has a slight echo to it, confirming the idea that this is an attempt to represent Humbert's mental state. This is also the longest voice-over in the film:

> No man can bring about the perfect murder. Chance, however, can do it. Just minutes ago she had said it wasn't loaded. What if I had playfully pulled the trigger then. [Now as if rehearsing a speech to the police] "She said it wasn't loaded; it belonged perhaps to the late Mr. Haze. She was having her morning tub. We had just finished talking about our plans for the future. I decided to play a practical joke and pretend I was a burglar. We were newlyweds and still did things like that to each other. Soon, as it happened, I called an ambulance, but it was too late!" Simple, isn't it, the perfect murder.

The commentary comes immediately after a scene in which Humbert and Charlotte have argued and she has stormed out of their bedroom. Throughout the monologue, Humbert loads the gun that he will presumably use on his shrewish wife. As he approaches the bathroom where Charlotte is drawing her bath, he continues:

> She splashed in the tub. A trustful, clumsy seal. And all the logic of passion screamed in my ear, "Now is the time." But what do ya' know folks, I just couldn't make myself do it. The scream grew more and more remote. And I realized the melancholy fact that neither tomorrow, nor Friday, nor any other day or night, would I make myself put her to death.

At this point, Humbert discovers Charlotte in the act of reading his journal. Moments later, fate accomplishes what he has been unable to do: Charlotte runs out into the street and is struck by a car. This is the clearest evidence that Humbert's commentary is most often addressed to the audience ("What do ya' know folks"), rather than consisting of diary entries.

The fourth time the audience hears Humbert's voice, it is later in the narrative as he makes his way to Beardsley, Ohio. The tone is again matter-of-fact and contains a curious (and impossible) directive to "forget Ramsdale, and poor Charlotte, and poor Lolita and poor Humbert." The commentary seems to indicate that a new narrative is about to commence, rather than a continuation of what has gone before. The direct address occurs over another montage sequence of travel images:

> You must now forget Ramsdale, and poor Charlotte, and poor Lolita, and poor Humbert, and accompany us to Beardsley College where my lectureship in French poetry is in its second semester. Six months have passed and Lolita is attending an excellent school where it is my hope that she will be persuaded to read other things than comic books and movie romances.

Apart from the necessary summarizing function of this commentary, there is a curious tone in Humbert's voice. The commentary gives the illusion of normality in his life with Lolita, but subsequent narrative events reveal that Humbert is unhappy, suspicious, and paranoid. None of this is communicated in the voice-over. The naïve view and mystification of reality in Humbert's voice-over is in sharp contrast to the information offered in the visuals. In the voice-over, there is never any hint of the dark, gloomy relationship that engulfs Humbert and Lolita. Humbert's tone is sunny, buoyant, and seemingly unaware of the fiction the viewers have been following.

This disjunction is perhaps most evident in the final voice-over. It follows several episodes in Beardsley that effectively dramatize the deteriorating relationship of Humbert and Lolita. Yet the sunny tone continues:

> The brakes were realigned, the water pipes unclogged, the valves ground. We had promised Beardsley School that we would be back as soon as my Hollywood engagement came to an end. Inventive Humbert was to be, I hinted, chief consultant in the production of a film dealing with existentialism, still a hot thing at the time.

The commentary never hints at the real reasons for leaving Beardsley, which revolve around the suspicions their relationship has aroused and Humbert's desire to find a place where he can play out his idyllic fantasy in isolation. The vocal inflection of Humbert's voice-over changes little throughout the film. It remains a generally neutral, if cultured and literary, commentary, unaware of the somber events unfolding in the visuals.

In many instances, the film's descriptive camera reveals an important moment relating to Quilty but conceals the information from Humbert. I have previously mentioned one example that occurs after Lolita leaves for Camp Climax, when the camera moves in on a framed picture of Quilty on the bedroom wall. This is clearly a form of emphasis meant for the viewer alone and just as clearly meant to exclude Humbert. Other instances include a scene in which Humbert talks to Quilty at a hotel. Quilty is framed with his back to Humbert and faces the camera (and hence the audience) in full view. Humbert is unaware of Quilty's identity. The staging of this sequence is emblematic of the ways in which the film's narrative excludes Humbert from most of Quilty's appearances. Quilty's other disguises, such as Dr. Zempf, are obvious to the audience but opaque to Humbert.

A disparity of information occurs not merely because Humbert is oblivious to the appearances of Quilty. It derives from a far more pervasive and all-consuming difference in world views. According to the voice-over commentary, Humbert sees the world in a very particular way that is at odds with the character's dramatized presentation. The character encountered through the commentary is, in many ways, a different person from the protagonist who populates the body of the film. Thus, the dramatization of Humbert's obsession seems to be occurring without the knowledge of the character who supplies the commentary's point of view. This difference between the generally characterless, uninvolved voice that the audience hears and the sympathetic character that it sees, provides the film with added ironic distance and a level of complexity it would otherwise not have.

In the commentary, Humbert gives the impression that he is knowledgeable, wise, friendly, and in complete control. In the dramatized portions of the film, by contrast, he is most often presented as one whose knowledge is at best fragmentary. He is often shown as foolish, angry, and desperate—decidedly not in control.

Though Humbert is ostensibly the first-person narrator, there is clearly another narrating consciousness in the film that organizes and controls its presentation. Seymour Chatman has written: "We must distinguish between the narrator, or speaker, the one currently telling' the story, and the author, the ultimate designer of the fable, who also decides for example, whether to have a narrator, and if so, how prominent he should be."[4]

The difference between the film's points of view, as presented in the voice-over commentary and as presented through the overall narrating function as viewed in the narrative action, is one of the film's most interesting and complicating factors. It elevates the seemingly simple and infrequent commentary to a new level of intricacy. Taken alone, the commentary operates on only a few informational and ironic levels. Taken with other narrative strategies, however, it becomes something more. It is through such combinations that *Lolita*'s narrative becomes more playful and elusive. Complexities in structure, narrative organization, and point of view help make *Lolita* one of Kubrick's most accomplished and resonant films.

This discussion reveals that Kubrick's films have remarkable consistencies in their narrative progression and are constructed in precise, structurally coherent ways. Despite the fact that *The Killing* and *Lolita* are not thematically similar and are of substantially different lengths, they share many characteristics in their narrative construction. I have already mentioned the fact that both films are constructed of thirty-five narrative units. Both films also have a crucial sequence at unit 12. In *Lolita*, there is the key sequence of Charlotte Haze's death, which moves the film to a different phase of its narrative progression. *The Killing* begins the crucial day of the robbery and enters the middle phase of its development at sequence 12. Another point of convergence in both films occurs at units 23 and 24. In *Lolita*, unit 23 takes Humbert and Lolita to Beardsley, Ohio and marks the beginning of the film's third and final movement. In *The Killing*, the start of the crucial seventh race and the robbery begins at unit 24. Finally, both films have something of a narrative climax or crucial development around units 28 through 30. *Lolita* includes Quilty's elusive car appearances at units 28 and 29. In *The Killing*, the climactic moments of the heist and the massacre occur at units 29 and 30.[5]

These plot convergences add weight to the argument that Kubrick is manipulating the traditional, three-act story structure. The films display a degree of consistency in their narrative construction, especially in the placement of emotional climaxes and other crucial narrative moments. They are appropriating and hyperbolizing the three-act dramatic structure of classical filmmaking. This manipulation of traditional rules of construction is an important aspect of the director's gradual transformation of the classical Hollywood model into a more modernist narrative style, especially evident in later films such as *2001: A Space Odyssey* and *The Shining*.

The question of subtextual meaning is as intriguing in *Lolita* as it is in *The Killing*. By structuring the film so that Quilty's appearances and traces of those appearances are in the foreground, Kubrick speaks, if rather indirectly, to the way his film generates meaning. A large part of the pleasure of watching *Lolita* has to do with the game analogy, and one of the most interesting games concerns these elusive appearances and the main character's obliviousness to them.

The viewer of *Lolita* is in a privileged position. He or she has much more information than the main character. An attentive viewer understands the significance of the dolly movement into Quilty's picture on Lolita's wall (at least, in retrospect) and of the ever-present car trailing Humbert and Lolita after they leave Beardsley, Ohio. The audience can always see through Quilty's impersonations, while Humbert always remains in the dark.

Why should Kubrick structure his film around these imperatives of presence and absence and around the main character's lack of information? It is not enough to claim that the film is more interesting or playful or enjoyable this way. It is also unsatisfying to claim that the original novel restricted the film's conception of Quilty's character. Once again, my speculation is related to the notion of cinematic reflexiveness. The "Quilty game," and all that this game implies, can be read as another way for the film's organizer of meaning, its creator, to speak (indirectly) to the viewer. One could relate this level of discourse to the notion that much of a film's meaning is hidden. As in any valuable work of art, the attentive viewer must reflect and dig below the surface for the layers of complexity that an artwork can give up.

The perceptive viewer has the reasonable expectation that many layers of a film's meaning will not reveal themselves on first viewing. The subtext that I relate to the film's structural insertion of Quilty is elusive and does not represent the most common thematic form in Kubrick's work. But Kubrick's films are intriguing precisely because they encourage this kind of speculation. The thematic operation of the films is often as complex as the formal organization and inextricably connected to it.

APPENDIX

Narrative Segmentation of The Killing

1. Marv Unger (Jay C. Flippen), Mike O'Reilly (Joe Sawyer), and George Peatty (Elisha Cook) are introduced at the racetrack, which will be the scene of the heist later in the film. The time is 3:45 P.M. Voice-over.

2. Officer Randy Kennan (Ted De Corsia) meets a loan shark in a bar. The time is 2:45 P.M., same day. Voice-over.

3. Gang leader, Johnny Clay (Sterling Hayden), is at his apartment with his "girl," Fay (Coleen Gray). The time is 7:00 P.M., same day. Voice-over.

4. Mike is at home with his sick wife. The time is 6:30 P.M., same day. Voice-over.

5. George is at home with his wife Sherry (Marie Windsor). The time is 7:15 P.M., same day. Voice-over.

6. Sherry meets her lover (Vince Edwards). No precise time is established, although viewers know it is later than segment 5. No voice-over.

7. The gang meets and discovers Sherry, who is listening in another room. George is roughed up. No precise time is given, although viewers know it takes place after segment 6. No voice-over.

8. George is at home with Sherry. No precise time is given, but it is still Saturday night or early Sunday morning, and so it must come after segment 7. No voice-over.

9. Johnny talks to Maurice (Kola Kwariani). It is the Tuesday following the previous Saturday of segments 1–8. The time is 10:15 A.M. Voice-over.

10. Johnny talks to Nikki (Timothy Carey). The time is unclear, but probably after segment 9. No voice-over.

11. Johnny rents a motel cabin. The time is unclear, but probably after segment 10. No voice-over.

12. Sherry and George are at breakfast. The time is 7:30 A.M. the following Saturday (all the following actions take place on this, the day of the heist). Voice-over.

13. A view of Red Lightning, the horse to be shot in a planned diversion at the racetrack. The time is 5:00 A.M. Voice-over.

14. Johnny talks to Marv at his apartment. The time is 7:00 A.M. Voice-over.

15. Johnny arrives at the airport. The time is 7:00 A.M. Voice-over.

16. Johnny is at the motel cabin. The time is 8:15 A.M. Voice-over.

17. Johnny is at the bus station. The time is 8:45 A.M. Voice-over.

18. Johnny slips a key in Mike O'Reilly's mail box. The time is 9:20 A.M. Voice-over.

19. Mike O'Reilly is at home with his sick wife. The time is 11:15 A.M. Voice-over.

20. Mike takes a key out of the mailbox and goes to the bus station where he takes a flower carton (containing a rifle) out of a locker. He hops on a bus to the racetrack where he works as a bartender. The time is 11:29 A.M. Voice-over.

21. Mike arrives at the track and puts the flower carton in his locker. Viewers see George take the rifle from the locker. The time is 12:10 P.M. Voice-over.

22. Mike pours beer for a customer. Marv appears drunk. The time is sometime after the first race. Voice-over.

23. Officer Randy Kennan makes a call to the police chief that his car radio is out of order. The time is 3:23 P.M. Voice-over.

24. Randy drives to the track and positions himself under the window. The seventh race begins approximately at 4:00 P.M. Voice-over.

25. Maurice is at the chess club. Viewers learn that he is to be in position at the track at 4:00 P.M. The time is 2:30 P.M. Voice-over.

26. Maurice begins his diversion at the track. Viewers hear that it is the start of the fateful seventh race. Johnny is in position. The time is 4:00 P.M. Voice-over.

27. Nikki is at his farm; he arrives at the track at 12:30 P.M. The film stays with Nikki until he shoots Red Lightning during the seventh race and is himself shot dead at 4:24 P.M. Voice-over throughout all of Nikki's actions.

28. Johnny buys a briefcase and positions himself for the robbery at the start of the seventh race. The time is from 2:15 to 4:00 P.M. Voice-over.

29. In the racetrack money room, George opens the door for Johnny and gets the gun out of the flower carton. The role of the various gang members becomes clear, except for Randy Kennan. Johnny throws the moneybag out the window. No voice-over.

30. The gang members wait for Johnny to arrive. They sit listening to a radio announcer describe details of the robbery. The radio announcer voices puzzlement as to how the duffel bag containing the money was removed from the track. Viewers see the bag come out of the window in a flashback. George announces the time. It is 7:15 P.M. He notes that Johnny was supposed to be at the apartment at 7:00 P.M. The two hoods (Vince Edwards, Joseph Turkel) break in. The sequence ends with the climactic bloody massacre.

31. Johnny reaches the motel cabin and takes the duffel bag of money out of the cabin. The time is 6:25 P.M. Voice-over.

32. Johnny arrives at the meeting place at 7:29 P.M. The police arrive. Johnny notices that something is wrong and drives away. Voice-over.

33. Johnny buys a large suitcase at a pawnshop and stuffs the money into it. The time is 7:39 P.M. (10 minutes later). Voice-over.

34. Sherry is at her apartment. George walks in covered in blood and shoots Sherry. The time is unclear but it is after segment 32. No voice-over.

35. Johnny meets Fay at the airport. He is informed that his bag is too big to be carried onto the plane. He is forced to check the suitcase, and it is placed on a small loading van. A small dog runs toward the plane on the runway. The baggage van swerves to avoid hitting the dog. Johnny and Fay look on in horror as the suitcase full of money flies open. They begin to leave, but Johnny resigns himself to his fate

and decides to give himself up. The time is unclear, but it is after segment 33. End of film; no voice-over.

Narrative Segmentation of Lolita

1. After opening credits, Humbert Humbert (James Mason) wanders through Clare Quilty's (Peter Sellers) mansion and shoots Quilty. Several transition shots (aerial/car shots, etc.) follow, and a title announces "Four years earlier." Character voice-over by Humbert begins at the end of the scene.

2. Humbert is introduced with some background information. Charlotte Haze (Shelley Winters) is also introduced.

3. Humbert, Charlotte, and Lolita watch a horror film at a drive-in movie.

4. Humbert teaches Charlotte how to play chess.

5. Humbert observes Lolita as she plays with her hula-hoop in the garden.

6. Humbert, Charlotte, and Lolita are at a school dance; Quilty is there in the company of Vivian Darkbloom.

7. Humbert is at home with Charlotte after the school dance. Lolita interrupts them while they are dancing.

8. Humbert is writing in his diary the morning after segment 7. This is the second sequence with Humbert's voice-over.

9. Charlotte and Lolita are at the breakfast table. Lolita takes breakfast up to Humbert's room where the two briefly discuss the diary. Humbert reads an extract from Edgar Allan Poe to Lolita.

10. Humbert and Charlotte are at the dinner table. Charlotte informs Humbert that Lolita will be going to summer camp (Camp Climax).

11. Lolita gets in a car to go to camp and gives Humbert a goodbye kiss. Humbert walks into Lolita's room and cries on Lolita's bed. Humbert reads Charlotte's letter. Scene ends with camera on Quilty's picture on the wall in full frame.

12. After Humbert's wedding to Charlotte, Humbert is writing in his diary. This is the third voice-over in the film. Humbert and Charlotte discuss God. Charlotte takes out a gun. She mentions her plans for Lolita who will be sent away to school, allowing Charlotte and Humbert to live alone. He contemplates murder; they argue. Humbert addresses the spectator. Charlotte discovers his diary. She is hit by a car, off-screen. Humbert discovers her body on the street outside their house.

13. Humbert is in the bathtub with his drink. Neighbors come in. They notice the gun and assume (wrongly) that Humbert wants to kill himself.

14. Humbert goes to Camp Climax to fetch Lolita and inform her of her mother's death.

15. Humbert and Lolita are in the car. Humbert tells Lolita that her mother is ill and in the hospital. The odyssey begins!

16. Quilty and Vivian Darkbloom are at the hotel. Quilty talks to Mr. Swine, the night manager. Quilty notices the arrival of Humbert and Lolita at the hotel.

17. Humbert and Lolita are in a hotel room.

18. Humbert is in the hotel lobby but does not notice that Quilty is also there. They go outside; Quilty impersonates a policeman ("just a normal guy" speech). Humbert does not recognize Quilty.

19. Humbert and a bellhop try to open a folding cot; Lolita is asleep in bed. Humbert is thwarted in his attempt to consummate their relationship.

20. Next morning Humbert and Lolita are playful. The implication is that their relationship is consummated here, off-screen.

21. Humbert and Lolita are in the car. He tells Lolita that her mother is dead.

22. In the motel room, Lolita is in tears. Humbert promises never to leave her.

23. Voice-over announces that they are in Beardsley, Ohio, six months later. Humbert paints Lolita's toenails (same action under opening credits). Lolita asks to be in the school play. Humbert refuses.

24. Humbert talks with Dr. Zempf, the school psychologist, impersonated by Quilty.

25. Backstage at the school play, Humbert discovers that Lolita has been missing piano lessons for weeks.

26. Lolita and Humbert have a tremendous argument. He proposes that they leave Beardsley. Lolita leaves the apartment.

27. Lolita is in a phone-booth, probably talking to Quilty.

28. Voice-over and car scenes as Humbert and Lolita travel across the country. A car follows them. Humbert notices he is being followed. They stop at a gas station. Humbert notices Lolita talking to someone in another car. They have a blow-out. The car behind them also stops. Both characters seem to be getting ill.

29. Lolita is in the hospital. Humbert brings flowers. He notices a pair of dark sunglasses.

30. Humbert is in a motel room. The phone rings in the middle of the night. It is Quilty in another impersonation.

31. Humbert goes to the hospital and discovers that Lolita has been checked out to the care of her uncle. Humbert goes berserk and has to be restrained.

32. Typewritten page of a "Dear Dad" letter. It is much later in time since Lolita is now married and pregnant. She is badly in need of money.

33. Humbert drives to Lolita's house. He takes a gun out of the car's glove compartment.

34. Humbert and Lolita are in her house. Lolita explains everything about Quilty to Humbert. He gives Lolita money after one final attempt to have Lolita leave with him. Lolita's "nice" husband is introduced. Humbert drives away.

35. Humbert walks into Quilty's mansion, echoing the opening scene. The film ends with Humbert shouting the words "Quilty, Quilty."

Endnotes

1. Tyvetan Todorov, *The Poetics of Prose* (Ithaca, New York: Cornell University Press, 1977), 32.

2. Seymour Chatman has defined the terms this way: "Story is the content of the narrative expression, while the discourse is the form of that expression" (Seymour Chatman, *Story and Discourse:* Narrative Structure in Fiction and Film [Ithaca, New York: Cornell University Press, 1978], 23.)

3. Alexander Walker, *Stanley Kubrick Directs*, expanded edition (New York: Harcourt Brace Jovanovich, 1972), 75.

4. Seymour Chatman, *Story and Discourse*, 33.

5. *A Clockwork Orange* interestingly enough has some striking similarities to both films in terms of narrative structure. It is also constructed of thirty-five narrative units. Unit 12 ends the first part of the film as Alex is about to be sent to prison. The film begins its third phase at unit 23 as Alex starts his life after the Ludovico treatment and his release from prison. At units 28–30, Alex is involved in the crucial scenes with the writer and attempts suicide. For a more complete discussion of the narrational strategies in *A Clockwork Orange*, as well as *Barry Lyndon*, see Falsetto, *Stanley Kubrick*, 21–27.

Paths of Glory

THOMAS ALLEN NELSON

Humphrey Cobb's *Paths of Glory* would seem to be an ideal source for the film maker of *Fear and Desire, Killer's Kiss,* and *The Killing.* Its style and narration develop an ironic contrast between public and private worlds, the fictions of officialese and the fluctuations of an indeterminate truth; the novel is gorged with passages of hallucinatory intensity depicting the actual and imagined horrors of war and others showing an empty and formal masking of that truth by characters who are ambitious. Throughout, Cobb's third-person narration remains all-knowing, ironic, and moralistic; in one scene with an obvious appeal to Kubrick's demonstrated interests, the narrator tells us that General Assolant (Mireau, in the film), who is obsessed with viewing war as merely a "question of percentages," does not take into account that "a battle is a thing of flux, and that you cannot measure flux by the debris that it leaves behind." Elsewhere, Cobb has a scene between Assolant and Colonel Dax that contains very cinematic and Kubrickian overtones. Dax feels that the general's problem is one of "seeing," that he is "always looking through lenses, lenses which are made of the insignia of rank"; consequently, Dax tricks Assolant into confronting the human reality of war through a periscope in the trench:

> The telescopic lenses seemed to spring the mass of bodies right into his face. The bodies were so tangled that most of them could not be distinguished one from the other. Hideous, distorted, and putrescent, they lay tumbled upon each other or hung in the wire in obscene attitudes, a shocking mound of human flesh, swollen and discoloured.

Cobb concludes his strong indictment of the politics of war with a "note" at the end of the novel that forces the reader to extend its lessons to life itself and to see the historical truth behind the fictional lie.*

---

*Cobb's NOTE (p. 265) to *Paths* reads as follows:
All the characters, units, and places mentioned in this book are fictitious.
However, if the reader ask, "Did such things really happen?" the author answers, "Yes," and refers him to the following sources which suggested the story: *Les crimes des conseils de guerre,* by R. G. Réau; *Les fusilles pour l'exemple,* by J. Galtier-Boissiere and Daniel de Ferdon: *Les dessous de la guerre révélés par les comites secrets* and *Images secretes de la guerre,* by Paul Allard; a special dispatch to the *The New York Times* of July 2, 1934, which appeared under this headline: "FRENCH ACQUIT 5 SHOT FOR MUTINY IN 1915; WIDOWS OF TWO WIN AWARD OF 7 CENTS EACH"; and *Le fusillé,* by Blanche Maupas, one of the widows who obtained exoneration of her husband's memory and who was awarded damages of one franc.

From *Kubrick: Inside a Film Artist's Maze* (Bloomington: Indiana University Press, 1982), pp. 37–53. Reprinted by permission.

It is interesting that Kubrick's *Paths of Glory* duplicates neither the nightmare landscapes of the novel nor those found in his earlier films. The film contains only two sequences where subjective tracking shots are used, and neither travels over a field of carnage; in places where the novel calls for an expressionistic film treatment, Kubrick's style remains objective and realistic, and when he extends scenes for which there is little descriptive authority in the novel, such as the attack on the Ant Hill, the court-martial, and the execution, his camera and mise-en-scène become truly impressive. And although he follows the novel's three-part division (before the attack; the attack and after; the court-martial and execution), Kubrick does not choose to work out its ironic patterns of fate. Cobb, for instance, begins and ends by focusing on two soldiers named Langlois and Duval, the first a veteran and survivor who is convinced that "no German shell or bullet has my number on it" and the other a recruit who dreams of glory and especially admires Langlois's medals, even though they were won in a lottery. At the end of the novel, Langlois (Corporal Paris, in the film), as the result of another lottery, is tied to a stake, with his medals on the ground at his feet, and Duval (who is not in the film) is a member of the firing squad that executes him. The novel abounds in such devices, most of which are anticipated far ahead of time, and which reveal a temporal and psychological straitjacket no less confining than the one in *The Killing*. Kubrick's film likewise downplays the conventional appeal of the novel's manipulation of time—which is very cinematic in its parallel "editing" and the "high noon" suspense countdown that precedes the attack and execution—and instead chooses to develop spatial complexities through a more deliberate handling of scene exposition. If *The Killing* represents Kubrick's first real success with a temporal film rhetoric, what Pudovkin might have called the "filmic representation" through action (story) and images of a theme (time), then *Paths of Glory* could be considered his early masterpiece of spatial film communication, one that extends the philosophic implications of the novel far beyond the logic of its liberal/moral preachments. Kubrick, in other words, uses the temporal and psychological framework of Cobb's novel to develop more fully and more satisfactorily than before an aesthetics of contingency, one which by its very nature requires that the exigencies of any given moment in filmic time (whether psychic or "real") be measured against the larger spatial and ambiguous dimensions of a disparate cinematic universe.*

Paths poses difficulties in assigning credit for its verbal ideas. Undoubtedly, both Calder Willingham and Jim Thompson helped Kubrick with the ironic and literate nuances of the dialogue, although *Barry Lyndon,* scripted by Kubrick with help only from William Makepeace Thackeray, plays with language in much the same way. And the use of narration stands as one of Kubrick's most distinctive film signatures. Kubrick freely admits that the collaborative experience of putting a film script together is essential to its success, as the significant contributions of Vladimir Nabokov to *Lolita,* Terry Southern and Peter George to *Dr. Strangelove,* Arthur C. Clarke to *2001,* and Diane Johnson to *The Shining* will testify. However, Kubrick's career illustrates his stated belief that the writer-director who masters both crafts produces consistently the finest work.

In *Paths of Glory* Kubrick combines, for the first time, a "sound" thematics—language, noise, music—with a visual complexity that illustrates his belief that film must achieve the ambiguity and "subconscious designating effect of a work of art" through images and music rather than words. It is evidence of Kubrick's early maturity as a film artist that he uses an off-screen narrator only at the beginning and yet maintains a documentarylike realism of style that develops a complexity of ideas. Following the credits and the playing of the French national anthem, and a title that identifies place and time ("France 1916"), the narrator—his tone anticipates the computer voices of *Dr. Strangelove's* narration and HAL of *2001*—briefly summarizes the beginning years of World War I as first a series of attacks and counterattacks and then a stalemate of "zigzagging" trenches and unchanging "battlelines." At the same time, the camera from a distance shows the arrival of General Broulard (Adolphe Menjou) outside a grand eighteenth-century chateau, which looks out onto a spacious but formal garden of walkways more appropriate for a ceremonial promenade than a casual stroll. Two lines of soldiers form a pathway for Broulard's entrance into a setting of splendor, which, ironically, houses the headquarters of the French regiment commanded by General Mireau (George Macready). In this first shot, the narrator's unemotional voice undercuts the patriotic implications of the *Marseillaise,* while visually the lines and paths anticipate later developments that will show a far more elaborate drama of zigzagging political forces, of psychological attack and counterattack, than the ones mentioned in the narration: the execution scene near the end of the film, for instance, will traverse this very setting and bring together the contrary but complementary worlds of the chateau and the trench; and the film will conclude on an ironic note as a frightened girl (Susanne Christian, since married to Kubrick) in the bistro sings a sentimental *German* song.

The first half of *Paths* (the end of this half can be marked by the film's initial fade-out, after the failed attack on the Ant Hill) further develops this ironic structure of oppositions and parallels between the chateau and the trenches, through which Kubrick will turn a system of clearly defined conflicts into a maze of paradoxical associations. A comparison of the aural and visual treatments of the first two sequences effectively illustrates this point. As the first scene begins, Broulard walks between the lines of soldiers and along the pathway into the chateau for a meeting with Mireau in the spacious and ornate room commandeered for his office and apartment; he compliments Mireau on the "pleasant atmosphere" of the room and on his taste in "carpets and pictures." Mireau, obviously pleased, confesses that the room is the "same as when I moved in" and that "I didn't have to do much." Broulard, with no visible indication that he appreciates the art of the setting or the humor of this exchange, then goes to the "top-secret" reason for his visit (it is not, after all, a social call, but Kubrick confuses the distinction between social formality and political manipulation). Mireau interrupts, "reading" Broulard's mind and abbreviating these formalities with his reference to the Ant Hill; after some smiling cajolements from Broulard, and an implied promise of promotion, Mireau slams a fist into his hand and exclaims: "We might just do it!" Kubrick cuts on this sound of fist and voice, first, to a bleak panorama of no-man's-land through a horizontal viewer and then to Mireau, who like Broulard on his way to the chateau, walks down a pathway lined with soldiers, but Mireau is in a trench where the lines are not as formal or exact, and instead of the *Marseillaise* or the voice of the omniscient narrator, we hear shells exploding and see dirt and debris falling from above. Once again the film is showing us a general officer visiting a subordinate, and at the same time implying a vertical line (i.e., chain of command) both ascending (to Broulard and the gods above) and descending (to Dax and the "insect" men below) outside the frame of any given scene. Mireau must stoop slightly to enter Colonel Dax's cramped bunker, but he does not neglect the verbal formalities of the chateau: He compliments Dax on the "neatness" of his quarters. The colonel (Kirk Douglas), unprepared for this visit, is naked from the waist up and washing from a decorative porcelain bowl (a memento from the chateau, expressive of his desire to stay clean in a dirty world). He conforms outwardly to the rules of protocol by putting on his tunic and addressing his superior officer as "sir," even though his bluntness of language ridicules these formalities. He plays on Mireau's empty rhetoric, turning "mice" into "mausers" and "pregnable" into a paradox of birth and death; when Major Saint-Auban (Richard Anderson) characterizes the fear felt by the huddled men as a herd instinct, an "animal sort of thing," Dax objects, defining it instead as a "human sort of thing." He completely asserts his verbal, as well as moral, superiority when he deflates Mireau's pomposity by citing Samuel Johnson's dictum that "patriotism is the last refuge of a scoundrel." Yet, despite Dax's fervor and his humane education, his final comment, "We'll take the Ant Hill," echoes, ironically, Mireau's resolution at the conclusion of the first sequence.

The film's deployment of camera and mise-en-scène, by contrast, provides a larger and more philosophic perspective from which to view and evaluate the psychological and verbal sparrings of these early sequences. When Broulard commits a *faux pas*, referring to the paintings in Mireau's apartment as "pictures," Kubrick is revealing not just Broulard's artistic illiteracy but his historical and moral illiteracy as well. (When Broulard returns to the chateau after the failed attack, Kubrick shows him traveling on a course parallel to that of a huge painting being carried in the background, but in the opposite direction.) Kubrick's use of the chateau as both primary setting and visual metaphor has little or no precedent in Cobb's novel. There, the chateau does not become a factor until the court-martial and has little descriptive status, except when the narrator alludes to its history by informing the reader that Napoleon once slept there. In Kubrick's film, it visually represents an architectural and philosophic embodiment of one period in human civilization and a timeless passion for aesthetic expression, and at the same time, it provides a commentary on the efforts of the characters to duplicate in their activities its formal properties while ignoring the implications of its beauty and vertical reach. Throughout the film, characters are shown walking down paths that lead either to a maze of personal ambition and delusion or to the endgame of death. In sequence one, as the generals circle an ornate round settee in the middle of the room, the camera moves with them to record the circular logic of both Mireau's thinking and Broulard's persuasion. We notice that Mireau, in his excitement over the prospect of personal glory, momentarily forgets formalities and pours himself a cognac without first offering one to his guest; and when he finally contrives a reason to believe in the likelihood of the attack's success, the camera stops its weaving motions and watches as the two men move into the background across a chessboard parquetry. While the vertical spaciousness of the chateau—as well as an implied scope of history and art—belies the horizontal and circular courses of its temporary inhabitants, the visual definition of the trenches leaves no doubt that their paths take a deadly straight and narrow course. Not only is no-man's-land visualized horizontally in that shot following sequence one, but literally it is part of a topography decorated by a series of horizontal trenches that look more like a surrealist graveyard than paths to glory. Above the trench line, instead of a suggestion of spatial expanses, Kubrick overexposes his film and clouds the air so much that the sky, which rains down shells of death, is also visually oppressing, like a ceiling or a coffin lid. Kubrick's first dolly/tracking shot—moving backward as it shows Mireau's progress through the trenches and past the three men who will later be scapegoats for his failure and vanity—captures a world dynamically in touch with the extremes of life and death but committed, along with the planners in the chateau, to a destructive and predetermined path.

Kubrick continues this ironic blending of explicit and implicit oppositions—of settings and action, words and images, a close-up versus distanced perspective—during the attack on the Ant Hill. Instead of prolonging the countdown to battle and extracting its full emotional and suspense value, as Cobb did, he cuts it short and stretches out the attack itself, perhaps to provide his "war" film with at least one traditional action sequence. Typically, however, Kubrick does not give the audience an uncomplicated moment of human conflict without the intrusion of forces far more sinister than those German soldiers who, if not seen, at least are heard from in the deafening roar of battle. For one thing, the film never explains until after the fact the purpose of the attack or the value, strategically, of the Ant Hill (no such ambiguity exists in the novel). Later, in the last scene between Dax and Broulard, we learn that the attack was necessitated by political, not military, pressures. Only at the end, therefore, does the audience, along with Dax, fully appreciate the extent of Broulard's powers; that, in effect, he was a political and very corporeal *deus ex machina* who watched Mireau watching Dax watching after his men, only Broulard mistakenly assumed Dax's motives were as callous as his own. Kubrick indirectly prepares the audience for this possibility when he contrasts Mireau's activities during the attack with Dax's actual movement into battle. For the second time a binocular view of the Ant Hill is shown from Mireau's always distant perspective, in this instance as he absurdly anticipates a victory celebration with smiles, glasses of cognac, and formal toasts to "France." Kubrick then cuts to the film's first subjective shot, a bold movement with Dax through a trench lined with soldiers on both sides and the sounds of bombardment overhead; the shot ends by moving into a ghostly cloud of smoke and dust. For the attack, Kubrick employed six cameras; one he handheld to bring Dax and the battle into vivid, zoom-close-up. The cameras primarily move on a horizontal path with the attack and capture a remarkable three minutes of film. No doubt, it is as realistic and exciting a battle as any ever put on film: but its real power comes from the sheer magnitude of the disorder and death, the cacophony and volume of the noise, and that Kubrickian overview which lifts it from the immediate fictional context into a larger conceptual one. Kubrick now shows us nightmares taking place in broad daylight and in "real" moments of film time; and the faint but insistent sound of Dax's whistle exhorting his men, at the moment when Mireau fulminates against an artillery commander who "humbly" refuses to open fire on his own men, stands as a poignant mockery of both the destruction falling from a godless sky and the verbal and moral corruption descending from the echo chambers of the chateau.

Yet nothing in part one of *Paths of Glory,* not even this stunning attack sequence, necessarily prepares us for the aesthetic and conceptual brilliance of the last half of the film. The twists and turns of a psychological/political labyrinth bend in even more sinister directions as the action moves entirely into the chateau. The film's visual and philosophical emphasis on horizontal and vertical forms, paths and lines, becomes even more pronounced and intricate as the two worlds of the film begin to express the paradoxical outline of a single world. The early scenes of part two, for instance, show that the trench world has come to the chateau and, ironically, that it is not as out of place there as were the formalities of the chateau in the trenches. Dax now visits Mireau in his "quarters," with Broulard present, and brings his moral rectitude and candid tongue into the parlors of euphemism. They sit at the very table where earlier Broulard began to lead Mireau down that path to the ill-fated attack on the Ant Hill. Only now there are three men, and in the framing of the scene Kubrick implies an emerging alliance between Dax and Broulard: A series of two-shots showing Dax left and Broulard right, with a large classical painting between and over them in the background, oppose Mireau's isolation in one-shot. Here Kubrick is suggesting that there are not only deceptive political maneuvers at play but complex cinematic ones as well. Broulard, assuming that Dax's concern for the men is cynical, supports the colonel's request that he be appointed defense counsel, and thereby prepares the way for Mireau's downfall—Mireau will become the scapegoat for the general staff. And while Kubrick is framing this relationship—ironically, one that Dax, like Broulard, misinterprets—he implies another between them and the "higher" work of art in the background. Not unexpectedly, neither the politics of the trench nor those of the chateau acknowledge its value as an emblem of civilized expression and aesthetic beauty. For both, it remains, like the chateau itself, an uncomprehended and unappreciated decoration. For the audience, however, it will be a source for both comprehending and appreciating Kubrick's cinematic art.

The three prisoners and the animal stalls that serve as their cell make the presence of the trench felt. Even now, with their humanity so palpable, the soldiers of the trench are viewed by the officers in the chateau as a lower form of life occupying the bottom rung of an imaginary Chain of Being. (Although, ironically, their last meal is delivered on an ornate silver tray.) Politically, as the scene involving the killing of the cockroach implies, they have no more status than the ants that crawl over the ground. Here and elsewhere Kubrick shows their common humanity, their courage and their fears, while, as he did in *Killer's Kiss* and *The Killing,* intensifying a sense of tragic pathos through their ensnarement in a fate at once political and metaphysical: Lieutenant Roget (Wayne Morris) has a cowardly inability to deal with the stresses of war and its magnification of human mortality, and Corporal Paris is a victim of that inability; Private Ferol (Timothy Carey) is a misfit, someone who does not conform to socially acceptable conduct; and Private Arnaud (Joseph Turkel) has been selected by lottery, which epitomizes the trench concept of life as a metaphysical crapshoot. Significantly, Kubrick shows us that the same struggles exist, in disguised form, in the corridors and salons of the chateau. Mireau's fear of failure and his desire for an empty glory, Saint-Auban's smugness and sycophancy, Broulard's subservience to unseen forces off-screen, and, yes, even Dax's fervor and naïveté, may not result in their walking down that formal path to an undeserved execution, but they just as surely do not ascend to the more comprehensive understandings embodied in the lessons of history and art that surround them, radiant but unseen. The officers' paths, too, run a horizontal course, as the formal structures of the court-martial and execution make clear.

More than any other scene in *Paths,* or before it in his other films, Kubrick's handling of the court-martial achieves an impressive merger of concept and form. From long shot, the camera shows a detachment of soldiers bringing the three accused men into a vast, elegant room. An enormously large landscape painting hangs high up on the wall, looming above their heads; light floods in from tall windows in the rear and to the right; while below, on the floor, are the ever-present chessboard squares of a marble floor. Again, the composition emphasizes the verticals of the chateau, but more strongly than before, while the painting overhead hints at an idealization of the trench landscape and, significantly, provides the one prominent horizontal presence in the shot. While space is enlarged, however, time is compressed. The court-martial proceedings begin at three o'clock in the afternoon and take up very little actual time, even though an elaborate consideration for the formalities of the occasion is evident. The Colonel Judge (Peter Capell) repeatedly chastises Dax for taking up too much of the court's "time" with technicalities that do not bear directly on the case (such as the reading of the indictment!). Formalities, not the "technicalities" of justice, are important here. And in the actual examination and cross-examination of the three men by prosecutor Saint-Auban and Dax, the court makes every effort to deny the reality of time: It will not allow Dax to offer as evidence the past histories of these men as soldiers, only what they did during the three minutes of the attack; and, of course, its primary purpose is to take from the prisoners a right to all future time. Yet this temporal evasion—an avoidance of the existential basis of life—takes on a spatial form as well. For the court to duplicate the vertical grandeur of its surroundings would be tantamount to its recognizing its own folly; such duplication would entail an enlargement of vision and perspective that would first lead to the court's acknowledging its own tragic absurdity. Kubrick's audience, however, does perceive this disparity, especially when it realizes that the court-martial itself assumes the formal properties of a battle on a gameboard. The camera work and composition leave little doubt about Kubrick's intentions here. On one side we have the battleline represented by the five judges, symmetrically composed with the Colonel Judge in the middle, framed by an archway in the background and the French flag overhead; on the other, the three prisoners, sitting in chairs, enclosed from behind like pawns by two lines of guards standing motionless in an attitude of parade rest; on the flank to their left, and parallel to the windows, is Major Saint-Auban's table and behind him General Mireau and a line of spectators; and finally, to the prisoners' right is Colonel Dax, opposite Saint-Auban and clearly outnumbered. This boxlike gameboard moves along horizontal paths, as the camera reveals when it pans back and forth behind the line of judges during Saint-Auban's speech and tracks behind the line of prisoners during Dax's. The court-martial, Kubrick implies, formalizes the world of the trenches, not the reaches of the chateau. The scene ends in darkness as the screen fades to black following the Colonel Judge's final words: "The court will deliberate."

The implication that the politics of the chateau and the horrors of the trench differ only in form and not in substance crystallizes in Kubrick's handling of the execution scene. It begins with a high-angle shot looking across the garden to the massive chateau in the background and down a wide path formed by Mireau's regiment connecting chateau with execution. As the three men and the priest (Emile Meyer) move toward the camera down this ceremonial walkway, the film not only visually links the vertical chateau to the horizontal trench, but reminds us that each side of a chessboard mirrors (and so reverses) the other. The film began with an expansive but formal composition of the area where now stands the place of execution, while in reverse angle it returns to a shot that forms a path to the very entrance where Broulard first tread another path into the chateau; similarly, the second half of the film thematically mirrors the first by demonstrating that an existential struggle with mortality and paradox persists even after the internecine conflicts of state. Kubrick cuts from the prisoners and chateau to a subjective shot moving toward the stakes. In this, the audience's first view of the execution area, Kubrick's camera creates both a sympathetic identification with the three men about to die and recalls Dax's movements into the smoky nightmare of battle, except that now the shot is more generalized and leaves the impression that we, too, move down that same path. Only in this background we are confronted with the ultimate mockery of the chateau's vertical thrust. Three narrow stakes, like the three figures that close in on Johnny Clay at the end of *The Killing*, form a line and rise upward and above the sandbags; and while the camera shows in their balanced spacing and proportion that the stakes not only face but imitate the chateau, the time-worn splendor at the other end of the pathway continues to preside over this horizontal labyrinth in silent contempt.

But once its formal mask is defined, Kubrick penetrates the artifice of the execution and reveals a human content that the judges of the court-martial refused to admit as relevant evidence. Tied to the stakes, the prisoners form a line that resembles their position at the court-martial, only now they are upright and about to face a firing squad rather than a kangaroo court. Major Saint-Auban stands before them and reads the formal sentence of the court, only now, in his hesitations, he expresses an uneasy awareness of death's presence; Sergeant Boulanger (Bert Freed) pinches the cheek of Arnaud, mercifully unconscious, who in the trenches had expressed his greater fear of pain than of dying, while Ferol, no longer confident that he has an edge over a cockroach, clings to the sacraments, and quite literally to the rosary, of the priest; and Corporal Paris makes that final existential choice and struggles to give his death some vestige of dignity; Lieutenant Roget then walks down the line of prisoners offering them blindfolds, ironically asking Paris to forgive him. And all the while, the drums continue to roll and off to one side a cart with three caskets waits. The last two shots reverse perspective and draw the audience even more deeply into the film's unresolved conflicts: the first offers a final look at the chateau and the path that connects it to the stakes, only now the double lines of a firing squad separate the prisoners from the spectators; the second reverses this angle and looks over the executioners' shoulders as they fire in unison at the three men. The audience, at once spectator and victim, watches death from afar and confronts it up close; and in the finality of that moment, it perceives that the same pathway that ends in death for Arnaud, Ferol, and Paris encloses the humanist Dax as well as the generals. It is a path beautiful in its symmetry and fearful in its meanings.

Alexander Walker calls *Paths of Glory* Kubrick's "graduation" piece, and no doubt it is a truly masterly film. It provides an early textbook of styles and preferences that will later be associated with a Kubrickian film signature. *Paths* shows the first signs of that passion for exact detail that establishes both the authenticity of a film and its expressiveness. Kubrick clearly wants to give each scene an interesting visual quality and at the same time to imply a latent coherence of emotion and idea. The imagery of the film blends grainy black-and-white realism and the documentary, handheld camera style of the attack (zooms and telephoto shots) with compositional effects achieved through deep focus and long camera takes. In every scene Kubrick is careful to provide an available-light look; when filming inside, he always identifies the "source" light, whether it is a naked bulb hanging in Dax's bunker, a candle on Roget's table, or the light-flooded windows of the chateau. He repeatedly gives value to unobtrusive objects in the background either through a brief compositional effect or as counterpoint. When Dax, for instance, meets privately with Broulard just before the execution, Kubrick slyly misleads the audience into thinking that the tables have been turned and that Dax's humanism yet may prevail over Mireau's vanity. The scene takes place in a library— walls lined with books, a warm fire burning in a fireplace, and carpets on the floor, all of which complement the intimate and liberal definition of Dax's character. Dax sips cognac and briefly plays Broulard's game before he plays his trump card—during the attack Mireau ordered artillery fire on his own positions. Broulard remains inscrutable and leaves Dax to wonder if, indeed, there is in the chateau even one spokesman for a humane politics. A china tea set in the background may provide the answer. The library is no different from any other room in the chateau; its books are decorative only, while the tea set at least has the virtue of contributing to the endless rounds of formal bartering which take place there. Also, *Paths of Glory* is Kubrick's first film to use music for ironic counterpoint. A typical example, besides those already mentioned, would be the ballroom scene on the night before the execution, which shows a party of French officers and ladies dancing to the "Artist's Life Waltz" of Austrian composer Johann Strauss. One aspect of Kubrick's artistry that is seldom recognized is the superb editing in the best of his work. Because his films give an audience so much to look at and listen for, the artful transitions from one scene to the next often go unnoticed. *Paths,* for instance, shows Kubrick's fondness for merging his "sound" thematics with an editing style that strives for continuity and juxtaposition within a single cut. Besides the examples already cited, the most notable instance of such a cut in *Paths* is that from the explosions of the firing squad to the tinkle of silverware at Mireau's breakfast after the execution. (This cut has to do with what will be a leitmotif in later Kubrick films. Like Buñuel, Kubrick has a surrealist's appreciation for both the primal and ritualistic significance of eating and food, which finds its fullest expression in the futuristic mise-en-scène of *2001.*)*

Paths of Glory marks the full emergence of a distinct film intelligence and, to a greater degree than in his earlier work, Kubrick makes his presence known and felt in the complex worlds of the film. Kubrick uses his spatial definition of conflict to integrate a series of disparate perspectives through which the audience can respond to the emotional or psychological directions of character and, simultaneously, understand the film's paradoxical blending of irony and affirmation. The conflicting characterizations of Dax and Broulard illustrate this merger of a receptive and generative aesthetics. After their final meeting, when Broulard has used Dax's evidence not to save three innocent men but to bring down one foolish general, Dax and the audience experience a catharsis of sorts in the scene where the German girl's song turns leers into tears. But by that time, through the library scene and that final confrontation in Mireau's apartment, the film has clearly shown that Dax and Broulard are victims of equally confining moralities. They, in fact, embody the polarities of the film itself: Dax's character represents that "close-up" and personal view of the trenches found in Cobb's novel, the one which believes in the importance of moral victories in a world without moral order; Broulard's is the impersonal and distant view of the chateau, one which mocks in its vertical politics a defunct belief in an ordered and purposeful cosmos. The first expresses all the right sentiments and glimpses life's contingencies, but lacks an appropriately expressive and objective form, while the second

---

*In the breakfast scene, the tables are turned on Mireau, literally as well as figuratively. He and Broulard each sit where the other sat in the two previous scenes in the apartment, while Dax sits between them. Mireau's downfall is initiated by Broulard: as he spreads jelly on a croissant, he says casually, "By the way, Paul," and goes on to reveal Colonel Dax's information about the artillery fire. In the library scene Dax uses a similar verbal tactic ("By the way, General Broulard, did you know that General Mireau. . .").

shows an appreciation of form without an understanding of life's existential substance. Each travels in ignorance through the splendor of the chateau, a setting that gives the film and its audience an historical perspective on the tragic and absurd meaning of life in time and, in addition, an aesthetic perspective on the endurance of that meaning in the forms of filmic space.

The Middle Period:
Dr. Strangelove *to*
Barry Lyndon

Out of This World

ROBERT BRUSTEIN

*D*r. *Strangelove** possesses a great many distinctions as a work of the imagination, but I should like to cite it, first and foremost, for valor: I think it may well be the most courageous movie ever made. It is certainly one of the funniest. A nightmare farce which proceeds from horror to horror, culminating in the annihilation of the human race after an American hydrogen bomb has been dropped on Russia, it is, despite its cataclysmic conclusion, a peculiarly heady, exhilarating experience. I can account for this partially by the fact that the movie pays absolutely no deference at all to the expectations of its audience.

Artistic courage always soothes the spirit and makes glad the heart, but when this quality enters as craven a medium as the American film one feels curiously exalted, ineffably happy. Then, too, there is something extraordinarily liberating in the nature of the movie itself. It is the kind of total theater that Antonin Artaud would have admired, with its dark

**Dr. Strangelove or: How I Learned to Stop Worrying and Love the Bomb,* produced and directed by Stanley Kubrick; screenplay by Stanley Kubrick, Terry Southern, and Peter George.

humor, its physical and anarchic dissociation. *Dr. Strangelove* is a plague experienced in the nerves and the funny bone—a delirium, a conflagration, a social disaster.

What Stanley Kubrick has done is to break completely with all existing traditions of moviemaking, both foreign and domestic. While the European art film seems to be inexorably closing in on the spiritual lassitude of certain melancholy French or Italian aristocrats, *Dr. Strangelove* invests the film medium with a new exuberance, expansiveness, and broadness of vision; compared with the sweep of this masterpiece, the weary meanderings of Resnais, Fellini, and Antonioni seem solipsistic and self-indulgent. Moreover, Kubrick's film is fun—this is its one debt to Hollywood. It is enjoyable for the way it exploits the exciting narrative conventions of the Hollywood war movie—say, *Air Force* or *Thirty Seconds Over Tokyo*—and even more, for the way it turns these conventions upside down, and cruelly scourges them. This is what is arrestingly new about the film: its wry, mordant, destructive, and, at the same time, cheerful, unmoralistic tone. We have heard this sound emanating from our comic novels, cabaret acts, satiric revues, living rooms, and dreams, but, although it rumbled a little bit under the conventional noises of *The Manchurian Candidate,* it has never before fully entered the mass media. With *Dr. Strangelove,* a subterranean vibration becomes a series of earthquakes, shattering cultural platitudes, political pieties, and patriotic ideals with fierce, joyous shocks. If the picture manages to remain open, it will knock the block off every ideologue in the country: even now, I suspect, Sidney Hook is preparing the first of fifteen volumes in rebuttal.

To avoid a repetition of Mr. Hook's embarrassing performance on behalf of *Fail-Safe,* where he wrote some eighty-odd pages of closely reasoned, technical argumentation to refute the premise of a cheap, best-selling fantasy, let me announce that *Dr. Strangelove* is frankly offered to the audience as a cinematic sick joke, and that it is based less on verifiable facts than on unconscious terrors. The film's source, a prototype for *Fail-Safe,* is Peter George's *Red Alert,* but the film writers have employed the novel very loosely, and the director has imposed on the finished screen play his own style and purpose. This style is Juvenalian satire; this purpose, the evacuation of fear and anger through the acting out of frightful fantasies. Kubrick has flushed a monster from its psychic lair—the universal fear of nuclear accident—and then proceeded to feed and nourish it, letting it perform its worst before your eyes. The consequence of this spectacle is, as the subtitle suggests, a temporary purgation: to witness the end of the world as a comic event is, indeed, to stop worrying and to love the Bomb.

The outline of the film is this: a psychotic right-wing general, convinced that the Communists are poisoning Americans through fluoridation, exercises emergency powers and sends a wing command to bomb the Soviet

Union. The President, trying to recall these bombers, learns that the Russians have perfected a deterrent, a Doomsday machine, which is automatically triggered to explode the moment a bomb is dropped on Soviet soil, spreading a shroud of fallout over the earth for a hundred years. After the general's base has been destroyed by American forces, and the recall code has been found, both nations cooperate to bring the bombers back or shoot them down. One damaged plane, however, its radio inoperative, manages to continue on to target. Through the invincible doggedness of the pilot and his crew, a hydrogen bomb is dropped on a Soviet missile complex—and apocalypse follows.

Kubrick handles this external action with ruthless documentary realism. The battle scenes, for example, which show Americans slaughtering Americans, are photographed through a grey morning mist (the same smoky tones so effectively used in Kubick's *Paths of Glory*) with a hand camera shaken by artillery explosions; and the flight of the bomber over Arctic wastes is a terrifying journey into the frozen unknown. At the same time, however, Kubrick is evoking savage ironies through the conjunction of unexpected images and sounds: the bomber, for example, proceeds to its destination (and to the destruction of the world) over a chorus of male voices humming "When Johnny Comes Marching Home."

The same blend of farce and nightmare is found in other scenes. During the credits, a B-52 bomber is fueled in the air through a phallic hose, while the sound track plays "Try a Little Tenderness." A looming shot of two monstrous hydrogen bombs, triggered and ready to go, reveals two scrawled messages on them. "Hi There!" and "Dear John." And the epilogue is composed of a series of nuclear explosions (a sequence borrowed, I suspect, from a similar filmed skit used in *The Establishment*), which flower soundlessly while a female voice croons "We'll meet again (don't know where, don't know when)."

What these images suggest is that our heroic postures and patriotic reflexes have become hideously inappropriate to modern weaponry—the same thing is illustrated by the conduct of the crew on the lethal bomber. Kubrick has sardonically included among these crew members the various ethnic stereotypes of Hollywood war movies: a Negro bombardier, a Jewish radio operator, a Texas pilot, etc., all of whom behave, in crisis, according to preconditioned movie patterns—they engage in sexual banter, become comradely, grow steely grim and fighting mad. When the order is received to proceed over enemy territory and drop the bomb, the Texas pilot, Major "King" Kong, takes off his helmet, puts on a ten-gallon hat, assumes an unctuous leader-of-men speaking style, and delivers an inspirational lecture to the crew about their duty to "the folks back home," while promising them all decorations, "regardless of your race, color or creed." When the plane is hit by a missile, he keeps it in action, flying low over jutting peaks; and when the bomb doors stick, he courageously climbs into the bomb bay, determined to fix the short circuit and complete his mission.

Kong finally clears the doors, and goes sailing down to target on the back of a bomb, waving his hat and whooping like a rebel. American heroism has become completely identified with American lunacy. So has American know-how—it is almost a structural principle of this film that our technology is wholly mad. Inside the bomber, for example, the camera peeks into complicated equipment and technical apparati—the instrument panel, the radar, the navigator's gear, the auto-destruct mechanism—all efficiently manipulated by this trained crew to create havoc and mass slaughter. The President's War Room, similarly, with its huge locating charts, is a model of gleaming competence and quiet decorum ("You can't fight in here," says the President to two dissidents, "this is the War Room"). Even the telephone works as an obstacle to survival. In one hilarious sequence, a British officer—having discovered the recall code—is trying to phone Washington with only minutes to go; but he lacks the necessary change, and the Pentagon will not accept collect calls.

If our technology is mad, however, then so are the technicians who create, control, and operate it. *Dr. Strangelove* is a satire not only on nuclear war and warriors, but also on scientists, militarists, military intellectuals, diplomats, statesmen—all those in short, whose profession it is to think about the unthinkable. Thus, the movie contains a large number of superb caricatures, all treated either as knaves or fools, but still recognizable as familiar American types.

These include two sharp profiles of General Walker-like military men: General Jack D. Ripper, played by Sterling Hayden in another of his stiff, interesting non-performances—his eyes fanatically narrowed, his teeth clenched on a huge cigar, as he drawls to an aide about how he confines himself to pure alcohol and rain water and refrains from sexual intercourse to protect his natural essences against the Communist conspiracy; and General Buck Turgidson, Air Force Chief of Staff, played by George C. Scott in a fine frenzy of muscle-flexing pugnacity—stuffing his mouth with wads of chewing gum, and flashing an evil smile as he outlines his plan to obliterate the "commie punks" entirely ("I'm not saying we wouldn't get our hair mussed, Mr. President, but I do say not more than ten to twenty million dead depending on the breaks").

Then, there are three magnificent satiric sketches by Peter Sellers: Group Captain Mandrake, Ripper's befuddled British aide; President Merkin Muffley, a bald, bland, liberal Chief Executive, educated and slightly effeminate (a *merkin* according to the OED, is a "female pudendum, "while *muffley* is an obsolete word for a pubic wig); and, finally, that eerie figure from the Bland Corporation, the German scientist, Dr. Strangelove.

Strangelove (formerly *Merkwuerdigichliebe*) is the most masterly character in the film, a composite portrait of Edward Teller, Werner von

Braun, and Herman Kahn, played by Sellers with an excess of mischief, and conceived by Kubrick in an excess of fury. Imprisoned in a wheel chair, his mechanical hand gloved in black, his face fixed in a perpetual smile, he stares through dark glasses and sibilates through false teeth, suggesting emotion only through a slight emphasis on certain phrases, the word *human* being particularly distasteful to him. Strangelove is the perfect synthetic man, and he comes to us by courtesy of a Universal horror movie. In his person, the Mad Doctor and the State Scientist merge—Boris Karloff with a computer, calculating the proper use of deterrents and the half-life of cobalt-thorium-G.

This is extravagant enough, but towards the end, Strangelove goes completely haywire. So does the movie, as if Kubrick, having breathed the air of the outer limits for the first time, were suffering from stratospheric drunkenness. The bomb has been dropped; the doomsday shroud is beginning to smother all life on earth; and Strangelove is outlining his plan for preserving "a nucleus of human specimens" at the bottom of mine shafts. His explanation is disarmingly rational but his mechanical hand has gone out of control. It shoots up in a Nazi salute, it punches him on the jaw, it strangles him, and finally it propels him right out of his wheelchair—whereupon he screams at the President, "*Mein Fuehrer,* I can walk!" The lunatic inappropriateness of the remark somehow sums up all the lunatic inappropriateness of the theatrics and celluloid heroics that have preceded it; and it makes the devastation that follows seem singularly fitting and just.

Dr. Strangelove is a work of comic anarchy, fashioned by a totally disaffected and disaffiliated imagination: it is thus the first American movie to speak truly for our generation. Kubrick has managed to explode the right-wing position without making a single left-wing affirmation: the odor of the Thirties, which clung even to the best work of Chaplin, Welles, and Huston, has finally been disinfected here. Disinfected, in fact, is the stink of all ideological thinking. For although *Dr. Strangelove* is about a political subject, its only politics is outrage against the malevolence of officialdom. Conservatives will find it subversive, liberals will find it irresponsible, utopians will find it bleak, humanitarians will find it inhuman—*Dr. Strangelove* is all these things. But it also releases, through comic poetry, those feelings of impotence and frustration that are consuming us all; and I can't think of anything more important for an imaginative work to do.

Dr. Strangelove and 2001: A Space Odyssey

ROBERT PHILLIP KOLKER

*D*r. *Strangelove* is that rarity among American film in which verbal language plays a major role. In fact it is a film about language that creates its own destruction, its own death, and the death of the world. In a film that delineates a love of destruction and death, a *Merkwürdigliebe* (Strangelove's German name), everything done and everything said manifests this love and hastens its consummation. What Kubrick, Terry Southern, and Peter George do in their script and what Kubrick does in his direction is create a series of linguistic and visual reductions and give the characters utterances which defeat meaning. Like the auto-destruct mechanism on the SAC bomber's radio, the characters' words undo and destroy themselves. The bomber, for example, is introduced by a very serious voice-over narration explaining the SAC system. When the film cuts to the interior of the plane, Major Kong (Slim Pickens) is reading *Playboy* and the communications officer playing with a deck of cards, images which immediately undercut the seriousness of the introduction. When the attack plan is confirmed, drums and trumpets begin playing "When Johnny Comes Marching Home," music that will accompany all the sequences in the bomber, creating a music-image complex that ultimately contradicts itself. No one comes marching home from this battle.

Major Kong prepares for "nuclear combat, toe to toe with the Russkies." He pulls out a cowboy hat, which he wears through the rest of the flight. He tells his men, "I reckon you wouldn't even be human beings if you didn't have some pretty strong personal feelings about nuclear combat. . . . If this thing turns out to be half as important as I figure it just might be, I'd say that you're all in line for some important promotions and personal citations when this thing's over with. And that goes for every last one of you, regardless of your race, color, and your creed. . . ." Both image and words clash with the seriousness of purpose expected from the situation: a bomber about to start Armageddon. The words in particular reduce meaning to a level of banality and cliché. Roland Barthes, speaking of linguistic structure in the works of Sade, writes that "he juxtaposes heterogeneous fragments belonging to spheres of language that are ordinarily kept separate by socio-moral taboo." Kubrick's characters in *Dr. Strangelove* do precisely the same thing. The socio-moral taboos they break are those which keep expressions of serious connotation apart from those that are banal. A drawling cowboy ought not be associated with the commander of an aircraft carrying a nuclear bomb. When this cowboy begins speaking, one does not wish to hear grammar-school commonplaces and locker-room psychologisms. When this is precisely what is heard, it is very funny because of the surprise, and very frightening, because of the gap between the utterance and the context, which demands other language. The serious is made light of and the ridiculous is made serious. The language circles upon itself, it has no subject or object, no detachable meaning. The meaning is the utterance itself and its own perfectly logical irrelevance and banality. Of course "human beings" have "strong personal feelings" about "nuclear combat" (does the topic arouse impersonal feelings in something other than "human beings"?). These men, however, seem to have no feelings about anything. They use language to express the obvious, the reductive, and the redundant, utterances that speak about feelings in ways that indicate their absence.*

This linguistic subversion continues throughout *Strangelove,* destroying meaning whenever it threatens to emerge. When the Russians discover the Americans are entering their air space, says General Buck Turgidson, clutching his book, *World Targets in Megadeaths,* "they are gonna go absolutely ape. . . ." Turgidson (George C. Scott) is particularly apt at laundering language of meaning, substituting jargon for information (hopes to recall the SAC bombers are "reduced to a very low order of probability") and speaking about the end of the world in the terms of a businessman ("I'm not saying we wouldn't get our hair mussed. But I do say no more than ten to twenty million killed. Tops. Depending on the breaks"). And the president himself, Merkin Muffley (Peter Sellers), a fussy little liberal with a vulgar name, well-meaning and unable to comprehend the mechanisms set in operation, delivers himself of a line that encapsulates the refusal of these men to understand their actions or the distance between these actions and the words they use to describe them. To Turgidson and the Russian ambassador, wrestling over a spy camera, he says, "Gentlemen, you can't fight here, this is the war room."

At the center of this is Jack D. Ripper, the mad general ("he went a little funny in the head—you know, a little funny," says the President to Premier Kissoff on the hotline) who put all the mechanisms of doom into operation. In his confusion of language, the psychotic ease with which he amputates and reconstructs meanings, he permits the entire structure of death to be erected, or, more appropriately, permits the structure,

---

*Over the newspaper office in the *Stars and Stripes* sequence of *Full Metal Jacket* is a banner that reads "First to Go—Last to Know: We Will Defend to the Death our Right to be Misinformed." Where *Strangelove* acts out the destruction of word and meaning, this film merely accepts it as a given.

already erected, to work itself out to completion. He is a fundamentalist anti-communist, filled with all the clichés that go with that aspect of the culture's dominant ideology. He is also rather confused sexually, believing that post-coital relaxation and depression are really a loss of vitality (he is not, as many critics say, impotent; his radical misunderstanding of normal psycho-sexual reactions is much more horrifying than mere sexual dysfunction and is part of the transfer and breakdown of meaning that informs the film).

I said Ripper is at the center of this, but that is an inaccurate metaphor for the film. *Dr. Strangelove* is about the lack of center; it is about a multitude of tangents glancing off non-concentric circles. That Ripper sets the mechanisms in operation is a convenience of plot and evidences, perhaps, some need on Kubrick's part to present a "human factor" in the proceedings. The inhumanity of the cold war and its destructive potentials are somehow mitigated if one can point to an individual who is mad and triggers those potentials into action. Happily, in the following films, Kubrick tries with some success to eliminate this essentially humanist desire to account for the world through the melodrama of the individual. However, Ripper is the most radical example in *Dr. Strangelove* of the dislocation of word and meaning, form and substance. His great speech is a concentrated collapse from the somewhat shared clichés of reactionary discourse into the crazed, subjective discourse of someone who is creating his own meanings. "Mandrake," he asks his barely comprehending aide, "do you recall what Clemenceau once said about war?"

> He said war was too important to be left to the generals. . . . But today war is too important to be left to the politicians. They have neither the time, the training, nor the inclination for strategic thought. I can no longer sit back and allow communist infiltration, communist indoctrination, communist subversion and the International Communist Conspiracy to sap and impurify all of our precious bodily fluids.

There is a perfectly logical movement to these words, just as there is perfectly logical movement to the mechanism of defense and retaliation that makes up the war machine. But the logic of both is internal only. The forms are correct, but what the forms signify is illogical and destructive. Ripper's speech ends in bathos, in perfect nonsense. The mechanisms of the war machine end with a different kind of anti-climax: the end of the world, the sapping of everyone's precious bodily fluids.

The appearance of Ripper as he makes his speech is a fine example of the way Kubrick creates an image that objectively comments on character and situation. The general is composed in closeup, from a low angle, his face brightly lit from below, against a black background. He is smoking a long cigar. This is the image of a man isolated in his own madness, yet protruding from his entrapment, threatening the viewer's space (which is represented, in this sequence, by Mandrake, who attempts a facade of calm and sanity in the face of Ripper's ravings). This appearance of Ripper is similar to a shot of Norman Bates in Hitchcock's *Psycho*. At one point Norman leans over the camera, his face emerging from the dark in an unexpected, and unsettling, angle. These two closeups of madness are similar in effect, but lead in different directions. The madness of Norman Bates is significant of a momentary, unknown, unpredictable terror, always lurking, seldom perceived. The madness of Ripper is the madness of the body politic, which should be easily perceived and perfectly predictable, for it results when individuals create a mock rationality based on language and gesture that appears logical and is in fact dead and deadly. Only the universality of his discourse makes it invisible. Norman's madness is local, the momentary eruption of violence in an unexpecting world. Ripper's madness is global. He is the disseminater of violence, the patriarch of a political and ideological structure whose purpose is to prepare the world for death.

Dr. Strangelove is a discourse of death. Its language and images, the movement of its narrative bespeak the confusion of life and death and the desire to see the one in terms of the other. The persistent sexual metaphor of the film emphasizes the reversal. From the copulating bomber that opens the film, to Ripper's confusion of sexual release with a subversive draining away of vitality, to the planned storage of sexually active men and women in mine shafts to await dissipation of the doomsday shroud, to Major Kong's riding his great, phallic H-bomb into the apocalyptic orgasm and the death of the earth, sexuality in the film is turned to necrophilia, which in turn is part of a greater mechanism of destruction over which the individuals in the film are powerless. The rage to create a controlling order undoes potency; the attempt to erect a structure of power results in the collapse of all structure. The patriarchy erects a world whose function is auto-castration.

If Jack D. Ripper is the mad father of this structure, Dr. Strangelove is the holy ghost, the spirit and mover of destruction. He is also the fascist machine, aroused by the word "slaughter," drawing life from death, becoming fully activated just as the apocalypse occurs. When the men in the war room think that the bombers have been recalled, Turgidson says a prayer: "Lord! We have heard the wings of the Angel of Death fluttering over our heads from the Valley of Fear. You have seen fit to deliver us from the forces of evil." On the words "Valley of Fear," Kubrick cuts to Strangelove sitting in his wheelchair, apart from the others, shrouded and crouching in darkness. The words of the prayer, like all the other words in the film, are undone, the image cancels their denotation, for everyone has been delivered into the Valley of Fear; and the Angel of Death becomes the figure around which all the others will cluster.

Through the creation of Dr. Strangelove, Kubrick comes to an important insight. At the peak of the last cold war, at a time when the great, grim myth of communist subversion was (as it still is) the operative force in America's ideology, Kubrick suggests that fascism is operating as the ghost in the machine. The glorification and celebration of power and death that feed politics and form the urge for domination define the fascist spirit. In the film it is resurrected in the body of Strangelove just at the point when death dominates the world. This is a chilling idea and perhaps difficult to comprehend for those who tend to look at fascism as a momentary histori- cal aberration that died with Hitler. Kubrick is suggesting that death was its disguise and that strength was drawn from its ability to hide in the guise of anti-communism and the cold war. This was a brave insight for the time. Its validity remains undiminished.

In *Dr. Strangelove,* the womb-like war room, with its halo of fluorescent light, its computerized wall maps, its faceless, unsmiling inhabitants, and the SAC bomber, with its multitude of neatly arranged buttons and switches and equally unsmiling inhabitants, are images of efficiency and progress that lead to a breakdown of control and reason. The efficient structures of progress become efficient structures of death. In *2001* the principal images of the future present in so many science fiction films are extended much further than they are in *Dr. Strangelove,* so far in fact that they acquire new meaning. *2001* is as much about science fiction, or at least our reading of the conventions and meaning systems of science fiction film, as it is about the search for some extra-terrestrial force. The design of the film combines the traditional components of linearity, cleanliness, and severe geometrical forms with an extraordinary sense of detail. The exteriors and interiors of Kubrick's spaceships seem to suffer from a *horror vacui.* Surfaces are intri- cately textured and articulated; interiors are filled with screens and buttons that do not merely flash, but flash complex verbal, mathematical, and graphic messages. At times the screen the audience watches is filled with other screens, themselves filled with information (one of the most dramatic episodes in the film, the computer HAL's murder of the hibernating astro- nauts, is done through words and graphs on a computer screen, flashing the stages of the astronauts' decline, ending with "Life Functions Terminated," a cold, mechanical machine message of death).*

Reviewers at the time of the film's release commented upon the minimal dialogue in the film, but they failed to point out just how much language, via print, computer graphics, mathematical formulas and configurations,

---

*There are other important machine communications: the viewer learns some of the details of the Jupiter mission from a television program viewed by Poole and Bowman in the space ship. Bowman learns the final detail, the need to discover the source of the monoliths, from a videotape that is played just as he finishes dismantling HAL.

does in fact appear. Visually these words and graphics are themselves clean and linear, presented (as are the credits of the film) in a typeface called Helvetica, a bold, uniform, sans-serif type introduced in 1952 and ever since used on posters, in road and building signs, and for other directional devices. Helvetica has been the favorite typeface for advertising and corporate communications. It is, in short, the typeface of the modern age and has achieved the status of having a meaning beyond what the words formed by it have to say. Helvetica, writes Leslie Savan, means "sanitized, neutralized, and authorized." "You see Helvetica," writes one designer, "and you perceive order." Form becomes an ideological event.

2001 is a Helvetica film. Not merely the verbal and mathematical images flashed on screens, but the total design of the film predicates a clean authority, an order of total mechanical, electronic perfection. But, as I said, Kubrick is not merely assuming the equation clean equals future equals better. He is examining the assumption and returning a verdict. That verdict is implicit in much utopian literature, explicit in anti-utopian fantasies of the twentieth century, and the cause of conflict in much American science fiction film: the future equals emotional and intellectual death. Perfect order and perfect function decrease the need for human inquisitiveness and control. A perfectly clean world is clean of human interference. But *2001* is no humanist's outcry against the diminution of the spirit, nor does it share the hysterical (and hilarious) equation of alien mind control with the International Communist Conspiracy implicit in many fifties science fiction films. There is not even the anger over human surrender explicit in its predecessor, *Dr. Strangelove.* The film exists as a leisurely, distanced contemplation of technological advance and human retreat, the design of man accommodated to and owned by his machines, neat, ritualized, without awe, without response. Gene Youngblood tries to make a case for Kubrick's prophesying a new consciousness in his bland, non-reacting scientists and astronauts, a sort of reverse nostalgia in which the future is reverie, "melancholy and nostalgia, not for the past, but for our inability to become integral with the present"—for loneliness in the face of progress. This, however, is wishful thinking; more appropriately, late nineteen-sixties wishful thinking, when passivity and withdrawal were regarded as one possible response to the irrationality of the corporate, technological State. Youngblood is right that Kubrick is presenting the human being as an outsider but wrong in implying that this is a psychological or metaphysical position. Kubrick's men are on the outside like the buttons and "read-outs" of their machines; which is to say they are not outside at all, but perfectly integrated into corporate technology, part of the circuitry. Everything—except, finally, the machine itself—works in perfect harmony. This is not humanity out in space, it is Pan Am, Conrad Hilton, ITT, Howard Johnson, Seabrook Frozen Foods (the corporate names that adorn the space station and spaceship), computers and their men and women. The people in the film lack expression and reaction not because they are wearing masks to cover a deep and forbidding anguish, as would be the case in a film by the French director Robert Bresson, for example. They are merely incorporated into a "mission" and are only barely distinguishable from the other components. They are sans-serif figures.

What then of the film's premise, the notion that the history of man has been guided by unknown, extra-terrestrial forces, represented by a dark version of a Helvetica character, the black, featureless monolith? Here the openness of the film is so great that there is a danger of falling through it. The only helpful way of dealing with it is in a dialectical fashion, seeing its contradictions clearly. History, one possible reading of the film would have it, is at the mercy of a god-like controlling power. The transmitters of this power, the monoliths, teach the use of weapons to kill; they lure humankind into technological perfection; they carry humanity to a transcendent stage of rebirth. Men, therefore, have a reason to be passive, for they are the servants of a higher order, slaves of a predetermined plan so precisely calculated that only a precise calculator, the HAL 9000 computer, realizes its full meaning and gets, quite literally, emotional about it and goes crazy (I don't mean to underplay this; I find the confrontation of HAL and Bowman, the latter undoing the computer's thought patterns while it cries "I can feel it," to be one of the most powerful and ironic sequences in the film—an agon between a man and a construction with a human voice in which the latter wins the viewer's sympathies).

But suppose the monoliths do not literally represent an existent higher intelligence? They may be read allegorically, as imaginary markers of humanity's evolution, dark and featureless because one of the valid connotations of the future is the unknown, a blindness to possibilities. Extending this further, the monolith becomes not a precipitator, but an obstacle to full development. After all, the first result of contact with it is killing. The ape touches it and learns to use a bone as a weapon. The wide-screen closeup of the ape's arm crashing down his new-found club is a prophecy of human savagery to come. The weapon may be a tool to control nature, indicated by the shot of a beast being felled; but it is also used to hold territory and to slay others. Kubrick attempts to present many mitigating situations. The apes are being attacked; they need to defend themselves. But they also take an undeniable pleasure in the kill. Brutality is aligned with pleasure, and the bone weapon is a mark of progress. In one of the most celebrated bits of editing in the history of American film, the bone, hurled into the air, becomes a spaceship. But this leap forward is no great leap at all. Kubrick's vision of space travel is spectacular, but deadly. The ape showed a manic joy in its discovery; the space travelers show neither joy nor sorrow; they are mere receivers of the data flashed on the various screens that surround them. The territory they conquer seems to offer no excitement, no danger to them (until one of the tools revolts). The ape used the tool, fashioned it into a weapon; now the tools and the men are hardly distinguishable.

When the bland Dr. Heywood Floyd touches the monolith discovered on the moon, the movement of his hand echoes that of the ape. The monolith emits a signal, and in the next shot shows the *Discovery* mournfully making its way toward Jupiter. The music, the deliberate track through the spaceship's centrifugal main hall, the quiet passivity of the astronauts give this sequence the air of a ceremonial, a detached, sad, and lonely aura. This is the end of man, alone in space, surrounded by the frozen, half-dead bodies of the other crewmen, and finally locked in combat with a machine of his own making. The isolation is complete, though Bowman and Poole take no cognizance of it. The situation is not unlike that in *Dr. Strangelove.* There the mechanisms of isolation were ideological. Here the ideology is not as apparent, but must be sought out in the deadpan faces and automatic reactions of the astronauts, the seductive perfection of the technology, in the red eye of HAL that watches over the proceedings and takes charge. As in *Dr. Strangelove,* the end of human subjectivity is prelude to the death of the person; but here Kubrick allows a further step, an indication of rebirth, of change. The old Bowman in his bed in the Jupiter room, looking up at the monolith, calls to mind a statement by William Blake: "If the doors of perception were cleansed, everything would appear to man as it is, infinite." The point-of-view shot from Bowman's position looking at the tablet presents it as an impenetrable mass, both promising something beyond it and enclosing that something at the same time. Once again, the monolith can be seen to signify an obstacle, a perceptual block that must be transcended.

This places the spectator, of course, on the brink of the metaphysical, a place the film begs us to enter and a place I would like to avoid. Any critical remarks on *2001* must note the suggestion of rebirth, how it moves from the dawn of man through his senescence and back to before the dawn. The enormously evocative images that constitute the film's final sequences point to possibilities of renewed intelligence, a return to a sense of curiosity. The fetus moving through space is the only image in the film of a human being unencumbered by things and, curiously, undiminished by surroundings. But it is, at the same time, an image of enormous solitude and powerlessness. Why is it there? Who is guiding events? The initial dilemma returns: either there is assent to the power of the images and to sensation, or to the suggestion of the narrative that some superintelligence is guiding our destiny. In either case, assent is acquired, and the openness of the film is suddenly threatened. The final sequences of *2001* are the most disturbing, for they are at once beautiful and overwhelming, vague and ambiguous, and suggestive of human impotence in the face of a higher authority. These images and their implications lead to some difficult and unpleasant conclusions.

Filming *2001: A Space Odyssey*

HERB LIGHTMAN

During my last trip to London a year and a half ago arrangements were made for me to meet with producer-director Stanley Kubrick who was at M-G-M's Borehamwood studio, working on his futuristic Super-Panavision spectacle, "2001: A SPACE ODYSSEY". I was looking forward to talking with him and perhaps standing by during the filming of a scene or two of this production, which was being filmed in great secrecy but which had already become a kind of legend among those working on it.

On the morning of the day set for our get-together, I received a call from Kubrick's secretary. It seemed that he had encountered a crisis in the cutting room which would keep him tied up for the entire day. Would it be all right if we switched our appointment to the following day, she wanted to know. Unfortunately it wouldn't, because I was scheduled to leave England the next morning.

The upshot was that I didn't get a chance to talk with him in depth about the production until after I had sat enthralled through a preview screening of the final cut. I was stunned by the scope and sheer visual beauty of this 70mm filmic excursion into the future, by the magnificent photography of Geoffrey Unsworth and John Alcott, by the technical perfection of its multitude of enormously complex special effects—but most of all by the uncompromising dedication of the creative genius who had devoted four years of his life and unstinting effort to the realization of this dream on film. Listening to him tell about how it was made, I found myself caught up by his enthusiasm, and tremendously impressed with the wealth of creative imagination which had been required to put it onto the screen.

"2001" is no mere science-fiction movie. In truth, to be really accurate, it is more like "science-fact" simply extended a few decades into the future. In his quest for complete authenticity in terms of present and near-future technology, Kubrick consulted constantly with more than 30 technical experts and the results, with the possible exception of an "up-tight" computer, are an accurate forecast of things to come.

A STORY FAR OUT IN TIME AND TECHNIQUE

In order that the enormity of the challenge may be fully appreciated, it is necessary, briefly, to synopsize the story of the film.

The picture opens with an awesome prologue entitled "The Dawn of Man" in which apelike pre-humans are seen (during an era occurring

Courtesy of *American Cinematographer*.

4,000,000 years ago) in action against spectacular natural backgrounds. Out of this rugged terrain there arises one morning a smooth, black, rectilinear monolith which first frightens the ape-men and then attracts them.

The time of the film then flashes forward to the year 2001, A.D. A United States envoy is sent on a secret mission to the moon to investigate a strange "made" object uncovered in an excavation of the crater Tycho. It turns out to be the same large monolith which we have seen in the previous sequence—except that now it is emitting a high-pitched signal apparently beamed at the planet Jupiter.

It is decided to send an immense spacecraft, the *Discovery,* to Jupiter for purposes of investigation. The gigantic vehicle is manned by two superbly self-controlled young astronauts (played by Keir Dullea and Gary Lockwood), with a back-up crew of three others resting in a state of quick-frozen suspended animation within "hibernaculums" that resemble mummy cases. The sixth personality aboard the spacecraft is an almost-human computer named HAL that talks in a dreamy voice and ultimately goes off the neurotic deep-end.

The main area of the *Discovery* is a huge centrifuge which rotates at the rate of three miles-per-hour to nullify the weightless effect by means of artificial gravity. Inside their space-age ferris wheel the astronauts do their roadwork and casually walk upside down.

When HAL makes an error in mechanical judgment, the astronauts decide to disconnect all but his most basic functions. However, the computer discovers the plot and, in a fit of all-too-human self-preservative frenzy, kills one of the astronauts when he goes outside of the mother ship to make repairs, executes the deep-frozen trio in their sarcophagi by cutting off their life support, and attempts to prevent the remaining astronaut from re-entering the *Discovery.* This plot is foiled when the cool young man, caught outside without his helmet, blasts his way through the vacuum of space into an air-lock of the mother ship.

With almost surgical objectivity he then proceeds to lobotomize the rebellious (and now contrite) computer by pulling out its "brain cells" one-by-one. Left as the sole survivor, he steers his course toward Jupiter. Approaching the huge planet he is drawn into a vortex of "psychedelic" color, rushing geometric corridors of infinite length and a galaxy of magnificently hued starbursts. Finally, he steps from the one-man pod into a lavish living-bedroom suite that boasts a luminous floor and Louis XVI furniture. He sees himself aging progressively until, as a very ancient senior citizen he reaches out in supplication toward the by-now-familiar monolith which stands at the foot of his bed.

The last sequence in the film shows a "starchild" embryo with glowing eyes which seems to emerge from the fusion of planets to go soaring through space in cosmic concert with the monolith.

THE BEHIND-THE-SCENES OF A GREAT FILM ADVENTURE

Knowing of the air-tight security which had attended filming of the special effects for this production, I was a bit apprehensive about asking Stanley Kubrick to discuss the intricate technology involved.

However, in my lengthy discussion with him (an occurrence which some journalists might aptly refer to as an "exclusive interview"), I found him to be completely cooperative. He answered my questions fully and often volunteered additional information, seeming actually eager to share his considerable know-how with the professional film-makers who constitute the great majority of the AMERICAN CINEMATOGRAPHER readership.

I had heard about the elaborate "command post" which had been set up at Borehamwood during the production of "2001." It was described to me as a huge, throbbing nerve center of a place with much the same frenetic atmosphere as a Cape Kennedy blockhouse during the final stages of Countdown.

"It was a novel thing for me to have such a complicated information-handling operation going, but it was absolutely essential for keeping track of the thousands of technical details involved," Kubrick explained. "We figured that there would be 205 effects scenes in the picture and that each of these would require an average of 10 major steps to complete. I define a 'major step' as one in which the scene is handled by another technician or department. We found that it was so complicated to keep track of all of these scenes and the separate steps involved in each that we wound up with a three-man sort of 'operations room' in which every wall was covered with swing-out charts including a shot history for each scene. Every separate element and step was recorded on this history—information as to shooting dates, exposure, mechanical processes, special requirements and the technicians and departments involved. Figuring 10 steps for 200 scenes equals 2,000 steps—but when you realize that most of these steps had to be done over eight or nine times to make sure they were perfect, the true total is more like 16,000 separate steps. It took an incredible number of diagrams, flow-charts and other data to keep everything organized and to be able to retrieve information that somebody might need about something someone else had done seven months earlier. We had to be able to tell which stage each scene was in at any given moment—and the system worked."

THE IDEAL OF THE "SINGLE-GENERATION LOOK"

A film technician watching "2001" cannot help but be impressed by the fact that the complex effects scenes have an unusually sharp, crisp and grain-free appearance—a clean "single-generation look," to coin a phrase. This is especially remarkable when one stops to consider how many separate elements had to be involved in compositing some of the more intricate scenes.

This circumstance is not accidental, but rather the result of a deliberate effort on Kubrick's part to have each scene look as much like "original" footage as possible. In following this pursuit he automatically ruled out process shots, ordinary traveling matte shots, blue-backings and most of the more conventional methods of optical printing.

"We purposely did all of our duping with black and white, three-color separation masters," he points out. "There were no color inter-positives used for combining the shots, and I think this is principally responsible for the lack of grain and the high degree of photographic quality we were able to maintain. More than half of the shots in the picture are dupes, but I don't think the average viewer would know it. Our separations were made, of course, from the original color negative and we then used a number of bi-pack camera-printers for combining the material. A piece of color negative ran through the gate while, contact-printed onto it, actually in the camera, were the color separations, each of which was run through in turn. The camera lens 'saw' a big white printing field used as the exposure source. It was literally just a method of contact printing. We used no conventional traveling mattes at all, because I feel that it is impossible to get original-looking quality with traveling mattes."

SMOOTH TRIPS FOR STAR-VOYAGERS

A recurring problem arose from the fact that most of the outer-space action had to take place against a starfield background. It is obvious that as space vehicles and tumbling astronauts moved in front of these stars they would have to "go out" and "come back on" at the right times—a simple matter if conventional traveling mattes were used. But how to do it a better way?

The better way involved shooting the foreground action and then making a 70mm print of it with a superimposed registration grid and an identifying frame number printed onto each frame. The grid used corresponded with an identical grid inscribed on animation-type platens.

Twenty enlargers operated by twenty girls were set up in a room and each girl was given a five or six-foot segment of the scene. She would place one frame at a time in the enlarger, line up the grid on the frame with the grid on her platen and then trace an outline of the foreground subject onto an animation cel. In another department the area enclosed by the outline would be filled in with solid black paint.

The cels would then be photographed in order on the animation stand to produce an opaque matte of the foreground action. The moving star background would also be shot on the animation stand, after which both the stars and the matte would be delivered to Technicolor Ltd. for the optical printing of a matted master with star background. Very often there were several foreground elements, which meant that the matting process had to be repeated for each separate element.

THE MECHANICAL MONSTER WITH THE DELICATE TOUCH

In creating many of the effects, especially those involving miniature models of the various spacecraft, it was usually necessary to make multiple repeat takes that were absolutely identical in terms of camera movement. For this purpose a camera animating device was constructed with a heavy worm-gear 20 feet in length. The large size of this worm gear enabled the camera mount of the device to be moved with precise accuracy. A motorized head permitted tilting and panning in all directions. All of these functions were tied together with selsyn motors so that moves could be repeated as often as necessary in perfect registration.

For example, let us assume that a certain scene involved a fly-by of a spaceship with miniature projection of the interior action visible through the window. The required moves would be programmed out in advance for the camera animating device. A shot would then be made of the spaceship miniature with the exterior properly lighted, but with the window area blacked out. Then the film would be wound back in the camera to its sync frame and another identical pass would be made. This time, however, the exterior of the spacecraft would be covered with black velvet and a scene of the interior action would be front-projected onto a glossy white card exactly filling the window area. Because of the precision made possible by the large worm gear and the selsyn motors, this exact dual maneuver could be repeated as many times as necessary. The two elements of the scene would be exposed together in perfect registration onto the same original piece of negative with all of the moves duplicated and no camera jiggle.

Often, for a scene such as that previously described, several elements would be photographed onto held-takes photographed several months apart. Since light in space originates from a sharp single point source, it was necessary to take great pains to make sure that the light sources falling on the separate elements would match exactly for angle and intensity.

Also, since the elements were being photographed onto the same strip of original negative, it was essential that all exposures be matched precisely. If one of them was off, there would be no way to correct it without throwing the others off. In order to guard against this variation in exposure very precise wedge-testing was made of each element, and the wedges were very carefully selected for color and density. But even with all of these precautions there was a high failure rate and many of the scenes had to be redone.

"We coined a new phrase and began to call these 're-don'ts'," says Kubrick, with a certain post-operative amusement. "This refers to a re-do in which you don't make the same mistake you made before."

FILMING THE ULTIMATE IN SLOW MOTION

In the filming of the spacecraft miniatures, two problems were encountered which necessitated the shooting of scenes at extremely slow frame rates. First, there was the matter of depth-of-field. In order to hold both the forward and rear extremities of the spacecraft models in sharp focus, so that they would look like full-sized vehicles and not miniatures, it was necessary to stop the aperture of the lens down to practically a pin-hole. The obvious solution of using more light was not feasible because it was necessary to maintain the illusion of a single bright point light source. Secondly, in order to get doors, ports and other movable parts of the miniatures to operate smoothly and on a "large" scale, the motors driving these mechanisms were geared down so far that the actual motion, frame by frame, was imperceptible.

"It was like watching the hour hand of a clock," says Kubrick. "We shot most of these scenes using slow exposures of 4 seconds per frame, and if you were standing on the stage you would not see anything moving. Even the giant space station that rotated at a good rate on the screen seemed to be standing still during the actual photography of its scenes. For some shots, such as those in which doors opened and closed on the space ships, a door would move only about four inches during the course of the scene, but it would take five hours to shoot that movement. You could never see unsteady movement, if there was unsteadiness, until you saw the scene on the screen—and even then the engineers could never be sure exactly where the unsteadiness had occurred. They could only guess by looking at the scene. This type of thing involved endless trial and error, but the final results are a tribute to M-G-M's great precision machine shop in England."

IT'S ALL DONE WITH WIRES—BUT YOU CAN'T SEE THEM

Scenes of the astronauts floating weightlessly in space outside the *Discovery*—and especially those showing Gary Lockwood tumbling off into infinity after he has been murdered by the vengeful computer—required some very tricky maneuvering.

For one thing, Kubrick was determined that none of the wires supporting the actors and stunt men would show. Accordingly, he had the ceiling of the entire stage draped with black velvet, mounted the camera vertically and photographed the astronauts from below so that their own bodies would hide the wires.

"We established different positions on their bodies for a hip harness, a high-back harness and a low-back harness," he explains, "so that no matter how they were spinning or turning on this rig—whether feet-first, head-first or profile—they would always cover their wires and not get fouled up in them. For the sequence in which the one-man pod picks Lockwood up in its arms and crushes him, we were shooting straight up from under him. He was suspended by wires from a track in the ceiling and the camera followed him, keeping him in the same position in the frame as it tracked him into the arms of the pod. The pod was suspended from the ceiling also, hanging on its side from a tubular frame. The effect on the screen is that the pod moves horizontally into the frame to attack him, whereas he was actually moving toward the pod."

To shoot the scene in which the dead astronaut goes spinning off to become a pin-point in space took a bit of doing. "If we had actually started in close to a six-foot man and then pulled the camera back until he was a speck, we would have had to track back about 2,000 feet—obviously impractical," Kubrick points out. "Instead we photographed him on 65mm film simply tumbling about in full frame. Then we front-projected a six-inch image of this scene onto a glossy white card suspended against black velvet and, using our worm-gear arrangement, tracked the camera away from the miniature screen until the astronaut became so small in the frame that he virtually disappeared. Since we were re-photographing an extremely small image there was no grain problem and he remained sharp and clear all the way to infinity."

The same basic technique was used in the sequence during which the surviving astronaut, locked out of the mother ship by the computer, decides to pop the explosive bolts on his one-man pod and blast himself through the vacuum of space into the air-lock. The air-lock set, which appears to be horizontal on the screen, was actually built vertically so that the camera could shoot straight up through it and the astronaut would cover with his body the wires suspending him.

First a shot was made of the door alone, showing just the explosion. Then an over-cranked shot of the astronaut was made with him being lowered toward the camera at a frame rate which made him appear to come hurtling horizontally straight into the lens. The following shot was over-cranked as he recovered and appeared to float lazily in the air-lock.

A FASCINATING FERRIS WHEEL

"2001: A SPACE ODYSSEY" abounds in unusual settings, but perhaps the most exotic of them all is the giant centrifuge which serves as the main compartment of the *Discovery* spacecraft and is, we are told, an accurate representation of the type of device that will be used to create artificial gravity for overcoming weightlessness during future deep-space voyages.

Costing $750,000, the space-going "ferris wheel" was built by the Vickers-Armstrong Engineering Group. It was 38 feet in diameter and about 10 feet in width at its widest point. It rotated at a maximum speed of three miles per hour and had built into it desks, consoles, bunks for the astronauts and tomb-like containers for their hibernating companions.

All of the lighting units, as well as the rear-projectors used to flash read-outs onto the console scopes, had to be firmly fixed to the centrifuge structure and be capable of functioning while moving in a 360° circle. The magazine mechanisms of the Super-Panavision cameras had to be specially modified by Panavision to operate efficiently even when the cameras were upside down.

"There were basically two types of camera set-ups used inside the centrifuge," Kubrick explains. "In the first type the camera was mounted stationary to the set, so that when the set rotated in a 360° arc, the camera went right along with it. However, in terms of visual orientation, the camera didn't 'know' it was moving. In other words, on the screen it appears that the camera is standing still, while the actor walks away from it, up the wall, around the top and down the other side. In the second type of shot the camera, mounted on a miniature dolly, stayed with the actor at the bottom while the whole set moved past him. This was not as simple as it sounds because, due to the fact that the camera had to maintain some distance from the actor, it was necessary to position it about 20 feet up the wall—and have it *stay* in that position as the set rotated. This was accomplished by means of a steel cable from the outside which connected with the camera through a slot in the center of the floor and ran around the entire centrifuge. The slot was concealed by rubber mats that fell back into place as soon as the cable passed them."

Kubrick directed the action of these sequences from outside by watching a closed-circuit monitor relaying a picture from a small vidicon camera mounted next to the film camera inside the centrifuge. Of the specific lighting problems that had to be solved, he says:

"It took a lot of careful pre-planning with the Lighting Cameraman, Geoffrey Unsworth, and Production Designer Tony Masters to devise lighting that would look natural, and, at the same time, do the job photographically. All of the lighting for the scenes inside the centrifuge came from strip lights along the walls. Some of the units were concealed in coves, but others could be seen when the camera angle was wide enough. It was difficult for the cameraman to get enough light inside the centrifuge and he had to shoot with his lens wide open practically all of the time."

Cinematographer Unsworth used an unusual approach toward achieving his light balance and arriving at the correct exposure. He employed a Polaroid camera loaded with ASA 200 black and white film (because the color emulsion isn't consistent enough) to make still photographs of each new set-up prior to filming the scene. He found this to be a very rapid and effective way of getting an instant check on exposure and light balance. He was working at the toe end of the film latitude scale much of the time, shooting in scatter light and straight into exposed practical fixtures. The 10,000 Polaroid shots taken during production helped him considerably in coping with these problems.

"FILM-MAKING" IN THE PUREST SENSE OF THE TERM

To say that "2001: A SPACE ODYSSEY" is a spectacular piece of entertainment, as well as a technical *tour de force,* is certainly true, but there is considerably more to it than that.

In its larger dimension, the production may be regarded as a prime example of the *auteur* approach to filmmaking—a concept in which a single creative artist is, in the fullest sense of the word, the *author* of the film. In this case, there is not the slightest doubt that Stanley Kubrick is that author. It is *his* film. On every 70mm frame *his* imagination, *his* technical skill, *his* taste and *his* creative artistry are evident. Yet he is the first to insist that the result is a group effort (as every film must be) and to give full credit to the 106 skilled and dedicated craftsmen who worked closely with him for periods of up to four years.

Among those he especially lauds are: screenplay co-author Arthur C. Clarke, Cinematographers Geoffrey Unsworth and John Alcott, and Production Designers Tony Masters, Harry Lange and Ernie Archer. He also extends lavish praise to Special Effects Supervisors Wally Veevers, Douglas Trumbull, Con Pederson and Tom Howard.

The praise, it would seem, is not all one-sided. M-G-M's Post-production Administrator Merle Chamberlin worked with Kubrick for a total of 20 weeks, both in London and in Hollywood, on the final phases of the project. A man not given to rash compliments, Chamberlin has this to say of the endeavor: "Working with Stanley Kubrick was a wonderful experience—a tremendously pleasant and educational one. He knows what he wants and how to get it, and he will not accept anything less than absolute perfection. One thing that surprised me is his complete lack of what might be called 'temperament.' He is always calm and controlled no matter what goes wrong. He simply faces the challenge with incredible dedication and follows it through to his objective. He is a hard taskmaster in that he holds no brief for inefficiency—and it has been said that he knows nothing of the proper hours for sleeping—but he is a fantastic film-maker with whom to work. I have been privileged to work very closely with David Lean on 'DOCTOR ZHIVAGO,' with John Frankenheimer on 'GRAND PRIX,' with Michelangelo Antonioni on 'BLOW-UP' and with Robert Aldrich on 'THE DIRTY DOZEN'—all terrific people and wonderful film-makers. But as a combination of highly skilled cinema technician and creative artist, Kubrick is absolutely tops."

From my own relatively brief contact with the creator of "2001: A SPACE ODYSSEY" I would say that this praise is not over-stated, for Stanley Kubrick, Film Author, epitomizes that ideal which is so rare in the world today: Not merely "Art for the sake of Art"—but vastly more important, "Excellence for the sake of Excellence."

Creating Special Effects For
2001: A Space Odyssey

DOUGLAS TRUMBULL

"2001: A Space Odyssey" was an extremely complex and difficult film to make, and naturally there are many interesting stories connected with the production. Probably the most important aspect of the film is its special effects, and in this article I shall try to relate some of the specific problems encountered in a production of this type, some of the techniques we used to create the effects, and a few other interesting points about the production as a whole.

One of the most serious problems that plagued us throughout the production was simply keeping track of all ideas, shots, and changes and constantly re-evaluating and updating designs, storyboards, and the script itself. To handle all of this information, a "control room," constantly manned by several people and with walls covered by pert charts, flow diagrams, progress reports, log sheets, punch cards, and every conceivable kind of filing system, was used to keep track of all progress on the film.

With a half-dozen cameras shooting simultaneously, some on 24–hour shifts, and different aspects of many sequences being executed at once, the problem of keeping apprised of each shot's progress was difficult at best. For the purpose of being able to discuss a shot without referring to a storyboard picture, each scene had a name as well as a number. For example, all scenes in the Jupiter sequence were named after football plays—"deep pass," "kickoff," "punt return," etc. Each of these terms called to mind a certain scene which related in some way to the name.

Early in production we began to realize that storyboards were useful only to suggest the basic scene idea, and as soon as a particular model or effect would come before the camera, something new would suggest itself and the scene would be changed. This change would often influence subsequent scenes. As each element of a shot was completed, a frame clip of the 35mm rush print would be unsqueezed and blown up to storyboard size with prints distributed to all of the people concerned. It was necessary to keep such an accurate record so that work could begin on other elements of the same shot. For example, each scene of the Discovery spacecraft required a different angle and speed of star movement, and a different positioning and action of the miniature rear-projected image in the cockpit.

Courtesy of *American Cinematographer*.

All moving images in the windows of the various spacecraft were rear projected either at the time of photography of the model, although as a separate exposure, or later after the model image had been duped using Technicolor Yellow-Cyan-Magenta Masters or "YCM's."

A few scenes show a miniature rear-projected image in the window of a spacecraft as the spacecraft is matted over an image of the moon. For this effect the foreground spacecraft was a still photograph mounted on glass and, using a bi-pack camera, the masters of the background image could be printed with a white backing behind the still photo—the photo silhouette producing its own matte. Then the photo and the rear projected image could be shot as separate exposures onto the same negative. To produce exactly the same movement on each successive exposure, all movement drives and film advances were selsyn synchronized. The mammoth device designed to produce this effect we nicknamed the "Sausage Factory," because we expected the machine to crank out shots at a very fast rate. This turned out to be wishful thinking, however, and shooting became very painstaking and laborious work. Another drawback to printing masters in this way was the fact that lens flaring caused by the white backing would partially print the image within the silhouette. Therefore only very dark backgrounds could be used for these shots.

One of our first serious special effects problems presented itself during the live action shooting. The interior set of the *Orion* spacecraft (which flew from the earth to the space station) and the interior set of the *Aries* spacecraft (which flew from the space station to the moon) were both equipped with pinhole star backgrounds outside the windows. These backgrounds were made of thin sheet metal with each star individually drilled, and were mounted on tracks to produce an apparent motion from inside. As shooting began it became apparent that when the stars had the correct intensity in the 35mm printdown, they were much too bright in a 70mm print. And, when the stars looked correct in the 70mm version, they would disappear altogether in 35mm. So star brightness became a compromise, and after all the problems encountered in trying to accurately control star intensity on the set, almost all stars shot subsequent to those interiors were photographed on the animation stand.

The Oxberry animation stand equipped with a 65mm Mitchell camera was used for shooting backgrounds of stars, Earth, Jupiter, the Moon, as well as for rotascoping and shooting high contrast mattes. All stars shot on the animation stand were spatter-airbrushed onto glossy black paper backing and were shot at field sizes of from six to twenty-four inches wide. Extensive tests were made to find the optimum star speed for each shot and great care was taken to control the action so that the stars wouldn't strobe. In almost all shots it was necessary for the stars to be duped, but this became a simpler problem because they required only one record instead of the usual three YCM's.

Backgrounds of the Earth, Jupiter, Jupiter's moons, and others were back-lit Ektachrome transparencies ranging in size from 35mm to eight by ten inches, and these were shot from much larger painted artwork. The Moon was a series of actual astronomical glass plates produced by the Lick Observatory. These plates were used only after nearly a year of effort at the studio to build a moon model—several attempts, in fact, by different artists, and all were unsuccessful.

It may be noted that in only a few effects shots in space does one object overlap another. The reason for this is that normal matting techniques were either difficult or impossible to use. The rigging to suspend the models was so bulky and complex that the use of the blue screen technique would have been very awkward. Also, the blue screen would have tended to reflect fill light into the subtle shadow side of the white models. It became a monu-mental task merely to matte the spacecraft over the stars, and the final solu-tion to this was meticulously rotascoped, handpainted mattes.

Since we couldn't afford to tie up the animation stand, or any camera, for very laborious and time-consuming rotascope jobs on so many shots, a unique rotascoping system was devised. Using ordinary darkroom enlarg-ers, equipped with carriers for rolls of 70mm film, each frame-by-frame image was projected onto specially marked animation peg boards, to which the projected image of the perforations had to be visually aligned.

We found that a star could not be allowed to penetrate the edge of any spacecraft image even to the very slightest degree, although it was unno-ticeable if the star was extinguished several frames before reaching that image. So to account for the poor tolerances in our visually registered sys-tem, each rotascoped cel was painted with a slightly oversized image.

All special effects work involves the standard problems of film steadi-ness, color correction, and matting, and "2001" was no exception. Since every effects shot necessitated the combining of multiple separate images onto one negative, absolute film steadiness was essential. After trying for months to find some rhyme or reason as to why some shots were steady and some weren't, we began the tedious task of comprehensive steady-tests on every roll of raw stock, every set of YCM's, and every roll of 35mm print-downs.

Another problem that gave us many headaches was the loss of black density due to multiple duped images being exposed onto one negative, and in a space film like "2001" the retention of blacks was very important. Part of this problem could be solved by ordering very dense sets of YCM masters to retain maximum contrast. Most original negatives were shot slightly over-exposed so that a higher printer light would be required to reproduce the image. This helped a little, but if carried too far would take the brilliance out of the whites. These precautions were only partially helpful and any shot involving more than two or three sets of masters would suffer a noticeable greying of the blacks.

The solution was to make at least one element in the scene an original unduped image. Aside from helping to retain the blacks, an original image is naturally preferable to a duped one, and in many cases great pains were taken to keep all elements of an entire scene on the original negative.

The first live action shooting on "2001" took place in the giant moon excavation set built on Stage H at Shepperton Studios. The set itself only included a small portion of terrain at one end for the astronauts to walk posed onto the held original negative.

The "held take" shots at the Moon excavation were relatively simple compared to the held takes of moving live action miniature projections. Many shots required that a weightless, gyrating astronaut be moving through space, matted over the stars. For this effect, a 65mm shot of the astronaut was projected onto a small white card, and the camera moved relative to that card to produce the apparent motion. Since this miniature projection was already a form of duping, although it remained sharp and brilliant due to the extreme reduction in size, it was important that this image not go through a further dupe generation. In order to retain the miniature projection as a held take, four separate but identical takes would be shot, using the "Sausage Factory" selsyn system to retain absolute synchronization. Only one of these takes would be sent to the lab for processing, where a 35mm rush print would be made to check color and movement, and a 70mm print would be made so that the rotascoping process could begin. Later, the other duped elements of the shot and the matted stars would be exposed onto one of the held takes, still leaving two more takes to iron out any problems which might have arisen in the first "marry-up."

The models in "2001" are probably the most precisely detailed ever constructed for a film. As soon as the overall design was completed on each model, construction was begun to produce the basic form of that spacecraft, and this process often took several months. Then the arduous task of detailing and painting the model would begin. Massive crews of model detailers worked around the clock for several more months to produce the finished results. Basic construction was of wood, fiberglass, plexiglass, steel, brass, and aluminum. The fine detailing was made up of specially heat-formed plastic cladding, flexible metal foils of different textures and thicknesses, wire, tubing, and thousands of tiny parts carefully selected from hundreds of every conceivable kind of plastic model kit, from boxcars and battleships to airplanes and Gemini spacecraft. A delegation from the production was sent to an international model exhibition in Germany to select the best kits available.

Every minute facet of each model had to be perfect, so that photography would not be restricted in any way, and during shooting the cameras came relentlessly close with no loss of detail or believability.

Each spacecraft was built to a scale which best suited that particular model, without any particular regard to scale relationship between models. Only the *Discovery* spacecraft and the pod were on the same scale, since they had to work so closely together. Very tricky calculating had to be done for the approach of the *Orion* spacecraft to the space station because both models couldn't be built to the same scale. Roughly, the *Orion* was three feet long, the space station eight feet in diameter, the *Aries* two feet in diameter, the Moon rocket-bus two feet long, and the *Discovery* fifty-four feet long with a thirteen-inch diameter pod. The main "command module" ball of *Discovery* was six feet in diameter, and for long shots another complete model of *Discovery* was built to a length of fifteen feet. All moving parts on the models were motor driven and extremely geared-down since most shooting was at a very slow rate due to the necessity for stopping down to small lens apertures to obtain maximum depth-of-field.

The Moon terrain models required considerable depth-of-field also, and in order to keep the distance from foreground to infinity within a focusable range, they were built with extremely forced perspective. Detail was graduated from very large foreground rocks and rubble to tiny mountain peaks and plains on the horizon in a total actual depth of about five feet. To reproduce in model form exactly what a drawing required, the drawing would be photographed as a 70mm-size transparency and projected onto the work area from the exact point at which the Super Panavision camera would be shooting, and with the same focal-length lens. In some cases we still couldn't hold the depth-of-field even with forced perspective, so the model would be shot as two four-by-five black-and-white stills, one focused on the foreground and one focused on the background. Large prints were made of each, cut out, retouched, pasted together, and then shot on the animation stand.

During the filming of what are probably best termed the "psychedelic" effects for the end sequence, we all joked that "2001" would probably attract a great number of "Hippies" out to get the trip of their lives. It seems now that what was once a joke is fast becoming reality, and as of this writing, I understand that each showing draws an increasing number of these people, who would probably prefer to just see the last two reels over and over again.

Stanley Kubrick strongly emphasized to all members of the production crew that he wished the specific techniques used in the last sequence to remain as unpublicized as possible, so out of respect for his wishes and in appreciation of the wonderful opportunity he gave me and others to experiment and produce these very costly effects, I will describe them only briefly without specific details.

As the black monolith vanishes into a strangely symmetrical alignment of Jupiter and its moons, the camera pans up and the "Stargate" engulfs the screen. For this infinite corridor of lights, shapes, and enormous speed and scale, I designed what I called the Slit-Scan machine. Using a technique of image scanning as used in scientific and industrial photography, this device could produce two seemingly infinite planes of exposure while holding depth-of-field from a distance of fifteen feet to one and one-half inches from the lens at an aperture of F/1.8 with exposures of approximately one minute per frame using a standard 65mm Mitchell camera.

After the Stargate, there follows a series of fantastically delicate, apparently astronomical cataclysms. The images implied exploding stars, vast galaxies, and immense clouds of interstellar dust and gas. Without revealing too much detail, I'll merely say that these effects involved the interactions of certain chemicals within a camera field of a size no larger than a pack of cigarettes.

The final series of shots before Keir Dullea ends up in his unusual predicament were done by shooting some fairly unusual aerial scenes, and then juggling the color filters in the YCM duping process. It took months of experimentation to find the key to this technique.

The live action sequences in "2001" involved so many different trick sets, rear projections, and stunts, that the only approach to writing about them is to handle each in the order in which it occurs in the film.

Filming of the "Dawn of Man" sequence took place entirely on only one stage at the studio. Distant backgrounds for all the action were front-projected eight-by-ten Ektachrome transparencies, using probably the largest front-projection device ever made, and constructed specially for "2001." The projector consisted of a specially intensified arc source with water-cooled jaws to hold the oversized carbons, special heat-absorbing glass, giant condensing lenses which would occasionally shatter under the intense heat, special eight-by-ten glass plate holders and positioning mounts, an extremely delicate semi-silvered mirror, and a specially built nodal point head so that the camera could pan, tilt, and zoom without fringing of the image.

To camouflage the varying light transmission rates between rolls of the front projection screen material on the giant 40- by 90-foot screen, the material was cut up into small, irregular pieces and pasted up at random so that slight variations in the transmission rates would merge with cloud shapes or be lost altogether in brilliant sunlight effects. Since the screen occupied an entire wall of the stage, and the front-projection rig was delicate and cumbersome, the sets were built on a giant rotating platform which covered most of the stage floor. Widely varying camera angles could then be obtained with no movement of the screen, and little movement of the projection rig.

During the testing of this front-projection system, it was found that the intense light and heat being poured through the transparency would burn off layers of emulsion in a matter of minutes. Additional heat filters were installed but the only real solution was to expose the plate only during the critical moments that the camera was running. Duplicate plates were used for various line-ups, tests, and rehearsals. Even with such an intense light source, the long throw from projector to screen required lens apertures of around F/2.

The first live action shots in the space sequence took place on board the *Orion* spacecraft during its journey to the space station. For long shots of the apparently weightless floating in mid-air, the pen was simply suspended on thin monofilament nylon strands. For the close-up reverse angle shots the entire end of the set was floated away, and an eight-foot diameter rotating glass was moved into position with the pen lightly glued to it. The stewardess merely had to pluck it off.

The movie being shown on the TV set in front of the sleeping passenger was a little more complicated. Kubrick wanted shots of a futuristic car, and close-ups of a love scene taking place inside. A crew was dispatched to Detroit to shoot a sleek car of the future which was provided by, I believe, the Ford Motor Company. The exteriors were shot in 35mm, but the interiors were shot without seats or passengers, as four-by-five Ektachrome transparencies. Using these as background plates for a normal rear-projection set-up, an actor and actress were seated in dummy seats and Kubrick directed the love scene. Shot on 35mm, this was cut together with the previous exterior shots, and projected onto the TV screen using a first-surface mirror.

In the cockpit of the *Orion* spacecraft, during its approach to the space station we begin to see a few of the 35mm animated, rear-projected computer displays on multiple screens. Throughout the space sequences these displays depict the activities of computers on board the *Orion, Aries,* Moon Rocket Bus, *Discovery,* and Pod spacecraft.

To produce thousands of feet of continually changing graphic readouts to cover the multitude of screens in "2001" would have been an impossibly long job using ordinary animation techniques. We terminated work with the local animation camera service, set up our own 35mm Mitchell camera with stop-motion motor, and with the help of a very talented and artistically oriented cameraman, we began the job of pasting up and juggling around artwork under the camera as we were shooting. In this way sometimes as much as a thousand feet of active, colorful, diagram animation could be produced in one day. Specific readouts showing docking alignments taking place, testing procedures under way, and other specific story points were not as fast and easy to shoot, however, and the job of producing all of the readouts for "2001" took nearly a year.

The interior of the space station was a giant curved set over three hundred feet long, and sloping up at one end to nearly forty feet. It may be noticeable that in the long shot of two men approaching the camera from the far end, their pace is slightly awkward, and this was due to the very steep slope at that end of the set. Most action took place in the more comfortable area at the bottom. The Earth image seen through the window of the space station was a rear-projected four-by-five transparency in a special rotating mount.

Aboard the *Aries* spacecraft on its trip to the moon, in the passenger compartment a stewardess is watching another TV screen, and again the action was directed and edited by Stanley Kubrick. The galley scene of this spacecraft where the stewardess comes in, picks up a tray, and then walks up the wall to exit upside down, was filmed using a rotating set with all lights and the camera secured to the rotating structure. The stewardess merely remained upright as the set and camera rotated around her.

The *Discovery* spacecraft included the most exciting sets of the production, and the most spectacular of these was the giant centrifuge. At a cost of over $750,000 the massive forty-foot diameter structure could rotate like a ferris-wheel. With the actors either standing, walking, or even running at the bottom of the set, cleverly thought-out camera angles made it appear that the actors could stand upright at any angle around the circular set.

In one of the most difficult shots Gary Lockwood was strapped into his seat and had to hang upside-down pretending to eat glued-down food while Keir Dullea climbed down the ladder at an angle 180 degrees opposed to Gary. As Keir began to walk around the centrifuge toward Gary, the centrifuge was slowly rotated until Keir and Gary were together at the bottom. The camera, which was locked down to the centrifuge floor, was then at the top. For other shots the camera was mounted on a specially made 360–degree tilting platform which was bolted to the floor of the centrifuge, and the camera operator sat in a ferris-wheel type seat which kept him upright at all times. Other shots were done with the camera mounted on a small rubber-tired dolly, which would be pulled by grips frantically clambering up the inside of the centrifuge as it rotated, trying to keep ahead of an actor shadow boxing at the bottom.

All lights and large banks of 16mm projectors also rotated with the set, so that exploding bulbs, loose junk, and reels of film constituted a serious hazard to people nearby. Hard hats had to be worn by everyone involved, and the control area from where the centrifuge was driven, and action directed by closed-circuit television, was netted over with chicken wire and heavy plastic.

The cylindrical corridor which linked the hub of the *centrifuge* to the rest of the ship, was constructed of two separately rotating sections, with the camera mounted securely to the corridor end. With the hub end rotating, the actors could walk down the static corridor and then step onto the hub as the port came to a position at the bottom. As soon as they stepped across onto the hub, it would stop and the corridor would begin to rotate in the opposite direction. From the camera's point of view the apparent rotation remained constant, but the actors seemed to be completely defying the law of gravity.

Other apparently weightless effects, which took place during the excursions outside the spacecraft, and in the "Brain Room," were created by suspending the astronaut on wires and then shooting from directly below so that he would cover his own means of support.

Several versions of the full-sized pod were used during the *Discovery* sequence. Three dummy pods were used in the pod-bay, two of which had operational doors, but only roughly mocked-up interiors. A separate interior pod set was built which included all the instrumentation, controls, and readout displays. Finally, a full-sized pod was built with completely motorized, articulated arms. It took ten or twelve men at long control consoles to simultaneously control the finger, wrist, forearm, elbow, and shoulder actions of the two pod arms, and the interior of that pod was a maze of servos, actuators, and cables.

Possibly one of the most unusual aspects of the live action photography on the interior sets of "2001" is that almost all lighting was an actual integral part of the set itself and additional lighting was used only for critical close-ups.

Mythic Patterns in *2001: A Space Odyssey*

DAVID G. HOCH

W hile it is true that Stanley Kubrick's *2001: A Space Odyssey* is primarily a visual experience, the narrative pattern, as the title indicates, follows that of the oldest stories known to mankind and hence invites the kind of interpretation that myth is subjected to.[1] Details are suggestive in the same way. The musical background of the opening and closing scenes used from Richard Strauss' *Thus Spake Zarathustra,* for instance, implies that the theme is related to Nietzsche's prophecy of the superman. Visually both sequences depict births following the pattern of the creation myth moving from darkness, formlessness, and void to light, form, and object. The first is a cosmogony of sorts: the camera pans from dark formlessness to light and the image of the earth—the mother of the ape-man, who represents mankind in the first part of the film. The sequence moves from the black of the monolith to the image of the allantoic sac containing the fetus of the cosmic child—the superman, who represents mankind in the stage of evolution following man. The monolith—a black, smooth, rectangular object—resembles another element of the traditional myths. It is like the faceless Uncreated Uncreating of the cabala or, in Paul Tillich's terminology, the God beyond God.

"The Dawn of Man," the first part of the movie, traces the development of consciousness from ape to man. The setting is appropriate to the birth of consciousness: the apes live in a hollow section of rocks—a womb-like enclosure—around a pool of water—the archetypal source of life. The first sequence shows the apes as beasts. They subsist as a part of nature; they eat, drink water and sleep; they scream ridiculously and impatiently at intruders. They are incapable of speculation and capable only of instinctive fear of everything outside the tribe. The moment of transformation or the call to the adventure of human consciousness comes with the appearance of the monolith. The apes scream wildly at it and dance in a frenzy. While investigating it, one touches it and looks with awe on it and on his hand. It is this look of awe that marks the transition from animal to man. Here he becomes conscious of himself as a living being. Subsequently the camera shows his imagining a boar's skeleton alive and himself in conflict with it. During this sequence he lifts a bone in his newly discovered hand from the skeleton and smashes its skull. The next sequence shows him generalizing the use of the bone as a tool. A repetition of the scene showing the intrusion of another tribe follows; however, instead of greeting

Reprinted by permission from *Journal of Popular Culture* (Summer 1970): 961–965.

them with impatient cries, the ape approaches their leader, strikes him with the bone, and kills him. Able to manipulate a tool, he is a man; and as a representative of mankind, he has answered the call to adventure.

The transition from prehistoric man to the man of the twenty-first century is effected visually by focus on the bone, man's simplest means of manipulating his environment; it becomes a spaceship, a highly complex instrument for overcoming a hostile environment. Although the setting is the twenty-first century, man in this portion of the movie lives in the same sort of world as we do. He flies in a Pan Am spaceship; he communicates with Bell Telephone, he uses his credit card. Like the ape and like twentieth century man, he is still in conflict with the other tribe—the Russians in the movie. The conflict, though, is less savage than either the ape's or twentieth century man's. The monolith has appeared again and its appearance sets the stage for a voyage into the unknown. The radio signal to Jupiter calls mankind to a new adventure in order to discover the significance of the transmission.

The astronaut David Bowman, who is the representative of mankind and the potential hero, is unaware of the real nature of the voyage he has undertaken aboard the spaceship *Discovery*. Like many of the mythological heroes, he does not know that he will undergo superhuman trials. On the voyage he is completely cut off from mother earth and headed for Jupiter—the symbol of the father. His task is to vanquish the beast formed by the spaceship *Discovery* and its brain the HAL computer. HAL is the embodiment of the diabolical portion of the human psyche; he is also the perfect servant. When Bowman wishes to have the headrest on his couch raised so that he can watch television, HAL raises it. Bowman, the representative of mankind, is reduced to complete dependence on the machine. It looks as though he has submitted completely to it. Because HAL is a "perfect" computer, he has emotions as well as intelligence. He feels that the voyage is too important to be entrusted to humans and so he kills Bowman's copilot and the five scientists in suspended animation aboard the ship. He locks Bowman outside the ship in a space pod. Bowman outwits HAL. In the fetal position he blasts himself from the womb-like space pod through the emergency air lock into a passage of the spaceship that looks like a birth canal. Like the new-born infant, he must withstand a number of seconds without oxygen and the force of being propelled into a different environment. When Bowman disconnects HAL, he proves that he is superior to the tool; he proves that he can exist independent of earth and as master of his own technology, which had nearly destroyed him. Just as the hero in the ancient myth must pass a test—slay a dragon, trick a goddess, be crucified—Bowman demonstrates that he is superior to the technological and diabolical extension of mankind. He is ready, then, for a transformation into a higher form of life.

In traditional myths, this is called atonement with the father. Since the third part of the movie is entitled "Jupiter and Beyond the Infinite," the symbolism of the setting would seem to corroborate this interpretation. The hero has traveled from the womb of mother Earth in part I and has arrived at the place of the father of the gods, Jupiter. In doing this he effects a resolution of opposites; that is, he transcends the categories of good and evil, time and eternity. The "Beyond the Infinite" of the title supports the validity of this inference. Since it is impossible to represent time-lessness with narrative, the sequence of events loses significance. This occurs when Bowman, aboard the space pod, is accelerated to an unimaginable speed as he approaches the planet Jupiter. Modern physics says, I am told, that as an object approaches the speed of light, time is slowed. To take an imaginative liberty with physics, were it possible for an object to reach the speed of light, then time would cease to exist for it. This is what happens to Bowman and this is why sequence breaks down. As the pod's speed increases, Bowman grows very old in a matter of a few minutes; when the pod slows down and stops, he gets out and finds himself inexplicably in a Regency bedroom. Exploring it, he turns and sees himself greatly aged walking into the bathroom. He then hears someone eating in the bedroom and sees himself still older. Then Bowman, eating in the bedroom, knocks over a wine glass, looks up, and sees himself in bed aged and shriveled up like a fetus. He then sees the monolith and is transformed into a cosmic fetus. This is all symbolic of atonement with the monolith as father and of rebirth as the green decor of the bedroom indicates. Because sequence is no longer significant, it happens in the same instant as the "light show" which precedes it.

The images in the "light show" symbolize the same process of rebirth. A few examples will demonstrate. Take the sequence in which a particle of light moves across the screen—seeming almost to swim through a fluid medium—and unites with a sphere; the sphere then pulsates and enlarges until it fills the screen. The process suggests a sperm fertilizing an ovum and the growth of a fetus. Another example is the use of Bowman's eye. When he begins to move, the viewer sees the lights of the instrument panel reflected in the plastic cover of his space helmet. When the acceleration takes place, the lights are transformed into geometric patterns and they seem reflected in Bowman's eye, which fills the screen. The viewer seems to be moving not outward but inward into the enlarged pupil of the eye. This is quite similar to the Oriental symbolism of transcendence which says (figuratively) that in order to achieve realization one must enlarge the pupil of the eye so that the body and personality no longer obstruct his view. Another important visual detail is the use of color negatives with the eye and other scenic details. This is particularly significant in the negative projection of a rocky landscape, which closely resembles the home of the apes in part I. It implies that mother Earth and father Jupiter are polar aspects of the same thing and that mankind in his journey has joined them. Like Bowman's atonement with the father in his confrontation of the monolith in the Regency bedroom, this union of opposites images the realization of a higher plane of existence.

Kubrick's *2001: A Space Odyssey,* then, follows the pattern of the monomyth with mankind as its hero. In part I when the ape becomes aware of himself as an ego, he is estranged from nature and becomes immersed in the polarized world of subject-object, good-evil; aboard the *Discovery* he does battle with and conquers HAL, the embodiment of the inhuman side of the Self; and in part III he reunites opposites and transcends the human ego. *The Space Odyssey* is a modern myth which in structure follows the pattern of all myths. The details, like those of a myth, have a number of psychological and philosophical meanings which when joined to the technical cinematic innovations in the movie contribute to its artistic thrust.

Notes

1. Joseph Campbell's analysis of myths in *The Hero with a Thousand Faces* (Princeton, 1968) forms a basis for this discussion.

A Clockwork Orange

STEPHEN MAMBER

A *Clockwork Orange* has fallen heir to the same controversies regarding film violence that blossomed with *Bonnie and Clyde* and seem never to have withered. Arguments against the film have consistently been based on moral grounds. Fred Hechinger, Education Editor of *The New York Times,* detected in it "the voice of fascism." Pauline Kael said the film conditions us to accept violence and charged Kubrick with "sucking up to the thugs in the audience." David Denby echoed this view in stating "Kubrick has provided a thug's rationale [for freedom]" and finding "no structure of values in Kubrick's recent films." Even in terms of his fidelity to Anthony Burgess' novel (or lack of it), Kubrick has generally been found wanting. The outcry against the film has been intense, and one would guess it likely to continue. Still, accusations in this case come cheap; the violence in every scene, indeed the varieties of violence, lead rather easily to such shrill charges. The supposed champions of morality and humanism, as well as those who would label Kubrick a misogynist, ought to look at the film more closely. *A Clockwork Orange,* despite its garish visual style and surface appearance of exploiting youth movie conventions, is no film to judge summarily. The issues, and Kubrick's treatment of them, run too deep.

1

Set at some unspecified time in the near future, the Burgess novel is narrated by Alex, a teenage hoodlum. He speaks in an argot called Nadsat, described by someone in the book as "Odd bits of old rhyming slang. A bit of gypsy talk, too. But most of the roots are Slav. Propaganda. Subliminal penetration." That last description is a useful clue to a primary function of the language, a seemingly impenetrable dialect when one first begins the book, but which eventually feels quite comfortable. Burgess re-orients us to language, approximating the conditioning processes at the heart of the book's concerns. Burgess also uses the strange sounding language as a distancing device, a means of discouraging immediate close reader identification with the narrator. Through this means Burgess moreover emphasizes class differences and points up the potentials for ingenuity in a socially damned group. With his penchant for lyrical Nadsat expression and his love of classical music, Alex is certainly not your run-of-the-mill punk, a point apparently lost on those reviewers (like *Time's* Jay Cocks) who have

Reprinted from *Cinema* (Winter 1972–1973):48–57, by permission of the author.

made the crudely inevitable comparison between Alex and Charles Manson.

Burgess is careful from the outset (but not too careful) to place Nadsat words in a recognizable context, so that the reader gradually acquires facility in this new tongue. When Alex talks of his "droogs" we immediately know he means his friends, and expressions like "kiss-my-sherries" do not need to be checked in the rather extraneous glossary appended to the paperback edition by the overly pedantic Stanley Edgar Hyman. The mystery of Nadsat, its appropriate Slavic harshness in describing scenes of violence, along with its frequent pop associations and word plays ("sinny" for cinema, "in-out" for copulation, "pee and em" for mother and father, "cancers" for cigarettes) is a forceful medium to express the ironies of free will versus mind control which are an important part of the book.

Divested of its linguistic ornamentation, the story is quite straightforward. After a frightfully convincing (but unquestionably satiric) expository period of beatings, rapes, and other assorted forms of violence, the book follows Alex into prison, where he is eventually given the opportunity to submit to the "Ludovico Technique" in order to gain his freedom. The treatment consists of exposure to films of harshly realistic violence, beginning with simple encounters and leading up to war, which coupled with drugs leads to complete aversion and outright sickness in the face of any such activities. Released from jail, Alex is subjected to a repeated pattern of encounters with his prior victims (including one of his friends, now turned policeman) and in each case is either beaten or tortured. Used as a political football by an opposition political party, Alex is driven to attempt suicide. After his unsuccessful try, the party in power (responsible for the administration of the Ludovico Technique) takes him under its wing, and his trauma has led to his being cured of his "cure." Given apparent official sanction to return to his violent activities, Alex has come full circle, perhaps.

The "clockwork orange" of the title appears in the book as a work-in-progress by the writer that Alex and his gang beat up (and whose wife dies as a result of her beating and rape), from which Alex reads: "The attempt to impose upon man, a creature of growth and sweetness . . . laws and conditions appropriate to mechanical creation." The metaphor cuts several ways, however, and has broader applicability than it might first appear. While the Ludovico Technique turns Alex into a clockwork orange, an apparently organic being whose inner workings are rigidly mechanized, it is certainly open to question as to whether Alex's return to free will at the end liberates him from a clockwork orange state or instead returns him to yet another form of it.

Burgess' gambit of having a writer writing a book whose title and "message" is identical to Burgess' book itself is not employed in the film, which has no mention at all of the title's meaning. In the book, besides leading

to a natural identification between Burgess himself and his Writer character, the device, like the language, establishes further distance for the reader from characters and events. The book-within-book forces an awareness
of authorial presence, and there are further references to writers in the
book as part of this distancing process. Street names include Amis Avenue
and Priestley Place, and one of Alex's gang wears a mask likeness of "a
poet veck [man] called Peebee Shelley." None of these things appear in
the film, since Kubrick establishes a formidable array of distancing devices
of his own.

The novel is symmetrically structured. In Frederick Karl's *A Reader's
Guide to The Contemporary English Novel,* there is a report of a seventh
chapter in the original English edition in the third and final part of the
novel, so that the book consists of three parts of seven chapters each, the
classical form of a musical concerto. That final chapter, according to Karl,
takes Alex a step closer to respectability and to "growing up." Karl's dissatisfaction with the chapter presumably mirrors Burgess' and Kubrick's, as it
is omitted in the later American edition and no trace of it appears in the
film. I will discuss the primary symmetries of the novel at a later point, as
the film extends them considerably. As preparation for that discussion, we
need to examine the connection made in the book between Alex and The
Writer, as this becomes an important consideration in the film, although
the matter is treated entirely differently.

Upon Alex's return to The Writer's house, he looks for a copy of his
book, *A Clockwork Orange,* so as to learn The Writer's name. As Alex
describes it: ". . . on the back of the book, like on the spine, was the
author's emya [name]—F. Alexander. Good Bog [God], I thought, *he is
another Alex.*" (Italics mine. Quote from paperback edition, page 136.)
The parallels are not much further developed in the book, beyond Alex
subsequently referring to The Writer as "F. Alex," although presumably the
final English chapter, with its suggestions of Alex's assimilation into the
system, might provide a clearer continuity between the two. Still, the initial connection is an important one, since Kubrick takes off from the suggestion in the book and incorporates it within a broad range of
symmetrical relationships.

2

Ironic, cyclical rebirth patterns have been present in earlier Kubrick
films, even the relatively impersonal *Spartacus.* In that film, while
Spartacus is crucified, a good deal is made of the possibility that his son,
who sees his father on the cross, may someday grow up to carry on the
fight more successfully. In *Dr. Strangelove,* the mad scientist's last words
before the apocalypse as he struggles out of his wheelchair ("Mein Fuhrer!
I can walk!") is a less-than-sympathetic view of a "cure," one well worth

comparing to Alex's. The atom bombs and the song "We'll Meet Again" have a duality of purgation to them, again suggesting (most ironically) a kind of rebirth. In *2001: A Space Odyssey,* the rebirth is literal. The Star Child, whatever its enigmatic, wistful-eyed meaning, is part of a cyclical process.

A rebirth pattern is present in *A Clockwork Orange* as well, strongly linked to symmetrical relationships on several levels. The argument to establish these relationships is somewhat labyrinthine, but relatively clear once we reach the end. This kind of argument, while familiar in literary criticism and French film criticism (e.g. Truffaut's famous piece on dualities in Hitchcock's *Shadow of a Doubt*), is often rather suspect in the eyes of an American audience as "reading too much in," but the case for symmetries in *A Clockwork Orange* and its fundamental importance to understanding Kubrick's way of communicating is too compelling to be ignored.

To begin at the most obvious point, the film can be divided into three parts: Alex's time before, during, and after prison (the same divisions indicated in the novel). The first and third parts share many common, though inverted, situations (besides lasting approximately the same length of screen time). In the first, Alex and his friends beat up a drunk. In the third, Alex is beaten up by the same drunk and a gang of *his* friends. The visit to The Writer's house, Alex at home with his parents, and Alex attacking his two friends are each repeated in the third part, to different result. This structural symmetry is pretty basic, but it serves as a useful starting point.

To extend the symmetries further, consider how Alex passes out of the clutches of the Ludovico Treatment. Before he undergoes the treatment, the doctor in charge describes it as being like death, so that the subject can then be transformed. Thus, Alex's purgation period after leaving prison, leading to his suicide attempt, is a kind of symmetrical transformation process (in that he is returned to his original state). That Alex is back where he started, rather than at a new point in terms of his own consciousness, is established (among other means) by repetitions of dialogue, like his identical reply to the same question of "Do I make myself clear?" from different government functionaries in the first and third parts of the film ("As clear as an unmuddied lake, sir. As clear as an azure sky of deepest summer. You can rely on me, sir."—too extended an identical reply to be accidentally repetitious). In other words, Alex is twice brought near death (the start of the Ludovico Technique, as the doctor describes it, and the suicide attempt) and twice reborn (his Ludovico cure, and the "cure" from his cure).

The transformational processes in the film are linked to changing roles for Alex in relation to violence. To oversimplify somewhat, in the first part of the film, Alex participates in violence; in the second, he watches it; in the third, it is inflicted upon him. At all three stages, both music and drugs are involved. I will leave to the reader a full consideration of all cases (the role of both music and drugs at each of the three stages), but note, for example, that in the first part Alex takes drugs (the "plus" in Milk-plus) to ready himself *for* violence, and in the second part, drugs are used to condition *against* violence. Kubrick, following Burgess' lead, turns the question of violence inside-out and back again, considering it from all possible points of view, and also in terms of reverse conditioning factors.

Alex, then, undergoes a three-stage transformational process in relation to violence: perpetrator to witness to victim. In order to understand the patterns of symmetry developing out of this process, we need to define them more clearly. As perpetrator, Alex exercises freedom of choice. Although he may be stimulated by music and drugs, he is free to do as he likes. When he is a witness to violence, he is immobile, and the acts he is forced to watch alter his attitudes toward violence, making his negative response automatic. The defining moment in the "victim" stage is not so much the physical violence directed frequently against him, but rather the use of his conditioning process to drive him mad, the scene where The Writer forces him to listen to Beethoven, thus leading to his suicide attempt. It is this *mental* violence which defines the three stages, because physical violence is so prevalent throughout the entire film. For instance, though Alex is heartily slugged with a milk bottle near the end of the first part of the film (during what I have called his perpetrator period), his free choice has not been disturbed. Presumably, if he wasn't sent to prison he would continue to inflict violence on others. While the Ludovico Technique itself is surely a form of violence, it is the process of establishing negative mental associations through forced witnessing of violence which is of primary importance. In the third part, it is not the physical beatings he receives at the hands of others which lead him to suicide, but the mental torture of hearing the now Ludovico-associated Beethoven music. Alex's relation to violence is defined by attitude rather than by action, and it is relationships between different character's attitudes towards violence which the film asks us to evaluate. In no sense is there ever a scene in *A Clockwork Orange* where violence is "gratuitous," where it is celebrated for its own sake.

The most important reoccurrence of these three stages relates to The Writer, who in fact undergoes equivalent transformational processes, but from a different starting point. Further, "the two Alex's" are linked to each other at their respective periods in the process. The Writer "progresses" as follows: witness to victim to perpetrator. To see how this occurs, I shall connect each of these stages to Alex's.

In the first part of the film, The Writer is bound up and forced to witness his wife's rape and beating. In his immobility, and through the distorted wide-angle shot of him watching, emphasizing his bulging eyes, he is later connected to Alex's Ludovico Technique witness period. (In that scene, Alex is also bound up and his eyes widely propped open). In both cases, music is associated with the subsequent aversion to violence (for The Writer, "Singin' in the Rain"; for Alex, Beethoven). The Writer's "victimization" begins with Alex's return to his house, with the shock induced by The Writer hearing "Singin' in the Rain" a second time. A distorted shot, both visually and aurally, of his response to hearing the song connects this moment to Alex's point of victimization, when his hearing Beethoven drives him to jumping out a window.

At the level of perpetrator, the two are most strongly and unmistakeably bound, and primarily through visual means. The opening shot of the film is a close-up of Alex staring directly into the camera, and then a long track begins, moving out to reveal Alex's friends and the whole Korova Milkbar. Alex is priming for a "bit of the old ultraviolence," his period of freely willed terror. The Writer's contribution to ultraviolence, his willful use of Beethoven to do Alex in, is introduced with precisely the same shot. We see a close-up of The Writer's face in the same position of staring directly into the camera, and then there is an identical track out, first to reveal the tape machine and speakers aimed at Alex, and continuing out to show his friend pushing billiard balls across a table. (The rolling of billiard balls is perhaps a small *hommage* to a favorite Kubrick director, Max Ophuls, as Robert Ryan performs the same action in *Caught*). The parallel movements beginning from identical close-ups (and the only two such shots in the film) establish without question a relation of equivalency between Alex and The Writer. Thus, Kubrick links the two quite closely, though not in the same manner as Burgess does in the novel.

The symmetrical connections between the two Alex's are more than structural conceits, as The Writer's similar process serves the function of further undercutting any possibility of exhilaration at Alex's final "cure." Alex's dual traumas (the Ludovico Technique, the attempted suicide) lead him to this supposed rebirth, The Writer's (watching the rape-beating of his wife, the second hearing of "Singin' in the Rain") to supposed insanity. In both cases, the outcome is the product of governmental whim, The Minister of interior deciding who gets committed and who goes free. Regardless of that element of choice (and since the Minister himself is governed by external forces), there is no more reason to assume that we are to gloat over Alex's outcome than we are to The Writer's. All are pawns in chess games of power and violence, "pieces" in Kubrick's elaborate master structure of reversals, alliances and attacks; in short, clockwork oranges.

3

Crucial to an understanding of *A Clockwork Orange* is an appreciation of the film's sense of deliberate parody, for this can lead to broader considerations of irony in the film as a whole, especially as it relates to Alex's final rebirth. While various critics have noted individual moments of parody, there has been no attention paid to just how far Kubrick goes in this direction (and I don't pretend to have picked it all up either). He quite clearly parodies specific films, genres, and writers all through *A Clockwork Orange.*

Take, for instance, the Korova Milkbar set. Its completely black-and-white motif and the passive nature of its patrons seem an obvious reference to the nightclub in *Blow-up,* where the *Clockwork*-like scene of musical instrument smashing took place. Likewise, the speeded-up sex scene between Alex and two girls recall the similar encounter in the Antonioni film. The two girls bear physical resemblances to the pair in *Blow-up,* and in fact, one of them, Gillian Hills, appears in both films. The all-white costumes and make-up in *A Clockwork Orange* have a theatrical quality akin to those of the mimes in *Blow-up,* and this is but one instance among many of theatrical parody.

Near the beginning of the film, Alex and his gang come upon another gang raping a girl on the stage of some sort of deserted auditorium, referred to as a derelict casino. Kubrick introduces the scene with a close-up of a fragile rococo floral design above the stage, and when he moves out to show the girl being stripped and thrown upon a mattress, the proscenium arch or other theatrical accoutrements are always visible. Pauline Kael specifically objects to this scene on moral grounds, clearly failing to recognize an obvious parody of Living Theater-like theatrical techniques. Besides the parody element, the scene might be a comment on the death of theater, or its impossibility in the "theatrical" time when *A Clockwork Orange* takes place.

The theatrical parodies go even further, as in the scene where Alex is tested after undergoing the Ludovico treatment, a scene which deliberately toys with theatrical mannerisms. A "performer" comes from behind a curtain, house lights dimming while bright theater lights and a spot-light go on, and he "plays his scene" where he forces Alex to lick his shoe. After he bows to the audience's applause and makes his exit, a second "actress" comes on, a nude girl whom Alex is now unable to approach. (Kubrick, however, omits the parody of medieval courtly love found in the novel, presumably because it is a literary parody rather than a cinematic one.) Once again, parody is enriched by this presentation of a new function of theater, the irony in the situation of a politician (The Minister of Interior, responsible for instituting the Ludovico Technique) using theater for his own purposes, as a means of persuasion. Like the gang rape scene in the casino, the lines between theater and life are seriously blurred, primarily through Kubrick's awareness of parody.

The scene of Alex's return to his parents' home after his release from prison is again a case of theatrical parody, this time of Pinter. Alex finds that someone else's things are in his room, but when he sees the fellow seated with his parents in the living room, he completely ignores him.

After engaging "pee and em" in some trivial conversation, he bends over his father's ear and says, "Hey dad. Who's that fellow sitting over there on the couch next to em?"—a very Pinteresque situation. A later scene when The Writer has prepared dinner for Alex, knowing he's the guy who attacked him earlier, is also acutely absurdist in like fashion, especially The Writer's near-hysterical readings of prosaic lines like "Food alright?" and "Try the wine."

Theatrical parodies merge into spoofs of musical comedy clichés in several scenes. The gang fight following the previously mentioned theatrical rape attempt is the first of many choreographed scenes of violence played to music. Its bravado movement and occasionally synchronized precision particularly suggest a parody of western saloon fights or the gang fighting in *West Side Story,* and indeed, one reviewer labelled the scene "Jerome Robbins gone mad." Alex's beating of The Writer and his wife as he "performs" a soft-shoe rendition of "Singin' in the Rain" is obvious musical comedy parody, and the *Blow-up*-like speeded-up group sex scene was aptly called an "insanely comic ballet" by Hollis Alpert. The hilariously appropriate hymn sung in the prison chapel ("I was a wandering sheep . . . I would not be controlled.") is a further form of musical parody.

Kubrick has as much fun with movie conventions, including occasional spoofs of his own films. The most important of these are Alex's fantasies, the first of which occurs while he is in his room listening to Beethoven. In it, he envisions such events as a hanging, a fire, an explosion, and a vampire or two. The use of fantasy here, besides preparing for the final fantasy "cure," seems a direct parody of the tame fantasy in films like Schlesinger's *Billy Liar*—another movie about an alienated working class youth. This is what teenage boys really dream about, Kubrick is saying, although of course he does so in purposefully inflated terms. In a later fantasy, as he reads The Bible in the prison library, Alex imagines himself (among other adventures) as a Roman soldier slitting the throat of an enemy. The close-up of knife going across throat is surely a close *Wild Bunch* quote. Another lovely movie parody is Alex's second visit to The Writer's house, a well developed horror movie spoof. In heavy rain (complete with an insert shot of lightning), Alex is forced to take refuge in the isolated home of a "mad scientist," seen rubbing his hands together (as thunder strikes) at the happy accident of the arrival of a "subject" for his experimentation. The horror parody is especially delightful in light of the term "horrorshow," a Nadsat expression of approval. To this point in the film, Alex has called lots of things "horrorshow," he's seen one (the Ludovico movies), and now he's really in one.

Kubrick's self-parody includes the hospital scene after Alex's suicide attempt when we hear loud breathing (a la *2001*) and assume it to be Alex's, only to have a curtain open (again a theatrical touch) to reveal that what we actually heard was a doctor and nurse making love. Kubrick has indulged in this playful sort of self-reference before, as in *Lolita* when Quilty says something like "I'm Spartacus. I've come to free the slaves." And while rather obvious, the dizzying, long circular track in the record store that ends with a *2001* album prominently displayed is a sure reminder of directorial personality. This sort of humorous self-reference is of a different order than the connections in *Clockwork* to earlier Kubrick films, especially *Dr. Strangelove,* although when one satire (*Clockwork*) refers to another (*Strangelove*), it's difficult to sort out intent entirely.

Parody is used in *A Clockwork Orange* primarily as a distancing device, to make us aware of a directorial sensibility apart from the narrative. Because parody is so obvious in the film, simply on this count arguments against *Clockwork* on a moral basis, that it calls for identification with and sympathy for a vicious inhuman character, seem excessively Puritan, rather facile, and a complete mis-reading of the film. Coupled with the ironies of Alex's final cure (and the sympathies a true cure would imply), parody is far too strong, I feel, for any criticism of Kubrick for championing violence to have secure foundation, although the moral argument deserves fuller discussion.

4

Patterns of symmetry and rebirth are, of course, only one aspect of the relationship between *A Clockwork Orange* and Kubrick's other films. Resonances from his earlier work are pronounced, especially from his two prior films. In fact, it is useful to consider *Clockwork* as the third part of a futuristic trilogy also encompassing *Dr. Strangelove* and *2001. Clockwork* refers to the two films repeatedly and often calls upon our ability to establish the necessary connections.

In *2001: A Space Odyssey,* as many have noted, after "The Dawn of Man" section there are no further views of life on Earth beyond occasional transmissions to space crafts. As in *Dr. Strangelove.* Kubrick in *2001* ignored "daily life" in favor of very limited specific locations which denied a social context. While there is a universe outside in *2001,* there is scarcely a "world" outside. (Kubrick's deletion of direct reference, contained in late drafts of the script, to the nuclear stalemate engendered by circling bombs belonging to the U.S. and U.S.S.R. is an example of this.) The ironies of hermetic power, whether in The War Room or the rocket ship, were placed above considerations of external observation. Kubrick dealt outwardly with particular hypotheses related to atomic holocaust and space travel, and thus was not concerned with conveying any kind of quotidian reality. Neither film sought to show what life in the future could be like, except in very limited terms.

A Clockwork Orange fills in the "meanwhile, back on earth," quickly placing itself in a parallel time period to *2001* during the attack on the drunk, the second scene in the film. Alex's stick in his stomach, the victim says, "What sort of a world is it at all? Men on the moon, men spinning around the earth, and there's not no attention paid to law and order any more." It will be difficult to look at *2001* now without visions of little Alex's running rampant in a world sharply contrasted to the antiseptic strictly functional space environment. The easily preferable extraterrestrial existence also implies a stronger degree of political irresponsibility when *Clockwork* is taken into account. *A Clockwork Orange* shows a few more reasons to leave Earth.

In the scene following the attack on the tramp, the derelict casino gang fight, there is one particularly striking shot—a long wide-angled composition as Alex's gang repeatedly clubs their prostrate adversaries—in obvious visual reference to the tribal battles in the first part of *2001.* Likewise, during the slow-motion sequence a short time later, there is a shot of Alex leaping into the air with club in hand (as he jumps into the river after Dim) that is very close to shots of the bone-wielding ape at the end of that *2001* section. Alex's club never becomes a tool, or a spacecraft for that matter, and the only transcendence in the film comes through shifts in levels of violence. Alex and his gang are pretty obviously apes anyway, but the connections to the pre-civilized period in *2001* are a bit more weight against favorable identification with their activities. There'll always be someone who will claim the apes are sympathetic in their violence too, but the obvious response to this far-fetched position is that Alex's actions cannot be justified on the basis of either survival or even the working out of territorial imperative. But whatever one's position vis-à-vis *2001,* these references do provide further distancing perspective.

The *Strangelove* aspects of *Clockwork* are almost too prevalent to make sense. The most useful connection (apart from the similar final cures) is the two films' common position in regard to the dangers of alliance between science and politics, essentially the initial hypothesis of both films. The relation in *Clockwork* is clearest at a point during Alex's post-Ludovico demonstration, when Kubrick includes a statement by The Minister of Interior not found in the book. An underling remarks to The Minister that they are really sticking their necks out with this whole Ludovico business. He replies that he has "complete faith" in Dr. Brodsky, developer of the Technique, and "If the polls are right, we have nothing to lose." This stressed assertion of political faith in technological efficiency puts us squarely in Strangelove country. In both cases, the collaboration leads to the exercise of power without moral considerations. The relationship between The Minister and Brodsky is very much akin to the President-Strangelove relationship. The similarity is strengthened by Brodsky's Strangelovian appearance, especially in the shots of him during the indoctrination process itself. He is often lit strongly from behind while in darkness, the same technique employed for Dr. Strangelove's first entrance to give him "an ogrelike image of malevolence," to use Alexander Walker's description of that moment.

The Writer, when seen during Alex's second visit to his house, is an obvious Strangelove parody (on top of the horror film aspects as well). Alex's first social call has left him wheelchair-ridden, and also with a partial paralysis similar to Strangelove's. His line deliveries, tightly controlled but teetering towards explosion, are nearly identical. I'll admit to some uncertainty as to why Kubrick makes this connection (the writer in the book lacks this physical affliction), unless the Strangelove character is intended as a parodied archetype of an amoral intellectual consciousness, in which case mutant offsprings are liable to spring up anywhere. In any case, I would still defend The Writer's Strangelove aspects because they close off the possibility of seeing the film as an attack against right wing or overly expedient government policies (an easy target), as represented by The Minister of Interior. It is quite clear that were The Writer's party in power, their supposedly more liberal regime would manifest Strangelovian characteristics in equally horrifying ways.

We could continue further about similarities to the earlier films, especially in terms of theme and visual style, but the above is hopefully sufficient to establish at least certain basic interrelationships between Kubrick's last three films. Of importance here is only the simple notion that the films *do* relate, that some ideas in *Clockwork* extend elements of *Strangelove* and *2001.* The notion of Kubrick's "sucking up to the thugs in the audience" would seem to deny that he had ever made a film before, or even that *Clockwork* is a film of ideas. Should the reader remain in doubt with regard to useful connections between the films, Alexander Walker's statement, for instance, that "Kubrick's chief concern in *2001* was the concept of intelligence and its transformations" (page 36) can be fruitfully extended. It is sufficient here to note that the connections with Kubrick's earlier films are yet another layer of argument over *Clockwork*'s already dense network of concerns. Those who see the film in terms of it being fascist, anti-humanist, or misogynist, put even less faith in the audience and its ability to abstract ideas from action than they accuse Kubrick of having.

5

While the discussion so far has centered in large part on distancing devices, there can be no denying that *A Clockwork Orange* packs a strong visceral wallop. If the "humanist" approach has any merit, its strongest case would be here, in that the way the film acts on you emotionally could override more subtle arguments put forth after the fact. In this area, we also need to consider questions of natural audience identification with a film hero (or anti-hero) and the way the film's violence acts on the viewer.

Many of the serious attacks on the film so far (Ricks, Denby, Sarris, Kael) have surprisingly agreed on several key points—that Alex in the film has been made more sympathetic than in the book, and that his victims become more repulsive. All conclude that this is part of a process leading to identification with Alex and a glorification of his initial violent acts and eventual cure. Were this view less prevalent, it would be easy to dismiss it; however, its continual reoccurrence forces further consideration.

Trying to recreate one's initial response to a film after repeated viewings is a difficult task, but despite everything said so far, one does respond at first with a certain lurid fascination to Alex's acts. His physical attractiveness and intimations of intelligence are surely factors to be reckoned with. Still, audience *identification* (rather than just interest) depends upon two factors—a realistic context and a character one either agrees with or aspires to be. In terms of context, the film seems to me so obviously a highly stylized work that on this level alone genuine identification would be impossible. Stylization does not preclude strong emotional impact, but it remains possible to separate shock from the idea of shock. Whether we speak of the eye-slitting in *Un Chien Andalou* or the pig slaughter in *Weekend,* these moments lose a certain degree of physical force when we realize *why* these acts are depicted. Directorial intent is too obvious a factor in many deliberately upsetting violent moments, and this is another element which works against audience identification with particular characters. Some critics really get stuck on this point, like David Denby, who can speak about Kubrick's "coldly repulsive and kinky style" and say "he's obviously trying to dissociate violence from feeling," yet still label Alex "an actual hero." If we can agree that Kubrick distances us from violence, how then can Alex be a figure of identification? It's as if we could identify with the Wicked Witch in *Wizard of Oz* because she's a more complex and interesting character than the munchkins.

A curious facet of this argument is that these critics always say that *other,* presumably less astute people identify with Alex, yet *they* see through Kubrick's sham and can remain detached. If Alex is made more sympathetic, why haven't they been taken in? Criticism which makes presumptions about the responses of others is condescending and ultimately useless unless supported by specific evidence. It would seem sufficiently difficult to work through one's own responses to this film than to evade issues by speaking for others.

To envision *Clockwork* as these critics would have preferred the film to be, it would seem that the film should have been much improved had Alex been more a bastard and his victims more innocently pathetic. Without arguing about the nature of character changes from book to film (though I would dispute there being any substantial differences), would this alter the film's meaning? Is the argument that less likeable characters are more deserving of rape, beating, and murder, and sympathetic characters more easily condoned for inflicting such punishments? *A Clockwork Orange* in no way argues that Alex is motivated to violence because of feelings of hatred or dislike toward his victims. He's just as ready to knife a friend as a complete stranger. Rather, during the first part of the film, there is very little distance between attackers and victims, which seems fair enough in light of the reversals in the third part of the film (and book). Kubrick, like Burgess, sees violence everywhere, and if there are no purely innocent victims, there are no completely evil villains. To dispute this view of life is fair enough (though the questions are more complicated than stated here), but this raises the argument above the level of placing sympathy with certain characters and against others. Because the Catlady, for instance, is not as helpless as in the book only serves to extend the question of violence beyond Alex himself, i.e. leads to a further distancing. We're not asked to root for one over the other, and to say that our sympathies *should* be with the victim is to ignore how equivocal the state of being a victim is in the film. No one in *Clockwork* is wholly innocent, but least of all Alex, whose violence, whatever might be said about his victims, is in no way justified.

If despite all, we are taken in at first by the attractiveness of stylized violence and do find Alex to be the most sympathetic character, there are just too many factors at work throughout the film to let this identification continue. Like Alex himself, the viewer goes through shifting relationships in regard to violence. It is Kubrick's intent, I feel, to have *Clockwork* function as its own Ludovico Technique, although this still carries with it the same ironic implications of "cure." The repeat of "Singin' in the Rain" over the final credits is surely a measure of our own conditioning; it is safe to say that no one who sees the film will ever feel quite the same about that previously innocent song. But this is only one part of our conditioning process. If we see violence through Alex's eyes during the first part or at least condone his acts in any way (though I don't think we do), then we, like Alex, must see the Ludovico Technique as itself a distancing device, through the film-within-film abstraction of violence. When his own victims turn attackers in the third section, then anyone who still identifies gets what he deserves. By the time Alex's friends-turned-police nearly drown him (in an excruciatingly long single take), the retribution for hero sympathy becomes pretty severe.

Because of the film's symmetrical structure, the shifting relationships of characters in regard to violence, the levels of personal and institutional violence, and the parallels between characters in regard to violence, there is no way (I hope!) to speak of either sustained directorial or audience sympathy for Alex. Add to this the function of stylization and parody, along with connections to other Kubrick films, and the assertion of fascist or anti-humanist tendencies becomes, at best, a gross oversimplification. To explore questions of violence is not the same as to approve violent acts. That the two have been so consistently confused by critics of *A Clockwork*

Orange is a measure of the volatility of the film's subject matter and the tendency to see in a film whatever one wishes to see. *A Clockwork Orange* is a complex work that yields no easy answers. To dismiss it because of Kubrick's supposed view of women, humanity in general, or the nature of society is an unproductive response.

The Décor of Tomorrow's Hell

ROBERT HUGHES

Some movies are so inventive and powerful that they can be viewed again and again and each time yield up fresh illuminations. Stanley Kubrick's A Clockwork Orange *is such a movie. Based on Anthony Burgess's 1963 novel of the same title, it is a merciless, demoniac satire of a near future terrorized by pathological teen-age toughs. When it opened last week,* TIME *Movie Critic Jay Cocks hailed it as "chillingly and often hilariously believable." Below,* TIME's *art critic takes a further look at some of its aesthetic implications:*

Stanley Kubrick's biting and dandyish vision of subtopia is not simply a social satire but a brilliant cultural one. No movie in the last decade (perhaps in the history of film) has made such exquisitely chilling predictions about the future role of cultural artifacts—paintings, buildings, sculpture, music—in society, or extrapolated them from so undeceived a view of our present culture.

The time is somewhere in the next ten years; the police still wear Queen Elizabeth II's monogram on their caps and the politicians seem to be dressed by Blades and Mr. Fish. The settings have the glittery, spaced-out look of a Milanese design fair—all stamped Mylar and womb-form chairs, thick glass tables, brushed aluminum and chrome, sterile perspectives of unshuttered concrete and white molded plastic. The designed artifact is to *Orange* what technological gadgetry was to Kubrick's *2001:* a character in the drama, a mute and unblinking witness.

This alienating décor is full of works of art. Fiber-glass nudes, crouched like *Playboy* femlins in the Korova milk bar, serve as tables or dispense mescaline-laced milk from their nipples. They are, in fact, close parodies of the fetishistic furniture-sculpture of Allen Jones. The living room of the Cat Lady, whom Protagonist Alex (Malcolm McDowell) murders with an immense Arp-like sculpture of a phallus, is decked with the kind of garish, routinely erotic paintings that have infested Pop-art consciousness in recent years.

The impression, a very deliberate one, is of culture objects cut loose from any power to communicate, or even to be noticed. There is no reality to which they connect. Their owners possess them as so much paraphernalia, like the derby hats, codpieces and bleeding-eye emblems that Alex and his mates wear so defiantly on their bully-boy costumes. When Alex swats at the Cat Lady's sculptured *schlong,* she screams: "Leave that alone, don't touch it! It's a very important work of art!" This pathetic burst of connoisseur's jargon echoes in a vast cultural emptiness. In worlds like this, no work of art can be important.

The geography of Kubrick's bleak landscape becomes explicit in his use of music. Whenever the woodwinds and brass turn up on the sound track, one may be fairly sure that something atrocious will appear on the screen—and be distanced by the irony of juxtaposition. Thus to the strains of Rossini's *Thieving Magpie*, a girl is gang-raped in a deserted casino. In a sequence of exquisite *comédie noire*, Alex cripples a writer and rapes his wife while tripping through a Gene Kelly number: "Singin' in the rain" (*bash*), "Just singin' in the rain" (*kick*).

What might seem gratuitous is very pointed indeed. At issue is the popular 19th century idea, still held today, that Art is Good for You, that the purpose of the fine arts is to provide moral uplift. Kubrick's message, amplified from Burgess's novel, is the opposite: art has no ethical purpose. There is no religion of beauty. Art serves, instead, to promote ecstatic consciousness. The kind of ecstasy depends on the person who is having it. Without the slightest contradiction, Nazis could weep over Wagner before stoking the crematoriums. Alex grooves on the music of "Ludwig van," especially the *Ninth Symphony,* which fills him with fantasies of sex and slaughter.

When he is drug-cured of belligerence, strapped into a straitjacket with eyes clamped open to watch films of violence, the conditioning also works on his love of music: Beethoven makes him suicidal. Then, when the government returns him to his state of innocent viciousness, the love of Ludwig comes back: "I was really cured at last," he says over the last fantasy shot, in which he is swiving a blonde amidst clapping Establishment figures in Ascot costume, while the mighty setting of Schiller's *Ode to Joy* peals on the sound track.

Kubrick delivers these insights with something of Alex's pure, consistent aggression. His visual style is swift and cold—appropriately, even necessarily so. Moreover, his direction has the rarest of qualities, bravura morality—ironic, precise and ferocious. "It's funny," muses Alex, "how the colors of the real world only seem really real when you viddy them on the screen." It is a good epigraph to *A Clockwork Orange.* No futures are inevitable, but little Alex, glaring through the false eyelashes that he affects while on his bashing rampages, rises from the joint imaginations of Kubrick and Burgess like a portent: he is the future Candide, not of innocence, but of excessive and frightful experience.

Stanley Kubrick on the set of *Fear and Desire*. Copyright © 1953 Joseph Burstyn.
Museum of Modern Art/Film Stills Archive (New York)

Elisha Cook and Marie Windsor in *The Killing*. Copyright © 1956 United Artists/
Harris-Kubrick.

Museum of Modern Art/Film Stills Archive (New York)

Kirk Douglas in *Paths of Glory*.
Copyright © 1957 United
Artists/Harris-Kubrick.
Museum of Modern Art/Film Stills Archive
(New York)

Timothy Carey (left, seated), Ralph Meeker (center, seated) and Joseph Turkel (right, seated) in *Paths of Glory*. Copyright © 1957 United Artists/Harris-Kubrick.
Museum of Modern Art/Film Stills Archive (New York)

Peter Sellers and Shelley Winters in *Lolita*. Copyright © 1962 Metro-Goldwyn-Mayer/Harris-Kubrick. *Museum of Modern Art/Film Stills Archive (New York)*

Sue Lyon and James Mason in *Lolita*. Copyright © 1962 Metro-Goldwyn-Mayer/Harris-Kubrick.
Museum of Modern Art/Film Stills Archive (New York)

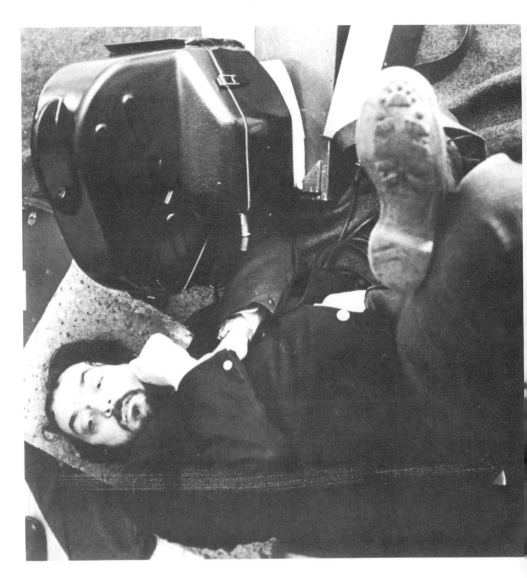

Stanley Kubrick takes a break during the filming of *A Clockwork Orange*. Copyright
© 1971 Warner Bros., Inc.

Museum of Modern Art/Film Stills Archive (New York)

George C. Scott (left) and Peter Sellers (right) in *Dr. Strangelove*. Copyright © 1963 Columbia Pictures/Hawk Films.

Museum of Modern Art/Film Stills Archive (New York)

Keir Dullea in *2001: A Space Odyssey*. Copyright © *1968 Metro-Goldwyn-Mayer*.
Museum of Modern Art/Film Stills Archive (New York)

Malcolm McDowell in *A Clockwork Orange*. Copyright © 1971 Warner Bros., Inc.
Museum of Modern Art/Film Stills Archive (New York)

Stanley Kubrick directing Malcolm McDowell and Miriam Karlin in *A Clockwork Orange*. Copyright © 1971 Warner Bros., Inc.

Museum of Modern Art/Film Stills Archive (New York)

Ryan O'Neal in *Barry Lyndon*. Copyright © 1975 Warner Bros., Inc.
Museum of Modern Art/Film Stills Archive (New York)

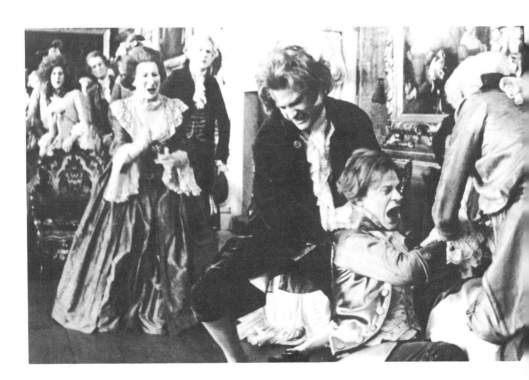

Ryan O'Neal attacks Leon Vitali in *Barry Lyndon*. Copyright © 1975 Warner Bros., Inc.
Museum of Modern Art/Film Stills Archive (New York)

Stanley Kubrick preparing for a shot during the filming of *A Clockwork Orange*.
Copyright © 1971 Warner Bros., Inc.

Museum of Modern Art/Film Stills Archive (New York)

Jack Nicholson (left) and Joseph Turkel (right) in *The Shining.* Copyright © 1980. Warner Bros., Inc.

Museum of Modern Art/Film Stills Archive (New York)

An agitated Jack Nicholson in *The Shining.* Copyright © 1980 Warner Bros., Inc.
Museum of Modern Art/Film Stills Archive (New York)

Vincent D'Onofrio (left), Matthew Modine (center, standing), and Lee Ermey (right) in *Full Metal Jacket*. Copyright © 1987 Warner Bros., Inc.

Museum of Modern Art/Film Stills Archive (New York)

Dorian Harewood in *Full Metal Jacket.* Copyright © 1987 Warner Bros., Inc.
Museum of Modern Art/Film Stills Archive (New York)

A contemplative Stanley Kubrick on the set of *A Clockwork Orange.* Copyright © 1971 Warner Bros., Inc.

Museum of Modern Art/Film Stills Archive (New York)

Juice from a Clockwork Orange

ANTHONY BURGESS

When it was first proposed, about eight years ago, that a film be made of *A Clockwork Orange*, it was the Rolling Stones who were intended to appear in it, with Mick Jagger playing the role that Malcolm McDowell eventually filled. Indeed, it was somebody with the physical appearance and mercurial temperament of Jagger that I had in mind when writing the book, although pop groups as we know them had not yet come on the scene. The book was written in 1961, when England was full of skiffle. If I'd thought of giving Alex, the hero, a surname at all (Kubrick gives him two, one of them mine), Jagger would have been as good a name as any: it means "hunter," a person who goes on jags, a person who doesn't keep in line, a person who inflicts jagged rips on the face of society. I did use the name eventually, but it was in a very different novel—*Tremor of Intent*—and meant solely a hunter, and a rather holy one.

I've no doubt that a lot of people will want to read the story because they've seen the movie—far more than the other way around—and I can say at once that the story and the movie are very like each other. Indeed, I can think of only one other film which keeps as painfully close to the book it's based on—Polanski's *Rosemary's Baby*. The plot of the film is that of the book, and so is the language, although naturally there's both more language and more plot in the book than in the film. The language used by Alex, my delinquent hero, is called *Nadsat*—the Russian suffix used in making words like fourteen, fifteen, sixteen—and a lot of the terms he employs are derived from Russian. As these words are filtered through an English-speaking mind, they take on meanings and associations unknown to Russians. Thus, Alex uses the word *horror-show* to designate anything good—the Russian root for good is *horosh*—and "fine, splendid, all right then" is the neuter form we ought really to spell as *chorosho* (the *ch* is guttural, as in *Bach*). But good to Alex is tied up with performing horrors, and when he is made what the State calls good it is through the witnessing of violent films—genuine horror shows. The Russian *golova*—meaning head—is domesticated into *gulliver*, which reminds the reader he is taking in a piece of social satire, like *Gulliver's Travels*. The fact that Russian doesn't distinguish between foot and leg (*noga* for both) and arm and hand (*ruka*) serves—by suggesting a mechanical doll—to emphasize the clockwork view of life that Alex has: first he is self-geared to be bad, next he is state-geared to be good.

The title of the book comes from an old London expression, which I first heard from a very old Cockney in 1945: "He's as queer as a clockwork orange" (queer meaning mad, not faggish). I liked the phrase because of its yoking of tradition and surrealism, and I determined some day to use it. It has rather specialized meanings for me. I worked in Malaya, where *orang* means a human being, and this connotation is attached to the word, as well as more obvious anagrams, like *organ* and *organise* (an *orange is,* a man is, but the State wants the living organ to be turned into a mechanical emanation of itself). Alex uses some Cockney expressions, also Lancashire ones (like *snuff it,* meaning to die), as well as Elizabethan locutions, but his language is essentially Slav-based. It was essential for me to invent a slang of the future, and it seemed best to come from combining the two major political languages of the world—irony here, since Alex is very far from being a political animal. The American paperback edition of *A Clockwork Orange* has a glossary of Nadsat terms, but this was no idea of mine. As the novel is about brainwashing, so it is also a little device of brainwashing in itself—or at least a carefully programmed series of lessons on the Russian language. You learn the words without noticing, and a glossary is unnecessary. More—because it's there, you tend to use it, and this gets in the way of the programming.

As the novel was written over ten years ago (and planned nearly 30 years ago), and the age of violence and scientific conditioning it depicts is already here, some people have been tempted to see it as a work of prophecy. But the work merely describes certain tendencies I observed in Anglo-American society in 1961 (and even earlier). True, there was not much drug-taking then, and my novel presents a milk-bar where you can freely ingest hallucinogens and stimulants, but I had only just come back from living in the Far East, where I smoked opium regularly (and without apparent ill effects), and drug-taking was so much part of my scene that it automatically went into the book. Alex is very unmodern in rejecting "synthemesc": his aim is to strengthen the will to violence, not enervate it. I think he is ahead of his time in preferring Beethoven to "teeny pop vesches," but Kubrick's film shows a way (especially in the record-store scene) to bridging the gap between rock music and "the glorious Ninth"— it is a clockwork way, the way of the Moog synthesizer.

Apart from being gratified that my book has been filmed by one of the best living English-speaking producer-directors, instead of by some porn-hound or pighead or other camera-carrying cretin, I cannot say that my life has been changed in any way by Stanley Kubrick's success. I seem to have less rather than more money, but I have always seemed to have less. I get odd letters from cranks, accusing me of sin against the Holy Ghost; invariably, I should think, masturbators, who, having seen the film, have discovered the book, used it as a domestic instrument of auto-erotic release, and then fastened their post-coital guilt onto me. Generally I am filled with a vague displeasure that the gap between a literary impact and a cinematic one should be so great, not only a temporal gap (book published 1962, film released ten years after) but an aesthetic one. Man's greatest achievement is language, and the greatest linguistic achievement is to be found in the dramatic poems or other fictional work in which language is a live, creative, infinitely suggestive force. But such works are invariably ignored by all but a few. Spell a thing to the eye, that most crass and obvious of organs, and behold—a revelation.

I fear, like any writer in my position, that the film may supersede the novel. This is not fair since the film is only a brilliant transference of an essentially literary experience to the screen. Writers like Mailer and Gore Vidal—who have seen novels of theirs turned into abominable pieces of film craft—are not in this position. But I can console myself by saying that *A Clockwork Orange* is not my favorite book, and that the works of mine that I like best are so essentially literary that no film could be made out of them.

As Kubrick's next film is to be about Napoleon, I find myself now writing a novel about Napoleon. God knows why I am doing this; there is no guarantee that he will use it, or even that the book will be published. Just the fascination of what's difficult, or an expression of masochism that lies in all authors, or a certain pride in attacking the impossible. My Napoleon novel will be very brief, and to write a brief novel on Napoleon is far more difficult than to write *War and Peace*. But you can take this present labor as a product of the *Orange* film, and by God it is a labor.

Otherwise, my life is unchanged. What really enrages me is two minor dimensions—it is people referring to both film and book as *THE Clockwork Orange*. Can't the bastards read? No, they can't, and that's what all the trouble is about.

All works of art are dangerous. My little son tried to fly after seeing Disney's *Peter Pan*. I grabbed his legs just as he was about to take off from a fourth story window. A man in New York State sacrificed 67 infants to the God of Jacob: he just loved the Old Testament. A boy in Oklahoma stabbed his mother's second husband after seeing *Hamlet*. A man in Kansas City copulated with his wife after reading *Lady Chatterly's Lover*. After seeing *A Clockwork Orange*, a lot of boys will take up rape and pillage and even murder.—The point is, I suppose, that human beings are good and innocent before they come into contact with works of art. Therefore all art should be banned. Hitler would never have dreamed of world conquest if he hadn't read Nietzsche in the Reader's Digest. The excesses of Robespierre stemmed from reading Rousseau. Even music is dangerous. The works of Delius have led more than one adolescent to suicide. Wagner's *Tristan and Isolde* used to promote crafty masturbation in the opera house. And look what Beethoven's Ninth Symphony does to Alex in *A Clockwork Orange*. If I were President of the United States, I should at once enact a total prohibition of films, plays, books and music. My book intended to be a delicious dream, not a nightmare of terror, beauty and concupiscence. Burn films—they make marvelous bonfires. Burn books. Burn this issue of ROLLING STONE.

Take the story as a kind of moral parable, and you won't go far wrong. Alex is a very nasty young man, and he deserves to be punished, but to rid him of the capacity of choosing between good and evil is the sin against the Holy Ghost, for which—so we're told—there's no forgiveness. And although he's nasty, he's also very human. In other words, he's ourselves, but a bit more so. He has the three main human attributes—love of aggression, love of language, love of beauty. But he's young and has not yet learned the true importance of the free will he so violently delights in. In a sense he's in Eden, and only when he falls (as he does: from a window) does he become capable of being a full human being. In the American edition of the book—the one you have here—we leave Alex dreaming up new acts of violence. We ought to feel pleased about this, since he's now exhibiting a renewal of the capacity for free choice which the State took away from him. The fact that he's not yet *chosen* to be good is neither here nor there. But in the final chapter of the British edition, Alex is already growing up. He has a new gang, but he's tired of leading it; what he really wants is to have a son of his own—the libido is being tamed and turned social—and the first thing he now has to do is to find a mate, which means sexual love, not just the old in-out in-out. Here, for a bonus, is how that very British ending ends:

> That's what it's going to be then, brothers, as I come to the like end of this tale. You have been everywhere with your little droog Alex, suffering with him, and you have viddied some of the most grahzny bratchnies old Bog ever made, all on to your old droog Alex. And all it was was that I was young. But now as I end this story, brothers, I am not young, not no longer, oh no. Alex like groweth up, oh yes.
>
> But where I itty now, O my brothers, is all on my oddy knocky, where you cannot go. Tomorrow is like all sweet flowers and the turning vonny earth and the stars and the old Luna up there and your old droog Alex all on this oddy knocky seeking like a mate. And all that cal. A terrible grahzny vonny world really, O my brothers. And so farewell from your little droog. And to all others in this story profound shooms of lip-music brrrrrr. And they can kiss my sharries. But you, O my brothers, remember sometimes thy little Alex what was. Amen. And all that cal.

America prefers the other, more violent, ending. Who am I to say America is wrong? It's all a matter of choice.

Kubrick and His Discontents

HANS FELDMANN

*B*arry Lyndon will almost certainly increase the confusion that has attended Stanley Kubrick's reputation since the release of *2001: A Space Odyssey*. For the technical aspects of his art, Kubrick is now generally acknowledged to be one of America's top three or four directors. But does the man have anything intelligent or intelligible to say; or does, as one reviewer has said with reference to *A Clockwork Orange*, his "intellectual poverty" limit his movies to "popfad art"? Since the recognized success of *Dr. Strangelove*, objections to Kubrick's obscurity, his enigmatic mind, his bleak view of man, his simplistic view of life, his boring mannerisms abound in the reviews of his films. *Barry Lyndon* seems destined to encourage the same ambivalent critical reaction. The preliminary reviews of the film almost unanimously praise its technical brilliance, but as often as not the reviewer ends by yawning with boredom. Is it, after all, anything more than a three-hour slide show for art-history majors? Stanley Kubrick apparently has nothing clear or profound or interesting or moving to say, but he says it magnificently. The assumption behind such critical evaluations of the film is that Kubrick's art exists merely as technique, that he gives us form without substance.

The confusion is compounded when one considers the source of his latest movie: Thackeray's first novel, *The Luck of Barry Lyndon*. It is not a very good novel, and Kubrick's deviations from his source are so surprising at times that one wonders what he saw in the novel to consider filming it in the first place. He excludes from the film a host of the novel's characters and he radically changes many others, notably Lady Lyndon and her son Lord Bullingdon. Reverend Runt appears in only one scene in the novel and has nothing to say. Hackton Castle's financial advisor, Graham, is entirely Kubrick's invention. So are certain scenes: Captain Feeny's robbery of the young Redmond on the Dublin Road, the duel between Bullingdon and Barry in the abandoned church, and the final scene in which Lady Lyndon, Bullingdon, Runt, and Graham are settling the estate's accounts and putting the castle back in order. In the novel, Lady Lyndon escapes from Barry without the aid of Bullingdon, who is in Canada at the time. Barry is forced into exile by the pressure of his debts and dies of delirium tremens after spending 19 years in Fleet Prison. He never loses a leg in a duel with Bullingdon.

Reprinted from *Film Quarterly* 30, no. 1 (Fall 1976): 12–19, by permission.

One thing is obvious from these deviations: Kubrick is not at all interested in faithfully reproducing another artist's interpretation of life. He has his own reading of life and he feels free to alter arbitrarily another artist's work in order to express his vision, his interpretation of his age. As an artist, Kubrick has developed at a remarkable pace, and it is interesting to follow his progress from the early melodramatic entertainment, *The Killing*, through the more subtle character studies in *Lolita* and *Paths of Glory*, to the nihilistic satire of *Dr. Strangelove*. This last movie alone earns him an artist's right to be taken seriously by his critics. To dismiss *Barry Lyndon* as a beautiful, but meaningless, piece of technical virtuosity, is to deny Kubrick the serious critical attention that is now his due.

In *Barry Lyndon*, Kubrick is making a significant statement about *his* age. In fact, along with *2001* and *A Clockwork Orange*, *Barry Lyndon* completes a trilogy on the moral and psychological nature of Western man and on the destiny of his civilization. *2001* itself is perhaps an emotionally and psychologically necessary response on Kubrick's part to the nihilism of *Dr. Strangelove*. The basic argument of the "Space Odyssey" is that mankind will survive the impending collapse of Western civilization. The film ends with an affirmation of life, an affirmation of the adventurous human spirit. Kubrick's affirmation, it is true, takes place outside of his cultural tradition, and the basic philosophical assumptions of the movie reject the Hebraic-Christian ideology that has functioned as the cohesive center of Western civilization for the past 2000 years. But if Kubrick rejects the Christian idea of God, he nevertheless believes a civilization can develop only if it is rooted in *an* idea of God. He would be very much surprised, he has said in a *New York Times* interview, "if the universe wasn't full of an intelligence of an order that to us would seem God-like." The "Space Odyssey" predicts man's imminent effort to re-establish contact with that divine intelligence.

In rejecting the claims of Western Hebraic-Christian civilization to significant order and meaningful form with the filming of *2001*, Kubrick does not submit to the Romantic argument that civilization corrupts the intrinsically good natural man. His view of man is clearly Freudian: the primal facet of the human personality is the id, the completely self-oriented structure that demands immediate gratification of its instinctual urges for food, shelter, and the propagation of itself. It is not moral or intellectual or sensitive to the needs or feelings of others. It simply is. Kubrick's fascination with this aspect of human personality can be traced from the prehuman creatures that achieve the miracle of conceptual thought at the beginning of *2001*, through the character of Alex in *A Clockwork Orange,* to the sublimated savages who inhabit the fashionable courts of Europe in *Barry Lyndon.*

Kubrick's trilogy is a disturbing study of a decadent civilization, decadent because the life-forms it has established for man to achieve the expression of his essential self are founded upon a false conception of the nature of man. Yet for all the bleakness that the critics have argued informs Kubrick's view of man, for all his negativism and pessimism, Kubrick is nevertheless struggling to strike an affirming note. Rebirth, renewal, the regeneration of the adventurous human spirit is the major dramatic point of *2001*. The civilization that begins when the prehuman creature, sitting before the skeleton of an animal, conceptualizes the thought that he can use an element in his environment as an extension of his will to gain dominion over his environment inevitably culminates with the astronauts voyaging through space on a mission to contact the suprahuman intelligence responsible for the monolith that has been uncovered on the moon. The immense distance between what man has become and what he began as is most dramatically expressed in the sudden juxtaposition of images that link the first two parts of the movie together: the image of the prehuman's ecstasy of savage gratification as he hurls the bone he has killed with into the air and the image of the spaceliner waltzing between heaven and earth. Conceptual thought, first used for the immediate gratification of the instinctual need for food, has ultimately delivered mankind to the threshold of some cataclysmic discovery about itself and about the universe which is its home.

But *2001* is not finally a panegyric to Western civilization; it is, on the contrary, a prophecy of its doom. The substance of a Kubrick movie is always delivered through the images projected onto the screen; seldom, if ever, is it delivered through the dialogue. The scenes of the surviving astronaut who lands upon Jupiter, dines at an eighteenth-century table, and lies upon his death bed are certainly intended by Kubrick to suggest the impending extinction of the civilization whose technology has put him there. The concluding scenes are emblems meant to suggest the brittleness of the whole of Western civilization. The most subtly suggestive scene is the eighteenth-century dining scene, for it balances two earlier eating scenes: the savage consumption of food by the prehumans, who rip the raw flesh from the bones with their teeth, and the meal on board the *Discovery*, when the astronauts dine on synthetic foodstuff prepared by the computer. The fragility and effeteness of civilization are emphasized when the astronaut shatters his crystal glass during the formal ritual that the act of eating has become in the eighteenth century. Kubrick clearly understands the acquisition of food to be the primal need of the instinctual man. In formalizing the act of eating, in disguising its essential bestiality with crystal and china and silverware and linen, man imbues the primal necessity with a dignity it does not intrinsically possess. The brittleness of the eating instruments which distance man from his instinctual self reflects the brittleness of what man has become.

Kubrick perceives that man, separated from his primal self, has become a mere mechanical force and is now little more than the instrument of the abstractions that he once conceptualized to serve him. This point he persistently and ironically enforces throughout the movie in the conflict he sets up between HAL and the astronauts. It is HAL who is the more human in his actions, the astronauts who are mechanical and faultless. HAL makes the mistake that jeopardizes the mission, commits murder, begs for his life. Neither astronaut, on the other hand, ever displays any emotion, and for Kubrick, mechanical man is a dead tree. Yet, the star-child that ascends into the cosmos at the film's conclusion emphasizes Kubrick's faith that man can renew himself, that he can in fact be "born again."

Thus, in spite of the film's many negative suggestions and overtones, the emphasis of *2001* is on birth and the regeneration of some primal human energy that urged man through a whole cycle of civilization. Two birthdays are celebrated during the course of the movie, the *Discovery* suggests a spermatozoon impregnating a cosmic womb, one astronaut has his umbilical life-lines cut and is hurled to his death in a reverse birth image, and the other astronaut dies just before the embryonic star-child ascends into the cosmos. The death of one way of life is the birth of another. Kubrick does not know what new directions reborn man will take, but he believes the new direction will be initiated by a reconnection with the "God-like intelligence" that informs the universe. The force manifests itself in the monolith that appears just before the genius among the prehumans thinks his thought and impels the species through the cycle of civilization that culminates with the astronaut upon Jupiter, which is named, appropriately enough, after the chief divinity in Roman mythology. The appearance of the monolith on the moon initiates the space odyssey, and its appearance again at the deathbed of the astronaut clearly suggests that the rebirth of the human spirit will establish the species upon a broader spiritual basis than that upon which it had previously existed.

The assumption upon which the argument of *2001* is based is that Western civilization is moribund, that its cultural forms and social institutions no longer provide man with the significant order that makes life meaningful experience. In his next two movies, Kubrick's principal interest is to study the relationship between the individual man and the cultural forms through which that individual must achieve the expression of himself. At the heart of *A Clockwork Orange* and *Barry Lyndon* is the great philosophical question that is at the heart of all great art: What is man, and what must he *do* with his life? The orthodox Christian answer, that man is the supreme creation of God and must do the will of his creator as it has been revealed to him to achieve the salvation of his soul, has lost much of its credibility in the post-Nietzschean, post-Freudian, post-Einsteinian world, with the result that cynicism and despair threaten the very will of man to survive. Albert Camus, for example, has insisted that the only philosophical question that requires an answer today is the question of suicide, and it is really not too extravagant a generalization to say that most of the significant art of the twentieth century is an effort by the artist to affirm life, to justify the daily effort required not to commit suicide. Kubrick continues to sound the life-affirming note with which he concluded *2001* in both *A Clockwork Orange* and *Barry Lyndon.*

HAL, Alex, and Redmond Barry comprise a strange trio of modern heroes, for they contradict all the virtues Western culture has taught man to respect. HAL is a mere machine, Alex a brutal and violent hoodlum, and Barry a cruel, dishonest scoundrel. Yet all three emerge from their films as the most attractive and sympathetic characters, and for the same reason: they all are the most *human* characters in their environments. Those critics who condemn Kubrick for playing some sort of trick on the audience by making Alex a sympathetic character have committed themselves to the cultural assumptions it is Kubrick's major effort to debunk. If the answer to the great philosophical question is that man is some special creation of God who should dye his hair blue, live in a plastic apartment hundreds of feet in the air, and spend his days accumulating the platitudes and pop art of his culture, then Alex is indeed a threat to the moral order of the universe.

That Alex is a threat to his social order is the point of *A Clockwork Orange,* for Kubrick presents him as the chief evidence that the significant order of civilization is collapsing. Alex is the Freudian id, the savage instinctual man who operates only to gratify his basic urges. Socially, morally, emotionally he is no more advanced than the prehumans at the beginning of *2001.* Although Alex has the ability to think conceptually, he uses the talent for no better purposes than do the prehumans, that is, for the immediate gratification of his instinctual urges. The difference is that Alex's environment is no longer hostile: his meat is butchered for him in invisible stockyards, his shelter is provided by a benevolent government, and his instinct toward self-propagation is gratified by accommodating females. Thus the expression of his instinctual self, no longer necessary for the survival of the self, is horrifying.

Anthony Burgess, who believes that the forms of Christian civilization are necessary to protect man from his instinctual self and therefore must be preserved, has lamented that Kubrick failed to understand the point of his novel. The fact is that Burgess, as well as the many movie critics who have appreciated the novel, has failed to understand the point of Kubrick's movie, which is grounded in a Freudian view of the dynamics of civilization. In *Civilization and Its Discontents,* Freud argues that a civilization progresses as it develops forms and institutions to restrict the free expression of the primal, asocial, instinctual id, or at least as it develops life-forms which permit the sublimation of its expression. Yet even the sublimated forms of civilization inevitably frustrate the vital, primal urges of the instinctual man; thus the "discontents" of Freud's title. Kubrick's discontents with civilization's forms are not only because they frustrate the instinctual man, but also because they deny that the instinctual self is intrinsic to man's nature. Kubrick insists upon this point throughout *A Clockwork Orange* by juxtaposing the brutal enactment of instinctual urges with sublimated expressions of those urges. The popular song "Singin' in the Rain," for example, is a sentimental, sublimated expression of the same urge that is compelling Alex to the act he commits while singing it. Beethoven's music is a "higher" expression of the same instinctual compulsions, and when Alex attacks the health-spa proprietress with the sculpture of a phallus, she counters by swinging a bust of the great composer at him. Political activity is also no more than the sublimated urge to overpower all that is outside the id. The final scene of the movie, in which the government minister attempts to win Alex's endorsement and frees him to the strains of Beethoven's *Ninth Symphony,* is perhaps overly contrived in its symbolism: the minister is metaphorically feeding his id as he is literally feeding Alex. Yet Malcolm McDowell's chewing performance in the scene projects all the libidinal energy that is Alex's vital characteristic and that somehow marks him as the healthiest individual in the movie.

If Freud is correct in arguing that civilization progresses as it develops forms and institutions to control the spontaneous expression of the id, then the converse becomes possible: a civilization in decline would be marked by the increasing ineffectuality of those forms to control the expression of the id and eventually by the unhampered re-emergence of the id itself. Alex is thus the chief manifestation of a collapsing civilization, as well as the chief threat to the continued viability of his culture's claims to meaningful forms. The thrust of Kubrick's insight, however, carries one step further. Although he presents Alex as the main force which is eroding the significant order of Western civilization, he also perceives that Alex embodies the libidinal energy which will drive the faltering human spirit through the collapse of that civilization. It is this characteristic which generates sympathy for Alex, which makes him the "hero" of the movie. Alex is the only character in the movie who is *not* a clockwork orange. He is the only character who never submits to the restricting and falsifying forms of his society, who never becomes the mechanical adjunct of moral or ethical or political abstractions, who operates always and only from his primal, instinctual, human self. He is by no means admirable, but Kubrick insists that he is a real part of every man.

"Any attempt to create social institutions on a false view of the nature of man is probably doomed to failure," Kubrick has claimed in his *New York Times* interview. That the forms and institutions of Western civilization deny the Alex in every man, and therefore can only deform the social man as he seeks to express his essential self through them, is the central theme of *Barry Lyndon.* Redmond Barry's failure to achieve selfhood in the terms prescribed by his society is his tragedy, and by extension the tragedy of Western man. Eighteenth-century Europe, the world in which Barry must achieve self-hood, represents for Kubrick, as it had at the end of *2001,* Western civilization at its most formal stage of development. Conformity to the innumerable codes of ritualized social conduct was essential for any man wishing to establish his value as a man. Barry, in his effort to become a "gentleman," accepts the validity of all the institutions of his day. Only once does he fail to act according to form, and that once destroys all his efforts to achieve his peerage, the highest life-form then available to man.

No critic will complain about the violence in *Barry Lyndon.* Yet numerically there are more violent scenes in *Barry Lyndon* than in *A Clockwork Orange.* Only in the scene in which Barry brutally attacks his stepson, however, does Kubrick present the violence as a savage phenomenon. The rest of the violent scenes are enacted according to rules which deny the source of the violent inspiration: in fact, the inspiration is falsified by being dignified with ritual. The scenes are countless: men and boys are shot, robbed, flogged, and beaten throughout the movie, but all according to forms which Western man had come to accept. In the British army, for example, Barry beats a fellow soldier to insensibility, but according to the rules of fair play—no biting, kicking, or scratching. First they are made to shake hands. The British soldiers march in straight ranks upon the straight ranks of French soldiers, whom they hope to impale upon their bayonets. In the Prussian army, men are made to walk the gauntlet for minor offenses. Major offenses are punished by mutilation. Kubrick, perhaps responding to the criticism of gratuitous violence in *A Clockwork Orange,* decided not to film any scene of mutilation.

The core of Kubrick's insight in *Barry Lyndon* is this: the forms of civilization, which are intended to repress or sublimate the savage nature of man, only work to deform the social man. Barry's tragedy is that, in seeking to achieve the expression of himself—to "become" himself—he submits to all the values and life-forms of his culture. Surely no one today would argue that man fulfills God's will best by wearing powdered wigs and false beauty marks or by demanding satisfaction for insults by ritualized murder. Yet the eighteenth century believed it had evolved the social forms which were the highest expression of God's cosmic scheme, and which best permitted man to achieve and express the dignity inherent in his nature. Barry, in submitting to the values of his culture in an effort to become himself, ends physically deformed and spiritually corrupt. Since he is as much Everyman as is Alex, his fate is the fate of Western man.

This perception that the forms and institutions of civilization corrupt and deform man is Kubrick's alone; it is not the eighteenth century's, nor is it Thackeray's. Redmond Barry narrates his own story in Thackeray's novel, a technique which keeps the fatuous arrogance of the man always before the reader. Thackeray is not objecting to the forms of civilization as much as he is objecting to man's abuse of those forms. The man himself is the principal target of Thackeray's satire. Kubrick's use of a disinterested narrator, on the other hand, and the somewhat wooden performances he demands from the principal actors, redirects the aim of the satire. The performances of Marisa Berenson and Ryan O'Neal, especially, emphasize the extent to which cultural institutions distance the social man from his primal, vital self. The many excellent supporting roles all are directed by Kubrick to expose the darkness at the heart of every man. Leonard Rossiter as Captain Quin, for example, is barely able to control his rage when he is cut by a glass flung at his head by the disappointed Redmond, and he is scarcely able to submerge his terror when he subsequently confronts Redmond in a duel. Man is "an ignoble savage," Kubrick has insisted. "He is irrational, brutal, weak, silly, unable to be objective about anything where his own interests are involved—that about sums it up."

This view of man, and the belief that the life-forms of Western culture do not permit man to achieve any real dignity, are most evident in the changes Kubrick has made in Thackeray's plot. The duel is the major social form which Kubrick uses to expose the false conception of human nature upon which Western civilization is structured. The movie begins and ends with duels, both invented by Kubrick: in the opening scene, Barry's father is killed in a duel, and Barry has his leg shattered in the final duel with his stepson. The duel between Barry and Captain Quin for the hand of Nora Brady is the only duel that appears in both the novel and the movie.

The final dueling scene is a masterful invention by Kubrick. In the novel, Bullingdon has gone to America to fight against the rebelling colonists. He does not return until after Barry's fortunes have been reversed. Lady Lyndon escapes the brutal Barry through the help of a former lover. To escape his creditors, Barry agrees to exile. His "luck" just winds down gradually. Thackeray invents no climactic scene to give point to the dissipated life of the hero. The message seems to be that false pride and hypocrisy will eventually destroy the man who fails to achieve a proper view of himself.

Kubrick's climactic scene is much more pointed, driving the various thematic strains he has been working with to their inevitable conclusion. The setting is an abandoned church, with pigeons (or are they mourning doves?) descending from the dark recesses of the roof's arches. Barry and Bullingdon confront each other in the nave and fire across the transept. The ritualized conduct is intended to assert the innate dignity of man, a dignity which is insisted upon by a religious ideology that Kubrick, with the abandoned church and the duel that mocks the crucifixion, finds to be empty and false. That the ritual expresses little nobility in man's character is emphasized by Bullingdon's emetic reaction to receiving Barry's shot after his own gun misfires. What is motivating Bullingdon is not the outrage to his intrinsic dignity, but his savage compulsion to destroy the man who has come between him and his inheritance, and between him and his mother. When Barry's leg is shattered by Bullingdon's second shot and he screams with pain, Bullingdon himself emits an uncontrollable cry of joy, and for a fleeting moment the id expresses its ecstatic gratification upon his face. He has conquered that which was opposed to him. The finest ironic touch in the scene, however, is the doves, symbolic birds of peace, descending from the darkness above like epiphanic tongues of flame to give the lie to the conception of human character which is working itself out in the duel across the crucifix formed by the intersecting nave and transept.

The true inspiration of Western civilization is not the imitation of God's cosmic scheme, but money. Barry loses his youthful quest for his first love because he is penniless and his cousin Nora opts for a man who can bring 1500 pounds a year into the family coffers. When Barry finally does marry, he marries only for money, and, as Lord Wendover says, anybody with a yearly income of 30,000 pounds and an estate ought to be a peer. The way to a peerage is the flagrant display of wealth—saying the right things about art, appreciating the right kind of music, knowing the best people, giving extravagant entertainments. Barry almost squanders his wife's fortune in his campaign for a peerage, under the distressed but stoical eye of Graham. It is saved when Bullingdon, the champion of Christian civilization, returns to demand satisfaction for the beating Barry had given him, the beating that was not according to form. In mutilating Barry, Bullingdon makes civilization safe for Money and the Church. Symbolically, of course, he has unmanned Barry, he has spiritually castrated him.

The final scene of the movie is also Kubrick's invention. Bullingdon and his mother are reunited and are settling the debts of the estate, once again under the frozen stare of Graham and the self-satisfied and watchful gaze of Reverend Runt. It is a highly suggestive tableau. Under the aegis of these two authorities. Capitalism and the Church, Western civilization marches its relentless way to the apocalypse of *A Clockwork Orange*. Barry, now impotent, accepts a cash compensation for his mutilation and exists with *his* mother, subdued past all further defiance.

It is not that Kubrick is suggesting the instinctual man be permitted unrestricted expression of himself, but that man recognize and acknowledge the savage in himself and develop cultural forms based upon the frank acceptance of that acknowledgment. Joseph Conrad, a writer known to Kubrick, has voiced a variant of Camus's only significant philosophical question. Stein, a character in the novel *Lord Jim*, claims that the real question is not "To be or not to be," but "How to be." He concludes, as Kubrick concludes, that man must "immerse" himself "in the destructive element," that is, man must embrace the savage in himself in order to control him. In the duel between Barry and his stepson, Barry is the true victor. Closer to his instinctual self than any other character in the story, Barry is able to control his rage and fire his pistol into the ground after

Bullingdon's pistol misfires. It is true that Barry is distraught over the death of his son Bryan, but O'Neal's performance in the scene does not in any way suggest his indifference to life. Instead, he struggles to control his fear and his rage. He is thus able to stand his ground to receive Bullingdon's second shot which shatters his leg. In so doing, he achieves a dignity that Bullingdon betrays with the joyful expression of gratified rage when he hears Barry's cry of pain. Although he is deformed by his civilization, Barry has achieved the only meaningful victory in the movie, the triumph over the savage in himself. It is only a passing victory, however. Kubrick's point is clear enough: man must embrace the Alex in himself to be whole again. He must reject his past, his cultural traditions, the dead moral scheme that falsifies life and deforms, rather than controls, the instinctual man.

The charge that Kubrick's later movies are devoid of meaning is thus nonsensical. The charge that he is ponderous and dull is comprehensible only if his ideas are ponderous and dull. The evidence of his trilogy on Western civilization supports the claim that he is one of America's top film directors. He is more than that. Stanley Kubrick is a critic of his age, one of its interpreters and one of its artists.

Kubrick's *Barry Lyndon*

ALAN SPIEGEL

Now that we are three-quarters done with this century, we should be ready to admit that some recent American films don't look like other American films. Precisely: the chief aesthetic distinction between some of the most original and provocative American movies of the late sixties and seventies—*2001, The Wild Bunch, The Long Goodbye, Badlands* and most other American movies has been the restructuring of narrative means and ends, that is to say, a disruption of the customary hierarchy in narrative form. The representative Hollywood film of the past subordinated the components of style—image, sound, rhythm, physical movement, etc.—to the promotion of character and drama, enlisted these components as functionaries in the service of narrative events. This procedure, familiar to the point of invisibility, defines the formal nature of the major tradition in the commercial cinema here and in Europe, a thriving tradition almost as old as Film itself.

There is, however, another kind of film which operates according to a different procedural concept. In its commercial format, this film has appeared intermittently in this country over the past decade and takes formal inspiration primarily from the innovations of the "new" European cinema (actually almost a quarter-century old), and secondarily from the experiments of the American non-commercial "underground" (even older than its European, "aboveground" analogue). This film proposes a new equilibration of means and ends, and the emancipation of the components of style from the hegemony of character and drama. What formerly was a centralized system in which style was ordered and harmonized by its relation to drama, now becomes a decentralized system in which discrete elements of style and drama float freely in shifting suspension, in which elements confront each other in glancing discord and irresolute debate. In a centralized system style dissolves into subject, in a decentralized system style itself becomes a subject; and one way you can tell some of the good new films from most of the good old ones is that the new film compels an awareness of the way it is being seen, a consciousness of the medium itself as part of your understanding of what this film means to be. In the past an American director might conceivably work in the decentralized manner—as for instance, Von Sternberg did in the Dietrich films—but not without jinxing his career, and rapidly achieving something like the singular infamy and totemic isolation of a carnival geek. Nowadays such a director's profession-

First published in *Salmagundi* #38–39, Fall 1977. Reprinted by permission.

al status might be just as tenuous as in the past, but just as certainly his very presence on the scene has become less exotic, and less noxious too.

Let's assume that in making these simple distinctions of procedure, I am not recycling the by now decrepit and essentially bogus agon between the "verbal" and the "visual" film. Bogus, because film has always been, like the Centaur, a bipartite amalgam with an aural-visual constant; the old "silents" were never really silent—not with all the words in those title cards and not with all that noise swelling from the big Wurlitzer. Nor conversely, were the famous dialogue comedies of the thirties composed of "just talk," and the patronizing tag "filmed theatre" was true only by analogy, never by percept—for the camera's view even in those "talk" films was still more varied, selective, and intimate than anything offered by the monotypic space of the stage. No, I don't want to exhume those issues: the formal difference between *The Long Goodbye* and *The Big Sleep* is not that the former has "fewer words" than the latter (it doesn't actually), but rather that the former, unlike the latter, shifts the attention of the viewer to the entire aural-visual complex as a semi-autotelic category. *The Long Goodbye* shreds its cinematic weave, presents each thread of its formal warp as separate, distinct, and on a par with each thread of its dramatic weft: a zonked camera somnambulates past the central axis of each narrative point, a torpid montage pulse defuses each climax into its opposite, a frost-blue color scheme drips ice water over the abrupt explosions of personality, a kibitzer's logorrhea tugs sideways against the straight-on logic of character and plot. A decentralized film may use images not only to reveal action but to make a pattern, just as it may use words not only to reveal motive but to contrive a sonance.

Now there is Stanley Kubrick's latest work, the remarkable and luminous *Barry Lyndon*. This film, like the decentralized film, also disrupts the old hierarchy in narrative form, also releases the full range of tonal and sensual potency in the aural-visual complex. But unlike the decentralized film, *Barry Lyndon* doesn't oppose style to drama, but rather subordinates drama to style, and so disrupts the old hierarchy by reversing it completely and creating a new order in which plot and character are harmonized and finally *placed* in relation to a formal design. That is why where *The Long Goodbye* seems "loose" and "open," *Barry Lyndon* seems "measured" and "finished" (indeed, the latter seems so even in a comparison with Kubrick's earlier and more amorphous *2001*). *Barry Lyndon* deploys its discords and aesthetic anomalies with deliberation and consistency, and in this way achieves a strict cohesion to which the Altman film of course never aspires.

Still, *Barry Lyndon* is one of those movies, like *The Long Goodbye* or almost any other film in the new manner, that isn't going to survive "translation" into another format; not into the raked-over, respliced dray-horse version working at the local rerun house; and not into the high contrast

Thus BL not a "decentralized" film, NB.

color vulgarizings of a 16mm. squeeze job; and least of all, into the pigmy scale, low definition, and acoustical soup that passes for "movies-on-T.V." (which is to say, movies-by-proxy, the electronic tracings of movies). Perhaps more than a little of a strong film in the conventional style, with its solid story and developed characters, can survive such conversions. But in any format that doesn't preserve the full visual and sonic integrity of the original, a film like *Barry Lyndon* forfeits the very terms of its value and significance, the flesh of its expressive life.

Too bad: this film deserves a longer and happier future than the one it may get—at least, a future considerably brighter than its present. As a work of sensuous beauty without ostensible moral or social palliation, it was found to be by many critics—as such works often are—both too much aesthetically (e.g., "a collection of paintings") and not enough dramatically (e.g., "boring"). Since I found it neither too much nor too little but very nearly dead-center (e.g., "a work of art"—but with qualifications, more of which later), I want to go on a bit about its special qualities—its form, meaning, problems, and the problems of its critics.

Now I don't see how you can find in *Barry Lyndon* the basis for much of what you may have read or heard about it; it isn't "cold," "boring," or—the current cant on Kubrick—"misanthropic"; it isn't without "humour," "character," or—a blind man's bluff—"montage"; and it certainly isn't—peace to (and shame on) reviewers everywhere—"a collection of paintings," "a series of stills," or—authentic desperation—"what the eighteenth century must have looked like." For some critics, the displeasure in what was thought to be present in this film was exceeded, and may have been partly determined, by the disappointment at what was in fact missing: a traditional treatment of traditional materials, that is to say, the immemorial salivations at the chiming of generic clichés. As a "costume romance" of the eighteenth century, *Barry Lyndon* is neither a romp nor a swashbuckler, neither *Tom Jones* nor *Scaramouche;* and indeed there are no country squires ho-hoing over tankards of ale, and no hawk-like profiles flying chandeliers across the width of the frame-lines. Nor is the absence of these knee-jerk posturings cause for national lamentation: sometimes all talk about the "perennial vitality" of the "classic" genre film simply boils down to the last bad movie that sent you home to read a book.

The events in *Barry Lyndon,* while dramatic in themselves, are not presented in the form of a drama, but rather in the form of a spectacle for the senses. A beguilement of eye and ear precedes the customary seizure of the emotions. As in so much of Kubrick's best work—indeed, it is perhaps his defining quality—the images that you see exist not simply as vehicles for a story, but as vibrant indicators of a film-maker's commitment to his medium, as select opportunities for the deployment of the camera, gravid occasions for strategies of composition, light, physical texture, and editorial rhythm. They are images which immediately place the eye in an empathetic relation to the sensible intelligence that has composed them for the eye's delectation. They are images that exist primarily to be seen.

While all of this is true to some degree of each one of this director's films, it is true to the greatest degree of his present film: *Barry Lyndon* is Kubrick's most extravagantly beautiful creation. Opulent and solemn, jewel-like and lucid, profuse and lordly, the beauty of the film is not at all unlike the beauty of Handel's music (of which we hear the majestic and sweeping Sarabande in various guises and emotional contexts throughout the film).

Neither precious nor ponderous—avoiding both the spun sugar figurines of *Elvira Madigan* and the bronze bookends of *Alexander Nevsky*—this beauty is nevertheless highly controlled, self-regarding, and caliper-calculated, and because of this, probably won't be to everyone's taste. Kubrick's concentration consorts awkwardly with the casual, seemingly throw-away manner of some of the Altman films or early Godard where the poetry trips us by surprise, where the ticklish insights catch us napping, where art seems to deny itself even as it is created. And viewers who think that this is the only way to make a serious film nowadays aren't going to admire what Kubrick has done here because he seems to have worked so hard to do it.

Actually of course there are many ways to do it, and what matters most is that Kubrick has done it his way—and splendidly: the deliberation of the effort is matched and finally surpassed by the originality of the achievement. The source of this originality is the singularity of the film's beauty—to come back to this—the special way this beauty makes its meaning to eye and ear. By this I mean precisely the *strangeness* of the way things are seen and heard, and for this reason, the imperviousness of the film's beauty to a comfortable assimilation by the viewer. You can hear this strangeness, for instance, in the hieratic pacing of the dialogue; how a silence falls at the completion of each character's statement—a beat or two of hushed tension—before the reply; and how these recurrent silences envelop the colloquies in a ceremonial rhythm. And you can see this strangeness in the dense and dusky distributions of light in the chambers, taverns, and gaming rooms of the interiors: in particular, the way in which the extraordinary candle flames, each fat tip surrounded by a great saffron aureole, seem to reshape themselves magically from one scene to the next—now globes, now goblets, now eggs, now bulbs, and now, most characteristically, a blurring of tears, the flickerings of mortality. Or stranger still, in some of these interiors, how layer upon layer of color, costume, and cosmetic—congestions of salmon, pink, and scarlet—pile up into a thick, almost infernal impasto of impacted materiality; the gleaming ruby lip rouge, the marmoreal face powder, the speckling of beauty marks, the flaring chestnut wigs, the intricate whorls and floral imbrications streaming down the lapels of the frock coats, and a singular detail, the heavy fur cuffs that droop forlornly about the wrists of a sad gambler. Or just as strange, how the numinous density of the interiors is balanced and reversed by the deep focus concision of the exteriors where a gem-cutter's eye catches the morning of the world with almost halographic lucidity, and each shining particle and plane of every radiant landscape appears as a separate and distinct entity—from the sharply contoured patterns of field, hill, and valley to the precisely differentiated tones and textures of cloud (modulating from pigeon grey at the granulated edges to gunmetal black at the solid center). Or finally, as enigmatic as anything else, the curious exaggerations of posture, gesture, and motion throughout; the way, for example, an exultant army captain in thigh-high jackboots jigs with his girl on a green lawn, leering through clenched teeth, arms akimbo, and pelvis thrust forward; or the way deep in the forest, an outlaw greets the camera with his back, and then swings around to reveal two big pistols clutched against his chest; or the way the hero removes his hat with a large sweeping motion of the arm—a gesture both passionate and decorous—before kissing his dying friend on the lips, and then falls sobbing on the dead man's chest.

Some of these postures, perspectives, and tonal surfaces doubtless allude to similar effects in the paintings of the eighteenth century—the camera notes a noblewoman's plumed hat angled like a Gainsborough above a small head, long neck, and arrogant backline, or a darkened chamber of lonely card players lit, as in Wright of Derby, by a small planet of candles, etc.—but no single film image coincides in its totality of parts with any single painting; and nothing in Kubrick's work resembles those unintentional comedies of literalist displacement like Minnelli's *Lust for Life* or Korda's *Rembrandt*, where the live action incessantly ices up and lap dissolves into and out of official art masterpieces. The use of period culture—music, costume, landscape gardening, as well as painting—is strictly a matter of fragments and generalized referrals which then appear in personal and thoroughly transformed contexts. *Barry Lyndon* isn't "a collection of paintings," but the invention of an autonomic culture. And what might otherwise have appeared as the woolgatherings of an archivist has been transmitted by a film-maker into a tribute to the farraginous nature of his medium.

Each image seals off direct access to its content by converting content into an object of formal admiration; the formalism, that is, insures the image as both visual enticement and proof against further intimacy. The beauty of the film is indeed strange as the formalism of the image sequestrates not only its dramatic, but also its historical utility. The particularities of history seem to take place in a blink of the camera's eye—the Seven Years War reduced to brief snaps of two elegant skirmishes (the outcomes of which we never see); the signal date "1789" glimpsed at the close and consigned to an ironic grace note on an annuity statement, the end of an epoch placed literally beside the point that the film itself is coming to an end. In spite of the fact that Kubrick's work at the very least equals the two richest recreations of the eighteenth century in film, Griffith's *Orphans of the Storm* and Renoir's *La Marseillaise,* it isn't really reminiscent of either of them. Both Griffith and Renoir seek out dramatic forms that translate the historical past into the immediate present, that burn up the distance between past and present in the fire of a continuing human struggle. Kubrick's aesthetics, on the other hand, seek to preserve not the immediacy, but the pastness of the past, its remoteness and irretrievability; and in this respect, his film is most like Welles' *The Magnificent Ambersons* and Ophuls' *Lola Montès,* those "period" films that project history into a Proustian *temps perdu,* that visualize the historical past not as an aspect of perdurable, human conflict, but as a textured cluster of private emotion, the sensible expression of memory and nostalgia.

What is true of history is equally true of the narrative that Kubrick has extracted from Thackeray's novel, *The Luck of Barry Lyndon*: neither history nor novel serves the film as its subject; rather, both provide materials out of which a subject is to be shaped. Events common to both film and novel, however, run roughly as follows: tricked into believing he has killed an affluent rival in a duel over his sweetheart, young Redmond Barry leaves his mother's side to become by turns a soldier in the British army, a soldier then a spy in the German army, then a gambler-at-large and a fortune hunter; whereupon, he marries the Countess Lyndon who provides him with a son, a stepson, a fortune, and a new surname. He bungles the fortune in a costly quest for a peerage, loses the son in a fall from a horse, fights bitterly with the stepson, and finally, is expelled from the estate *sans* wife, fortune, and surname, back to the side of his mother. Thackeray has made of these events a picaresque for cynics, a social satire which charts the rise and fall of a jackanapes. Kubrick, by contrast, has made not a satire, but a virtually abstract contemplation of human suffering and loss: the story of a man who cannot get what he wants or keep what he gets as the function of a formalist construction. The film's true subjects then become mortality and art, grief and cinematographics, human ruin "ingested" by the plenitude of an aural-visual ordering of film. Actually these motifs generalize upon a current of imagery that has flowed through all of Kubrick's work, and the dialectics of his present film recall sequences and icons from the past: for example, a great baroque chateau that harbors the death-dealing decisions of the French high command (in *Paths of Glory*), or a wizened and dying astronaut smashing a dish in a Louis XVI drawing room (in *2001*), or perhaps most memorably, a love-sick James Mason pumping bullet holes into a Gainsboroughlike portrait of a lady (in *Lolita*). But in *Barry Lyndon,* the fusion of art and human suffering is more than a matter of isolated images: it has become a structural concept that both determines and permeates the emotional ambience of an entire film—a paradoxical ambience that is characteristically sadly beautiful, beautifully sad, an aesthetic, almost Vergilian gaze upon the sheer fragility and benighted fretfulness that resides at the core of all creaturely striving. *Barry Lyndon* is about "the tears in things."

Kubrick has done to Thackeray's fiction what Thackeray himself could not do—or by his own admission could not bring himself to do out of weariness and dissatisfaction with this, the earliest of his novels—and that is, transform a lively, but garrulous and often shapeless narrative into a coherent structure. By many excisions, deft condensations, and fresh inventions (e.g., the extraordinary climactic duel between Barry and his stepson Bullingdon, with its gripping montage-cadence, belongs to Kubrick not Thackeray, whose narrative fizzles out in a splutter of anti-climaxes), the director constructs a shape that is a model of unity, symmetry, and abstract formal relationship. The film splits into two equal parts—the first corresponding to Barry's rise, the second to his decline—in which the major sequences in one part duplicate, reverse, and finally harmonize comparable sequences in the other—producing at the close an overall effect of minor variants within a major aesthetic stasis; the boxing match in part one, for example, balances the public throttling of Bullingdon in part two: in part one, Barry's victory over a bully earns him the admiration of his soldier companions, in part two, Barry is himself the bully and his "victory" defines him as a social outcast in the eyes of the assembled gentry; the loss of Barry's elderly friend Captain Grogan in part one balances the loss of Barry's child Brian in part two: in one, Barry weeps as a "son" to a "father," in two, as a father to a son; Barry's duel with Captain Quin at the beginning of part one balances against his duel with Bullingdon at the end of part two: in one, Barry, placed at the left side of the frame, is the young challenger against an older authority figure, and wins, in two, Barry has moved to the right side of the frame, is himself the challenged and older authority figure, and loses. Like most autotelic forms, *Barry Lyndon* seems to feed off itself, secretes the materials upon and with which it is to be made and understood. Events reproduce themselves, and the second time round, they are not only mirrored, but reversed. Serpentlike, the tail of the film feeds itself back into the mouth of its head as the ending both doubles and reverses the beginning: thus in the penultimate scene, we see Barry, once more a fatherless son in a position of dependency upon his widowed mother; and then in the final scene, we see in reverse a widowed Countess Lyndon in a position of dependency upon *her* fatherless son, Bullingdon. The microstructure of this ending replicates the macrostructure of the entire film, and the phrase "they are all equal now"—from the written epilogue which appears after the last scene—refers to more than just the death of the characters.

The mode of *Barry Lyndon* is emblematic, not analytic, and the treatment of character follows the treatment of structure as the extreme stylization of act and speech deprives personality of its idiosyncrasy and psychological nuance. Rarely are we provided with a conventional, sequential account of any character's specific motives, and the various Oedipal rivalries that emerge during the course of the film assume simple, generalized, even transpersonal shapes. While Thackeray's Barry is a braggart, a bully, a stereotype of the Irish temperament, Kubrick's Barry is none of these: his "positive" and "negative" acts keep rhyming off each other—his cruelty to Bullingdon against his love for Brian, his infidelity to Lady Lyndon against his reconciliation with her, etc.—so that a final judgment of his character becomes tentative, and ultimately, I think, superfluous. The director has thoroughly neutralized his hero's identity to create neither a rogue nor an innocent, but a human shape that approaches the conditions of an artifact. Who Barry is, what he wants, and what we are to make of him, are issues of psychology and morality that resolve and finally conciliate themselves into how and where Barry stands in film time and film space; his career and character development translate into exteriorized patterns of posture, gesture, choreography within a frame, and position within a tableau. Barry's "rising action," for instance, characteristically plants him alone, far back in deep space (on country roads, in forests, palace chambers, and army camps) and then marches him forward along the central axis of the frame, bringing him to a full stop in the foreground, where he often encounters a knot of figures who then either aid or hinder the pursuit of his fortune.

His "social success" usually finds him motionless in the foreground, sometimes standing stiffly (e.g., at his wedding), often sitting stiffly (at parties and dinners, in clubs and drawing rooms), often in frontal position, never alone, always enclosed by clusters of friends, relatives, and/or household attendants. His "social expulsion" pushes him back—either alone (once again) or with his child—into the middle distance, isolating him (on bridges, lawns, and once in a boat on a lake) amidst the vast reaches of an all-but-deserted estate. And after the funeral of Brian, his "fall" is depicted neither as a defect of character nor a force of circumstance, but quite literally as a deficiency in personal carriage, as the recurring inability to stand erect: we see a broken Barry hoisted like a sack of grain between two servants and carried from a hall; a drunken Barry seated in a club with head lolling on chest and feet forked apart like an open scissors; a wounded Barry shot down by Bullingdon; and finally of course, a crippled Barry who exits from the film on crutches.

Everywhere the methodology of the film attempts to transform a continuous action into a finished design, something happening into something remembered, a subject enacted into an object contemplated. To effect this transformation, the film makes special use of two devices—the camera and a narrator. Thackeray immerses the reader in the events of his novel by allowing Barry to tell his own story. Kubrick removes the viewer from the events of his film by rarely allowing the commentary of his anonymous narrator to synchronize precisely with any given action. The voice of the narrator, genial, ironic, and remote, is the voice of a collective memory, a public recollection of private passions. His oblique commentary distances the action by characteristically either generalizing from it (transforming action into homily) or expounding upon its past and future extensions; thus, after an interlude of intense passion, we see Barry leave the farmhouse of a young German girl while the narrator tells us that this girl has loved in this manner many times before; or we see Lord Lyndon fumbling for his pills while the narrator reads his obituary; or we see Barry riding with his son while the narrator reminds us that Barry is destined to be "childless." The primary function of the commentary, then, qualifies, challenges, and "mutes" the present tense condition of the visualized action; finally determines the status of the action as the ineffable, transient, and sometimes irregular inflection of lives already packaged by memory. If the action is affecting, it is so not in spite of the narrator, but precisely because of his presence, and if the perspective of the narrator is limited, so too is that of the action. Each contains insights denied the other; the action reveals the intimacies of the part, the narrator the ironies of the whole. But the union of word and deed produces not contradiction, but enrichment, a contribution to our special sense of film space—we hear "far" even while we see "near"—and film time—the event seems to be "finished" (temporally as well as aesthetically) even while it is happening.

If the temporal provenance of the action is the present and that of the narrator is the past and the future (i.e., the historical overview), the stance of the camera itself—the third active presence in this multiplex work—seeks to elude the temporal continuum altogether, and reside in the condition of formal meditation, of timeless repose as a maker of self-reflexive images. The provenance of the camera is the provenance of art, and indeed at certain times, this provenance is threatened: during the boxing match, the fight with Bullingdon, and Lady Lyndon's attempted suicide, as if "overcome by grief" or "shattered by violence," the camera capitulates to the human turmoil, enacts its subject, shifts to hand-held position, and dramatizes a dizzy, rushing space. But once the moment is past, the camera quickly "composes" itself and proceeds, as before, to propitiate and formalize the action in a regular succession of elegant, even-keeled compositions. Even as Barry leaves the film the camera continues to guard his suffering as he momentarily abandons his crutches and moves toward the door of a waiting coach, seemingly about to fall—only to be *caught* and held fast in a freeze frame.

This gesture epitomizes the relation between film form and human loss that is sustained throughout *Barry Lyndon*, and so too does the backward camera glide (i.e., a reverse zoom), perhaps the film's single most affective visual strategy. Over and over, like the incremental repeti-

tions of a ballad, at the beginning, middle or end of a scene, in the grand-
est, saddest, most elegiac of motions, the camera slowly pulls back (from
near to far), and takes leave of the human struggle; that is to say, the
motion of the camera begins in drama and ends in spectacle, starts off
with an action and finishes with a design, converts human value to aesthetic value and a utilitarian image into a self-reflexive image. Still, this
motion is not to be understood as a simple change from one perspective
to another, but rather as a dilation of space, a widening of the frame that
sustains continuity between the close-up and the long view, between
tumult and repose; and the grief of what has been left behind at the
beginning of the motion carries over into the end of it. I do not think that
Kubrick has ever made a film more suffused with feeling than *Barry
Lyndon,* although I must stress the fact that this feeling does not arise
from what the characters do to each other, but from what the form of the
film itself does to the characters—and finally to us. Characters and situations are taken away from us even in the midst of their happening; the
camera withdraws from that to which we would cleave close—and in this
respect, our sorrow is collateral to Barry's: we too can never get what we
want or keep what we get, and the motion of the camera is the measure
of our bereavement. Indeed I know of no film within recent memory that
urges us, as this one does, to so passionate an understanding of the
supernal poignancy and tantalizing opacity that abide at the heart of the
ontology of any film, that compels so completely our assent to the truth
of Virginia Woolf's early vision of film—surely one of the most sensitive
"amateur" responses ever recorded.

> We behold them [subjects in film] as they are when we are not there. We see
> life as it is when we have no part in it. As we gaze we seem to be removed
> from the pettiness of actual existence . . . Watching the boat sail and the
> wave break, we have time to open our minds to beauty and register on top
> of it the queer sensation—this beauty will continue and this beauty will
> flourish whether we behold it or not. Further, all this happened, ten years
> ago, we are told. We are beholding a world which has gone beneath the
> waves. ("Movies and Reality")

This presence ("life as it is"), this absence ("we are not there"), this
beauty ("the boat," "the wave"), this loss ("a world . . . gone") are the
meaning of *Barry Lyndon.*[1]
Having said all this, I must now report that I did not find the second
half of the film to be the equal of the first. To be sure, there are marvelous
episodes throughout—among them, the funeral and the final duel—but
much of this section does not lend itself to visual spectacle; it is essentially
an abortive psychodrama—a rococo skeleton of *Hamlet* retold from
Claudius' viewpoint—and keeps begging questions of individual motive
(e.g., Barry's brutality toward the child Bullingdon) to which its formalist

method of presentation won't provide any precise answers. In one important episode, the death of Barry's son, Kubrick actually loses confidence in his form, abjures his customary distance, dramatizes the scene in a series of conventional close-ups, and splashes about in a puddle of old-fashioned death-bed melodrama. This decision was a mistake, and so too I feel was the casting of Ryan O'Neal as Barry. Certainly the body is right—sloping shoulder blades, hefty torso, and splay feet—a rustic even in a castle. And the face is emotionally apt—a soft, blond potato with a spoiled boy's pout, the preferred love-thing of a doting mother. But this particular face is also an historical and cultural anachronism: it is still too full of California dreaming. At this time in his career, O'Neal brings all the wrong associations (i.e., contemporary juvenile romance) to his role. Perhaps in the future different roles will retroactively modulate these associations, but for now his persona has been fudged for a culture of elegance by low slung cars, junk food, and a smear of zinc oxide at the mouth. Shadow boxing with a brogue (and losing like Gable in *Parnell*) can't conceal the fact that this persona doesn't belong in either Ireland, Georgian England or anywhere else in the eighteenth century.

But none of these objections really qualifies my enthusiasm for what is remarkable in Kubrick's film. Many viewers, however, have found it impossible to accept the aesthetic terms in which this film operates and some of them continue to explain *Barry Lyndon* as a failed example of an altogether different and more traditional mode of cinema. It's hard for any of us to break out of our inherited and automatic habits of movie-going which have taught us to expect and appreciate essentially one kind of film experience, but not many others. And four decades of the traditional Hollywood sound film have not made it easier for any of us to decode the language of films like *Barry Lyndon* and *The Long Goodbye* (not to speak here of innumerable others); and some film critics haven't helped much either.

No help at all, for example, was the film critic who found *Barry Lyndon* to be "anti-film" and "destructive of the vitality and uniqueness of the *whole* film art." Since I am not sure that a phrase like the "*whole* film art" really means anything at all, I am hard put to understand how only one film can be "destructive" of what probably doesn't exist in the first place. But I would imagine what this critic actually means by the "*whole* film art" (and I hope I'm wrong) is one kind of film—the centralized film that traditionally subordinates style to drama, as opposed to the kind of film that reverses these priorities; and it is this latter film that he has termed "anti-film." The truth is, however, that there are many different categories of film, and good, bad, and indifferent films exist within each category; surely it is this plurality of categories that constitutes what can legitimately be called—if anything can—the "*whole* film art." And surely this critic does not need me to tell him (for in the past he has been one of the most perceptive observers of film) that one advantage the critic has over the polemicist or theorist is that he does not have to choose on principle one category of film over another, that he may select or reject specific films in any category, and do so not on the grounds of some theory of cinema, but on the basis of his personal experience of the depth and intensity of thought and feeling contained in each specific film.

In the past, my own experience of specific American films has convinced me that much of the best work has indeed been done in the centralized mode (partly because in the past, most American films have not been made in any other mode). In the present, however, recent experience of specific American films has assured me that few works in any mode have been as rich or interesting as the best films of Kubrick and Altman. And on the basis of this experience, I have no way of understanding how virtually the same critics can disparage films like these with one hand and then with the other boost films like *Dog Day Afternoon* and *One Flew Over the Cuckoo's Nest,* those standardized and rather slovenly made, "hard-hitting" showboats, notable only for the declamations of their respective stars. Are these two representative of the "vitality and uniqueness of the *whole* film art"? Aside from a new sexual frankness, haven't we been ordering Hollywood soufflés like these for at least a quarter of a century? A soupcon of craft, a dollop of actor's fustian, and a gallon of Broadway-style humanism (e.g., exchanges of "heart," and hysterias of loyalty and betrayal, especially between male buddies). And can we not finally have an indefinite moratorium on the fifties plot conflict—which makes these confections jell—of whether or not a rebel hero will knuckle under to conformist authorities? *Dog Day* has only one directorial "touch" (editor Dede Allen's filch from the climax of *Intolerance* as she cuts to the hands of the policemen trembling at their weapons *after* the order to desist), and *Cuckoo's Nest* has none (just an unfortunate ragtag of actors chosen for their blemishes and gargoyle features stammering at each other in a succession of mug shots); and both are as moribund as their numerous, socially conscious progenitors like *The Snake Pit* (for the atmosphere in *Cuckoo's Nest*), and *Brute Force* (for the warden-inmate conflict also in *Cuckoo's Nest*), and *On the Waterfront* (for the betrayal of a "brother" in *Dog Day*), and *The Defiant Ones* (for the all-male love affairs in both films), and so on, and so forth right into Janus-faced America's maudlin myth crypt.

You see how easy and essentially unfair it is to rattle on in this manner about a category of film of which one, from time to time, begins to weary. But works like *Barry Lyndon* and *The Long Goodbye,* categories of film we have hardly begun to understand, are rarely treated much better than this by those who should know better. Still, I take pleasure in the fact that Kubrick's film exists, and further pleasure in the hope that it will outlive our resistance to what it is and how it makes its meaning.

Notes

1. One may qualify, corroborate, or counter all or part of the foregoing by reading the other articles on this film that have been steadily appearing in quarterlies and film journals. I recommend in particular Michael Dempsey's excellent review, *"Barry Lyndon"* (*Film Quarterly*, Fall '76), and Mark C. Miller's frequently brilliant readings in *"Barry Lyndon* Reconsidered" (*The Georgia Review*, Winter '76) and "Kubrick's Anti-Reading of *The Luck of Barry Lyndon*" (*Modern Language Notes*, December '76). Miller's writings on this film are the most exhaustive and meticulous to have appeared thus far. I don't think it in any way diminishes the richness of his work, however, to say that I disagree with some of his major contentions. Miller, for example, finds the film's narrator to be "unreliable." I find this judgment hard to accept, even when imagining it to be true. If the narrator is "unreliable," he then becomes, by virtue of this fact, not an anonymous voice above the action, a detached witness, but rather a character within the action, an engaged participant. But if he is such a character, why isn't he characterized? Why are none of the many forms of first person syntax ever included in his commentary? Any narrator who is unreliable shifts the burden of narrative attention to himself—but why then doesn't Kubrick's narrator enforce such a shift? Thackeray's narrator is of course involved, unreliable, and named "Barry Lyndon": Kubrick's nameless narrator is not involved and I find his commentary reliable as far as it goes and in precisely what it says (what it does not say—a great deal—is "said" by the image itself, see above). Miller also feels that Barry is essentially "an innocent deprived of guidance," and often resorts to an elaborate and sometimes contradictory calisthenics of logic and language to defend some of his hero's misdeeds. Miller, for instance, finds Barry's flogging of the child Bullingdon "oddly fitting (as well as upsetting)" because Barry associates the "boy's coldness" with the "loveless uprightness of the Prussians." Even if this association were not far-fetched—I find no evidence for it—it becomes oddly unfitting (as well as amusing) when Miller later contends that Barry "stares" at Bullingdon in the final duel, "recognizing himself." If so (and here the association is eminently plausible), does he then also recognize in himself "the loveless uprightness of the Prussians"? If so, to what degree is he still "a misunderstood innocent"? Perhaps this is one moral issue in which Germany should not be implicated at all. In general, I think that Miller, in trying to free Barry from the "scoundrel" charge (and rightly so), has imagined motives where there aren't any, and inadvertently invented, instead of a "scoundrel," an Oliver Twisted Barry, the protagonist of a male weepie (e.g., "Barry is always at heart a helpless innocent at the mercy of those who watch him"). Any final judgment on Barry's character must, I think, remain equivocal, for his conduct takes place in the aesthetic, not in the moral or psychological, arena.

Photographing Stanley Kubrick's
Barry Lyndon

JOHN ALCOTT

A mong all the film-makers of the world, there is no one quite like Stanley Kubrick.

To be more accurate, there is no one even *remotely* like him.

An early dropout from formal education, largely self-taught, but possessed of a razor-sharp intelligence and a voracious curiosity, he has, since the late 1950s steadily risen toward the very pinnacle among the rarefied ranks of world-famed film producer-directors.

Behind him there are ten feature motion pictures, each one totally different from the others in both content and style. He has never twice made the same type of film.

What sort of man stands behind this astounding body of work? Nobody seems to know—for he is such an intensely private person, living and working, since 1961, encapsulated with his family in a manor house outside of London, that he has become—reluctantly, one suspects—a kind of legend, a disembodied enigma, making public his *persona* solely in terms of what he puts up there on the screen.

He cares nothing for personal publicity and is all but inaccessible to journalists—which is understandable, considering how many so-called "journalists" hanging onto the fringes of the film world are such unprincipled swine.

Yet, to those few whom he respects and trusts, he comes across as completely free of pretensions, totally honest and forthright.

When, in 1968, after "2001: A SPACE ODYSSEY" had burst like a rocket across the screens of the world, Editor Herb Lightman personally asked Kubrick to share the "secrets" of the film's stunning technical expertise with *American Cinematographer* readers, he graciously and generously did so, explaining each unique and dazzling effect in the most precise detail, holding back nothing (see *American Cinematographer,* June 1968).

To say that Kubrick is "dedicated" is to sell him short, considering that in Hollywood a dedicated producer is all too often one who foregoes his weekly poker game in order to count the preview cards of his latest movie.

The term "complete commitment" comes closer to describing Kubrick's symbiotic relationship with film—but "total immersion" is even more apt. Taking as long as four years to make a single film ("2001", for example), he eats, sleeps and breathes the project, once into it. An almost fanatical

Courtesy of *American Cinematographer*

perfectionist, he drives his co-workers seemingly beyond the limits of their endurance toward heights of achievement they never imagined, let alone hoped to attain.

Stanley Kubrick does not simply create films—he creates entire *worlds* on film. In "DOCTOR STRANGELOVE" he creates a world at once hysterically funny and nightmarish, a quite plausible preview of the beginning of the end of life on this planet. In "2001" he creates a world of the not-so-distant future—cold and computerized, with robot-like astronauts reaching almost mindlessly out toward the cosmic unknown. In "A CLOCKWORK ORANGE" he creates a 1984-ish world of senseless violence that is only a silly millimeter away from the chronic craziness and terrorism that prevail globally at this very moment.

And now comes "BARRY LYNDON".

In this latest epic effort, currently caressing selected screens, he translates into cinematic terms the first novel of William Makepeace Thackeray to create a pastel, pictorial 18th-century world of lush country estates, doll-like women and dueling men.

The film's central character is a slightly thick, hungrily ambitious young Irishman who longs to pull himself up by his low-born bootstraps into the airy-fairy world of the nobility—and almost succeeds in doing it.

The lavishly mounted production, released by Warner Bros., runs 3 hours and 4 minutes, and cost $11 million—every dollar of which is visible on the screen.

In its bare bones the rise-and-fall saga of an 18th-century Sammy Glick, "BARRY LYNDON" is also practically a documentary of how people lived in the Ireland and England of that period—their manners and morals, their values and amours, their personal duels and large-scale battles.

It is a film on a grand scale which abounds in meticulous technical craftsmanship and—even more important—the tender loving care of Stanley Kubrick and his loyal co-craftsmen.

In his cover story for the December 15, 1975 issue of *Time* magazine, noted film critic-historian Richard Schickel wrote: "In it, he [Kubrick] demonstrates the qualities that eluded Thackeray: singularity of vision, mature mastery of his medium, near-reckless courage in asserting through his work a claim not just to the distinction critics have already granted him but to greatness that time alone can—and probably will—confirm."

Underlying this statement is the realization that Kubrick has taken a basically talky novel and magically transformed it into an intensely visual film.

Schickel went on to write: "The structure of the work is truly novel. In addition, Kubrick has assembled perhaps the most ravishing sets of images ever printed on a single strip of celluloid. These virtues are related: the structure would not work without Kubrick's sustaining mastery of the camera, lighting and composition; the images would not be so powerful if the director had not devised a narrative structure spacious enough for them to pile up with overwhelming impressiveness."

The operative phrase out of that assertion is: "the most ravishing set of images ever printed on a single strip of celluloid."—which is quite possibly true, because "BARRY LYNDON" is a delicious feast for the eye. Each composition is like a painting by one of the Old Masters, and they link one onto the other like the tiles of a wondrous mosaic.

Pictorially, the elegant result emerges from a close collaboration between Kubrick (no mean photographer himself) and Director of Photography John Alcott, BSC.

Aside from the sheer beauty of the images, the problems of getting some of them onto the screen were considerable and unique. In the following interview, conducted by the *American Cinematographer* Editor, John Alcott discusses those problems, as well as the techniques utilized to make "BARRY LYNDON" the pictorially beautiful film that it is:

QUESTION: *You've worked with Stanley Kubrick on three pictures:* "2001: A SPACE ODYSSEY", "A CLOCKWORK ORANGE" *and now* "BARRY LYNDON". *Can you tell me a bit about that working relationship?*

ALCOTT: We have a very close working relationship, which began on "2001". I had been assisting Geoffrey Unsworth on that picture and then, when Geoff had to leave after the first six months. I was asked to carry on—so it was Stanley Kubrick who gave me my break. Our working relationship is close because we think exactly alike photographically. We really do see eye-to-eye photographically.

QUESTION: *What about the preplanning phase of* "BARRY LYNDON"?

ALCOTT: There was a great deal of testing of possible photographic approaches and effects—the candlelight thing, for example. Actually, we had talked about shooting solely by candlelight as far back as "2001", when Stanley was planning to film "NAPOLEON", but the requisite fast lenses were not available at the time. In preparation for "BARRY LYNDON" we studied the lighting effects achieved in the paintings of the Dutch masters, but they seemed a bit flat—so we decided to light more from the side.

QUESTION: *You photographed both* "A CLOCKWORK ORANGE" *and* "BARRY LYNDON" *for Stanley Kubrick and, obviously, the photographic styles of these two pictures were quite different from each other. Comparing the two, purely as a point of interest, how would you describe those stylistic differences?*

ALCOTT: Well, "A CLOCKWORK ORANGE" employed a darker, more obviously dramatic type of photography. It was a modern story taking place in an advanced period of the 1980's—although the period was never actually pinpointed in the picture. That period called for a really cold, stark style of photography; whereas, "BARRY LYNDON" is more pictorial, with a softer, more subtle rendition of light and shadow overall than "A CLOCKWORK ORANGE". As I saw it, the story of "BARRY LYNDON" took place during a romantic type of period—although it didn't necessarily have to be a romantic film. I say "a romantic period" because of the quality of the clothes, the dressing of the sets, and the architecture of that period. These all had a kind of soft feeling. I think you probably could have lighted "BARRY LYNDON" in the same way as "A CLOCKWORK ORANGE", but it just wouldn't have looked right. It wouldn't have had that soft feeling.

QUESTION: *How did you translate "that soft feeling" into cinematic terms, and what technical means did you use to achieve it?*

ALCOTT: In most instances we were trying to create the feeling of natural light within the houses, mostly stately homes, that we used as shooting locations. That was virtually their only source of light during the period of the film, and those houses still exist, with their paintings and tapestries hanging. I would tend to re-create that type of light, all natural light actually coming through the windows. I've always been a natural light source type of cameraman— if one can put it that way. I think it's exciting, actually, to see what illumination is provided by daylight and then try to create the effect. Sometimes it's impossible when the light outside falls below a certain level. We shot some of those sequences in the wintertime, when there was natural light from perhaps 9 o'clock in the morning until 3 o'clock in the afternoon. The requirement was to bring the light up to a level so that we could shoot from 8 o'clock in the morning until something like 7 o'clock in the evening—while maintaining the consistent effect. At the same time, we tried to duplicate the situations established by research and reference to the drawings and paintings of that day—how rooms were illuminated, and so on. The actual compositions of our setups were very authentic to the drawings of the period.

QUESTION: *In other words, then, you would take your cue from the way the natural light actually fell and then you would build that up or simulate it with your lighting units in an attempt to get the same effect, but at an exposurable level?*

ALCOTT: Yes. In some instances, what we created looked much better than the real thing. For example, there's a sequence that takes place in Barry's dining room, when his little boy asks if his father has bought him a horse. That particular room had five windows, with a very large window in the center that was much greater in height than the others. I found that it suited the sequence better to have the light coming from one source only, rather than from all around. So we controlled the light in such a way that it fell upon the center of the table at which they were having their meal, with the rest of the room falling off into nice subdued, subtle color.

QUESTION: *In creating that particular effect, did you use any of the light actually coming through the windows?*

ALCOTT: No, it was simulated by means of Mini-Brutes. I used Mini-Brutes all the time, with tracing paper on the windows—plastic material, actually. I find it to be a little bit better than the tracing paper.

QUESTION: *Was most of the picture shot in actual locations, or did you have to build some sets?*

ALCOTT: Oh, no—every shot is an actual location. We didn't build any sets whatsoever. All of the rooms exist inside actual houses in Ireland and the southwest of England.

QUESTION: *What about the physical problems of shooting inside those actual stately homes?*

ALCOTT: Well, we did have problems, although they didn't affect me too much. For instance, many of those stately homes are open to the public. We couldn't restrict the public from going through—so we had to cater to them. We would use certain rooms with visitors virtually walking past in the corridor. They would simply close off that one room and have the public bypass it. However, at times our shooting schedule would be limited to the point where we had to work when they weren't touring. They would go around in groups and we would virtually shoot when they were changing over from one group to another. In many of the locations, though, we had complete freedom of the house. We didn't really have too many problems, except for having to build very large rostrums for the lighting in certain rooms. I also had rostrums built around the exterior windows. They could be wheeled out of the way for reverse angles when we were shooting towards the windows and wanted to show the view outside, as well. Such was the case in the sequence that takes place in Countess Lyndon's bedroom.

QUESTION: *Did you have to gel the windows, or were you using a daylight balance?*

ALCOTT: In the actual interiors, most of the time, we did gel the windows, although there were a very few instances when we didn't do it. We had neutral density filters made, as well—ND3, ND6 and ND9—so that we had a complete range to accommodate whatever light situation prevailed outside the windows. Also, on all the exterior shooting, I never used an 85 filter.

QUESTION: *What was your reason for not using the 85?*

ALCOTT: One reason was to get an overall consistent balance

throughout the entire picture. In that sense, I tend to use it as I use forced development—that is, in every scene (including those that don't actually need it), in order to maintain a consistency of visual character throughout. The second reason was simply that the exterior light was sometimes so low that I needed the extra two-thirds of a stop. Although we mostly used the zoom lens outdoors, there were many instances in which we ended up shooting wide open with the Canon T/1.2 lens.

QUESTION: *In other words, the light was sometimes so dull, so overcast that you had to open up that lens all the way. Is that right?*

ALCOTT: Oh, yes—all the way. That was especially true in the holdup ambush sequence. We started off with a good day and there was plenty of light in the beginning, but the last part of that sequence was shot with the T/1.2 lens wide open. In order to match the brilliance of the normal daylight one had to be very fully exposed. I needed that fast lens.

QUESTION: *Can you tell me to what extent you used diffusion in shooting* "BARRY LYNDON"?

ALCOTT: When I went around looking at locations with Stanley we discussed diffusion among other things. The period of the story seemed to call for diffusion, but on the other hand, an awful lot of diffusion was being used in cinematography at the time. So we tended not to diffuse. We didn't use gauzes, for example. Instead I used a No.3 Low Contrast filter all the way through—except for the wedding sequence, where I wanted to control the highlights on the faces a bit more. In that case, the No.3 Low Contrast filter was combined with a brown net, which gave it a slightly different quality. We opted for the Low Contrast filter, rather than actual diffusion because the clarity and definition in Ireland creates a shooting situation that is very like a photographer's paradise. The air is so refined, I think, because Ireland is in the Gulf Stream. The atmosphere is actually perfect and we thought it would be a pity to destroy that with diffusion, especially for the landscape photography.

QUESTION: *That's rather refreshing. There seems to be a tendency these days, despite the nice sharp lenses that are available, to just fuzz everything out as a matter of course.*

ALCOTT: Yes, it's done a lot. I've even done it myself in shooting commercials. We did discuss the possibility for "BARRY LYNDON", but then we thought: "Well, it's been done before so many times; let's try for something different. Let's go into low contrast." We tested many filters and of all those we tested the Tiffen Low Contrast filters came out the best qualitywise. With the Tiffen filters we didn't lose any quality whatsoever, even when shooting wide open, in fact. They were the best.

QUESTION: *Did you use any of the 5247 color negative, or was it all 5254?*

ALCOTT: We used the 5254, because the 5247 wasn't available even at the time when we finished shooting. It came out something like two months after we had finished the main shooting of the film. Now I find that, because of the fineness of the grain with the 5247, I would have had to use a No.5 Tiffen Low Contrast filter in order to get the same effect I got using the No.3 with the old stock.

QUESTION: *Do you find, as many other cinematographers have found, that the 5247 negative has an inherently higher contrast than the 5254?*

ALCOTT: Well, they say it's higher contrast, but I really think it's not so much the contrast as the fact that the grain is so much finer. If the grain is finer, this will increase the apparent contrast. In other words, you've got to dress and color your sets to accommodate the film stock. Even the tiniest ornaments which are red will kick out on the new stock, whereas on the old stock they wouldn't. This is because of the finer grain. It's the color, in fact, which is building up the contrast. However, I can't understand why anybody wouldn't go for the finer grain, because that's what it's all about. The thing is to try to make it work by knocking down the contrast in some other way. We must either modify the lighting or design the set in a way to tone it down. For instance, in some of the interiors used for shooting "BARRY LYNDON" there were lots of white areas—fireplaces and such. If you put a light through a window these would stick out like a sore thumb, as they say. So, most of the time, I covered them with a black net—the white marble of the fireplaces, the very large white three-foot-wide panels on the walls, and the door frames that were white. I covered them with a black net having about a half-inch mesh. You could never see it photographically, unless you were really close to it—but in the long shots it wasn't visible at all. It did wonders in toning down the white. I also used graduated neutral density filters on certain light parts of the set when the illumination was coming from a natural light source and there was no way to gobo it off. For example, if the light source were coming from the left and hitting something that it was not possible to put a net over, I would put a neutral density filter on the right side—an ND3 or ND6, depending upon the brightness.

QUESTION: *You would actually use graduated neutral density filters for shooting interiors? That's not done very often, is it?*

ALCOTT: I don't think so—no. I know that when I use them now in different types of work that I do, some of the people on the set wonder what I'm up to, using graduated filters for interiors. But they work very well indeed. In fact, we had a matte box made to accept the three filters on the Arriflex 35BL. Incidentally, we used the Arriflex 35BL all the way through the picture.

QUESTION: *Can you give me some of your impressions of that camera?*

ALCOTT: I think it's a fantastic camera. To me, it's a cameraman's camera—mainly because the optical system is so good. Some optical systems give you a much more exaggerated tunneling effect than others, and I even came across someone the other day who prefers that long tunneling effect because it makes him feel like he's in a cinema. Personally, I prefer it when my eye is filled with the actual picture image. You find that this only really occurs with the Arriflex 35BL. Another feature I like about the camera is that you've got the aperture control literally at your fingertips. It's got a much larger scale and, therefore, a finer adjustment than most cameras. This feature is especially important when you're working with Stanley Kubrick, because he likes to continue shooting whether the sun is going in or out. In "BARRY LYNDON", during the sequence when Barry is buying the horse for his young son, the sun was going in and out all through the sequence. You've got to cater to this. That old bit that says you cut because the sun's gone in doesn't go anymore.

QUESTION: *Instead, you try to ride it out by varying the aperture opening during the shooting of the scene?*

ALCOTT: Yes, that's why the Arriflex 35BL offers such an advantage. It's got a finer aperture adjustment—more so than most other cameras—which allows you to cater to light variations while you're actually shooting. On most lenses there's not a great distance between one aperture stop and the next. There isn't actually on the Arriflex 35BL lenses either, but it's the gearing mechanism on the outside that offers the larger scale and, therefore, the possibility of more precise adjustment. It's like converting a 1/4–inch move into a 1–inch move.

QUESTION: *What about the use of the zoom lens in this film?*

ALCOTT: Oh, yes—we used it a great deal. The Angenieux 10–to-1 zoom was used on the Arriflex 35BL, in conjunction with Ed DiGiulio's Cinema Products "Joy Stick" zoom control, which is an excellent one. It starts and stops without a sudden jar, which is very important, and you can manipulate it so slowly that it almost feels like nothing is happening. This is very difficult to do with some of the motorized zoom controls. I find that this one really works.

QUESTION: *What types of lighting equipment did you use?*

ALCOTT: We used Mini-Brutes and we used a lot of Lowel-Lights—all the time. I used the Lowel-Lights in umbrellas for overall fill. I always use the umbrellas—ever since "A CLOCKWORK ORANGE".

I find that the Lowel-Light has a far greater range of illumination from flood to spot than any other light I know of. In fact, it's the only light of its type that gives you a fantastic spot, if you need it, and an absolute overall flood. Also, when you put a flag in front of most quartz lights you get a double shadow—but not with the Lowel-Lights. But then, of course, they were designed by a cameraman.

QUESTION: *What about the use of the moving camera in "BARRY LYNDON"?*

ALCOTT: We used it in certain sequences, but not too many. We had one very long tracking shot in the battle sequence, with the cameras on an 800–foot track. There were three cameras on the track, moving with the troops. We used an Elemack dolly, with bogie wheels, on ordinary metal platforms, and a five-foot and sometimes six-foot wheel span, because we found that this worked quite well in trying to get rid of the vibrations when working on the end of the zoom. It seemed to take the vibration out better than going directly onto the Elemack.

QUESTION: *Do I understand that you were racked out to the end of the zoom on that tracking shot?*

ALCOTT: Yes, virtually all closeups made from the track during that battle sequence were on the 250mm end of the zoom.

QUESTION: *That really is living dangerously.*

ALCOTT: I made a test beforehand with the camera traveling on an ordinary track and one with this base, and the difference was quite amazing. That's what got us round to building these platforms and using the Elemack with the bogie wheels on the four corners. They are really quite handy for doing all kinds of shots.

QUESTION: *What would you say was your most difficult sequence to shoot in this film?*

ALCOTT: I think the most difficult bit was the scene in the club when Barry comes over to confront the nobleman sitting at the other table, is given the cold shoulder and then goes back to his own table. That involved a 180–degree pan and what made it difficult was the fluctuations in the weather outside. There were many windows and I had lights hidden behind the brickwork and beaming through the windows. The outside light was going up and down so much that we had to keep changing things to make sure the windows wouldn't blow out excessively. This was most difficult to do, because any time I changed the gels on the windows, I also had to change the lights outside in order to avoid getting too much light inside and not enough outside. I would say that was the most difficult shot in the whole picture, in terms of lighting. What complicated it further was the fact that this was one of those stately houses that had the public coming through and visiting at the same time we were shooting.

QUESTION: *Did you use much colored light during the filming?*

ALCOTT: Yes, many times. An example that comes to mind is the scene in Barry's room after he has had his leg amputated. I used a light coming through the window with an extra 1/2 sepia over it in order to give a warm effect to the backlight and sidelight. In other words, a 50% overcorrection. A similar effect was used on Barry in the sequence when his boy is dying. In some instances I let the natural blue daylight come through in the background without correcting it. The result looked pleasing and it created a more "daylight" sort of effect.

QUESTION: *I can't recall any night-for-night shots in the picture. Were there any, perhaps, that didn't appear in the final cut?*

ALCOTT: There weren't really any night shots. There's that one twilight scene of Barry by the fire meditating after he's joined up, but that was shot at the "magic hour" and wasn't a true night shot.

QUESTION: *Now we come to the scenes which have caused more comment than anything else in this overall beautiful film— namely the candlelight scenes. Can you tell me about these and how they were executed?*

ALCOTT: The objective was to shoot these scenes exclusively by candlelight—that is, without a boost from any artificial light whatsoever. As I mentioned earlier, Stanley Kubrick and I had been discussing this possibility for years, but had not been able to find sufficiently fast lenses to do it. Stanley finally discovered three 50mm f/0.7 Zeiss still-camera lenses which were left over from a batch made for use by NASA in their Apollo moon-landing program. We had a non-reflexed Mitchell BNC which was sent over to Ed DiGiulio to be reconstructed to accept this ultra-fast lens. He had to mill out the existing lens mounts, because the rear element of this f/0.7 lens was virtually something like 4mm from the film plane. It took quite a while, and when we got the camera back we made quite extensive tests on it.

This Zeiss lens was like no other lens in a way, because when you look through any normal type of lens, like the Panavision T/1.1 or the Angenieux f/0.95, you are looking through the optical system and by just altering the focus you can tell whether it's in or out of focus. But when you looked through this lens it appeared to have a fantastic range of focus, quite unbelievable. However, when you did a photographic test you discovered that it had no depth of field at all—which one expected anyway. So we literally had to scale this lens by doing hand tests from about 200 feet down to about 4 feet, marking every distance that would lead up to the 10–foot range. We had to literally get it down to inches on the actual scaling.

QUESTION: *You say that the focal length was 50mm?*

ALCOTT: It was 50mm, but then we acquired a projection lens of the reduction type, which Ed DiGiulio fitted over another 50mm lens to give us a 36.5mm lens for wider-angle coverage. The original 50mm lens was used for virtually all the medium shots and close shots.

QUESTION: *And those scenes were illuminated entirely by candle-light?*

ALCOTT: Entirely by the candles. In the sequence where Lord Ludd and Barry are in the gaming room and he loses a large amount of money, the set was lit entirely by the candles, but I had metal reflectors made to mount above the two chandeliers, the main purpose being to keep the heat of the candles from damaging the ceiling. However, it also acted as a light reflector to provide an overall illumination of toplight.

QUESTION: *How many foot-candles (no pun intended) would you say you were using in that case?*

ALCOTT: Roughly, three foot-candles was the key. We were forcing the whole picture one stop in development. Incidentally, I found a great advantage in using the Gossen Panalux electronic meter for these sequences, because it goes down to half foot-candle measurements. It's a very good meter for those extreme low-light situations. We were using 70–candle chandeliers, and most of the time I could also use either five-candle or three-candle table candelabra, as well. We actually went for a burnt-out effect, a very high key on the faces themselves.

QUESTION: *What were some of the other problems attendant to using this ultra-fast lens to shoot entirely by candlelight?*

ALCOTT: There was, first of all, the problem of finding a side viewfinder that would transmit enough light to show us where we were framed. The conventional viewfinder would not do at all, because it involves prisms which cause such a high degree of light loss that very little image is visible at such low light levels. Instead, we had to adapt to the BNC a viewfinder from one of the old Technicolor three-strip cameras. It works on a principle of mirrors and simply reflects what it "sees", resulting in a much brighter image. There is very little parallax with that viewfinder, since it mounts so close to the lens.

QUESTION: *What about the depth of field problem?*

ALCOTT: As I suggested before, that was indeed a problem. The point of focus was so critical and there was hardly any depth of field with that f/0.7 lens. My focus operator, Doug Milsome, used a closed-circuit video camera as the only way to keep track of the distances with any degree of accuracy. The video camera was placed at a 90–degree angle to the film camera position and was monitored by means of a TV screen mounted above the camera lens scale. A grid was placed over the TV screen and by taping the various artists' positions, the distances could be transferred to the TV grid to allow the artists a certain flexibility of movement, while keeping them in focus.

It was a very tricky operation, but according to all reports, it worked out quite satisfactorily.

Kubrick's Anti-Reading of *The Luck of Barry Lyndon*

MARK CRISPIN MILLER

"There'll be no screenplay of 'Barry Lyndon' published, because there is nothing of literary interest to read."[1]

Since the completion of *2001: A Space Odyssey*, Stanley Kubrick has repeatedly suggested that his films are inapplicable to verbal formulations. "I tried to create a *visual* experience," he said of *2001* in 1968, "one that bypasses verbalized pigeonholing and directly penetrates the subconscious with an emotional and philosophical content. . . . I intended the film to be an intensely subjective experience, that reaches the viewer at an inner level of consciousness, just as music does."[2] Commenting on *A Clockwork Orange* in 1971, Kubrick referred to "something in the human personality which resents things that are clear, and, conversely, something which is attracted to puzzles, enigmas, and allegories."[3] "The most important parts of a film," he said in a discussion of *Barry Lyndon* in 1975, "are the mysterious parts—beyond the reach of reason and language."[4]

No one would question the relevance of such statements to most of Kubrick's work since *Dr. Strangelove* (1964). *2001* at first resembles a conventional science fiction thriller, but abandons its "plot" midway through the action. The mystery of the monolith is never solved in the traditional manner; there is no climactic discovery, no conclusive explanation. Instead, the viewer is left to ponder images and sequences that connote the futility of logic and the primacy of some higher intelligence. As the film deals with the limitations of human perception, it leaves the realm of familiar convention and aspires to a subliminal effect. *A Clockwork Orange* is similarly innovative. It baffles our sympathies, merging victim with aggressor, imposing beauty and comedy on savagery; it seems founded on the logic of dreams. Its images connote, among other things, the futility of enforcing a socially acceptable response to violence; and, as with *2001*, such a simple response to the film itself is impossible.

A Clockwork Orange and *2001* are anti-conventional. They elude ascriptions of genre and formulations of statement. *Barry Lyndon* seems at first entirely conventional, a picaresque tale uncomplicated by inexpressible elements. Furthermore, it is based on a Victorian novel, Thackeray's *The Luck of Barry Lyndon,* from which Kubrick has adapted a narrative voice-over far more intrusive than any he has ever used before.[5] Given Kubrick's

Modern Language Notes, 91, no. 6 (1976):1360–1380. Reprinted by permission of the author and The Johns Hopkins University Press.

stated emphasis on the non-verbal, it seems odd that he should choose to make a film that depends so much on words. If we are to understand how the meanings of *Barry Lyndon* lie "beyond the reach of reason and language," we must compare the film to Thackeray's novel, and consider the cinematic effect of Kubrick's changes. Like *2001* and *A Clockwork Orange, Barry Lyndon* deals with the inadequacy of language itself; and like those earlier films, it makes simple judgments impossible.

I. CHANGES IN PLOT

Kubrick's story is simpler than Thackeray's. Part I of the film deals with the protagonist's "rise." Young Redmond Barry must flee his Irish home after shooting Captain John Quin in a duel over the affections of Nora Brady, Redmond's cousin. On his way to Dublin he is robbed by highwaymen. Suddenly impoverished, he joins the British army, which needs recruits for its engagement in the Seven Years War. He is sent to fight the French, but after Captain Grogan, his friend and protector, is killed in battle, Redmond deserts, posing as an officer. On his way to neutral Holland, he spends some time with Lischen, a German girl whose husband is away at war. After leaving her, Redmond meets the Prussian Captain Potzdorf, who discovers his ruse and forces him to join the Prussian army. Eventually, Redmond wins the confidence of his superiors, who use him to spy on the Chevalier de Balibari, an old Irish gambler posing as a Frenchman.

Redmond confesses the plot to the Chevalier, but pretends to help the Prussians by working as the Chevalier's servant. The Prussian authorities finally move to expel the Chevalier from the country; but Redmond, disguised as his employer (who leaves on his own), is expelled instead. The two outcasts roam Europe as professional gamblers, working every fashionable court and spa. At one such place, Redmond meets and woos Lady Harriet Lyndon, whose aged husband Sir Charles Lyndon has a fatal seizure at the card-table.

Part II presents the protagonist's "fall." Redmond marries Lady Lyndon and becomes Barry Lyndon by the king's permission. He and his mother move to Castle Hackton, the Lyndon estate. Lady Lyndon bears her husband a son, Bryan, whom Barry loves passionately; there is no love, however, between Barry and Lord Bullingdon, Lady Lyndon's son by her first marriage. Acting on his own mother's advice, Barry cultivates the friendship of certain prominent men in the hopes of obtaining a peerage. He spends much of his wife's fortune to this end. At a musicale, Bullingdon enters the room with Bryan and publicly condemns his stepfather. Barry flies into a rage and beats his stepson before the audience of horrified aristocrats, who thenceforth avoid him. Bullingdon leaves home. Bryan dies

after falling from a horse, which bereavement drives his parents into helpless depression. Bullingdon returns, challenges Barry to a duel and
wounds him in the leg. Barry loses the leg, and is forced to leave England
on pain of imprisonment for debt.

Thackeray's novel is more densely constructed, filled with episodic
adventures which Kubrick omitted, for they are much too long and
involved to provide material for any cinematic endeavor other than farce.
Thackeray's Barry is not robbed by highwaymen, but by the victim of such
a robbery: he escorts a Mrs. Fitzsimons to safety after she has been robbed
on the road, takes up residence at her house, and gradually loses all his
money to the woman and her husband. Captain and Mrs. Fitzsimons make
no appearance in the film. While serving with the British army in
Germany, Thackeray's Barry is knocked unconscious in a petty quarrel,
then finds himself in Lischen's house, recuperating beside a wounded officer. With Lischen's help, he convinces the household that the wounded
man is Barry himself, delirious with fever; he steals the officer's uniform
and leaves unimpeded. In the film, Barry finds an officer's uniform and
papers unattended, as if by accident, and quickly steals them; Lischen,
whom he meets thereafter, has nothing to do with the theft.

Kubrick also omits the nasty episode of Barry's attempt to win the
Countess Ida from the Chevalier de Magny (a stratagem that leads tortu-
ously to gruesome reprisals), and the complicated plot whereby Barry
steals the affections of Lady Lyndon from her lover, Lord George Poynings.
Barry's downfall in the novel is the result of further elaborate machina-
tions, and Kubrick also does away with these.

Complicated stratagems in films tend to supersede the characters as
objects of attention. If the hero devotes himself to clever subterfuge, the
viewer will try to figure it out, follow its steps, determine its consequences. In films such as *Rififi, The Great Escape, The Day of the Jackal*
and Kubrick's own *The Killing*, characterization becomes less important
than the details of careful dissimulation; the subtleties of personality
emerge before and after the precise event. In the best of such films, the
characters become most interesting when the stratagem has failed. In films
such as *The List of Adrian Messenger* and *The Sting*, the stratagem is all.

By deleting Thackeray's most involved episodes, Kubrick places the
film's emphasis on the protagonist's inner life; we attend to Barry's feelings and responses, not his actions. Kubrick's changes in Thackeray's story
emphasize Barry's passivity: the film's hero seems incapable of the self-
seeking ingenuity that inspires the career of Thackeray's Barry. This passivity makes the protagonist seem enigmatic, for if he is not an independent
agent, then we cannot expect him to express his desires through the usual
manifestations of the will. He may do what he is told and expected to do,
but his reasons for acting dependently may be very complex.

Kubrick's omission of the novel's farcical episodes has another effect on the film: the tone of *Barry Lyndon* is subdued, quiet, melancholy, whereas the novel's adventures radiate a boisterous crudeness.

II. "A SORT OF WOEFUL TENDER IMPRESSION"

The film's melancholy is indistinguishable from its loveliness; "every frame is a fresco of sadness," writes Andrew Sarris.[6] Society in *Barry Lyndon* projects a sense of solitude and bereavement. Characters are isolated from one another in their decorative groups and self-conscious poses. Houses are not homes, but funereal mansions whose vast spaces seem to discourage human contact. Civilization itself is a tragic necessity, blocking the heart's disruptive impulses with a sad apparatus of restraint.

Redmond Barry is always at odds with this staid world; his assault on Bullingdon at the musicale is the disastrous consummation of a lifetime of subtler disruptions. However, he is no happier than the society which he invades. His life is a history of loss. He is dispossessed at the outset when his father is killed in a duel, which is the first thing we see. Fatherless in the dynastic society of the late eighteenth century, he seeks permanence, stability, a firm grounding, but none of his efforts can effect his integration into the world of men and women, families and estates. He loses Nora, Grogan, Bryan, Lady Lyndon. Absence seems inevitable in his career; death is his pervasive adversary.

Thackeray's hero is also dogged by woe, but there is none of the film's stately melancholy in the novel; there is more of Rowlandson than of Gainsborough in the spirit of the book. As Kubrick's Barry is not a conventional rogue, neither are Kubrick's other characters the picaresque caricatures described by Thackeray's narrator. For instance, in the novel Mrs. Barry is a grasping harridan whose uncouthness embarrasses her son, despite his dependence on her:

> To say truth, I was rather afraid, now that I lived in a very different sphere to that in which she was accustomed to move, lest she should come to pay me a visit, and astonish my English friends by her bragging and her brogue, her rouge and her old hoops and furbelows of the time of George II., in which she had figured advantageously in her youth, and which she still fondly thought to be at the height of the fashion. So I wrote to her, putting off her visit; begging her to visit us when the left wing of the castle was finished, or the stables built, and so forth.[7]

Kubrick's Barry never betrays any ambivalence toward his mother, who is present at his wedding and at every fine social function thereafter. Although she does appear out-of-place among the English aristocrats, the incongruity is subtle. And Mrs. Barry is an adaptable creature in the film:

she loses "her brogue" with the passage of time, and only takes to applying "her rouge" *after* coming to live among the painted English.

The image of Lady Lyndon is similarly softened in the film. Thackeray's narrator describes a pretentious prig:

> She was a goddaughter of old Mary Wortley Montague, and, like that famous old woman of the last century, made considerable pretensions to be a blue-stocking, and a *bel esprit*. Lady Lyndon wrote poems in English and Italian, which still may be read by the curious in the pages of the magazines of the day. She entertained a correspondence with several of the European *savans,* upon history, science, the ancient languages, and especially theology. Her pleasure was to dispute controversial points with abbés and bishops, and her flatterers said she rivalled Madame Dacier in learning. Every adventurer, who had a discovery in chemistry, a new antique bust, or a plan for discovering the philosopher's stone, was sure to find a patroness in her. (243)

There is nothing so ridiculous about Kubrick's Lady Lyndon, a reserved and mournful character who keeps her misery barely hidden beneath an air of exhausted elegance. In the novel, she gratifies Barry's cruelty with tearful entreaties for kindness; in the film, she is as enigmatic as her husband, and as fully misunderstood.

Kubrick also expunges the melodramatic bravura of Barry's account. Redmond Barry's uncle declares a toast to the engagement of Quin and Nora:

> At the third toast, it was always the custom for the ladies to withdraw; but my uncle stopped them this time, in spite of the remonstrances of Nora, who said "O, pa! Do let us go!" and said, "No, Mrs. Brady and ladies, if you please; this is a sort of toast that is drunk a great dale too seldom in my family, and you'll please to receive it with all the honours. Here's CAPTAIN AND MRS. JOHN QUIN, and long life to them. Kiss her, Jack, you rogue; for 'faith, you've got a treasure!"
>
> "His already?" I screeched out, springing up.
>
> "Hold your tongue, you fool—hold your tongue!" said big Ulick [Redmond's cousin], who sat by me; but I wouldn't hear.
>
> "He has already," I screamed, "been slapped in the face this morning, Captain John Quin; he's already been called coward, Captain John Quin; and this is the way I'll drink his health. 'Here's your health, Captain John Quin:'" and I flung a glass of claret into his face. I don't know how he looked after it, for the next moment I myself was under the table, tripped up by Ulick, who hit me a violent cuff on the head as I went down; and I had hardly leisure to hear the general screaming and skurrying that was taking place above me, being so fully occupied with kicks, and thumps, and curses, with which Ulick was belabouring me. "You fool!" roared he—"you great blundering marplot—you silly beggarly brat (a thump at each), hold your tongue!" (84–85)

There is none of this rough-and-tumble Cruikshank frenzy in Kubrick's version of the scene. Redmond comes to the table at which the family sits dining; characteristically, he is late, out-of-place. Quin and Nora sit across the table. Redmond studies uneasily his cousin's discomfiture, his rival's smugness. Quin speaks quietly to Nora, then to her father, who stands up and announces the engagement. Redmond stares in disbelief as Quin bends to kiss Nora for the benefit of all the seated spectators (among whom Kubrick places us, by shooting the entire sequence from the points-of-view of others seated at the table). Mr. Brady proposes a toast; all, except Redmond, rise to drink the couple's health; all sit. Mr. Brady scolds Redmond for failing to join in. Redmond pauses, stands, holds up his glass: "Here's my toast to you, Captain John Quin," he says quietly, and tosses his glass in his rival's face.

The women leave in consternation; Quin backs away from the table, fussing angrily with his wet face and cut forehead. "The captain's nose was bleeding," says Thackeray's Barry, "as mine was—*his* was cut across the bridge, and his beauty spoiled forever" (85). In the film, Quin suffers from nothing more than a tiny cut over one eye; and there is no mad brawl after the incident. Redmond announces calmly that "Mr. Quin may have satisfaction any time he pleases, by calling on Redmond Barry, Esquire, of Barryville," and makes his exit.

Kubrick seems to have sifted from the novel those details which the narrator, mendacious and ashamed of unmanly feeling, has added to his story years after the event. In recounting his departure from Lischen's house, Thackeray's Barry is more interested in the details of deception than in the effect of cutting short whatever intimacy he and the girl might have discovered:

> (I shall pass over my adieus with my kind hostess, which were very tearful indeed), and then, making up my mind to the great action, walked upstairs to Fakenham's room attired in his full regimentals, and with his hat cocked over my left eye. (128)

Kubrick's treatment of the departure from Lischen's house suggests that there has been great intimacy between Redmond and the girl. Redmond had introduced himself as "Jonathan Fakenham," but on the morning of his departure, Lischen's farewell nullifies this dissimulation: "*Auf wieder-sehen*, Redmond." In the film, there is no busy plotting to distract hero or viewer from the separation, which is allowed reverberations of tenderness.

In the novel, moments of loss are painful not for their pathos, but for their ugliness. We consider sad incidents through a satirist's eyes:

> When my kind friend Fagan was shot, a brother captain, and his very good friend, turned to Lieutenant Rawson and said, "Fagan's down; Rawson, there's your company." It was all the epitaph my brave patron got. "I should

have left you a hundred guineas, Redmond," were his last words to me, "but for a cursed run of ill luck last night at faro." And he gave me a faint squeeze of the hand; then, as the word was given to advance, I left him. When we came back to our old ground, which we presently did, he was lying there still; but he was dead. Some of our people had already torn off his epaulets, and no doubt, had rifled his purse. Such knaves and ruffians do men in war become! (13)

When Redmond's "kind friend" Grogan is shot down in the film, his corpse is not ravaged, nor do his last words refer only to money. Redmond carries his wounded friend from the battlefield and sets him down in a nearby copse. "I've only a hundred guineas left for you, my lad. I lost the rest at cards last night," laughs the dying man with difficulty. Then: "Kiss me, my boy! For we'll never meet again." Redmond leans down and kisses Grogan on the lips, then lies across the dead man's chest, sobbing as if his heart would break.

Kubrick eliminates the sordid aspects of Thackeray's story and restores the emotional undercurrent to moments of death and departure. He has thoroughly restrained the action, deliberately avoiding the light-hearted shenanigans of the Osborne/Richardson *Tom Jones* (1963), a change that has offended some of the film's critics, including Pauline Kael:

> If you were to cut the jokes and cheerfulness out of the film "Tom Jones" and run it in slow motion, you'd have something very close to "Barry Lyndon." Kubrick has taken a quick-witted story, full of vaudeville turns (Thackeray wrote it as a serial, under the pseudonym George Fitz-Boodle), and he's controlled it so meticulously that he's drained the blood out of it. The movie isn't quite the rise and fall of a flamboyant rakehell, because Kubrick doesn't believe in funning around. We never actually see Barry have a frisky, high time, and even when he's still a love-smitten chump, trying to act the gallant and fighting a foolish duel, Kubrick doesn't want us to take a shine to him.[8]

Asking for "vaudeville turns" in *Barry Lyndon* is like asking for a pie-fight in *Hamlet*. But Kael's complaint reveals more than a misunderstanding of Kubrick's intentions; it reveals a misconception of Thackeray's novel, which does not evince much "funning around."

Despite its frequent bluster, *Barry Lyndon*'s narrative is, finally, unhappy and unamusing. Whatever pleasure we might take in his anecdotes of bullying and deceit is diminished by our awareness of his final state: his questionable triumphs are all in the past; he speaks as one who has lost all he describes; he ends up, by his own admission, a "poor, lonely and broken-hearted man" (383). But the sadness pervading Thackeray's novel derives from something subtler than our objective knowledge of the protagonist's finish.

Barry Lyndon is a stage Irishman, given to the exaggeration that "is a practice not unusual with his nation" (52), as the novel's "editor" points out in a footnote. This stock character, we assume, is comic; but this assumption, according to Thackeray, is wrong. Thackeray wrote the following analysis of the Irish a few weeks after beginning Barry Lyndon in 1844:

> A characteristic of the Irish writers and people, which has not been at all appreciated by the English, is, I think, that of extreme melancholy. All Irish stories are sad, all humorous Irish songs are sad; there is never a burst of laughter excited by them but, as I fancy, tears are near at hand; and from "Castle Rackrent" downwards, every Hibernian tale that I have read is sure to leave a sort of woeful tender impression. . . . You may walk all Ireland through, and hardly see a cheerful [landscape]; and whereas at five miles from the spot where this is published or read in England, you may be sure to light upon some prospect of English nature smiling in plenty, rich in comfort, and delightfully cheerful, however simple and homely, the finest and richest landscape in Ireland always appeared to me to be sad, and the people corresponded with the place. But we in England have adopted our idea of the Irishman, and, like the pig-imitator's audience in the fable (which simile is not to be construed into an opinion on the writer's part that the Irish resemble pigs, but simply that the Saxon is dull of comprehension), we *will* have the sham Irishman in preference to the real one, and will laugh at the poor wag, whatever his mood may be.[9]

Here the visions of director and novelist converge. Thackeray's Irishman bears the traits of a stock figure, but his story is more woeful than amusing, closer in tone to Kubrick's film than a careless reader may realize. Only once does Kubrick's hero speak of himself with the braggadocio characteristic of Thackeray's narrator, and this is in a context that commonly encourages such fantasy. Barry tells his young son a bedtime story about an attack he supposedly led on a French fortress. The account is improbable and naively grisly, like most fairy tales, and recalls the Irish bluster that Thackeray considered melancholy: "And you should have seen the looks on the Frenchmen's faces, when nineteen rampaging he-devils, pell-mell, cut-and-thrust, jumped over the wall!" Later, Barry sits at his son's deathbed; Bryan asks him to "tell the story about the fort"; and Barry begins the same tall tale, but its swaggering tone belongs to a happier context in which that tone was not taken seriously. Now its exaggeration seems out-of-place; it is a purely verbal magnification of Barry's worth, and so meaningless now that his only creation, his living son, lies dying. Barry breaks off in the middle, and gives way to his grief. Perhaps Kubrick was thinking of Thackeray's remarks on the melancholy Irish when he decided to reintroduce this story into the film's saddest moment.

More important than this, however, is the tension between the style of Barry's story and the style of the film itself. The tale calls up no memorable image because its events are amplified beyond apprehensible proportions. We have no clear impression of what Barry describes, whereas our impression of the context in which he tells the story is strong, nearly overwhelming. The same is true of Bryan's deathbed utterances. The child's last words are patently sentimental. Taking each of his parents by the hand, he asks them to "promise not to quarrel, but to love each other, so that we may meet again in heaven, where Bullingdon says quarrelsome people never go." This recalls the death of little Paul Dombey. If it were a literary scene, comprised only of the dying boy's words, it might not seem very sad to a modern reader. But Kubrick never shows us the child's face as he is speaking. Instead, he shows us the parents' reactions, the boy's pale hand on the coverlet, images of grief more eloquent and affecting than any statement. And what is sad about the repetition of the bedtime story, aside from its covert allusion to a happier time, is Barry's inability to tell it.

Kubrick cuts from Barry's grief-stricken face to Bryan's funeral procession. Dozens of mourners follow the funeral carriage, a sheep-drawn toy coach in which Bryan had ridden on his birthday. Reverend Runt leads the procession, reciting John 11:25 in a loud, clear voice. It is a noble intonation of the text, but his actual words have no meaning. His voice has the stirring effect of a subsidiary musical instrument beneath the full strains of Handel's dolorous sarabande. This piece also dominates the film's opening and closing credits, and now complements the tragic spectacle of the orderly bereaved. The shot of the funeral comprises a beautiful image of misery, "a fresco of sadness," sad because beautiful: its effect depends on the visual-aural entirety of the cinematic event.

Kubrick's changes in tone suggest a crucial attitude toward cinematic style. Our immediate response to film style precedes the perceptive act of decoding the statements of montage, and precedes the act of choice afforded us by the successful use of *mise-en-scène*. Certainly, Kubrick edits and composes to work from his images and sequences as many meanings as possible; but his great technical skill allows him to determine the quality of each cinematic moment, to imbue every frame with a certain "mood" or "flavor." "Style" is what determines the quality of the moment: it is what we respond to first of all.

Writing on the problems of directing his version of Nabokov's *Lolita*, Kubrick made this statement in 1961: "Style is what an artist uses to fascinate the beholder in order to convey to him his feelings and emotions and thoughts. These are what have to be dramatized, not the style."[10] Once these things have been dramatized, they will be conveyed to the viewer, again, through style. Here it is important to point out the simple difference between cinematic and literary style: cinematic style is non-verbal. The sadness of Bryan's death derives from Kubrick's use of visual and aural elements, not from the child's deathbed remarks. The cinematic relationship between speech and image is one of antagonism. Words become distractions from the full suggestiveness of film style, and from the ambiguous plenitude of images which that style delivers.

This brings us to Kubrick's most important change in Thackeray's novel, the transformation of a first-person autobiographical account to a nonsynchronous third-person commentary.

III. THE UNRELIABLE NARRATOR

The narrator imposes on the action a retributive formula, lending a superficial "rise and fall" schema to the film's two-part structure. This formula dictates that pride goeth before a fall, implying that the hero's misfortunes are all his own fault. The narrator sees his hero as a conventional picaresque upstart: he speaks for a genre, and therefore misses whatever subtleties rest uneasily with his conventional interpretation.

For instance, he sees Barry's search for deep fulfillment as a picaresque search for wealth and prestige, although there is no visual evidence that Barry ever covets any such worldly item. The narrator obscures Barry's mysteriousness with predictable ascriptions. When young Redmond watches Quin's regiment parading before the people of Barryville, the narrator assures us that the boy's "heart burned with military ardor," but nothing in Redmond's demeanor supports this claim. Redmond watches the soldiers unresponsively. He is expressionless because at this early moment he has not yet learned that the people around him want an exciting display. It is not until he stands and challenges Quin that he reveals any histrionic self-consciousness. He is unimpressed by the stilted manners of Quin's troops. Later, when Redmond rides toward Holland in Fakenham's uniform, the narrator says that the youth "resolved never again to fall from the rank of a gentleman." Again, nothing in the image supports the claim; and immediately after the narrative assertion, Redmond encounters Lischen, for whom he relinquishes the fiction of social prominence in favor of the kind of intimacy he always seeks.

The narrator resembles the pitiless spectators of Barry's career, who react with the self-protective disapproval of the privileged. When a Prussian colonel calls Redmond "idle, dissolute, and unprincipled" and tells him that "for all your talents and bravery, I am sure you will come to no good," he speaks for a society that distrusts the outsider on principle. The narrator's opinion of Redmond is no fairer, although it is always more gently phrased. He tells us that Redmond soon became "very far advanced in the science of every kind of misconduct" among the Prussian soldiers, but we never see any evidence of such corruption. Kubrick allows the action to discredit the literary framework of narrative opinion, which is nothing more than a structuralization of slander.

Kubrick implies that we modern viewers are potentially just as unfair as the eighteenth-century spectators within the film. This implication inheres in the use of the narrator, who speaks *for* the audience *within* the film, and *to* the audience *in front of* the film, bridging the gap between the most superficial viewers in each. For instance, if we rely on the narrator, we will understand no more about Redmond's marriage than his enemies do: like them, we will assume that it is based entirely on materialistic drives. The narrator's treatment of this marriage is a good example of the authoritative libel that passes for insight.

When Redmond Barry first sees Lady Lyndon, he is seated opposite the Chevalier at a small table overlooking a parterre at Spa. He and the Chevalier are richly dressed; they take tea silently, as if unhappily. A group approaches from the far end of the segmented terrace: Lady Lyndon, Sir Charles Lyndon, their son Bullingdon, the tutor Reverend Runt, and an attendant who pushes Sir Charles' wheelchair. Sir Charles is an old, bent, powdered invalid, faintly ludicrous as he handles the steering mechanism of his little vehicle. In his wig and make-up, with his bulbous nose and puffy cheeks, he resembles a dropsical old woman. Runt's face is white as snow, his nose sharp as a pen, his hat and suit all somber black: this prim and bloodless figure also appears desexualized. And Bullingdon is a small child, austere and dignified beside his seated father. Lady Lyndon is young and beautiful. Although lacking in vitality, she seems unlike her sexless company; her sumptuous dress glows at the lightest end of a spectrum that darkens to brown in Sir Charles' coat, to indigo in Bullingdon's suit, ending in Runt's funereal clerical attire.

Redmond stares at them in fascination. There seems to be no suitable match for Lady Lyndon in this group; Redmond might become the missing mate. But Redmond's attraction to the woman is based on more than sexual desire. It also involves Sir Charles, the sedentary old man at Lady Lyndon's side.

Throughout the film, sedentary old men confront Redmond with the fact of his fatherlessness; he stands before them, trying in various ways to win their acceptance. He stands before his uncle, whose own sons sit nearby, and challenges Captain Quin. (This is a doubly ambiguous gesture, because Quin is yet another older man sitting before the solitary boy.) Later, Redmond stands before Herr von Potzdorf, the Prussian Minister of Police, whose nephew, Captain Potzdorf, occupies the filial place next to the old man. Redmond pretends great loyalty to the Prussian government, hoping to win the approval of the men who deprived him of his freedom. He stands before the Chevalier, posing as a Hungarian servant. Unlike Mr. Brady and Herr von Potzdorf, the Chevalier sits alone, unaccompanied by any filial figures; and, also unlike the other men, the Chevalier looks at the young man standing before him and accepts him, whereupon Redmond tearfully confesses the entire plot, joining the old man on whom he has been sent to spy. The narrator prefaced this startling act with some facile and contradictory explanations, failing to perceive the real cause of Redmond's emotional, unpredictable act: for Redmond, the fatherless outcast, finds his father in that sedentary outlaw.

Now he sees another such figure, but no longer feels impelled to present himself as a son, for his "father" sits beside him. The time has come for Redmond Barry to become Barry Lyndon: self-begotten, a father in his own right. The Chevalier has ceased to be necessary; he will stand at Barry's wedding, then disappear. And now the old man in the chair is not to be embraced, but cast aside. Redmond longed to be a filial figure at the side of such a man; now Barry wants to be in that man's place: "He wants to fill *my shoes*!" shouts Sir Charles to his companions at the card table when, a few scenes later, Redmond stands before him, goading the invalid with a pose of innocence.

Redmond's attraction to Lady Lyndon, however, is not merely a consequence of oedipal aggression. There is a sympathy between this Irish outcast and the aristocratic object of his love. They seem bound together by silence. Intimacy and performance are at odds throughout *Barry Lyndon*. Quin and Nora perform for each other, delivering conventional remarks that take the place of affection. Redmond always finds it necessary to wear a mask in order to win acceptance, and yet no real intimacy is possible as long as the mask fulfills its mediating function. What little we see of Redmond's courtship suggests an attraction based on the freedom to enjoy a quiet interaction, a relationship absolved from the obligations of disguise.

Nevertheless, there are insurmountable differences between these representatives of opposed nations and social classes; primal needs and vague temperamental affinities will not necessarily ensure mutual esteem. Immediately after their wedding, Redmond and his wife ride to Castle Hackton in a coach. Redmond placidly draws on a fine pipe, filling the carriage with smoke. Lady Lyndon blinks, tries to wave the smoke away, then asks her husband to stop for awhile. He persists, and she asks again. He draws deeply, blows the smoke in her face, laughs gently, kisses her, and then keeps smoking.

Although considerably less offensive than the event described by Thackeray's narrator,[11] this is an upsetting moment. And the effect is compounded by Bullingdon, who, sitting with Runt in a separate coach, disparages his new father: "He seems to me to be little more than a common opportunist. I don't believe he loves my mother at all. And it hurts me very much to see her make such a fool of herself." Kubrick cuts to a close-up of the couple's newborn baby, then zooms slowly back to reveal the mother and father grouped lovingly around the child. Their closeness suggests that

Bryan's birth has introduced a new intimacy into their relationship. But Kubrick then complicates this conclusion by cutting to a whore-house where Barry sits embracing two prostitutes, kissing each of them hungrily. Kubrick continues to zoom back from this action, having cut from family to bordello in mid-zoom: the continuous movement suggests that Barry's domestic happiness and passionate infidelity are expressions of the same urge.

Barry craves the whole world for a family; his warmth denies the meaning of propriety, and so he seeks immediate closeness everywhere. Because he desires intimacy rather than pleasure, his encounters with women generate a familial aura. At supper with Lischen and her child, he discovers a momentary family; and a furtive tryst with one of his wife's maids seems more domestic than lewd: he holds the girl in a close, protective embrace as Bryan's baby carriage stands behind him.

Lady Lyndon, out walking with Bullingdon and Runt, sees this happen; Bullingdon consolingly takes her hand, and they return home, but not before Barry sees that his lapse has been discovered. Some time later, he comes into his wife's room to apologize. Lady Lyndon sits in a tub, grieving over her rejection. Barry stands before her; "I'm sorry," is all he says, a tender, unadorned admission. She takes his hand as if in forgiveness; he bends to her, thus conquering the distance between them. They kiss. The moment recalls and redeems the first scene with Nora, when that cold cousin, dissatisfied with Redmond's unexciting display, bent to kiss him after calling him a liar.[12] Lady Lyndon's acceptance of her erring husband is complete: she loves him as a mother loves her son, an equation given subtle pictorial support by her apparel. The cap she wears in her bath recalls the bonnet Mrs. Barry wore the day she kissed young Redmond goodbye.[13]

This marriage is a complex union, charged with intimacy, fraught with oedipal meanings, complicated by incompatibility. It is ambiguous. The narrator reduces it to a picaresque adventure. When Redmond first sees Lady Lyndon, the narrator implies that Redmond's motives are purely materialistic. Over the images of the Lyndon family's promenade and Redmond's fascinated gaze, the narrator recites a list of Lady Lyndon's titles and holdings, and alludes to Sir Charles' poor health, suggesting that the woman's pedigree and imminent widowhood were all that Redmond cared for. These insinuations are grossly misleading. Redmond cannot know, when he first sees this woman, the facts which the narrator recounts. And surely the hero, a professional gambler who has visited all the courts of Europe, has observed a great number of wealthy women more easily attainable than Lady Lyndon.

Similarly, after the smoking incident, the narrator makes a claim that only corroborates our unpleasant first impression: Lady Lyndon would soon mean no more to her husband "than the elegant carpets and fixtures which would form the pleasant background of his existence." At the time, this seems a safe prediction, but it assumes that no change can occur with the passage of time, and that Barry's playful insolence reflects nothing more than contempt. The narrator's claim agrees with Bullingdon's interpretation of his stepfather's motives, but it is irrelevant to the development of the marriage as it is presented on the screen. The narrator says nothing of Barry's apology because it is an intimate expression of complex feeling, inapplicable to the narrator's cynical reading. The viewer who fails to watch carefully, with an open mind, will understand no more than Bullingdon does. For that bitter son never outgrows his early antagonism. His first impression of "a common opportunist" becomes a disastrous *idée fixe* that stunts and sours his maturity.

One day he refuses to give Barry a kiss. In reply to his mother's order that he kiss his father, he says coolly: "My father was Sir Charles Lyndon." Barry whips the boy, and promises further punishment of any further intractableness. But the boy remains intractable all his life. Kubrick cuts from the chastisement to a close-up of the adult Bullingdon, sitting at his mother's feet, holding her hand, watching a magic show arranged for Bryan's birthday. Bullingdon was a grave and handsome child; as a grown-up, he is gawky and sallow, wearing a constant expression of truculent anxiety. On one level, he is his stepfather's nagging double, troubling Barry's life as an emanation of fatherlessness. Seen another way, he is a superficial viewer, resolute in the certainty of his cruel interpretation of events. It is to the likes of him that the narrator directs his confident appraisals.

IV. REPORT AND EVENT

Kubrick's changes in Thackeray's plot enhance the protagonist's enigmatic quality by making him a passive figure, one whose actions do not illuminate his inner life. Redmond Barry leads a sad existence in a sad world: Kubrick's style conveys this melancholy in a way that "fascinates the beholder," whereas the narrator only encourages the beholder to form opinions. The style and the narrative framework are at variance.

This tension between report and event dramatizes the difference between the literary and cinematic modes. Cinema is the only art form that exists in space and time simultaneously; unlike the novel, it is dynamic, it cannot be stopped. In reading, we can slow down, speed up, flip ahead, pause to reflect. But cinema is ongoing. The viewer's reflective pauses interrupt his experience of what is happening before him. Whenever the narrator intrudes to interpret or predict, he mimics the reader's reflective pauses; once we recognize the inappropriateness of the narrator's responses, we can begin to stop bringing to bear on the film experience a literary habit of mind.

Words and images have an uneasy relationship. When the narrator's authoritative voice cuts across the action, we stop watching insofar as we think about his remarks. The brief retirement within that succeeds the contemplation of language makes the fullest perception of film impossible. As we mull over the narrator's description of Lady Lyndon's pedigree, we forget to see what she looks like when Redmond first observes her.

This antagonism also works the other way. The cinematic event devaluates the importance of words. Many viewers, engrossed in the action, pay little attention to the commentary. And the more deeply engrossed the viewer becomes, the less vulnerable he becomes to the narrator's suasion. The narrator is discredited in two ways: temporally and contextually. When the narrator predicts Barry's indifference to his wife, he is proven wrong by the sequence of events. The passage of time renders the verbal report meaningless. When the narrator explains Redmond's breakdown before the Chevalier as the result of homesickness, the Chevalier being another Irishman, he is proven wrong by the image itself, considered in the context of "Ireland" as we remember it from the early part of the film. The Chevalier looks and sounds like no one from Redmond's Irish experience: he is outlandishly arrayed (the Irish were simply and monochromatically dressed), and he speaks German with a French rather than an Irish accent. The film's nuances temporally and contextually invalidate the crude fiction which the narrator uses to simplify every issue.

This fiction is an imposition of a conventional literary formula on the sensory plenitude of film. Kubrick exposes the paucity of the narrator's phrases by playing their inexhaustible referent against them. The viewer must make a choice between the large affective experience and the thin ironies of the disembodied voice. By exploiting the tension between event and report, Kubrick reveals the great possibilities of his art.

There is more than an aesthetic preference implicit in Kubrick's exaltation of cinema. Kubrick's vindication of cinematic plenitude entails a philosophical position on the effectiveness of language as a means of discovering truth. Kubrick's characters always fail to understand what they discuss: the scientists' bland observations never come to terms with the enigma at the heart of *2001;* for all his cultivated self-analysis, Humbert Humbert is powerless to curtail or satisfy his passion for Lolita; General Broulard in *Paths of Glory* and Alex in *A Clockwork Orange* speak voluminously about their actions without ever comprehending them; and the urbane narrator in *Barry Lyndon* reveals nothing but his own ignorance. These blind, voluble creatures unwittingly challenge the assumption that accurate language can ever be possible. They impose on baffling reality the simplistic formulas of their own discourse: they resemble the limited viewers whom Kubrick endeavors to educate. Kubrick uses the fullness of cinema to tease the viewer out of explication with "puzzles, enigmas, and allegories" that defeat the brief certitudes of speech.

Notes

1. Stanley Kubrick, quoted by Jon Hofsess in "How I Learned to Stop Worrying and Love 'Barry Lyndon,'" *The New York Times* (Jan. 5, 1976).
2. Quoted in Norman Kagan's *The Cinema of Stanley Kubrick* (New York, 1972), p. 145.
3. Quoted in Alexander Walker's *Stanley Kubrick Directs* (New York, 1971), p. 45.
4. Quoted by Hofsess in *The New York Times*.
5. Kubrick uses different kinds of voice-over narratives in four earlier features: *The Killing, Lolita, Dr. Strangelove,* and *A Clockwork Orange.*
6. Review of *Barry Lyndon* in the *Village Voice* (Dec. 29, 1975).
7. William Makepeace Thackeray, *The Luck of Barry Lyndon,* ed. Martin J. Anisman (New York, 1970), p. 308. Subsequent page references will be included in the text.
8. "Kubrick's Gilded Age," *The New Yorker* (Dec. 29, 1975), 50.
9. "A Box of Novels," written in February, 1844, for *Frasers,* and reprinted in Thackeray's *Works,* 24 vols. (London, 1886), XXIII, 49–50. For a similar analysis of the Irish, see the *Irish Sketch Book:*

> The delightful old gentleman who sang the song here mentioned could not help talking of the Temperance movement with a sort of regret, and said that all the fun had gone out of Ireland since Father Mathew banished the whiskey from it. Indeed, any stranger going amongst the people can perceive that they are now anything but gay. I have seen a great number of crowds and meetings of people in all parts of Ireland, and found them all gloomy. There is nothing like the merry-making one reads of in the Irish novels.

Reprinted in Thackeray's *Works,* ed. Lady Richie, 26 vols. (London, 1911), XXIII, 70.
10. Quoted in Kagan, p. 80.
11. "The first days of a marriage are commonly very trying; and I have known couples, who lived together like turtle-doves for the rest of their lives, peck each other's eyes out almost during the honeymoon. I did not escape the common lot; in our journey westward my Lady Lyndon chose to quarrel with me because I pulled out a pipe of tobacco (the habit of smoking which I had acquired in Germany when a soldier in Bülow's, and could never give it over), and smoked it in the carriage; and also her ladyship chose to take umbrage both at Ilminster and Andover, because in the evenings when we lay there I chose to invite the landlords of the Bell and the Lion to crack a bottle with me. Lady Lyndon was a haughty woman, and I hate pride, and I promise you that in both instances I overcame this vice in her. On the third day of our journey I had her to light my pipe-match with her own hands, and made her deliver it to me with tears in her eyes; and at the Swan Inn at Exeter I had so completely subdued her, that she asked me humbly whether I would not wish the landlady as well as the host to step up to dinner with us" (302).
12. Having hidden a ribbon in her bodice, Nora commands Redmond to find it. He separates her clasped hands, sees that the ribbon is not there, and gives up. She guides his hand to the ribbon: "Why are you trembling?" she asks. "At the pleasure of finding the ribbon," he answers, pulling the prize from her dress. "You're a liar," she says, and then kisses him. Later, Potzdorf parodies this scene. Having determined that Redmond is an imposter, Potzdorf stands up from the table where he dines with Redmond at a German

officer's club. Redmond is dazed at the realization that he is being arrested, and protests that he is a British officer. "You are a liar!" shouts Potzdorf, towering over him.

13. There is a similar oedipal detail in the scene between Redmond and Lischen, who also wears a bonnet. Having found that her husband is away at war and that she is lonely, Redmond, sitting beside Lischen at the dinner table, bends and kisses her hand. This gesture and the placement of the two recalls Redmond's last moment with his mother: he sat to her right at a small table, and bent to kiss her hand after assuring her that he would be safe in Dublin. Lischen too has just expressed concern for his safety: "And it must be very danger for you, to be in the war."

The 1980s: The Shining *and* Full Metal Jacket

❖

Kubrick's Shining

RICHARD T. JAMESON

C amera comes in low over an immense Western lake, its destination apparently a small island at center that seems to consist of nothing but treetops. Draw nearer, then sweep over and pass the island, skewing slightly now in search of a central focus at the juncture of lake surface and the surrounding escarpment, glowing in J. M. W. Turner sunlight. Cut to God's-eye view of a yellow Volkswagen far below, winding up a mountain road through an infinite stand of tall pines and long, early-morning shadows; climbing for the top of the frame and gaining no ground. Subsequent cuts, angling us down nearer the horizontal trajectory of the car as it moves along the face of the mountainside. Thrilling near-lineup of camera vector and roadway, then the shot sheers off on a course all its own and a valley drops away beneath us. More cuts, more views, miles of terrain; bleak magnificence. Aerial approach to a snow-covered mountain crest and, below it, a vast resort hotel, The Overlook. Screen goes black.

Did Stanley Kubrick really say that *The Shining*, his film of Stephen King's novel, would be the scariest horror movie of all time? He shouldn't have. On one very important level, the remark may be true. But that isn't the first level people are going to consider (even though it's right there in front of us on the movie screen). What people hear when somebody drops

First published in *Film Comment*, (July-August 1980). Reprinted by permission. Copyright © 1980 Richard T. Jameson.

a catchphrase like "the scariest horror movie of all time" is: You joined the summer crowds flocking to *The Amityville Horror*, you writhed and jumped through *Alien*, you watched half of *Halloween* from behind your fingers, but you ain't seen nothing yet! And a response: OK, zap me, make me flinch, gross me out. And they find that, mostly, Kubrick's long, under-populated, deliberately paced telling of an unremarkable story with a *Twilight Zone* twist at the end doesn't do it for them—although it may do a lot of *other* things to them while they're waiting.

So Kubrick, who is celebrated for controlling the publicity for his films as closely as the various aspects of their creation, is largely to blame for the initial, strongly negative feedback to his movie. Maybe he didn't know, when *The Shining* started its way to the screen several years back, that the horror genre would be in full cry, the most marketable field in filmmaking, by the time his movie was ready for delivery. But he could have seen that, say, a year ago. And still he pressed on with the horror sales hook, counting on it—along with his own eminence—to fill theaters, and to pay off the $18 million cost of the most expensive Underground movie ever made.

The action of the film can be synopsized in terms that seem to fulfill the horror movie recipe. Jack Torrance (Jack Nicholson)—sometime school-teacher, shakily-ex alcoholic, and would-be writer—signs on as caretaker of this resort hotel in the Colorado Rockies, deserted and cut off from human contact five months of the year. Sharing the vigil will be his quiet-spoken, rather simple wife Wendy (Shelley Duvall) and their just-school-age son Danny (Danny Lloyd).

Danny secretly possesses the gift of "shining"—the ability to pick up psychic vibrations from past, present, and future, long-distance or closer-up. Before he ever gets to The Overlook, he is receiving messages from "Tony," the make-believe playmate who is Danny's way of accounting to himself for his special powers. The Overlook has framed its share of bad scenes since its construction in 1907, and more of the same—indeed, some of the same—seem to be in store for the Torrance family.

Jack has no acknowledged powers of shining, but he appears to be in tune with the hotel in his own way. Supposedly, he plans to take advan-tage of his undemanding work schedule as caretaker to get into "a big writing project" he has outlined, and periodically we see or hear him typ-ing away. But we also begin to get ample indication that he will follow in the footsteps of the previous caretaker, Grady, a steady-seeming fellow who chopped up his wife and daughters one winter's day and then blew his brains out.

This likelihood is apparent from the first. Among the prime sources of irritation to horror-zap buffs is that Kubrick (writing with novelist Diane Johnson) has thrown out most of Stephen King's ectoplasmic and other-wise preternatural inventions—most of the more outré ghosts, the demon-ic elevator, the deadly drainpipe, the sinister hedge animals (an insoluble special-effects problem?)—to concentrate on the three principal characters and The Overlook as a collection of abstract spaces. He has also—and not entirely for reasons of cinematic streamlining—dispensed with virtually all of Jack Torrance's troubled history, so that his "motivations" and the degree of his complicity with whatever forces inhabit the hotel become much more elusive. Neither is Torrance permitted a very traceable descent into madness—he simply arrives there. Moreover, Kubrick has decentralized Danny as psychic focus of the action and target of acquisition (because of his gift of shining) for the hotel's master demons, encouraged Jack Nicholson in the most outrageous displays of drooling mania, and directed Shelley Duvall so grotesquely that Wendy Torrance becomes nearly as much a case for treatment as her husband. He has, in short, deprived the audience of any real opportunity for identifying with his characters in their hour (rather, 146 minutes) of menace, thereby violating conventional theory on how to bring off a jolly good scareshow.

Now it can be told: *The Shining* is a horror movie only in the sense that all of Kubrick's mature work has been horror movies—films that constitute a Swiftian vision of inscrutable cosmic order, and of "the most pernicious race of little vermin that nature ever suffered to crawl upon the surface of the earth." The Stephen King origins and haunted-house conventions notwithstanding, the director is so little interested in the genre for its own sake that he hasn't even systematically subverted it so much as displaced it with a genre all his own. And why should this come as a surprise? Who bothers to characterize *Dr. Strangelove* as "an antiwar film," or sees merit in rating *2001: A Space Odyssey* as "an outer-space pic," or finds particular utility in considering *Barry Lyndon* as "a costume picture"? *The Shining* is "A Stanley Kubrick Film," and as such it makes impeccable—if also horrific—sense.

It seems poetically apt that, at the time Stanley Kubrick was describing arabesques round space stations and star corridors and the history of human consciousness in *Space Odyssey*, Michael Snow was making *Wavelength*, "the *Birth of a Nation* in Underground films" (Manny Farber's phrase). A 45–minute film "about" a loft, it consists of a single continuous zoom across 80 feet of horizontal space, beginning with a full view of the room and ending on a closeup of a photograph on the opposite wall. Actually, a dissolve is necessary to get to a second, very brief shot of the photo, which we didn't even recognize as a photo when the shot/film began: a wave about to break on the shore. Formal pun: Optically move down the length of a room to look at a picture of a wave (the dissolve enabling specific perception and "understanding" after the comprehensive inventory of the whole space)—and the name of this moving picture is *Wavelength*.

I've no doubt that Kubrick has seen *Wavelength*, and not just because his new film ends with a shot that moves down a corridor and into a photograph, after which we dissolve for still closer scrutiny of the photo's elements. After all, he appropriated the visionary techniques of Jordan Belson, another Underground filmmaker, for *2001*. And maybe the avoidance of orthodox motivational analysis in his treatment of characters has its analogue in Snow's cheeky rebuke to our susceptibility to melodrama in *Wavelength*, when a wounded man staggers into the empty loft, collapses on the floor, and is summarily lost sight of—and left unaccounted for—as the zoom penetrates deeper into the room-space, leaving him outside the frame of visibility.

To be sure, Kubrick is a track man rather than a zoom man. Indeed, his tracking—in this film, freed of all physical restraints thanks to the development of the Steadicam—has long since become notorious, if not infamous, among critic types: an obscurely embarrassing fetish. ("Of *course* there's a lot of tracking—he's Kubrick! So what else is new?") Nevertheless, the tracking in *The Shining* is consecrated to a good deal more than satisfying the director's lust for technology, or providing a grand tour of a Napoleonically lavish set. It personifies space, analyzes potentiality in spatial terms, maps the conditions of expectations within a neo-Gothic environment that is finite, however imposing its scale. And if this sounds like an arid exercise to pass off as a popular entertainment, consider that Kubrick twice provides the formal nudge of Roadrunner cartoons heard playing on a television offscreen somewhere. Tell a casual filmgoer that he's caught between comic and emotional hysteria because Wile E. Coyote's multifariously misfired stratagems describe a systematic reinterpretation of spatial and temporal possibility, the trading-off of kinetic and potential energy, and he'll think you're pulling his chain; but that's still why he's laughing.

The Steadicam sits low, mere inches off the floor behind Danny Torrance as he rides his tricycle round and round the ground floor of the hotel early in the film. We follow him for a complete circuit, incidentally getting our bearings on what's where in relation to what else (kitchen, office, lobby entrance, the Colorado Lounge where Jack does his writing). Kubrick gets away with this establishing tracking shot because even the most antifetishistic observer must find the technical achievement exhilarating, and also because the action is punctuated with one of those vivid, lushly particular moment-of-cinematic-discovery effects that has virtually an atavistic appeal: the clump-*whoosh*, clump-*whoosh* sound as the child trikes, with blithe relentlessness, across the polished floor and deep-pile carpet.

Yet even as we get off on this wonderful movement, we look for it to disclose more. Will the kid round a corner and run smack into a ghost? Every turn, every new avenue of perception, is approached with anticipation; and nothing happens. Anticipation, anticlimax, anticipation. It has a lot to do with the quality of the Torrances' lives.

For Jack Torrance's life has nowhere to go. The wrinkle in Kubrick's haunted-house concept is not that The Overlook Hotel, with its layer on layer of sordid, largely silly (in Kubrick's selection from King) atrocity, taints Jack—it is the setting he was born to occupy, the snow-walled zone in which he can achieve an apotheosis he is clearly unequipped to achieve in any other way. To be a writer, for instance, is not within Jack's grasp. It is sufficient self-justification that his former wage-earning job of school-teaching got in the way of his writing; or that his wife Wendy so little comprehends the reality of writing (she thinks he just needs to get into the habit of doing it every day) that he can stay points ahead simply by being more sophisticated on the subject than she. The Overlook's spaces mirror Jack's bankruptcy. The sterility of its vastness, the spaces that proliferate yet really connect with each other in a continuum that encloses rather than releases, frustrates rather than liberates—all this becomes an extension of his own barrenness of mind and spirit.

Those spaces draw Jack. Kubrick sees to it that they draw us as well. It's not merely a matter of corridors obsessively tracked. Virtually every shot in the film (whether the setting be The Overlook or not) is built around a central hole, a vacancy, a tear in the membrane of reality: a door that would lead us down another hallway, a panel of bright color that somehow seems more permeable than the surrounding dark tones, an infinite white glow behind a central closeup face, a mirror, a TV screen . . . a photograph. From the moment we lose the consoling sense of focus and destination supplied by that island picturesquely centered in the lake, we are careening through space.

There's a moment quite early in the Torrances' residency when Wendy and Danny go to explore the Overlook Maze, a carefully sculpted hedge as old, and very nearly as large, as the hotel itself. Kubrick cuts from them to Jack, drifting in an eerie lope through the hotel interior. He stops at a table bearing a scale model of the Maze outside. A low-angle shot of Jack registering bemused interest is followed by a downward gaze, absolutely perpendicular, at the Maze. This frame is pure geometry until we notice two figures (cartoonlike or real?) moving, and casting individual shadows, in the central aisle. The overhead view has been descending steadily (camera movement? zoom?) since the cut to it, and faintly, like mouse squeaks, we begin to pick up Wendy-and-Danny voices.

What is the scale here? Are we looking at the table model or the actual Maze? If the actual Maze, those figures are the real Wendy and Danny foreshortened from a great height, as in the film's opening aerial views; perhaps Kubrick has just reverted to his fond, God's-eye view that turns the world into a chessboard. If the scale model, then those figures are grotesque projections of Wendy and Danny—projected in Jack's imagination, or somehow appallingly duplicated in a demonic, child's-toy accessory of the hotel. Or is the actual Maze rightly enough, the real Wendy and

Danny diminished by distance, being seen by Jack in sympathetic phase with the hovering spirit of the "Overlook" itself? We can't be sure. Any or all of the above might be true (and the descending view never gets far enough to plug us back into life-sized visual relation to mother and son; that is achieved only by a cut back to them seen from normal eye level). We aren't sure where we stand in this game. And it won't be the last time.

In a moment of intense distraction sometime later, Jack lurches into the hotel bar, the Gold Room, and climbs onto a stool. The place is empty, not only of people (of course . . .) but also of booze, which the management always removes during the off-season to cut insurance costs. Still, it's the sort of space in which Jack used to find solace. And now, having awakened from a nightmare of Grady-like atrocity, and having been accused of hurting his son as he (inadvertently?) did once before, he sags with self-pity and sighs, "God, I'd give anything for a drink! Give my god-damned soul for just a glass of beer!"

Up to this point we have been observing Jack from a diagonal, behind the bar but some distance down its length. Now we cut to a position directly opposite him. He drags his hands down over his face and then peers straight at us. His face is brightly—too brightly—flooded by the warm glow of a lighting strip built right into the bar; and now the fluorescence is increased by a sudden, hail-fellow-well-met grin. "Why *hello*, Lloyd!" And Jack slides into a well-rehearsed litany of worldweary wisdom, a soliloquy pretending to be a monologue, delivered to a composite image of all the bartenders in his past. *We* have been cast as "Lloyd." The role is bizarre, but not intolerable. Then Kubrick reverse-cuts and there, where we figuratively stood, *is* Lloyd (Joseph Turkel).

Jack goes on talking; he isn't the least surprised that Lloyd is visible, for real, and pouring him a bourbon, as a matter of lovely fact. We are now the ones distracted. Here at last is an authentic Overlook ghost, vouchsafed to us ever so naturalistically (if eerily gilded by the lambency of the Gold Room) without benefit of any "shining" from Danny. Not only that: we have no way of knowing (and never will know) whether this is the first time in a month or more of occupancy at the hotel that Jack has seen Lloyd. Nor is there any consolation in the fact that, when Wendy arrives on the scene a moment later, neither Lloyd nor his bourbon is in evidence.

Kubrick makes limited, straightforward use of the standard reality/illusion device of mirrors in *The Shining*. But as narrative details, the bits and pieces of many possible Overlook stories, accumulate, and as the editorial design of the film becomes increasingly oblique and suggestive, more and more one feels trapped in an infinity of facing mirrors. Identity and reference are deliberately confused: Wendy comes to tell Jack, "There's a crazy woman in the hotel," and he giddily responds, "Are you out of your fucking mind?!" It is only the first tremor in an extraordinary concatenation that escalates toward the final crisis.

The brutalization of Danny (of which Jack had been accused) took place in the mysterious Room 237, whose vibrations had tempted the boy several times previously. We watched through his eyes as he passed through the door, but were spirited away by Kubrick's cutting to Wendy, who in turn led us to Jack in the throes of "the worst nightmare I've ever had," the gory murder of his family. Hence, though technically innocent, Jack has been formally implicated in whatever transpired in 237.

As Jack answers Wendy's summons to investigate the room, we suddenly find ourselves locked in on the compartmentalized logo of a television news program. A slow zoom-out, and we are in the Miami home of Dick Hallorann (Scatman Crothers), the Overlook's black cook, who also "shines," and who had earlier established rapport with Danny in one of the few sequences free (up to a crucial point) of the central-vacancy principle. Reverse-cut and zoom-in on Hallorann as he suddenly registers horror.

Cut to a closeup of Danny Torrance, shivering in a trance, a froth of spittle on his lips (as Jack had visibly drooled when coming out of his nightmare). Then the camera begins describing a subjective penetration of Room 237—Danny shining to Dick about his experience? Dick remembering an experience of his own in 237 (his fear of the room having been planted earlier)? Not until we see an adult Caucasian hand reaching out to push open the bathroom door can we be sure exactly what is happening.

Beyond the bathtub curtain, a hazy figure moves, then draws the curtain aside. A nude woman, young, lovely, but mannequinlike, looks across the room at the camera for a moment—and then we reverse-cut to Jack Torrance in the doorway. The young woman rises, steps from the bath, pauses. Cut again to Jack, who slowly begins to leer in anticipation and starts toward her. They embrace, kiss—and over her shoulder Jack beholds the reflection of a thick, ancient, partially decomposed hag in his arms. He backs away; the hag advances, cackling, arms extended. Intercut with this are images of the same old woman seen from above, lying dead in the tub, then beginning to stir to life. It is a perspective Jack never had, but presumably either Danny or Dick Hallorann did; a reality from the past (Danny's, Dick's, or one still more distant) is juxtaposed against the immediate reality of Jack's experiences in 237 at that moment. Who and which is where and when? And does it matter?

Jack Torrance returns from the encounter denying that there was anything to see in 237. Moreover, he seeks to placate Wendy with the resonant cliché, "I'm sure [Danny]'ll be himself again in the morning." (But he won't: he'll be "Tony.") Wendy isn't buying; she insists they get Danny out of the hotel. Threatened for the first time with separation from The Overlook, Jack explodes: "You've been fucking up my whole life! But you won't fuck this up!"

Storming off, Jack finds the hotel corridors strewn with balloons and confetti, and the sound of a '20s dance band floating on the air. A fluid lateral track brings him from the hallway into the Gold Room once more. The nightclub is full of subdued revelers in period dress. Jack passes among them, affecting unconcern about his caretaker togs, and adjusting his stride to approximate an elegant dance stroll. Good old Lloyd is on duty, there's bourbon for Jack's glass, and "the management" has given instructions that "Your money is no good here, Mr. Torrance." Jack, though unremarked by the assembly as he has surely been unremarked through life, will momentarily be assured: "You're the only one that matters."

But *The Shining* is something much more complex than an exercise in solipsism. Lloyd's respectful salute upon both of Jack's visits—"What will it be, Mr. Torrance?"—is tinged with quiet irony. And Jack, far from being able to join the party, is instead shunted off from it: a collision with the waiter, a spilled drink, and his and the camera's course is deflected into . . . another powder room.

As he has so often played hyperkinetic sequences off against grindingly slow ones, here Kubrick condemns Jack to a long, maddeningly static and formalized talk scene—off the back hall of life, as it were, like the seedy servants'-quarters he is given to occupy in this luxury hotel—while the music and the crowd murmur on the other side of the red, red wall. It is a conversation that self-destructs in its logic: the waiter, Jack's interlocutor, is none other than Mr. Grady (Philip Stone), the former caretaker, who in short order assures Jack 1) that he has never seen him before, 2) that he himself has no memory of ever having been the caretaker, 3) that Jack has *always* been the caretaker—"I should know, sir, I have always been here"—and 4) that he indeed had to "correct" his family when they interfered with his caretaking!

Roles shift in other ways: Grady is the unctuous servant deferring to his superior at the same time he becomes the steely master of the scene and issues the Overlook's definitive warning that Jack is now expected to "correct" his own family. He even introduces Jack to the quaint snobbery of his anachronistic, English-accented cultural frame: Danny has tried to bring "an outside party, a *nigger*, a nigger *cook*" into the action; and Jack repeats "A '*nigger*'?" (a superb reading by Nicholson) in a tone that suggests he is not used to considering negritude an offense, is on the verge of disbelieving laughter, and yet is also fascinated by the new ripple of self-congratulating possibility here. Whose sensibility is in charge? What role does Jack play in the Overlook narrative that would have Grady as its center? Indeed, how many of those other guests out in the Gold Room are "the only ones that matter" in *their* scenarios—cut off from Jack and from us the way the promising panoply of possibilities in a dream are lost when we detour into a peripheral line of development that never carries us back to the main scene?

Surely this distraction of the self is Hell, not the seamy, vicious gestures by which the lost soul expresses its violence. Jack Torrance is presented with an oneiric environment in which only he matters—and then he doesn't matter at all. This is the final vacancy. This is the bankrupt script. This is the horror that we feel when Wendy Torrance, come to look for her husband in his writing den, at last manages to see the Overlook manuscript, the outpourings of his creativity: the endless reiteration, in myriad configurations, of the same formulaic line, the same lyric bad joke—"All work and no play makes Jack a dull boy." Jack the dull boy becomes Jack the bright boy when, having done murder at last, he rises into a previously neutral frame: this time the vacancy is fulfilled in his wide, white, shining face.

Has there ever been a more perverse feature film than *The Shining* in general release? No one but Kubrick could have, would have, made it. Certainly no one but Kubrick could come as close to getting away with it. And it is impossible to suggest another contemporary star besides Jack Nicholson who could have served to hold its ferocious strategies together. Both director and star have been criticized for showcasing a mugging, transparently implausible geek performance. Transparent is the operative word. The devastating subtlety of Nicholson's Torrance lies in its obviousness. We watch Jack Nicholson—and we *will* watch Jack Nicholson, note every raised eyebrow, every mongrel twitch of limb—from the fatuous, blatantly phony man-of-the-worldliness and patronizing deference in the opening interview scene (Barry Nelson—a Kubrick casting coup—as the Overlook manager), through the smarmy tolerance of Wendy's naïveté, to the raging, aggressively self-defensive rationalizations of his contractual eminence in the Overlook establishment. Scarcely a reviewer has failed to sneer that Nicholson has regressed to playing AIP mad scenes—but that's *it*, that's what works: Nicholson the Roger Corman flake become Nicholson the easy-riding superstar, Bad-Ass Buddusky, J.J. Gittes, R.P. McMurphy, super-hip, so sardonically self-aware that he cuts through the garden variety of cynical Hollywood corruption like a laser, and lays back bored.

Jack Nicholson plays Jack Nicholson playing Jack Torrance playing Jack Torrance as King of the Mountain. Everything Jack Torrance says in the extremity of his derangement is pixillated in the viciousness of its banality ("Heeeeeeere's *Johnny!*"); his loathsome bum jokes are gauntlets flung in the face of his significant others, his family, his audience—and they are loathsome most of all because they rebound on him, because he tells them badly as he played the furtive madman badly. But not Jack Nicholson. Nicholson plays the badman badly *brilliantly*.

And Kubrick, the king of his own cinematic mountain, the lone, hush-hush contriver of Skinner boxes for the contemplation of his fellow creatures, or his idea of them? Kubrick flings the stingingest gauntlet of them all. He makes a horror movie that isn't a horror movie, that the audience has to get into and finish for him.

The Maze: shivers of goosepimply expectation from the audience. But the Maze is quite benign. Indeed, Danny Torrance knows it like his own hand. Danny the Kubrick Child gets free of bathrooms, slides magically down a personal snowhill, leads the Daddy Monster a merry chase through that Maze. And the Maze, hole after hole opening before us as the Steadicam rushes down tunnel after tunnel, is not a trap but an escape hatch. Child's play: Danny backs up in his own footsteps in the snow, nobody else's; but Stanley Kubrick will not permit the viewer to share in the reversing of relentless tracks.

Danny and Wendy will escape, but we stay behind with the monster of banality. We track into the frozen moment of time in a film where time, finally, is as abstract and terrible as space. Once a Kubrick monster threw a bone into the air and became man; now the man regresses to monster, grunting, incapable finally of even pronouncing its own bad jokes. Illumination is poisonous: we cannot learn: "we have always been here." The hole—the photograph that the last track penetrates—is the screen. The face grinning imbecilically out at us is our own. Shining.

The Overlook Hotel

PAUL MAYERSBERG

Jack Torrance applies for the job as caretaker at the Overlook Hotel high in the Colorado Rockies during the winter months. Jack is warned that a man can get very lonely up there. He laughs it off. He is also told, if not actually warned, of a murder by a previous winter caretaker, Mr Grady, who apparently went mad and killed his wife and daughters with an axe. Jack smiles and says that nothing like that will happen to him.

What follows when Jack brings his wife, Wendy, and his small son, Danny, to The Overlook, is not the unfolding of a narrative so much as a series of glimpses into the real and imagined lives of Jack, Wendy and Danny. And also the lives of previous inhabitants of the hotel. A sequence of events suggests that Jack Torrance is going mad. But this is not quite true. Jack Torrance is crazy by the time he gets to the hotel. He is crazy for choosing the caretaker's job. Like an updated Henry James story, *The Shining* depicts a state of mind in which 'the story' is as much a figment of the character's imagination as it is of ours.

Events that seem to take place in the present may be re-enactments or simply memories of the past. To take *The Shining* at its face value is a mistake. It has no face, only masks, and it has no value, only implications. *The Shining* belongs firmly in the tradition of *The Turn of the Screw* and *The Beast in the Jungle*. If the setting of the film had been an hotel in Yorkshire or a deserted winter retreat in Maine, the nature of the piece would be even more apparent.

The film opens with an extraordinary shot. An island, apparently in the middle of a lake or a river, seems to be moving towards us, floating on the surface, perhaps driven by an unseen machinery. It is an optical effect. In fact the lake is so still that the camera moving towards the island makes it look as if the island itself is moving. This unsettling image sets the tone of the film. The following sequence of aerial shots, tracking Jack's car up into the snowy Rockies, is equally disorienting. At one point the camera sweeps away from the road, literally over the edge of the mountain. At precisely that moment the main title of the film appears, just when we are lost over the edge.

Over the edge, and over the top is Jack Nicholson's performance as Jack Torrance. But not really. Shelley Duvall's performance as Wendy Torrance, like Nicholson's, shows very little true development. This is not an oversight on the part of the director or actors. Jack and Wendy arrive at the

First published in *Sight and Sound* (Spring 1972): 62–66. Reprinted by permission.

Overlook Hotel with their personalities fully formed. They are like two characters picked off park benches. One look at them and you know they're nuts. Pinter's plays are peopled with similar caretakers.

The Shining is not about internal character development. It questions the extent to which a character shapes his environment or to which the environment shapes him. Does the place drive you crazy or are you crazy to live in the place? Are these people ghosts already dead, having been driven to crazy deaths? Or are they ordinary folk infected by the frightening past of the monster hotel?

Jack claims to be a writer. To be a writer is a way of escaping mundane reality. He wants to write a project, not a book. His life seems to have amounted to nothing. He's a modern man. People turn to writing as they turn to astrology when they don't know where they are going. Jack is deeply frustrated. He is obviously intelligent, some of his phrases are quite vivid, his silences are either empty or profound. When it comes to the act of writing he has no discipline. This is a reflection of his past; he clearly could never stick at any job. His writing project is vague, that is to say he has no idea what to write about.

In the past he has turned to drink. The hotel is dry. Jack's visits to the bar and his conversations with the ghostly barman are banal. Jack is a lost soul. When he orders the first drink of the day it's 'The hair of the dog that bit me.' He is doomed to repeat himself. 'I'd give my soul for a drink,' he says. And so he does. Then he confesses his life as drunks confess to their barmen. It seems that in a fit of drunken anger Jack has beaten his young son, Danny. It is obvious that he will do it again. The answer to a drink is another drink.

Jack Nicholson's performance is a splendidly Gothic reworking of Ray Milland's in *The Lost Weekend.* All alcoholics see things that aren't there. They say things they don't mean. They become people they are not. At least on the face of it. Perhaps, though, alcohol is a way of becoming the man you think you ought to have been.

In the loneliness of the Overlook Hotel Jack Torrance becomes an earlier inhabitant of the place. But not exactly. Grady, the earlier caretaker, killed his daughters and wife with an axe and shot himself. When Grady 'visits' Jack, 'accidentally' spilling a drink over the revenant, he takes him to the men's room, a blood red airport lounge. Grady goads Jack, as the new caretaker, to kill Wendy and Danny in the correct Overlook manner, that's to say with an axe. Jack reasons with himself that this must be the correct procedure. His contemporary frustration must be answered with tradition. Later, Jack, ever conventional, gets a fireman's axe and goes about his business. But Jack does not succeed and nor does he shoot himself as Grady did.

So the parallel with the past, real or imagined, is deliberately inexact. Why? Because the world has changed. This is the comment of *The Shining* on the facile convention of horror writing and film-making. In most films the present reproduces exactly the past. But not in *The Shining*. As in life, things turn out quite differently in this horror story.

Jack never 'sees' Grady's two doll-like daughters and no one ever 'sees' Grady's wife. The daughters are 'given' to Danny, the little boy who has the shining, as 'friends' of his own age. The little girls beckon him and tease Danny in his psychic state. Like Danny, Jack absorbs from the hotel what is appropriate to his own age and his own life. Wendy sees nothing. She does not even understand until very late just how dangerous Jack is, when he actively attacks her, or just how psychic her son is until he writes the word 'Redrum' on the door of her bedroom knowing that when she wakes she will see it in the mirror as 'murder.'

Everyone has certain psychic powers. The limitations are within our own personalities. Even in a psychic sphere we see only what refers to us in our own situation. Only with difficulty can we see what is beyond us. Danny sees an elevator door leaking and then flooding with blood. This staggering image has no relation to any scene in the film. But why should it? Danny has had a glimpse of the future. The flooding of blood has yet to come. As everyone knows who has visited a clairvoyant, the past, the present and the future are often indistinguishable. We are impressed by observations about the past, but often mystified by por- tents of the future.

The Overlook Hotel will continue its life as a building after our charac- ters have left. The floating furniture in a sea of blood is a scene from the never-to-be-made *The Shining 2*.

The psychic powers of young Danny and of Hallorann, the black cook, who leaves the hotel at the start to go to his home in Florida, are genuine. The two recognise each other from the first. The act of recognition, the act of one person seeing in another what he understands, is crucial to our understanding of the characters in *The Shining*.

Danny has an imaginary friend called Tony. Tony is represented by Danny's index finger wiggling, like a seductive come-on. Tony also has a voice, which seems to come through Danny's mouth. The joking reference to *The Exorcist* is one of many in a film that satirises horror movies. Tony is the ventriloquist's dummy who may eventually come to control his young master in the manner of *Dead of Night*. Tony warns Danny and also entices him. Is Tony out to destroy Danny? We cannot tell.

In one scene, after Danny has gone into the forbidden room 237 and he appears like a ghost before his parents during a terrible row, it is never certain how Danny acquired the bruises on his neck and arms. Wendy blames Jack because Jack has already attacked his son. We blame whoever it was in room 237. Danny won't speak about it. Jack says, 'Maybe he did it to himself.' That is the least credible explanation but it is possible that Tony did it. Or do we do it all to ourselves in the end?

As Danny stands watching the terrible argument between his parents it is as if he is watching their first encounter, not the primal sexual scene, but the primal psychic scene. In any case, Danny is silent about his visions and adventures. He cannot express himself in words, perhaps because he is too young, perhaps because his experiences are non-verbal. Apart from Tony, the only person who understands Danny is Hallorann, two thousand miles away in Florida. When Danny becomes most frightened that his father will attack and perhaps kill him, Hallorann, in his strange, long apartment in Florida, shines it. Hallorann then flies back to Colorado and drives through the blizzard to get to the Overlook Hotel. His shining costs him his life.

It seems that Hallorann is impelled by his relationship with Danny. But there is another level to Hallorann's perceptions. He is presented from the start as an asexual Negro. He lives alone, but in his Florida apartment he has a photograph of a naked black girl on the wall facing his bed, and another nude over his bed. It so happens that the scene which drives Hallorann finally back to Colorado is not what happens to Danny in room 237, but what happens to Jack in 237 when he visits the room afterwards.

Forced by Wendy, Jack fearfully goes alone into the room. Its colours are ridiculously garish, dominated by a sensual purple. Jack goes into the bathroom. He becomes aware that behind the shower curtain in the bath is a figure. The figure pulls back the opaque curtain and stands up. It is a naked woman. She steps out of the bath. Jack smiles, no terror here, as the woman walks towards him and puts her arms round him. They kiss. As he pulls back from the embrace he sees that he has been clutching an old woman covered in marks that are a cross between leprosy and tattoos. The old woman laughs at him. Jack is horrified. A trick with time: somehow the old woman is still in the bath as Jack is embracing her across the room. When Wendy asks Jack about room 237, he replies that there was no one there.

This is the strangest scene in the film. It has no reference to earlier events, and it seems completely unconnected with any of the characters. Yet it serves as an important link between all the characters in this psychic drama. It would be wrong to insist on a single interpretation of this scene, but in looking at it it exposes the heart of Kubrick's method in the film.

First, it is a rewrite of the shower scene in *Psycho*. In *Psycho* it is the lady in the shower who is threatened by the monster outside. In *The Shining* this is reversed. Jack is the 'monster', scared by what might emerge from the shower behind the curtain. This reversal of well-known horror conventions is one of many in the film. Later there is a reference again to *Psycho* when Jack menaces Wendy by climbing up the stairs. It is Wendy who has the weapon in her hand, the baseball bat, but it is she who is backing away, frightened by the empty-handed Jack. Underlying many sequences in *The Shining* is a critique of the whole genre of horror movies. The character of Jack Torrance himself is presented as the innocent, not knowing what he is getting himself into, whereas he is in fact the threatening element.

Secondly, the woman turning from slim youth to grotesque age is perhaps symbolic of everyone's most feared destiny, growing old. To watch your own body over a period of years disintegrate before the mirror is an essential horror story for all of us. Fear of old age grips Jack Torrance by the throat as does fear of losing his mind. Growing old and losing your senses, time passing, is a frightening notion that is inescapable.

Thirdly, it is the only overtly sexual scene in the movie. *The Shining* is a strangely chaste horror story. Part of this comes from Jack's sexual indifference; he is always glancing at women, including his wife, but he never actually does anything to them. Lack of sexual drive is characteristic of a paranoid personality. The young naked woman also seems asexual. She looks like one of those models who pose in seedy lunchtime photographic clubs.

Fourthly, the marks on the old woman's body, which so repel Jack, are difficult to identify. When she rises out of the bath in a shot that seems to refer to Clouzot's *Les Diaboliques,* she seems diseased. Then the marks look as if they had been applied like paint. There is also a hint that this woman has come from another world or an earlier civilisation.

All these interpretations have a certain validity without getting near totally to describing the scene. It may come down to the simple fact that the scene in room 237 is no more nor less than a nightmare of its creator. But one of the extraordinary aspects of *The Shining* is the way the simplest events in bright light conjure dark fears, guesses and portents. The movie is constantly ironic, if not downright satirical. The humour of *The Shining* puts it close to *Lolita* and *Strangelove* in Kubrick's work. As in much of Hitchcock and Buñuel, and to some extent Polanski, there is an underlying crazy comedy which is also deadly serious.

The central horror of *The Shining* is family life. For a child there can be few characters more frightening than his angry father. Danny, despite his stoicism, is terrorised by his father. Wendy is terrorised by her violent husband. Jack is frustrated to the point of rejection and violent aggression towards his family. It is a nice picture of American home life.

The Shining, the least admired major American film in the past year, is an accidental but none the less effective reworking of *Kramer vs. Kramer,* one of the most admired films of the past year. Both treat the collapsing single child family. Kubrick makes no attempt to deal with this subject from the social point of view. The psychology is dealt with in broad strokes; the characters, with the exception of Danny, are grotesque masks. There are, of course, real people behind the masks, but who they are is like saying what will they become. The three people alone in the overlit Overlook Hotel are similar to the three characters in Sartre's play, *Huis*

Clos. They are in the hell of each other. Danny sees his father as an eye-rolling lunatic. Jack sees Wendy as a weak, whining housewife, and Wendy sees nothing. Until the end of the story she seems completely devoid of psychic power. It is almost as if *The Shining* is showing that bright people are more capable of understanding telepathically than less bright people.

The family hierarchy, Dad, Mom and kid, is very strong. The equivalent hierarchy in the Overlook Hotel itself is the idea of the maze in which they are lost, both inside and out. The more intelligent you are the easier it is for you to solve the puzzle of the maze. The only character who can get out of the maze is Danny. Not because of his psychic ability but because of his high intelligence. They seem to go together in Kubrick's behaviourist view. The maze is not treated in the manner of *Marienbad*. In *Marienbad* the labyrinth of the hotel is a philosophical question. It cannot be solved. It can only be apprehended and interpreted. In *The Shining* the maze is a Sunday morning puzzle, and the most intelligent member of the family will always come up with the correct solution first.

There is a sense in the Overlook Hotel that it represents the world after the bombs have gone off; the loneliness, the incredible store of food, ways to survive.

The Shining may be the first film of the post-nuclear age to come. A bizarre follow-up to *Strangelove*. The music of Penderecki, the *Dies Irae* of the Auschwitz Cantata, creates an exactly post-Apocalyptic tone. The music of Ligeti and Bartók is music for the world that followed the Second Vienna School of Strauss and Mahler. The Ligeti has a mocking tone as if laughing at all past music and at people with notions of fixed values. The Bartók is wonderfully lyrical, but who, among ordinary filmgoers, would hear the strong music of Béla Bartók and think instinctively that it is lyrical and dance-like? But there was a time when Beethoven's *Grosse Fuge* was considered unacceptable and esoteric by his own publisher.

The Shining has a lot in common with post-war music. It seems technically brilliant and yet fundamentally heartless. It seems deliberately clever and yet remains enigmatic. Kubrick has tried to bridge a gap which has occurred in the language of film. How can you express dissonance and fragmentation, the essential features of our present lives, in a manner which respects traditional harmonies? Can disorder ever be expressed in an orderly way? Kubrick has reached the limits of conservative film art in *The Shining*. It used to be thought that the antonym of art was nature. But this Shakespearian opposition is no longer true. Art and nature are both by definition devoted to order. The opposite of art is enigma.

The Shining is not an enigmatic film. It is actually about enigma. That is why Kubrick is instinctively drawn to technology in his work, camera technology in particular. The machine is better able to cope with enigma than the human hand. Most enigmatic paintings from Cimabue's Crucifix to de Chirico's piazzas somehow suggest the presence of a machine. *The Shining* is about this machine that cannot be seen. It is, if you like, the machine in the ghost.

Shining denotes the ability to communicate telepathically, to see backwards into the past and forwards into the future. *The Shining* is nothing more nor less than a metaphor for the cinema itself. Film has the shining. Danny is probably the director of the movie. He is certainly identified with the camera. The Steadicam tracking shots through the hotel corridors and then in the maze evoke the exhilaration of a small boy racing about on his tricycle. He imagines himself to be a machine.

In *The Shining,* Kubrick plays with the Steadicam like a toy. It is essentially childlike. He wants to find out all the things he can do with his latest acquisition. Danny's visions are represented in cuts, in montage, so the boy is not only the camera he is also the movieola. The director-child is seeing his own parents and the world around him. In a way the hotel becomes his doll's house, like the model in Albee's *Tiny Alice,* and his father and mother are turned into his neurotic children. If they go crazy from time to time he can still control them with his superior intelligence and visionary ability. Film, after all, is the art of seeing and showing from a fresh point of view. But the boy is not an artist. He is before art, and after it. Picasso said it took him ten years to draw like Raphael and a lifetime to draw like a child. There is the child in all of us. There is the artist in all of us, and to varying degrees we are all capable of shining.

If the cinema was born around 1900 then he is eighty years old today. *The Shining* reminds us how far the cinema has come and how much it has stayed the same. It shines bits of an enigmatic film future which in the last image turns out to be a still from the past. There is no immutable order of experience when the past becomes a picture of what might have been.

Photographing Stanley Kubrick's *The Shining:*
An Interview with John Alcott

HERB LIGHTMAN

QUESTION: *Starting from the beginning, can you tell me how much pre-production planning time you had for your assignment as Director of Photography on* THE SHINING?

ALCOTT: Stanley Kubrick gave me the book to read about ten months before we were to start shooting and, although I had several other shooting assignments in between, this gave me time to be constantly in touch with him and check on the situation regarding the set that was going to be built—whether it should contain ten windows or only five windows, whether the fireplace should be located in one part of the room or the staircase in another—which proved to be a great asset for me in developing a visual concept for the film. This kind of direct contact prevailed throughout pre-production and I would always make a point of visiting him whenever I was back in England in order to see how the set construction was progressing.

QUESTION: *Did you have a chance to study sketches or renderings of the sets before construction began?*

ALCOTT: What we did at the very beginning was to have all of the sets built in the form of cardboard models. They were painted in the same colors and had the same scenic decor as we intended to use in the film and I could actually light them. With this concept of using artfoam cardboard models I could light the set with ten windows and then with five windows and photograph it with my Nikon still camera, using the same angle we would use with our motion picture camera. That would give us some basic idea of how it was going to look on the screen. We went all the way through the film like that, even for the sets which were built perhaps two months after we started shooting. All of the major sets—the hotel lobby, the lounge, Jack's apartment, the ballroom and the maze—were built in model form first, so I was able to do some careful planning. By this time we were probably about four months from our starting date and I would make it a point to visit the sets at least once a week, even though I had other commitments. Meanwhile, my two gaffers, Lou Bogue and Larry Smith, were doing the enormous amount of wiring necessary for the sets.

Courtesy of *American Cinematographer.*

QUESTION: *Do I understand correctly that most of the lights used for the photography were actual practicals in the sets?*

ALCOTT: Yes, the lights were wired as actual practicals. They were part of the hotel. The gaffers started their work about four months prior to shooting because there was an awful lot of internal wiring to be done, and I would check at least once a week to make sure everything was going fine. They had to wire a great many wall brackets and chandeliers. For example, in the main lounge and the ballroom there were 25–light chandeliers which contained FEP 1000–watt, 240–volt lamps (the same lamps that are used in the Lowel-Lights). Each five of the lamps were connected to a 5 Kilowatt dimmer, so that I could adjust every chandelier to any setting I wished, and this was all done from a central control board outside the stage. The service corridors, which were outside the hotel lobby and the main lounge, were all lit with fluorescent tubes.

QUESTION: *Fluorescent lighting always presents its own special set of problems. How did you cope with those?*

ALCOTT: Because the humming of the fluorescent tubes does indeed create a problem, all of the controls and ballasts and transformers were taken outside into the corridors of the studio, so there was no sound problem whatsoever. But this called for another great wiring job, because every tube had to have two wires going up and two wires coming back again. However, at least we eliminated the humming. We had no color temperature problem because the fluorescent tubes we were using were the Warm White Deluxe Thorne tubes, the ones which I've found in all my tests that come closest to matching incandescent lighting at 3200° K. In America I use the General Electric equivalent of these tubes.

QUESTION: *You mentioned that the dimming of the practicals was controlled from a central board outside the stage. Can you tell me how this worked out during actual shooting?*

ALCOTT: They were all on dimmers on the board and I could control the whole situation by remote control through the use of a walkie-talkie. This was especially convenient for the Steadicam shots— and there were an awful lot of them. I could change the light settings of the chandeliers as the Steadicam was traveling about the set simply by talking to the control room. This happened in several instances and it was a great help.

QUESTION: *The main lounge of the Overlook Hotel, which was built inside a huge sound stage at EMI Studios in England, nevertheless had very large windows which seemed to face the outdoors and let in a great deal of diffused "exterior" light. Can you tell me how you achieved that lighting effect?*

ALCOTT: Creating that exterior lighting was quite a project. We had the Rosco people make up an 80– by 30–foot backing of one of the Rosco materials which had the diffusing quality of tracing paper. They welded together the sections of material to give us this complete one-piece backing. The set for the lounge had a kind of small terrace outside with trees behind it. Then came the backing, and behind the backing there were mounted 860 1000–watt, 110–volt Medium Flood PAR 64 lamps. That was a lot of lamps and a lot of light—and a lot of *heat!* I mean, you just couldn't walk from one end to the other between the lights and the backing. You just couldn't make it.

QUESTION: *How were the lights mounted?*

ALCOTT: They were mounted on 40–foot tubular scaffolding and they were all built upright and placed at two-foot intervals. Each lamp was on a pivoted ball-bearing mount and they were all linked together, so that I could vary the light from a control inside. For example, we could start the shot off with the Steadicam pointing in one direction. I could have the light pointing toward me and then, by the time the Steadicam had traveled through the service corridor and around the back of the set and come in again, I could have the lights coming back again. This was possible because all the poles were linked together with one rod. You just turned the handle and the whole bank turned together. I remember going to a meeting and saying to Stanley, "The ideal thing for me would be if the lamps were on ball-bearings." And he said, "Put them on ball-bearings. If it's going to work, do it." It gave us a terrific advantage, because I could very easily alter the direction of not just the whole bank of lights, but different poles and different parts of the backing, which, again, could turn in one piece. It was a great asset.

QUESTION: *Assuming that all of this was worked out well in advance of actual production, how did things change as you approached your shooting date?*

ALCOTT: What happened was that when we eventually got the sets built—and some of them were as much as eight weeks in building—I started pre-production full time. This was three to four weeks before we started shooting, which enabled me to basically light all the sets before the cameras rolled. What I did was something that I had never done before: I lit all the sets and shot all my tests with the Nikon camera. I found that I could get around much easier and quicker and I could shoot 36 tests on one roll of film. Whereas, if I'd had a crew and motion picture camera wandering around on sets, it would have taken a lot more time. I did this purely as a lighting test and I could shoot varied tests with the different lighting effects, different settings, less chandeliers, more chandeliers, some on, some off, and so on. I did this continuously with all the sets and I used to view the results the next day. If I didn't like something I could go back and decide on something else. By the time we actually started shooting the picture, virtually all of the sets were basically lit, so there was no kind of lighting that had to be done that hadn't been done beforehand. As I say, I had never worked this way before, but I found it a great help and it left me with much more time than I'd ever had before.

QUESTION: *Didn't having almost all of the sets built in advance also add up to a great advantage for you?*

ALCOTT: Yes, I was very lucky in that respect. On most pictures all of the sets are not built in advance. They are built, struck and built again. But during the entire filming the sets were up continuously. Therefore, it was simply a matter of going from one set to another.

QUESTION: *With so many sets up at one time, how did you keep track of your lighting logistics?*

ALCOTT: When I was about to do all of my tests, I had the Art Department make me plans of every set on foolscap-type sheets that I could file with all of the lights in the different positions. I could mark them down at the settings I established, so that when I came back to each set I would just give the setting plan to the control room and get them to make their settings accordingly. Then I would go around and check my measurements, because sometimes they weren't always true, but basically they were there and it just meant making a final adjustment here or there to get back to the same situation we had left about two weeks before. Working in that way, I found that I had to make a plan and I had one for probably every slate number I shot. I found it to be invaluable.

QUESTION: *How did your lighting plan work with the Steadicam shots?*

ALCOTT: Because most of the lighting was done within the set itself, using the practicals, if the chandeliers and light brackets were behind us, I would turn them up to a higher light level than the ones that I was photographing within the view of the camera, then, by the time the Steadicam had come around, I'd have changed the setting, reversed the whole situation. This had to be down on the plan, as well, depending upon whether we were going to come back and intercut something or pick it up somewhere. For example, we had problems with shooting all of young Danny's scenes, because he was only allowed to shoot 40 days out of the whole year. His time was from nine in the morning until four in the afternoon, and if his time ran out we would suddenly have to abandon his shooting and go on to something else. We would come back to it maybe not even the next day. It might be the next week, because it would have been silly to come back and pick up just that one scene and then lose a day of his shooting time.

QUESTION: *I noticed when I visited the ballroom set at EMI Studios that the walls were covered mainly with a gold metallic material and the lighting seemed to be almost entirely indirect. Could you tell me about that lighting?*

ALCOTT: There were three troughs on either side of the ballroom and in each trough there were 150 100–watt domestic light bulbs. I had those on dimmers, as well, and, again, they were operated from the control room. They were on a 240–volt system, but most of the time I had them dimmed down to 60 or 70 volts, which threw a kind of golden glow and that's the kind of light I used for the sequence when Jack comes into the ballroom and it's all back in the 1921 period. The bar was translucent glass and the back of the bar was lit by 100–watt bulbs which were banked in boxes of 25 to each panel. The band was lit in a special way. For each person playing an instrument I used one Lowel-Light, just to pinpoint them out. In that set I had to rig the chandeliers up high because they reflected back so much from the mirrored surfaces of the walls that, at certain points, they looked unattractive. There were other times when they became very attractive, so I had to make up my mind that in certain scenes they would be on and in other scenes they would be off.

QUESTION: *Most of the sets you have discussed have been the huge public rooms of the hotel. What about the smaller sets—Jack's apartment, for example?*

ALCOTT: Jack's apartment was lit, again, by fluorescent tubes, the same tubes I mentioned before. And inside all the practicals were wired, again, with the FEP 1000–watt, 240–volt lamps. So basically the rooms of this set, too, were lit by means of the actual practicals, supplemented sometimes with fill. I used to hang a little fill light behind the archway into the bedroom and the small lounge that they had. But basically the illumination came from a top hanging light and the table lamps by the bed and dressing table were actually the practical lights themselves. Again, outside the windows we had a translucent backing with the 1000–watt lamps behind it, but it was a much smaller backing than the other one— only about 20 by 30 feet.

QUESTION: *What about the lighting of the maze?*

ALCOTT: The maze was lit by the type of lights that are used for floodlighting in garden centers and that sort of thing. They were 1500–watt floods made by Thorne. That sequence was lit solely with those lights, with just a fill running behind. Garrett Brown did all the Steadicam work for us, including all that running around in the maze. I basically tried to place the lights so that everything was always in-picture that gave us a highlight, something which would expose the film properly. Of course, we had the snow all over the maze, which was very bright and gave us a lot of luminosity. I was usually stopped down to T/5.6, and even sometimes T/8 in that maze—and that was normal development. The whole picture was normally developed, which is the first time I've shot a picture with normal development throughout. We wanted depth of field, so it might have seemed logical to force the development, but we had so much light coming through the windows from the backing that I could work at a T/2.8 to T/4 aperture most of the time and that gave us sufficient depth. We weren't quite sure at the time whether it would be a good idea to force the development because of the new stock, but we had made one or two tests and the forcing had added more contrast. So we went ahead with normal development and it worked out just fine.

QUESTION: *Can you comment a bit on the use of the Steadicam?*

ALCOTT: As I've said, Garrett Brown did all of the work with the Steadicam and it was used a great deal on this picture. It was used for most of the traveling shots you see when the Torrances are being shown around the hotel. For me, seeing the picture all cut together emphasized what a wonderful piece of equipment it is to use in that type of setting. Garrett is the ideal operator for it. Being such a tall man, he can go anywhere, and he seems to be so fit. It's quite incredible. He really is a perfectionist at the art of the Steadicam and I have great admiration for his work. This particular film is a great showcase for the device because the story takes place in a very large hotel and one could only explain it being large and complex by traveling through it, and one could only travel through it the way we did by using the Steadicam. Otherwise, I don't know how we would have done it.

QUESTION: *I would say that the kitchen set alone presented a kind of obstacle course for the Steadicam. Isn't that so?*

ALCOTT: Yes, the kitchen set was a maze in itself with all that equipment. When one travels through the kitchen in the first sequence, there are twistings and turnings in and out amongst the ovens and the kitchen furniture—a kind of backtracking. I don't think you could find a dolly that could do that. The Steadicam was an ideal piece of equipment in that instance. We used it often in shots where you would have to start off from a very difficult position and continue on to where you perhaps could use a dolly, but Garrett would end up on a composition as precise as anyone could have done it with a dolly and a Worran head. I must say it was terrific.

QUESTION: *How were the shots done of the boy running around in his little racing car?*

ALCOTT: That was the Steadicam, with Garrett operating it from a wheelchair made up for use on *A Clockwork Orange*. It has the same basic construction as a wheelchair, but it was designed so

266 ◆ HERB LIGHTMAN

that one could place different platforms on it, lie on it, stand up on it, sit on it and do all types of things while it was traveling around the hotel.

QUESTION: *The exterior sets, including the rear facade, were built on the back lot at EMI Studios. Can you tell me what kind of lighting was used for the night shots?*

ALCOTT: The lights in the parking lot on the outside of the hotel were ordinary streetlight-type fittings with 2000–watt quartz bulbs in them. They were far too bright for the camera, but the heat was too intense for any gelatine to take them down, so I had some perforated metal which I could use on the camera side of the lights. If there were a moving camera shot that showed two sides of the light, I would use the perforated metal sheet on two sides of the light. It acted actually as a neutral density barrier, because although the light flared out, it flared out around the metal sheet. In other words, the many holes were flaring into one another and becoming just one bright light—but not as bright as it would have been without the shield. The streetlights that did not show on-camera were left free of the perforated metal shields in order to provide maximum set illumination. They were used for all the exterior lighting except for the lights on the outside of the hotel. I wanted to light the hotel so that it looked weird and mysterious, but, at the same time, wasn't lit by an unknown source. So I imagined that the hotel would have floodlights on it, as most hotels do (especially at skiing resorts)—at the same time lighting it up, but not making it look too pretty. Then I also used smoke for the night exteriors, which again gave it a more mysterious look and softened the lights so that they weren't so contrasty. The result was a kind of glow that was in keeping with the film itself, and especially the attitude of the hotel, as well. Although I used smoke, the intention was not to produce the effect of fog, but of cloud.

QUESTION: *What kind of camera equipment did you use in photographing* THE SHINING?

ALCOTT: Again, on this picture, we used the Arriflex 35BL. We had one of them that was used solely for shooting as our main camera, and the other one was geared up for Garrett Brown to use on the Steadicam. He used that 35BL the whole time throughout the picture. The only time he used the Arriflex 2C was for the running shots in the maze. It was very difficult running in all that snow, which was actually a layer of salt and polystyrene about a foot deep. The Arri 2C made it much easier for him.

QUESTION: *What kinds of filters did you use in shooting* THE SHINING?

ALCOTT: I didn't use any filters on this film, because it was supposed to look different. It was supposed to have a hard look to it and it needed a lot of contrast. There was supposed to be no attractive softness about it. The daylight was soft, of course, and the windows just naturally flared a bit, but without the use of the low contrast filters which I'd used on previous productions. In the sequence where Shelley finds out that Jack has been typing not a story, but the same phrase over and over, it was supposed to be early morning and I wanted to create a kind mistiness to suggest the early morning effect. That was the only time I used smoke within the set, except for a very slight amount in the ballroom sequence where Jack goes in and finds the whole crowd there:

QUESTION: *Did you order corrected or one-light dailies on this film?*

ALCOTT: All the dailies were printed on one light, not so much because we didn't want them graded, but because I'd already decided during our testing period what type of printing lights I wanted. Therefore, I thought it best to stick to the one-light system, because then, if something was a bit off, I could tell whether it was anything to do with me. Most times in a situation where I am working on location, I like the laboratory to correct for me, because I'm usually working with mixed light or light from a source that is out of control altogether. In such a case I like to see how the laboratory handles it. But in a studio situation like this it was much better for me to have control over the laboratory and know that the printing lights that had been chosen were continued all the way through. Then, if something wasn't right, I could alter it the next day—two points here or two points there.

QUESTION: *What variations did you make in the color temperature of the light to enhance various moods of the film?*

ALCOTT: In the beginning of the film I used just the ordinary straight daylight system. I'm referring now to the 860 bulbs shining through the backing outside the windows. When the Torrances first arrived and checked into the hotel, the whole thing was lit that way, without any color filter whatsoever. Then, when it started to snow, I changed the whole lighting system to a full blue. I put a full blue on all the windows, and by that I mean that the gels were actually sandwiched in between two pieces of glass. So I had a double pane put on all the windows and that's why it wasn't just a simple thing to make the change. It took the construction people at least a day to change all those windows in that large lounge (and also in the lobby) to a full blue, but it created a cold daylight effect for the snow sequences and gave me a much better contrast between the warm light of the chandeliers and the cold light coming through the windows.

QUESTION: THE SHINING *is shot very straight. In other words, the visual treatment is devoid of all of the usual mysterioso effects that are conventionally used in horror films. That being the case, is there any instance in which you shot what might be termed a "special effect" in the camera?*

ALCOTT: There is a sequence looking down from the balcony with Jack at the typewriter and the fireplace in the shot. I wanted to get a full fire effect, a nice big glowing fire in the fireplace, but I didn't want to reduce the general lighting in any way because I needed the depth of field. So I shot the scene all the way through without the fire burning, then rewound the film, killed every light on the set, lit the fire, opened the lens up to T/1.4 and shot the fire by itself—which gave me a nice glowing fire. It was something I thought would be different to do and it was worth a try anyway. But I think that's really the only kind of "special effect" we did in the camera.

QUESTION: *Did you use any type of video assist on the cameras while photographing* THE SHINING?

ALCOTT: Both Arri 35BLs were fitted with video cameras which enabled us to watch the scenes as played. This was especially valuable with the Steadicam, because everybody was virtually in the picture and the only way to view the scene was from outside in the corridor somewhere. Without the video set-up it would have been impossible to see what you had until you actually saw the rushes. I found also that the device which Garrett Brown has on the Steadicam for stop and focus control is great. I especially found the stop control to be extremely valuable in cases where it was an advantage to change the stop within the scene. I found that it was very good to be able to hold the control and be away from the camera, but watch the picture on the TV monitor. Most of the time it is very difficult to know what the camera is viewing when it is panning or tilting especially. You have some idea, of course, but with the TV monitor in front of you it's easy to judge to the finest degree of stop control. I just hope that perhaps in the future all camera manufacturers will bear this in mind and incorporate it into their designs.

QUESTION: *Did you use any HMI lighting on this production?*

ALCOTT: I think once, in Danny's bedroom for a moonlight effect, but that was the only time. In fact, I haven't used HMIs an awful lot until this picture that I am doing now (FORT APACHE), but I must say that I find them very good. I think one has to be careful as to which make of lamp one chooses and which company one rents them from, because they have to be in tip-top condition. They've got to be maintained to their fullest. They're not like an ordinary light that you can hire out and switch on and as long as it comes on it's alright, because it isn't with an HMI. There are contacts and various other things that must be absolutely perfect, because if they are not, that's when flicker can occur without being the fault of the frequency. In other words, it's not always the frequency that gives the problem; it's the connections and the bad maintenance of the lamps. But I always carry a frequency meter with me anyway, as a safeguarding factor. I think a frequency meter is one of the most valuable things one can have these days if you are going into HMIs, or even if you are going into fluorescent light for lighting, because in the northern part of England, for instance, you will often get a very weird type of voltage and you'll never get rid of the flicker.

QUESTION: *From what you've told me, most of your actual photographic light came from the practicals built into the set. Would you say that you used that kind of light more on this film than on your other films?*

ALCOTT: When it came to sticking with the actual lights that were built into the set, the chandeliers and other practicals, the answer is that I did use such lighting in this film more than in anything I've done before, but I had to do this for a very special reason—and that was the Steadicam. Because of the Steadicam there was no way I could have used any floor lights. I couldn't have any ceiling lights because the hotel lounges, if you noticed, are built in such a way that they are fixed; they are solid; they are there for keeps. The hotel was actually built wall-to-wall. As you went out of a hotel door you went into the studio corridor; it was that close. At any rate, in most instances, the lighting was what existed within the actual setting. I would use the chandeliers as my overhead lighting when they weren't in the picture. In other words, I would use them as a supplementary light for the practicals which appeared within the scene. I'm speaking now of the wall brackets and the small chandeliers in the outer rooms of the main lounge.

QUESTION: *But as "real" as practical lighting is, we both know that, from the aesthetic standpoint, it's not always the best light with which to photograph a scene. That being the case, weren't there times when, to insure the quality of the image, you had to use extra units to supplement the existing practical lighting?*

ALCOTT: In instances where I could use additional light—for instance, under the table when Jack is on the floor groveling after he's had his nightmare—I did use additional lights. But these would be basically Lowel umbrellas with Lowel-Lights inside them, and I would supplement that with a full blue in order to get the same daylight effect. The fact is that under the table there was no light, no matter what I put through the chandeliers. Sometimes I would have to boost the daylight in instances where I needed the extra depth, as well. So the answer is that yes, I did use supplemental light in quite a few instances, when it was called for. By "called for" I mean if it was not possible to use the light existing within the set itself. But whenever possible I did use the existing fixtures for supplemental lighting. For example, if Shelley was talking to Jack in the mid part of the lounge, I would use a wall bracket with tracing paper to soften the light falling onto her and I would bring it up to give the required amount of exposurable light. All of our lights were on dimmers using increments from 1 to 10. If my general level were 4, I might bring the supplemental light up to 6 and then put on a quarter-orange or half-orange to keep the color temperature consistent.

QUESTION: *You mentioned before that in the ballroom set the chandeliers tended to pick up as reflections in the metallic gold walls. Did the metallic materials cause any other problems that you can recall?*

ALCOTT: No, not really. In fact, it rather added to the whole effect. It reflected my light, which gave the set an overall golden quality. If I was fortunate enough, in the position the camera was in, to have the chandeliers on without any reflection, then I was fortunate enough to have the light of the chandelier bouncing off the mirrored surface, giving me an overall fill. The six troughs I mentioned—three on either side—gave me an overall top fill for basically the whole set. The practical small brackets around the ballroom I kept at a very low level because, being right next to the reflective material, they tended to burn out. I didn't use them as a lighting source at all and they were much more effective as viewing practicals. On the dimmer scale of 1 to 10, the setting for those wall brackets was about 3. Each table had its own separate table light—an ordinary 25-watt bulb—but it was just enough, with the white tablecloth, to lend a luminosity to the features of the people seated around the table. That sequence had a period look to it—which, of course, it was meant to have.

QUESTION: *You said that you used a bit of smoke in there. Was that all it took? You didn't have to augment it with any fog filters?*

ALCOTT: No, just the smoke—and it was very, very light indeed. In fact, I tended to put it just in the background. You get to the point with smoke that no matter what you do in the foreground, it just never shows. So that's why I used it on virtually just the background half of the set. The light from the troughs gave it an overall glow which softened it, as well. Then, of course, there was the hard light at the bar coming from the cabinets behind the bartender. The bar was sort of a set of its own within a large set, but the hardness of that light made the rest of it look much softer, more of an illusion. Had there been no bar there at all it would have been flat and uninteresting. It needed that contrast in the foreground to give it the depth that it had.

QUESTION: *I gather from what you've told me that whenever you needed a cold look it was a matter of filtering tungsten with blue gels. Were there ever any times during the shooting when you lighted for daylight balance with arcs, using white carbons?*

ALCOTT: No, there was no time that arcs were used to create a daylight effect. The only time I used arcs was in the sequence where Shelley is running through the hotel just before she exits. She runs through the corridor into the lobby when she finds all the skeletons. I shot that with open arcs to get the very hard shadows which I found effective. And one other time, in the sequence where Scatman is phoning from his apartment in Florida, I used an open arc with a full blue filter to create a hard blue light, but that was intended more for a night effect. The only other light was the red practical burning in the background, which gave it a kind of separation.

QUESTION: *The long establishing shots of what was supposed to be the Overlook Hotel actually were scenes of a real hostelry [The Timberline Lodge, Mt. Hood National Forest, Oregon]. Did you have the benefit of seeing those shots from the actual location before you had to light the hotel exteriors built on the EMI back-lot?*

ALCOTT: Yes, plenty of time, and it was very helpful. I should like to comment on the wonderful sequence which Greg MacGillivray shot from the helicopter in the first sequence of the picture. It was a great introduction to the film and some of the most beautiful helicopter work I've ever seen.

QUESTION: *In working with Stanley Kubrick on* THE SHINING—*which marked the fourth feature that you've done with him—did you adopt any different method or approach to working together, or was it basically the same working pattern that you've sort of established over the years?*

ALCOTT: I think that, as time goes on, Stanley becomes more thorough, more exacting in his demands. I think that one has to go away after having done a film with him, gather knowledge, come back and try to put that knowledge together with his knowledge into another film. He is, as I've said before, very demanding. He demands perfection, but he will give you all the help you need if he thinks that whatever you want to do will accomplish the desired result. He will give you full power to do it—but, at the same time, it must work. Stanley is a great inspiration. He does inspire you. He's a director with a great visual eye.

QUESTION: *Did you have much opportunity to discuss with him the visual style he wanted for this particular vehicle?*

ALCOTT: He said he wanted it to have a different approach from that of previous films. He stated that he wanted to use the Steadicam extensively and very freely without having any lighting equipment in the scenes. In other words, he suggested that we let the practical lighting work for us without using any actual studio lights. It wasn't easy. In fact, at first it was quite worrying, because while I had visions of how it could work, I wasn't sure it would actually come into practice. Even though you might prelight certain pieces of sets and lighting models, you can't tell what is actually going to happen when you get artists in position. This you can never visualize until you are given a set-up, which causes you to light it. By then the sets have been built and it's too late to change much.

QUESTION: *How would you sum up the working rapport that has developed between you and Stanley Kubrick, having worked together on four features in succession?*

ALCOTT: I feel that when you're with Stanley the working relationship benefits from picture to picture. We've worked together since about 1965 and in working with him there is always a different outlook, a different idea: "Let's try something different. Is there any way we can do it differently? Is there any way we can make it much better than it was before?" I feel that when you have as much time as I had on THE SHINING to make sure the sets are right and that the Art Director is building them to your lighting design, as well as his own design, it is a great privilege. You don't have that privilege with someone who lacks the experience and the visual perception that Stanley has. He is willing to bend over backwards to give you something you may desire in the way of a new lighting technique and this is a great help. If you have somebody who is working that way it makes the job so much easier for you. I don't think there is anything really different that has developed in our working relationship. He may be more demanding than he was before, but that makes it very easy for you when you go on to your next picture. To use an analogy in reference to our British game of Cricket: It's like practicing with five wickets and playing three. You defend five and then when you come to defend three, it's much easier.

The Steadicam and "The Shining"

GARRETT BROWN

To date it cannot be said with complete conviction that the Steadicam has revolutionized the way films are shot. (Maybe it really should have slowly-moving parts underneath!) However, it certainly had a considerable effect on the way THE SHINING was shot. Many of Kubrick's tremendously convoluted sets were designed with the Steadicam's possibilities in mind and were not, therefore, necessarily provided with either flyaway walls or dolly-smooth floors. One set in particular, the giant Hedge Maze, could not have been photographed as Kubrick intended by any other means.

I worked on THE SHINING in England at the EMI Studios in Borehamwood for the better part of a year. I had daily opportunities to test the Steadicam and my operating against the most meticulous possible requirements as to framing accuracy, the ability to hit marks and precision repeatability. I began the picture with years of Steadicam use behind me and with the assumption that I could do with it whatever anyone could reasonably demand. I realized by the afternoon of the first day's work that here was a whole new ball game, and that the word "reasonable" was not in Kubrick's lexicon.

Opening day at the Steadicam Olympics consisted of thirty-or-so takes of an elaborate traveling shot in the lobby set, interspersed with ballockings for the air conditioning man (because it was 110 degrees in the artificial daylight produced by 700,000 watts of light outside the windows) and complaints about the quality of the remote TV image.

Although I had provided a crude video transmitter so that Kubrick could get an idea of the framing, I quickly realized that when Stanley said the crosshairs were to be on someone's *left* nostril, that no other nostril would do. And I further realized that the crudeness of the transmitted image simply prolonged the arguments as to the location of the dread cross-hairs. Had I known on that first day that we would still be debating questions of framing a year later, long after the air-conditioning worked, I might have wished to become an air-conditioning man or a caterer . . .

THE SETS

I first met Stanley Kubrick during FILM 77 in London when Ed DiGiulio, president of Cinema Products Corporation, and I took the latest

Courtesy of *American Cinematographer*.

model out to Borehamwood to demonstrate it. At this time, THE SHINING was in its early pre-production stages. Stanley had engaged Roy Walker to design the sets, and we provided them with some food for thought by going over the various maneuvers that were then possible and, at Kubrick's request, demonstrating the accuracy with which one could hit marks in order to pull focus in the neighborhood of T/1.4.

Throughout the following summer there were sporadic early morning phone calls from Kubrick and preliminary arrangements were made for my services, ostensibly to commence in December of 1978. In fact, the start date had been put back well into the spring when I was notified that I had won the Bert Easey Technical Award of the BSC. I decided to fly from Los Angeles to London to accept the award in person and to show Stanley some of our latest wrinkles. Cinema Products had just constructed the prototype of the new "Universal II—raised monitor" Steadicam and we had also devised the means to *suspend* the 35BL from the Steadicam platform, thereby permitting a whole new range of lens heights from about 18 inches to waist high. Kubrick seemed particularly pleased with the possibilities for low-lens shooting.

This time I was taken for a quick tour of the sets, including the monumental exterior set of the Overlook Hotel and the vast and intricate "Colorado Lounge" set with its interconnected corridors, stairs, and rooms on two levels. My excitement mounted as we progressed around corner after corner, each unexpected turn offering further possibilities for the Steadicam. Originally we had decided that I would rent some of the more exotic equipment to Kubrick and just come to England briefly to train an operator. However, as we continued, I became convinced that here was a unique opportunity for me. Kubrick wasn't just talking of stunt shots and staircases. He would use the Steadicam as it was intended to be used—as a tool which can help get the lens where it's wanted in space and time without the classic limitations of the dolly and crane.

The kitchen set was enormous, with aisles winding between stoves and storage racks. The apartment sets were beautifully narrow. Suite 237 was elegant and ominous. The Overlook Hotel itself became a maze; absurdly oversized quarters for the players, yet ultimately claustrophobic. Here were fabulous sets for the moving camera; we could travel unobtrusively from space to space or lurk in the shadows with a menacing presence.

I guess I wanted to be there myself because Kubrick is, let's face it, The Man. He is the one director working who commands absolute authority over his project from conception to release print. The ultimate technologist, but more, his technology serves a larger vision which is uniquely his own. He is a film-maker in the most pure sense of the word. I learned a great deal about the making of movies from simply being on hand for the stupefying number of discussions which sought to improve one aspect or another of the production.

PROGRESS

During the year of production which followed, the science of air-conditioning was reinvented and you can be certain that just about every other branch of human learning was at least reexamined insofar as it touched upon the doings in Borehamwood. Laboratory science, lighting, lenses, and the logistics of lunch—all were scrutinized daily. For example, the offending video transmitter was soon replaced by adapting Ron Collins' AC-operated unit into a much smaller DC version (which has been a mainstay of my Steadicam services ever since). I was determined to remain unencumbered by wires, so the propagation of the signal became the next drama.

Although Stanley knows an astonishing amount about an astonishing number of things, his grasp of antenna theory is weak. He is, however, a formidable opponent in an argument—with or without the facts—so some bizarre theorems were actually tested and a disturbing number of them actually worked. By switching to various antennas hidden behind the walls, we were finally able to provide Stanley with acceptable remote wireless video nearly anywhere within his sets. To annoy him we would indicate the forest of TV antennas aimed at the studio from suburban Borehamwood and imply that the TV signal was escaping the sound stage and being watched by a gaggle of "Monty Python" women every morning:

"Oooob, poor Mr. Brown! . . . That take seemed perfectly good to me!"

Somewhat later, our imitation ladies got even more sophisticated:

"Ooh, must be the 24mm Distagon!, see how it's vignetting in the viewfinder!"

The infant science of the Steadicam advanced during the year. With the expert assistance of Mick Mason and Harold Payne of Elstree Camera Hire, we constructed a number of new mounts to adapt the Steadicam to various wheeled conveyances. After one ride on the converted skateboard and one push on the custom sackbarrel, both went into the "Bin of Whims" never to be seen again. However, Ron Ford's elaborate motion picture wheelchair proved more enduring. We made the first prototype of the "Garfield Bracket" to adapt the Steadicam arm to a Mitchell mount on the wheelchair. This was also useful on the Elemack and we later made use of the Elemack leveling-head on the wheelchair.

On the theory that one should ride whenever possible in order to concentrate on operating and forget navigating, I promoted every opportunity to use the chair. In a number of instances it was the only way to get the lens right down to floor level.

I think that useful progress was made in the area of operating technique. I had a chance to refine my own abilities in the most direct possible way. By repetition! (With playback!) Stanley made a number of useful observations and speculations about the interaction of the human body with machine such as this. Just how good can it possibly be? How close to the exact repeatability of a dolly shot? More than most filmmakers he knows the limitations of the dolly, and when it was necessary to have phenomenally good track, he rebuilt an entire 300–foot plywood roadway three times to get it smoother. During one difficult shot, Kubrick said gloomily that the Steadicam would probably get the credit for all the dolly moves in the picture anyway!

Although he would admit that I could produce a printable take by any reasonable standard within the first few tries, Stanley would seldom respond with anything but derision until about take 14. He did not appear to be comfortable until we were well beyond take 20. Since the editing was to occur entirely after the filming of the production, he wanted at least two and preferably three perfect takes on each scene. Basically this was fine with me. Although most retakes were for other reasons, I could see a gradual improvement in my operating with each playback. I learned the route like a dancer learns a difficult piece of choreography and I could relegate more and more of the navigating to my subconscious and attend to the rhythm of the shot. To be fair, Kubrick later admitted that in selecting takes he went for performance every time and that many were technically indistinguishable. (He has been known to mutter, upon sitting through twenty identical passes in the lunchtime screenings, "Damn crosshairs, they get me every time!")

THE "TWO-HANDED" TECHNIQUE

Throughout the production I worked on what we now call the "two-handed technique". I found that if one hand strongly holds the Steadicam arm and is used to control its position *and its height,* the other hand is able to pan and tilt the handle with almost no unintentional motion in the shot. Whereas before the act of booming up or down would always seem to degrade slightly the steadiness of the image, now one can maintain the camera at any boom height and yet not influence the pan or tilt axis at all. This understanding has been the key to holding the beginning or end position of a shot so still that one must examine the frame line carefully in order to find any "float" at all. Kubrick was often able to use the head or tail of a Steadicam shot as his master for at least a portion of a dialogue scene. Even if I got caught in an awkward position because of an unexpectedly quick stop in the action Kubrick would count the beads of sweat, cast a practiced eye on the twitching of a calf muscle and wait until he judged that discs were about to fly like frisbees before he would quietly call "cut".

THE 35BL

In the beginning I was somewhat apprehensive about shooting an entire picture with the 35BL on the Steadicam, not to mention that it was for Kubrick. It did not prove to be as difficult as expected. My style of operating is fairly relaxed anyway, and with the chance to put the camera down and watch a replay on each take, one could continue indefinitely or until the next tea and bacon-roll arrived. Unfortunately there was a new MacDonalds nearby, so the evening break went through that phase, much to the disgust of the English crew. (The BL does become somewhat more burdensome with a full cargo of Big Mac's on board.)

One advantage of the 35BL is its mass. It's about 10 pounds heavier than the Arri IIc, but it allows a noticeably quieter frame. Also the BL is less affected by gusts of wind. All in all, I came to prefer it to the Arri IIc for general shooting.

CLOSE QUARTERS

From the beginning, Kubrick intended to shoot within some of the more constricted sets without flying out walls as often as usual. Since he wished to use wide lenses, in particular the Cooke 18mm, he used the capability of the Steadicam to rapidly boom up and down to avoid distorting the sets. As someone approached and passed the camera we held the proper head-room by changing the height of the lens rather than tilting and risking the keystoning of the verticals on the set. Throughout the shooting I kept an additional spirit level mounted fore-and-aft on the Steadicam so that I could keep an eye on the tilt axis.

The Steadicam can reverse its direction rapidly and without any visible bump in the shot so one can back into a doorway or alcove and push out again as the actors pass by camera. In addition, since there are no geared-head handles in the way and no need for an operator's eye on the viewfinder, one can pass the camera within an inch of walls or door frames. The combination makes a formidable tool for shooting in tight location spaces. Of course, John Alcott was left with the lighting problems that result from this kind of freedom. However, I never heard him complain and he always managed to solve these difficulties in his usual imperturbable way. John personally flew in flags and dealt with some of the camera shadow problems that arise when you are seeing 360 degrees around a room.

In the Torrance apartment in Boulder, I had a shot bringing Wendy and the doctor back along the corridor from the bedroom, backing around in a curve, booming up, then way down as they sat on the sofa, finally holding still for 1/2 page of dialogue. There is nothing about this shot that would attract the undue attention of the audience, however the lens is just where Stanley wanted it throughout. This is exactly the kind of shooting that I am most interested in. I have an increasing reluctance to suggest to a director that I might be able to smoothly jump out of the window and land shooting. It may be a sign of getting older or perhaps it just represents the maturing of my taste for the moving camera.

In the Kitchen set, one of the best shots for the Steadicam in the picture involved backing up ahead of Scatman Crothers (Halloran, the chef), Shelley Duvall (Wendy) and Danny Lloyd (Danny) as the three take a winding path through rows of immense restaurant machines and huge stoves and racks of dishware. Even if there had been room to wheel a dolly along this path, the camera would have been required to stay more or less centered, which would have meant some very sudden pans as the camera's axis swung around corners. In my case I took the least disturbing "line", like a race driver going through turns, and so the result has an unearthly tranquility about it which seems to best fit the requirements of that particular scene. In short, with the Steadicam, one can choose to pivot on any axis: far ahead of the lens, the nodal point of the lens, the filmplane, or some point far aft of the camera. In the case of this shot, I was able to pivot my camera around an imaginary point halfway between me and the actors, and prevent violent swings from side-to-side as we made the turns.

In Jack and Wendy's winter quarters in the Overlook, there were many spectacular opportunities for the Steadicam as the various players passed through the entrance hallway. For example, as we followed Wendy leaving the apartment, she would descend the three stairs just before the door and the camera would boom smoothly down in sync with her move. Then, as she passed through the door, I would boom up to negate the fact that I was now descending the same stairs, and then squeeze the matte box through the door just as it was closing. On several occasions I preceded Jack (Jack Nicholson) or Danny through the door and made the above maneuver in reverse. Obviously it is important that the camera doesn't make an unmotivated dip or rise just before or after the actor gets to the stairs. It feels better if the camera can be disembodied and not required to climb stairs itself! Other shots that stick in my mind: the-over-the-shoulder on Jack as he climbs the stairs above the lobby to find Halloran, the very believable moving P.O.V.'s as Jack or Danny enter room 237.

SPECIAL MOUNTS

One of the most talked-about shots in the picture is the eerie tracking sequence which follows Danny as he pedals at high speed through corridor after corridor on his plastic "Big Wheel". The sound track explodes with noise when the wheel is on wooden flooring and is abruptly silent as it crosses over carpet. We needed to have the lens just a few inches from the floor and to travel rapidly just behind or ahead of the bike.

I tried it on foot and found that I was too winded after an entire three-minute take to even describe what sort of last rites I would prefer. Also, at those speeds I couldn't get the lens much lower than about 18 inches from the floor. We decided to mount the Steadicam arm on the Ron Ford wheelchair prototype that Stanley helped design years before and still had on hand.

This is a very useful gadget. It can be properly steered in either direction with a simple set-up change, and the seat can be mounted low or high depending on the requirements of the shot. We arranged it so that rigging pipes could be fastened anywhere on the frame, and Dennis (Winkle) Lewis, our very able grip, constructed an adapter for the Elemack head. The Steadicam arm was fastened to the Mitchell mount, and I could sit on the chair and easily trim the leveling head to remove any imbalance in the "float" of the Steadicam.

With Stanley's BL in the underslung mode we were now prepared to fly the camera smoothly over carpet or floor at high speed and with a lens height of anything down to one inch. The results, as can be seen, were spectacular. In addition, the whole rig wasn't so massive that it would be dangerous if the little boy made a wrong turn and we had to stop suddenly. Of course, we immediately constructed a platform so that the sound man and our ace focus-puller, Doug Milsome, could ride on the back.

Now the entire contraption got to be quite difficult on the high speed corners. Dennis had to enlist relays of runners to get us around the course. Finally we had an explosive tire blow-out and the chair "plummered in", barely avoiding a serious crash. Afterward we switched to solid tires and carried no more than two people.

Stanley contemplated this arrangement and decided that the chair should have a super-accurate speedometer, and while we're at it so should the Moviola dolly and the Elemack. Then we could precisely repeat the speed of any traveling shot, etc. (More control over a capricious universe!) I was afraid that I would be lumbered with some kind of outboard wheel to precisely regulate my own speed, so I was happy that nothing came of this particular idea. (Although I would have enjoyed knowing how many miles I *didn't* run because I had the wheelchair rig!)

We used this set-up frequently in the weeks to come. In the fall I took a leave of absence for a month due to a prior commitment to shoot on ROCKY II. An English operator named Ray Andrew very capably took over for me on this occasion and several others when I was required to commute back and forth from England to the U.S. Ray made a shot from the wheelchair in which the lens is one inch above the floor, moving slowly beside Jack's head as he is being dragged toward the larder by Wendy. We also used the wheelchair with the lens at normal height to shoot a number of ordinary tracking shots through the corridors. The wheelchair was particularly useful when the camera had to move very slowly. If we needed to crab we mounted the arm on the Elemack dolly or the Moviola.

The operating technique in the chair also involves two hands: one for the arm, and one for the handle. You can easily jib over to the left and right, as well as boom up and down to compensate for slight variations in the course. We used this ability again to straighten out the camera's path and cut corners in order to make these shots easier to watch. The only tricky aspect of shooting from the chair is that starts and stops tend to be dramatic. It is a little like carrying a full punch bowl in a decelerating rickshaw!

WIRELESS FOCUS AND IRIS PULLING

I brought to England the first prototype of Cinema Products' sensational 3–channel wireless servo-lens-control, and Doug Milsome appeared to enjoy using it. He has a marvelous eye and something like a physicist's knowledge of optics. I don't think that we shot a soft frame in all the time I was on THE SHINING. He made up focus and iris strips on the servo-control for all the lenses. A surprising percentage of my shots on the picture involved iris pulls. We would commonly dial anything from 1/3 to 1½ stop changes and the results were undetectable on screen. Since we were often rushing through narrow spaces Milsome had to train his eye to pull focus from positions other than just abeam of the lens. We would get tangled in fantastic shifting choreographies and a wrong turn would find Doug outside the studio front gate, still gamely dialing the servo!

Kubrick has a fanatical concern for the sharpness of his negative. He resurrected the "harp test" for his lenses and then went beyond that to invent a bizarre variation on the harp test which positions one focus chart *every inch* for fifteen feet out from the lens.

The cameras were steady-tested nearly every week, and the dailies projectors (which belonged to Kubrick) were frequently torn down and rebuilt to cure unsteadiness due to wear. In addition, we shot with matte-perf film and our prints were made on the one and only captive printer at Rank that seemed to produce steady prints!

All this produced so much data that the results were subject at times to some confusion. The depth on one of the two BL's was packed by a few tenths on the theory that the film "liked" the image to bite somewhat into the emulsion. Lenses which were front-focused "preferred" one camera; back-focused lenses "preferred" the other. A master chart explained the feelings of each individual lens. It would be an exaggeration to say that I understood this system completely but I must point out that I never saw sharper dailies, so the lenses obviously prefer the long-suffering Milsome as focus-puller.

THE MAZE

The giant Hedge Maze set must be one of the most intriguing creations in the history of motion pictures. It must also be one of the most pernicious sets ever to work on. And folks, every frame was shot with the Steadicam. In its benign "summer" form, the Maze was constructed on the old MGM lot outdoors at Borehamwood.

It was beautiful. The "hedges" consisted of pine boughs stapled to plywood forms. It was lined with gravel paths, and contained a center section (although built to one side of the set) which was wider than the rest. It was exceedingly difficult to find one's way in or out without reference to the map which accompanied each call sheet. Most of the crew got lost at various times and it wasn't much use to call out "Stanley" as his laughter seemed to come from everywhere! It was amusing to be lost carrying nothing more than a walkie-talkie. It was positively hilarious if you happened to be wearing the Steadicam.

We determined by testing that the 9.8mm Kinoptik looked best, and that the ideal lens height was about 24 inches. This combination permitted a tremendous sense of speed and gave the correct appearance of height to the walls. The distortion was negligible when the camera was held level fore-and-aft. Much of the shooting consisted of fluid moves ahead of or behind Wendy and Danny as they learn their way through the Maze. Some of the best moments came as we followed them right into a dead end and back out again in one whirling move. I also made some tripod-type shots in the center of the maze since it would have been time-consuming to lug in the equipment to make a conventional shot.

Stanley mostly remained seated at the video screen, and we sent a wireless image from my camera out to an antenna on a ladder and thence to the recorder. For the first time I found the ritual of playback a burden, since I had to walk all the way out of the maze and back. We had made an early attempt to leave certain passages open to the outside. However, we found that we were constantly getting disoriented and a terrific shot would inadvertently wind up staring out one of the holes.

I discovered at this time that young Danny Lloyd weighed exactly as much as the camera, so we made a chair out of webbing and he would yell with delight as he swooped along riding suspended from the Steadicam arm. (I was sorry that I hadn't thought of that one before my own son weighed as much as a BNC!)

The maze was then struck and reerected on stage 1 at the EMI Studios. Roy Walker's men proceeded to "snow" it in with two feet of dendritic dairy salt and Styrofoam snow crusted on the pine boughs. The quartz outdoor-type lights were turned on and a dense oil-smoke atmosphere was pumped in for eight hours a day. Now the maze became an unpleasant place in which to work. It was hot, corrosive and a difficult spot in which to breathe. The speed of the shots stepped up, since everything now happened at nearly a run. To lighten the load we switched to the Arri IIc from Joe Dunton Cameras and constructed a special underslung cage for it.

The "snow" was difficult to run on. I constantly had a fill light clattering around my legs, and I had to navigate by the sound of muffled curses ahead as the lighting and focus-pulling intrepids fell over one another in the salt. I think that the most difficult shots on the entire picture for me were the 50mm close-ups traveling ahead of Jack or Danny at high speed. Milsome deserves a lot of credit for keeping on his feet and keeping them sharp.

For a special shot of the boy's running feet which required a lens height of three inches we made up a copy of my earliest "Steadicam": no arm, just camera, battery and magazine, connected in a balanced arrangement so I could run along "hand-held" with the lens right on the deck.

In the beginning we wore gas masks of various vintages. However, I found that I couldn't get enough air to support the exertion of getting from one end of the Maze to the other. We never measured the linear distance from the entrance to the center, but I am sure it was a hell of a long way. This was the only time on the picture that I sometimes had to call a halt to the shooting until I could get enough breath to move again.

Stanley, meanwhile, watched the deteriorating video pictures from outside the set, like a wrathful Neilson family suddenly given absolute power over the programming. The faster we had to move, the worse it got. I sometimes thought wistfully of breaking an ankle in the salt. It required enormous force to pull the camera around the turns and a degree of luck to find the right path while essentially looking backward. In addition, we were all acutely aware of the danger of fire and how difficult it would be to get out of the maze if the lights went out, with *real* smoke and burning Styrofoam—a genuine nightmare!

The footage, however, looked sensational and the sequence is tremendous in the picture, so it is all, as they say, worthwhile. Some of the best stuff was slow-moving. As Danny backs up stepping in his own footprints to fool Jack, I had to back up ahead of him *also in his footprints!* To accomplish this I had to wear special stilts with Danny-shoes nailed to the bottom so I wouldn't make the footprints any bigger!

As it turned out, there were very few stair-climbing shots in the picture. Ray Andrew shot one which worked extremely well as Wendy backs up the stairs swinging a baseball bat at Jack.

I made a "stairs" shot which is my all-time favorite. We are moving ahead of Wendy up three flights of stairs, starting rapidly, and smoothly slowing down until we are just barely moving ahead of her as she comes upon Harry Derwent and his strange doggy companion doing the unspeakable! A fabulous shot, despite the fact that we did it 36 times—

multiplied by three flights equals climbing the Empire State Building with camera . . .

When I finally saw it on the silver screen I was glad to have made the climb, if for no other reason than . . .

"Because it was there!"

The Displaced Auteur: A Reception History of *The Shining*

DENNIS BINGHAM

With recent writing on authorship by Dudley Andrew, James Naremore, and Timothy Corrigan, and with the books on directors in the Cambridge Film Classics series, auteurs are now inching back toward center stage in film studies.[1] Historically Andrew Sarris viewed auteur study as the decipherment of a film's interior meaning; Peter Wollen's Foucauldian approach posed the auteur as a set of codes that indicate a film's structuring catalyst; and Roland Barthes embalmed the author, retaining him/her only as a transmitter for cultural wavelengths.[2] The idea of the auteur as a creator of meaning faded from Anglo-American film studies in the late 1970s and throughout the 1980s. The auteur was taken seriously, or taken for granted, mostly as a pattern of signifiers. This was especially true of those Hollywood directors who could be treated as individual arbiters of classical style.

The effects of the auteur theory on American filmmaking, on the other hand, were seen first in the film school generation who in the early 1970s comprised a Hollywood New Wave. Eventually, Corrigan argues, the auteur became a brandname label in the marketplace of the 1980s: "Auteurs have become increasingly situated along an extratextual path in which their commercial status as auteurs is their chief function as auteurs."[3] By the 1980s film reached a three-way crossroads. Ideological criticism in the academy maintained the auteur as a structuring absence, with Bazin's prescient designation of Hollywood movies as "a cinema with . . . the ripeness of a classical art" winning out over the "aesthetic personality cult" founded by his protégés, the early auteurists.[4] Auteurist holdouts such as Robert Phillip Kolker insisted upon fundamental differences among "New American Cineastes," with Scorsese an artistic subversive and Spielberg a conservative.[5] In the industry, writes Andrew, money "not only equalize[s] Spike Lee, Ridley Scott, and Robert Bresson at the Video Rental store, but . . . places even the most intentional auteur . . . inside a system that is larger than he, a system that quickly and crudely exchanges his value on the market in its own way."[6] While this is nothing new—Alfred Hitchcock was a brandname before auteurship was even theorized—once auteurs arrived, authorship became one more dissonant element to be assimilated and exploited by the Hollywood system.

This essay was written specifically for this volume and is published here for the first time by permission of the author.

That system includes genres. The *auteur*ist romance whereby directorial genius "transcends genre" eventually gave way to a business practice that valued *auteur* directors mainly for their proficiency at delivering generic goods in a deluxe edition. Ed Guerrero explained, "After a fifteen-year period of experimentation and creative auteurship, in the work of such maverick Hollywood directors as Robert Altman, Stanley Kubrick, and Arthur Penn, the film industry returned to producing big-budget films that reestablished with a vengeance a thematically and formally conservative, linear, illusionist style called 'the cinema of recuperation.'"[7]

No director was caught in these transitions more than Stanley Kubrick, as the tumultuously confused release and reception of *The Shining* (1980) amply demonstrates. A big-budget adaptation of a popular novel by Stephen King, *The Shining* combined a transcendent auteur, the period's most colorful star actor, and a novelist known for delivering the generic goods. Those who had looked closely into Kubrick films such as *2001: A Space Odyssey* and *Barry Lyndon* could have foreseen that in *The Shining* Kubrick would subvert the novel's and the genre's outward conventions in order to explore the possibilities of meaning and expression on many levels. However, in a pre-release article on Kubrick, journalist John Hofsess depicted a director desperate for a commercial hit and resorting to escapist fare directed to a thrill-happy audience. "Years from now," wrote Hofsess, "when the films of 1980 have become pop-culture history, *The Shining* is likely to be viewed as further evidence of the degree to which pure escapism dominated the entertainment scene during this downbeat economic period."[8]

While the idea of a great film artist "reduced" to making horror movies eclipses the myth of the auteur whose brilliance overcomes the lowliest of genres, it does reproduce auteurist disdain for the popular audience. Contempt for "vulgar" tastes could be felt in the film itself, Kubrick's rendition of a base genre. Richard Schickel in *Time* called it "a daring thing the director has done, this bleaching out of all the cheap thrills . . . , taking a book by an author who is at the center of the craze for the supernatural, and turning it into a refusal of and subtle comment on that loopy cultural phenomenon."[9]

This assumption of "slumming" surfaces even in some later scholarly assessments. To Kolker, *The Shining* is "loud, broad, and—on an immediate level at least—quite explicit."[10] Even Brian DePalma, promoting his horror film *Dressed to Kill* in 1980, weighed in on auteurs like Kubrick who make horror movies: "They think it's a sleazy form and they're doing it to make money so they can go out and make more message pictures. They condescend to the genre, they don't understand it, they have no passion for it. And so they make terrible movies. I mean I was amazed by *The Shining*, right from the first job-interview scene."[11]

The Shining was met in 1980 by confusion and rejection from mainstream reviewers and lukewarm response from audiences. As the film moved out of its initial release, auteurist discoveries of theme and style emerged from the "little" film magazines, leading eventually to canonization, itself tentative and contentious, in the film establishment inside and outside the academy. The film's overall reception shows Kubrick's initial failure to fit cleanly into any of the categories of reading, except a broad and ill-defined auteurism, prescribed by the academy and the "mainstream." Stephen Mamber in 1991 pithily summed up the reasons for the critical response: "Kubrick, of course, is the know-it-all who rubs our noses in horror movie conventions until we wonder why we ever went to one in the first place. Stretched-out suspense, intrusive comedy, unexplained escapes, multiple motives, even title cards that move from the merely ominous to the madly random and unspecific—all point not to a failed horror film, as so many reviews stupidly labeled it, but to a deliberately subverted one."[12]

The critical reception was followed, though not necessarily in a causal way, by poor audience word-of-mouth. "There was probably no other film this year," wrote Myron Meisel in *Film Comment*'s annual review of box-office grosses, "with stronger box-office elements, or a film of its box-office potential that had fewer commercial goods to deliver . . . It drew torridly for five weeks, then dropped to a pittance for subsequent runs."[13] "Did Stanley Kubrick really say that *The Shining* . . . would be the scariest horror movie of all time?," asked Richard T. Jameson. "He shouldn't have. On one very important level, the remark may be true. But it isn't the first level people are going to consider . . . Kubrick, who is celebrated for controlling the publicity for his films as closely as the various aspects of their creation, is largely to blame for the initial, strongly negative feedback to his movie . . . He pressed on with the horror sales hook, counting on it—along with his own eminence—to fill theaters, and to pay off the $18 million cost of the most expensive Underground movie ever made."[14]

In the case of *The Shining*, therefore, we see how the conventions of commercial cinema and the aspirations of the *auteur* and his followers can bring about a veritable train wreck of clashing expectations. I have offered elsewhere a textual reading of *The Shining* that explores the ways the film deconstructs white American masculinity and its tensions within the "nuclear" family with help from Jack Nicholson's star persona and acting style.[15] In this study I will examine the myth of the auteur by means of reception, a method for understanding a film's meaning, and in this case, the meaning of "Stanley Kubrick." I will explore the response to the film as influenced by advance publicity, the expectations that audiences brought with them to the theater, and finally the ways in which critics made sense of the film as it drew farther from the circumstances of its original expectations.

Reception work is one of the latest strategies in film studies' emphasis on what happens when people watch movies. "Reception studies," writes Janet Staiger, "is not textual interpretation. Instead, it seeks to understand textual interpretations as they are produced historically . . . Reception studies tries to explain an event (the interpretation of a film), while textual studies is working toward elucidating an object (the film)."[16] Key concepts in any reception study are the horizon of expectations, the biographical legend of an artist, and reading formations.

First formulated by the German literary theorist Hans Robert Jauss, the "horizon of expectations" applied to film refers to the audience's knowledge of other works by the director and starring the actor, conventions of the genre, advertising and publicity for the film—anything that contributes to what audiences expect the work to be. Pertinent to *The Shining* is a statement about literary parodies such as *Tristram Shandy* and *Don Quixote* which "evoke the reader's horizon of expectations, formed by a convention of genre, style, and form, only in order to destroy it step by step."[17] Such works set up an "aesthetic distance" in which audiences are alienated by differences between their expectations and what the work actually presents.[18] On the horizon is the persona of the artist. Boris Tomasevskij wrote that "the biography that is useful to the literary historian is not the author's curriculum vitae or the investigator's account of his life [but] the biographical legend created by the author himself. Only such a legend is a *literary fact*."[19]

Various groups await and respond to the work in their own ways. Barbara Klinger calls these groups "reading formations."[20] Some reading formations that responded to *The Shining* have been Kubrick followers with an auteurist orientation, the target mass audience, mainstream reviewers, academic reviewers, and horror fans. Thus for these reading formations overall, the most important expectations were those concerning genre and the biographical legend of Stanley Kubrick. In the 1960s no young American director benefitted more from the new myth of the *auteur* than Kubrick. The biographical legend of the Bronx-born Kubrick that Kolker called "close to the European standard of the film *auteur*, in complete control of his work, overseeing it from beginning to end"[21] began to accumulate soon after the critical and commercial success of *Paths of Glory* in 1958. A 1959 *Film Quarterly* article on independent filmmakers highlighted Kubrick's insistence on independence from a studio during a film's production and remarked on his participation to that time in the writing, editing, and camerawork, an involvement that impressed the writer with "a strong feeling of unity and single-mindedness in his films."[22]

In the next half-dozen years, Kubrick was dismissed from one actor-controlled film (Marlon Brando's *One Eyed Jacks*), replaced a fired director (Anthony Mann) on another (Kirk Douglas's *Spartacus*), and experienced what he considered the thanklessness of delivering an impersonal and mammoth Hollywood production. He went to England in 1961 to make *Lolita* and ended up settling outside London with his family. His next film, *Dr. Strangelove, or How I Learned to Stop Worrying and Love the Bomb*, won acclaim from establishment critics, editorial writers, and young audiences in metropolitan areas and college towns.[23] Thus, by 1964, at age thirty-five, he had established himself as the quintessential new directorial hero in the age of the auteur. Aloof and enigmatic, a self-taught Renaissance man without a university degree, he released films through the studios but brooked no interference from them, separating himself physically from Hollywood by one wide continent and an ocean. Unlike the directors of the Classical Hollywood generation who eschewed the label of "art," Kubrick was the closest auteur study got to an image of the filmmaker as a lone artist in a garret.

Kubrick's films lent themselves perfectly to auteurist sensibilities and analysis, with one exception. The auteur himself was nowhere to be found in films which appeared to have been handed down from on high, with interior meaning buried so far beneath the spectacular surfaces (in *2001* and *Barry Lyndon*, in particular) as to keep the essentially New Critical method of *auteur* analysis busy indefinitely.[24] Kubrick's films announce themselves as creations, but without the palpable presence of a creator. This, I feel, is at the heart of the confused critical receptions of his films beginning with *2001*. Such influential and formally conservative reviewers as Stanley Kauffmann of *The New Republic*, David Denby of *New York*, and Stephen Harvey of *Saturday Review* were skeptical of Kubrick for a battery of reasons: his "no publicity" policy during production, his personal inaccessibility to the American press, his refusal to make his films available for early press screenings, and the paradoxical "self-indulgence" of this absent self.

Kubrick is also a problematic figure for academics, only partly because of the discredited auteurist baggage his reputation has carried. The Film Studies reception shows the problems the new academic profession has had reconciling what Fredric Jameson calls "classical modernist" auteurism with post-structuralist approaches that find the auteur irrelevant to concerns of ideology and signification. "The problem with Kubrick studies," wrote Judy Lee Kinney in 1984, "has been the failure to define a proper historical or theoretical context for the body of film work. This task has been made more difficult because Kubrick's idiosyncratic reputation has simultaneously encouraged and frustrated an auteur approach to the films."[25] As auteurism became obsolete, Kubrick's films failed to qualify in Film Studies' other categories. They did not belong to the classical Hollywood paradigm, to the "New Hollywood Cinema," to cinemas on the margins, or to styles thought of as experimental. If *The Shining* or *Barry Lyndon* were signed by Jean-Luc Godard, Wim Wenders, or even Jim

Jarmusch, they might be studied as brilliant revisions of classical film style instead of looked on askance as curiosities. The only role for Kubrick is a dated one of the auteur as wily trickster who puts one over on the film industry, the authors whose novels he adapts, media reviewers, interviewers to whom he makes his films sound incredibly conventional, and the audience whose expectations he confounds.

Moreover, the absence of Kubrick from the public eye for years at a time and from the texts themselves made the films for auteurists both existential and deterministic, activating what Foucault called "the religious principle of the hidden meaning . . . and the critical principle of implicit significations, silent determinations, and obscured contents."[26] In the 1960s and 1970s Kubrick was cinema's best example of the author as "an analogue of God, the creator and source of the world."[27] This can be seen in Kubrick's legend as the all-controlling creator, the pitiless distancing of his films' narration (with the helicopter shots that open *The Shining* or the slow reverse zooms of *Barry Lyndon* often referred to as "God's-Eye Views"[28]), the production photos showing him as a bearded, contemplative figure, and the long, Beckettian periods disciples spend "waiting for Stanley," hoping for a new film or even just word of a new film.

In a survey of Kubrick's relationship with Hollywood financing, Robert Sklar demystifies the myth of the solitary, subversive Kubrick who refuses to allow studio executives to see his films until days before release. "It seems quite clear," reports Sklar, "that both distributor and director wanted to make a film that could be marketed in . . . [the] high-potential manner [of] . . . 'saturation' booking, a big national advertising campaign, pre-release payments from exhibitors, and guaranteed playing time in theaters."[29] Interviewer John Hofsess was left with the impression that "Kubrick would like to prove to any doubters in the film industry that he can make an American film while residing in England. . . . He also would like to prove that he can make a film that does just as well as any of those by the so-called 'new Hollywood' directors."[30]

Media anticipation of *The Shining* began building far in advance of the film's completion. Jim Albertson in the Fall 1978 *Cinefantastique* harked back to a 1966 interview in which Kubrick said that he "would like to make the world's scariest movie, involving a series of episodes that would play upon the nightmare fears of the audience." From this, Albertson concluded that "Stanley Kubrick is going to scare the hell out of us." Peter S. Perakos added that "one need not 'shine' to expect Stanley Kubrick's film, upon completion, to evidence poetic genius."[31]

Improbable expectations combining hell-raising fright and "poetic genius" were mounting, fueled by a report on the film's production by Aljean Harmetz in *The New York Times*. Harmetz interviewed Diane Johnson about the writing of the script. Kubrick's basic decision, said Johnson, was "that the movie be completely scary." She defined this, however, in negative terms: "To be completely scary means that your suspension of disbelief can never be tampered with by some implausibility." Johnson spoke, misleadingly as the film turned out, about creating a convincing illusion of reality in gothic horror. She also pinpointed a theme that would be picked up by many of the film's defenders in the years after its theatrical run: "The material of this movie is the rage and fear within families."[32] Thus much of the deconstructive subtext that would make the film baffling to many commentators—that Kubrick would have his film say the "not said" of horror films, except that *The Shining* would not directly say it, but would embed it in subtext—was leaked a year and a half before release, in between statements that made the project sound utterly conventional. Johnson announced to the world that she and Kubrick read Freud's "The Uncanny" and Bruno Bettelheim's *The Uses of Enchantment*, providing grist for later, "serious" analysis.

All of the evidence indicates that Kubrick and Warner Brothers keyed *The Shining* to maximum financial success. The distributor implemented a massive and expensive advertising campaign geared toward the key demographic group of young adults between the ages of 18 and 34.[33] The ad tagline, "A masterpiece of modern horror," obliquely suggested auteur, genre, and, as it turned out, the modern*ism* (or post-modernism) of the former's approach to the latter.

The mainstream critical response reflects splits in the film itself between text and subtext, genre and auteur, "commercial goods" and thematic and stylistic cues to be found in the oeuvre of the auteur. The reviews which were angry and negative tended to be bothered by the portentiousness of the film's style applied to formulaic horror material, and by Kubrick's tendency to drop plot and character details out of the novels he adapts. "Eager to impress us with the importance of his subject," wrote David Denby in *New York*, "he flashes titles like 'Tuesday' and '4 p.m.' onto a darkened screen as if he were chronicling the preparations for D-Day."[34] *Variety* was baffled as to "why a director of Kubrick's stature would spend his time and effort on a novel that he changes so much it's barely recognizable, taking away whatever originality it possessed while emphasizing its banality."[35] Tom Allen in the *Village Voice* asserted that "in his last three adaptations . . . Kubrick has eviscerated the affective surfaces of novels while retaining their shrunken plotlines like misshapen scarecrows, warning off other predators that the book has already been ravished."[36] Reviewers who thought the horror film a worthwhile genre took Kubrick to task for what some of them saw as a failure to take the genre seriously enough to make it work. "Kubrick hasn't flunked an abstract exam," pronounced Stanley Kauffmann in *The New Republic*, "he's flunked the elemental test for a horror film. *The Shining* doesn't scare."[37]

The question of whether or not Kubrick might be up to something transgressive or parodic, when it was considered by the negative review-

ers, was usually eliminated, especially when the reviewer seemed overcome by the expectation of "epics" and "masterpieces" created by the publicity and the pre-release press coverage. Kauffmann, who recognizes
Brechtian alienation devices when European directors employ them,
expects from *The Shining* classical immersion in a horror diegesis. He
complains, "Stanley Kubrick's . . . *The Shining* has two good shots in it,
and he spoils them both." The first shot referred to is the moment in the
opening credit sequence when the helicopter shot following Jack
Torrance's yellow Volkswagen wanders off the trail (an early instance in
which the "God's Eye" blinks, showing that the conventional indicators of
visual narrative authority cannot be trusted here—a way in which Kubrick
both reminds us of his presence and vacates the text as a master of the
gaze and of his characters' fate). The other shot Kubrick spoils for
Kauffmann is the one in which after Wendy has discovered Jack's insane
"All work and no play" manuscript, the camera dollies in on Wendy from a
distance and from Jack's point of view. Other horror films probably would
have kept Wendy in the foreground but had Jack pop suddenly into the
shot or cut to him in a way that would make Wendy and the audience
jump in surprise. Thus it is a very familiar convention that Kubrick
"spoils." In following Jack's point of view, Kubrick not only destroys the
shock effect but shows Jack taking for himself the omnipotence to which
he is presumably entitled as a male in patriarchal society: every time we've
seen the same dolly shot before it has been the "objective" camera tracking
in on and objectifying Jack himself.[38] While Kauffmann expects performance of the genre (he compares *The Shining* unfavorably to *The
Exorcist*), Stephen Harvey in *Saturday Review* states that "*The Shining*
breaks every one of [the] rules so insistently, one can't help wondering if
Kubrick was trying to turn this property into a parody of the genre."[39] But
having hit upon this lead, Harvey doesn't pursue it.

While the vehemence of the negative reviews dominated the film's
reception, there were sympathetic reviews. These generally praised the
film's stylistic traits, such as the use of Steadicam, the employment of
music by Penderecki, Bartók, and Lygeti, and what Jack Kroll of *Newsweek*
called "one of the greatest sets in movie history—an astonishing catacomb
of corridors, rooms, lobbies, lounges, giant kitchens, and basements."[40]
Kroll's review is unusual in that it praises the film on the terms of its publicity, embracing the film on the level of spectacle and plot, and significantly, never mentioning Stephen King.

Other positive reviews found meaning in Kubrick's body of work.
Richard Schickel in *Time* repeated the theme of alienation and refusal
from the negative reviews. Calling it "a movie of false clues and red herrings," Schickel, in a review tentative in its judgments, adheres to
Kubrick's stated desire to counter "the assumption that a film, unlike a
book, a painting, or a piece of music, should require only a single

encounter to be absorbed and understood."[41] Turning the film over to auteurists, Schickel writes, "it may be that this is a canonical work, something that only those who find Stanley Kubrick to be one of the world's great artists will respond to." Schickel recognizes the film's "refusal of and subtle comment on" the horror genre, but leaves full analysis of the film to future work; thus "Kubrick has made a movie that will have to be reckoned with on the highest level." Janet Maslin in two articles in *The New York Times* tried to separate the film's troubling "loose ends" from the things which make it "a vibrant, provocative work." Maslin finds the film vastly more interesting on a second viewing.[42] She also notices a sympathy toward the female character new in Kubrick's work, finding a nascent feminism in such scenes as the one in which "Wendy sits in the hotel's elegant lobby, propped before a television set during a blizzard . . . watching Jennifer O'Neill play the ultimate in mindless femininity, in *Summer of '42*." Maslin also is one of the first to suggest an undercurrent of domestic frustration and violence. "The Overlook is something far more fearsome than a haunted house. It's a home."[43]

The theme of trouble in the family drove Andrew Sarris's appraisal of the film nearly six months after its release. "When I finally saw the film," he said, "I felt that many critics and viewers had missed the whole point . . . What really turns off audiences is the messy state of the family from the word go . . . *The Shining* would have been a more comforting horror film if the father-son conflict could have been blamed on the devil, or a mental illness, or a Freudian fury, or even a malignant invader from outer space. Instead the family structure generates its own psychic poisons with just a little help from an exotic setting."[44]

As the film's reception entered specialized film magazines and academic journals, critics explored levels of the film beyond the baffling literal level. In the semi-journalistic *Film Comment* where auteurism continued to find a home, Richard T. Jameson sorted through the horizon of expectations to find that "*The Shining* is a horror movie only in the sense that all of Kubrick's mature work has been horror movies—films that constitute a Swiftian vision of inscrutable cosmic order . . . The director is so little interested in the genre for its own sake that he hasn't even systematically subverted it so much as displaced it with a genre all his own."[45]

Flo Leibowitz and Lynn Jeffries in *Film Quarterly* echo this suggestion: "One suspects that the 'failings' in *The Shining* are related to Kubrick's interest in deliberately redirecting the audience's attention elsewhere." They then pick out a red-white-and-blue color scheme and a multitude of Native American motifs in the production design (these, they say "cannot be merely accidental. There are too many of them"), seeing the Overlook Hotel as a symbol of America itself. The family becomes a site of tension between the American dream of masculine self-reliance and family responsibilities that are perceived as a drag on freedom. Even the Donner Party anecdote early in the film is then a metaphor for "what can happen to families under the pressure of the myths of success and masculinity treated in the film." The critics also note that those who shine or who aid those who do are women, children, and blacks, "three of America's traditional victims."[46]

To Leibowitz and Jeffries the three primary levels of the film, fantasy, family, and shining, necessarily impinge on the drama at key points, resulting in miscuings of the audience. These critics isolate what will become apparent as two lines of inquiry into the film. Many of the critics interested in themes such as the psychodrama of the family in the context of American culture, treat the elliptical, obscurantist surface of the film as virtually a container for what Kubrick has to say about these things. Such critics disregard the film as sheer experience, the level on which many reviewers found it so lacking, and search for the movie's meaning. Others defend what they see as the film's subversive surface, extolling it as parody or pastiche, sometimes even wondering if there is any point to Kubrick's elaborate effort to frustrate a thrill-seeking spectator. Larry W. Caldwell and Samuel J. Umland in 1986 noted this split in the "serious" critiques of *The Shining*: "While the meaning is seen as ultimately serious, indeed pessimistic, the presentation is conceded to be partly playful." They argue that

> Kubrick's manipulation of the play metaphor, together with its adjuncts— stereotyped characters and plot, banal dialogue, allusions to fairy tales and cartoons, as well as his self-reflexivity—suggest that *The Shining*, as an object to bear "meaning," cannot sustain the ponderous social psychology which film scholars have imputed to it. They insist that comic parody, à la Kubrick, must be deadly serious in intent, or by extension, that the meaning can remain intact even after the form has been rendered silly.[47]

Signs of play, which are everywhere in the "adjuncts" Caldwell and Umland mention, might appear not to mesh with the director who reads Freud and Bettelheim in preparing his film and who is renowned for deliberateness and for multiple takes that may seem designed to wring any "playfulness" out of the mise en scène.[48] Nonetheless the "play" metaphors go on, opposed by "seriousness": Mario Falsetto, discussing the film's central performance, writes that "clearly Nicholson is having too good a time for some critics to take his work here seriously."[49] To Paul Mayersberg, "the humour of *The Shining* puts it close to *Lolita* and *Dr. Strangelove* in Kubrick's work. As in much of Hitchcock and Bunuel, and to some extent Polanski, there is an underlying crazy comedy which is also deadly serious."[50]

Countering Caldwell and Umland's views are critics who maintain that there is a point where comic subversion and serious intent meet and that point is parody. Stephen Mamber includes *The Shining* with a group of four films he calls "difficult, seemingly 'bad' films [which] "using parody techniques . . . push the limits of the acceptable, especially in redefining the ways the films are to be viewed."[51] (The others are *The King of Comedy* [1983, Martin Scorsese], *Body Double* [1984, Brian DePalma], and *The Purple Rose of Cairo* [1985, Woody Allen]). Mamber defines four characteristics of "multiple intertextuality" found in post-modern parody: "1. Inclusions of television, 2. Use of source music, 3. Film historical quotes, 4. Inversions of star types."[52] Thus Roadrunner cartoons from Danny's TV often undercut the feeling of terror and shift the action to the anarchic, regressive level of the coyote and the roadrunner. The "happy news" chatter of TV anchors allows Kubrick to undermine a horror film's accumulation of foreboding details with cheerful inanity, at one point letting a news item about a woman missing "since leaving for a hunting trip with her husband" curdle into a self-reflexive sick joke.

About Kubrick's well known use of source music, Mamber writes, "*The Shining* never reaches the repellent glories of the use of 'Singin' in the Rain' in *Clockwork Orange*, but there's never been a more obtrusive and overstylized prototypical horror movie synthesizer score than the one that beats down on us . . . with nearly every footstep and glance."[53] Film historical quotes, usually muted in Kubrick, are emphatic here: the voice of Tony, the "little boy who lives" in Danny's mouth, unmistakably recalls *The Exorcist*; Kubrick evokes his own filmic past when Jack tauntingly calls Wendy, "light of my life," a line from the first paragraph of Nabokov's *Lolita*.

The film most persistently quoted is *Psycho*, the movie with which Kubrick's would most likely be compared, and one which in its day both overturned and established some horror movie conventions. Not only are Bernard Herrmann's screaming violins reprised ironically and Hitchcock's use of an ultimately meaningless day and time marker ("Phoenix, Arizona, Friday, December the eleventh, two forty-three p.m.") extended, but Mayersberg points out that the Room 237 scene, in which Jack's apparition of a beautiful woman who turns into a zombie is intercut with Danny's transmission to Halloran of *his* experience in Room 237, "is a rewrite of the shower scene in *Psycho*. In *Psycho* it is the lady in the shower who is threatened by the monster outside. In *The Shining* this is reversed. Jack is the 'monster', scared by what might emerge from the shower behind the curtain. . . . Later there is a reference again to *Psycho* when Jack menaces Wendy by climbing up the stairs. It is Wendy who has the weapon in her hand, the baseball bat, but it is she who is backing away. . . ."[54] Finally, stars are inverted in the Nicholson-improvised "Here's Johnny!," the supreme example of Kubrick's strategy of disorientation: do we scream or laugh?

As Mamber indicates, parody itself can subvert genre conventions and the ideology they represent. Stephen King himself has talked about the conservative appeal of horror.[55] In *A Theory of Parody* (1985), Linda Hutcheon points to Mikhail Bakhtin's discussion of the medieval "subversive carnival," which operated with the approval of civic and religious establishments as a temporary release from "the prevailing truth and from the established order."[56] The paradox involves parody's capacity for being conservative or subversive. Parody can restore a form by imitating and effectively paying respect to its conventions, but it can also deconstruct and disable it.

Relating the latter point to post-modernism, Hutcheon defines the "postmodernist parodic film" as one which shows "both a respectful awareness of cultural continuity and a need to adapt to changing formal demands and social conditions through an ironic challenging of the authority of that same continuity."[57] Hutcheon says that the position of filmmakers inside the commercial system presents to them "the possibilities of the positive oppositional and contestatory nature of parody. Postmodernist film does not deny that it is implicated in capitalist modes of production . . . Instead, it exploits this 'insider' position in order to begin a subversion within, to talk to consumers in a capitalist society."[58] Hutcheon takes issue with Fredric Jameson's insistence that in a post modern world in which norms are obsolete and culture is recycled, not created, parody cannot be a viable form. Jameson's Marxist position is that in "post-industrial capitalism . . . , as individualism begins to atrophy . . . as the sheer difference of increasingly distinct and eccentric individualities turns under its momentum into repetition and sameness, as the logical permutations of stylistic innovation become exhausted, the quest for a uniquely distinctive style and the very category of 'style' come to seem old-fashioned."[59] The result is "pastiche," which

> like parody, [is] the imitation of a peculiar or unique, idiosyncratic style, the wearing of a linguistic mask, speech in a dead language. But it is a neutral practice of such mimicry, without any of parody's ulterior motives, amputated of the satiric impulse, devoid of any laughter. . . . Pastiche is thus blank parody, a statue with blind eyeballs: it is to parody what that other interesting and historically original modern thing, the practice of a kind of blank irony, is to what Wayne Booth calls the "stable ironies" of the eighteenth century.[60]

Jameson ties Kubrick's *The Shining* to what he sees as a trend in the 1970s toward Hollywood "genre pastiche." Encompassing such films as *Rosemary's Baby, McCabe and Mrs. Miller*, and Kubrick's own *Paths of Glory, The Killing*, and *2001* (which Jameson sees as pastiches of the war film, the crime film, and science fiction, respectively), pastiches "use the pregiven structure of inherited genres as a pretext for production which is no longer personal or stylistic."[61] Among the purposes of the pastiche is "to display the virtuosity of the practicioner." To Jameson, the auteur is a rogue mechanic who rebuilds an old engine out of used parts, rather than a creator of something new and "idiosyncratic" after the fashion of the modernist impulses behind the auteur theory.

Thus the shrieking violins from *Psycho*, the gimpy leg of the psychotic Jack with its Igor echoes (already parodied in Mel Brooks' *Young Frankenstein* [1974]), and references to Johnny Carson and the Roadrunner are the recapitulations of an exhausted culture and, especially, of its history: "The Jack Nicholson of *The Shining* is possessed neither by evil as such nor by the 'devil' . . . but rather simply by History, by the American past as it has left its sedimented traces in the corridors and dismembered suites of this monumental rabbit warren."[62] *The Shining* is thus Kubrick's answer to the audiences who did not respond to his previous film, *Barry Lyndon*. Rather than attempt historical representation, *The Shining* shows the present as the meeting point of past, present, future, a feat also accomplished by *2001* (a point Jameson does not make).

There is a fine line between parody and pastiche. Given the popularity of Stephen King and the full-throated revival of the horror film at the time of *The Shining*'s release, horror was hardly a "dead form," even if it does cavort with death. Kubrick forced audiences to abhor the very conventions they had come to the movie to see. Perhaps the artistic model for interpreting *The Shining* is not Jameson's pastiche of dead styles or so-called "silly parody," but the theatre of Bertolt Brecht. In a discussion of "satiric parody" Hutcheon explains that "the work of . . . Brecht has perhaps been the best modern model for the use of parody to satiric ends. . . . In *Arturo Ui* Brecht used parody as a mode of distanciation to create the epic theatre's critical attitude. It destroys the psychological motivation by which the audience might explain away the brutal reality of corruption and violence that must, instead, be faced,"[63] just as Jack Torrance does not simply go mad, but is shown to be part of a process of violence, colonization, and patriarchy throughout American history and centered in the American family.

The analogy to Brecht is not so simple, however. This is a point made by P. L. Titterington, who sees in Kubrick's style an ambitious attempt to combine in cinema Brecht's theater of distanciation and reflection with "the theatre of total, overwhelming emotional involvement conceived by Artaud." He continues: "[Kubrick] tries to work simultaneously through the two extreme and opposing modes of awareness in art, with the traditional middle ground of plot and psychological presentation severely, and possibly dangerously, restricted." Thus the Artaudian side works with the full production values of the American cinema, hoping to engage an audience on the level of spectacle, inviting them "to question and critically assess the experience . . . [of] images [which] cannot in themselves explain what we are seeing." The Brechtian side forces us "at the same time to question and critically assess the experience. . . . Kubrick seeks to create works that will engage the whole of our nature in our response."[64] As Brecht was frustrated throughout his life by audiences who responded to his plays in a conventional spirit, so film parodies, writes Mamber, "risking comparison to the originals . . . can easily be thought of as 'bad' by the unparody-minded, a risk openly engaged."[65]

On the other hand, some critics noted that *The Shining* opened in the midst of a cycle of critically acclaimed family melodramas such as *Kramer vs. Kramer* (1979, Robert Benton) and *Ordinary People* (1980, Robert Redford). In these films sensitive fathers, filling a vacuum left by mothers who leave their sons (*Kramer*) or smother them in repression (*People*), learn to play *both* parental roles—the nurturing mother and the symbolic father in whose image the son develops. *The Shining* and the family melodramas were seen as two sides of the same coin, a point made by Vivian Sobchack: "If the horror film shows us the terror and rage of *patriarchy in decline* (savaged by its children or murderously resentful of them), then the popular family melodrama shows us a sweetly problematic *paternity in ascendance*."[66] Indeed a 1981 article by Greg Keeler argues, as Sobchack puts it, that "the mad, murderous 'bad father' . . . carr[ies] out all of the negative patriarchal fury and paternal desire repressed by the nurturant 'good father' in . . . *Kramer vs. Kramer*." Keeler writes, "No matter how one views the differences between these films, there is no doubt that the nuclear family has to disintegrate in order for the characters to survive, either physically or psychologically."[67]

However, the Kramer family is in crisis because the wife flees the bourgeois marriage to make her own life, leaving the breadwinner husband to carry the burden of parenting. *Kramer* is profoundly a patriarchal reaction to feminism, which is shown as a destabilizing threat to an order invested with an almost eerie ability to adjust to the absence of the woman. On the other hand, "In *The Shining*," writes William Paul in 1994, "the father clearly feels stultified, blames it on the family, and seeks his independence. But seeing the film in these terms simply shows how *Kramer vs. Kramer* appropriates a pop feminism by assigning to a woman qualities not unusual for a man in American culture. What is darkest about *The Shining* is not the return of those qualities to a male, but rather the way the film turns what Freud called 'family romances' inside out."[68]

Accordingly, Diane Johnson's revelation that "The Uncanny" and *The Uses of Enchantment* lurk in *The Shining*'s subtext gave critics license to tease out causes for the film's baffling effects. Christopher Hoile wrote in 1984 that "most critics . . . seem to feel that [Kubrick] has provided so much psychological motivation for the events . . . that he has rendered unnecessary the presence of the supernatural and extrasensory perception, thereby draining the horror."[69] *The Uses of Enchantment* (1976), Bettelheim's argument that fairy tales are healthy and necessary for the development of a well-adjusted child, and "The Uncanny" (1919), Freud's demonstration that a return of the repressed is at the heart of tales of horror and the supernatural, can be seen, according to Hoile and Paul, as structuring Kubrick's portrayal of the fantasy lives of son and father.

Both works are important and complementary to each other because they "discuss man's relation to an animistic universe," a universe central to Kubrick's theme of "the resurgence of the primitive through the doors of what is supposedly more advanced."[70] Freud's notion of the "uncanny" is based on a wordplay with the German "heimlich" (literally, "home-like"), which after a lengthy survey of definitions, Freud concludes "is not unambiguous, but belongs to two sets of ideas: . . . on the one hand, it means that which is familiar and congenial, and on the other, that which is concealed and kept out of sight."[71] To Freud the "uncanny" connects to déjà vu, repetition compulsion, and the "double"; it is the revelation of an eerie, frightening, alien thing that nonetheless seems familiar and welcoming—or vice versa. Thus as Jack is driven mad and murderous by the Overlook Hotel, he "has the feeling I've been here before" and pronounces the hotel "homey." He can be said to consciously respond to the bartender's and Delbert Grady's appeal to his male ego at the same time that he is unconsciously drawn to what the cinematography and art direction present as luscious, warm, and enclosing physical surroundings—the manifestations of a repressed desire to return to the womb.[72]

Paul identifies the film's largest contradiction in the oedipal struggle between Jack and Danny: Jack's delusion that he is the overseer (with class and racial overtones that have been noted by Cook and Jeffries and Leibowitz) clashes with Danny's power of shining, also defined as a power of sight, which Jack simply doesn't notice, or "overlooks." The latter ties in with the mythology of David and Goliath and Jack the Giant Killer discussed by Bettelheim and with Freud's description of E. T. A. Hoffmann's story of "The Sand-Man," a monster who puts out children's eyes.

To Bettelheim and Freud the consciousness of the child is much closer to animism than the adult is. Thus, wishing, doubling, projecting one's fears on to others, and free movement between illusion and reality are "natural and therapeutic for the child . . . but uncanny to the adult who has surmounted the animistic stage."[73] Thus Danny copes with a frightening world through childlike fantasy, as Jack's fantasies draw him deeper into an American history of dark genocide. "I cannot recall a single fairy tale," writes Bettelheim, "in which a child's angry wishes have any consequence; only those of adults do. . . . It is as if the fairy tale, while admitting how human it is to get angry, expects only adults to have sufficient self-control not to let themsleves get carried away, since their outlandishly angry wishes come true."[74] Jack mixes up getting carried away with following orders. He can even be said to have made the standard "three wishes" of the fairy tale: he summons up Lloyd, the bartender from the hotel's (his?) past; he sees a nude young woman in the bathroom in Room 237 ("As every besieged husband must," writes Kolker, "he looks for an affair"[75]); and he somehow wills open (through his double, Delbert ["Doubled"?] Grady) the door of the storage room into which Wendy has locked him.[76]

Jack experiences the past as the present while Danny, through *his* double, "Tony," "shines" the present and future. Danny also explores and learns his own physical surroundings in a way that Jack does not. In addition, Danny gleans a child's understanding of the past in Bettelheim's terms of fairy tales: "'Once upon a time,' . . . 'A thousand years ago, or longer,' . . . 'Once in an old castle in the midst of a large and dense forest'—such beginnings suggest that what follows does not pertain to the here and now that we know. . . . The old castles, dark caves, locked rooms one is forbidden to enter, impenetrable woods all suggest that something normally hidden will be revealed, while the 'long ago' implies that we are going to learn about the most archaic events."[77] Thus the story that Hallorann, the cook who shares Danny's "shining," tells him about events leaving "traces of themselves" connects the "once upon a time" distancing of the fairy tale (and much of popular film) to Jack's possession by the "sedimented traces" of "History," as Fredric Jameson would have it. In other words, "The Uncanny" helps account for Jack's delusion and seduction by the hotel. *The Uses of Enchantment* helps account for Danny's fairy-tale child's-eye view. Wendy, the woman not in the thrall of visions and obsessions, is rooted in reality, a situation that can be read as an advantage, or not.

Both Hoile and Paul read *The Shining* as a recasting of the Oedipus myth (Paul's discussion is in a chapter entitled "The Revenge of Oedipus"). "As Laius in the myth of Oedipus, a father feeling threatened by his son tries to kill him only to be killed at a crossroads as the prophesy is fulfilled and the son runs off with his mother."[78] Both writers make much of the hedge maze, which Paul takes "as a metaphor for the mind itself . . . , a puzzle connecting sight—and particularly acute powers of vision—to knowledge." Writes Hoile, "Just as Torrance had led his family into the maze of the hotel, Danny leads his father into the garden maze. . . . Torrance is now on Danny's territory." Paul adds, "By the end of the film, [Danny] has the best knowledge of the hotel, as well as the maze, a knowledge that will save his life."[79]

Thus, this 1970s Oedipus (the name means "swollen foot," a mark of the child's mutilation by the father), uses his feet to trap his father in the maze, retracing his steps in the snow in order to head off a father blind to all "traces." Relatedly, Paul sees in Kubrick's film childlike fantasy exceeding the Freudian Oedipus Complex: "There is an almost naked Oedipal pattern outlined in Kubrick's film (albeit not with the proper resolution for Freud): the father is killed, and the child goes off with the mother." In Freud's scenario "the father . . . always occupies something of an ambivalent role in the life of the son, but in the Freudian scheme this ambivalence is created entirely in the son's fantasy life. The father does not actually wish to castrate his child; this is merely an outward projection of the son's anxiety. A strict Freudian interpretation of this movie would therefore have to see it as pure wish-fulfillment . . . [But] what if the father is in fact murderous?"[80]

Paul's treatment of *The Shining* marks a coming full circle in the film's reception by 1994. Paul, after all, is celebrating as important, culturally expressive forms the disreputable "animal" comedies and "gross-out" horror films of the late 1970s and 1980s, the very movies that crowded "creative auteurship" out of the theaters and created the climate in which Kubrick's "masterpiece of modern horror" was received with befuddlement. Paul treats *The Shining* as a horror film, assuming an automatic kinship between the film and more conventional shockers such as *The Other* (1972), *The Brood* (1979), and *The Exorcist* (1973). His approach—in a book emphasizing form and genre in order to get past content-oriented objections to works he feels are important—is nearly identical to that of earlier excavators of meaning like Hoile, David Cook, and even Andrew Sarris, Mr. "Interior Meaning." Paul simply "forgets" that *The Shining* was ever not thought of as a horror film. He assumes a fusion of genre, artist, theory, and the artwork, as seamless as the integration assumed among, say, the Western, John Ford, Frederick Jackson Turner, and *The Man Who Shot Liberty Valance*.

Of course, the reason for confusion and for wildly differing assessments of the film's meaning, each feeling somewhat incomplete, lies in Kubrick's refusal to work along the cause-and-effect linear pattern of classical cinema. David Bordwell and Janet Staiger's characterization of European art films as "a cinema of psychological effects in search of their causes,"[81] fits Kubrick's films perfectly. Kubrick is known for removing concrete motivation and causal details from his screenplays. Michael Bérubé in a 1994 analysis of *2001* finds that the details of the plot are left so unexplained that Kubrick might have "put the screenplay through a shredder at the last minute."[82] Bérubé finds that the silences of *2001*—and by extension, other Kubrick films—are themselves a discourse connected to repression of an institutional kind: "Silence is not an absence of discourse, but an integral part of discourse—just as ignorance is not something lying at the outer borders of the map of knowledge (marked 'here be tygers'), but something licensed and sustained by specific regimes of knowledge that tell you implicitly you don't need to know or shouldn't want to know."[83]

In loading the films with subtext, Kubrick not only does not "say" things, he empties the film of a "speaking subject," transferring his enunciating entity to the "system" that drives the machines that drive the characters. About *2001*, Bérubé writes that "Kubrick's critics have come to agree that the movie is better off without narration; though Kubrick's commentators tend to like the decision because it allows us to concentrate on the visual and 'poetic' aspects . . . , one might also add that in striking the narration, Kubrick has stripped the film of omniscience, leaving omniscience instead to the intelligences responsible for the monoliths,"[84] or in *The Shining*, to the powers responsible for luring Jack back to the hotel, the ones from whose point of view the camera advances on the frustrated man in the Navajo-decorated lounge.

The silences and the missing omniscience are caused by the auteur's own absence from his film, a point made by Stephen Mamber: "Absent power figures are a Kubrick staple, whether it's which general is in charge, or who stuck that monolith there anyway, or where that narrator went in *The Killing* and *Barry Lyndon*. The most absent figure is, of course, Kubrick himself, whose mythic image as a castle-inhabiting control-freak is the only media creation able to rival his own power-mad figures. Behind all those hotel doors setting ghastly images in motion, dripping blood out of elevators, providing the unexplained means of escape to frequently trapped characters, lies the director himself, a parody puppeteer in the shadows."[85]

Thus a decade and a half later, Kubrick's singular horror film is variously appreciated for the limitlessness of possibility created by the filmmaker's complex silence. Patrick McGilligan in his 1994 biography of Jack Nicholson writes, "Time has sided more with the crank minority who, even then, felt that *The Shining* ranked with Kubrick's finest." "If you haven't seen *The Shining* recently," wrote Vincent Canby in *The New York Times* in 1993, "rent the video sometime soon. In some eerie fashion, it gets better every year."[86] Although the Canby/Maslin/Caryn James era of *Times* movie reviewing has usually given the work of ambitious auteurs a more careful reading than the rest of the media (in short, time caught up with the sympathetic 1980 *Times* appraisals of *The Shining*), McGilligan's word choice tells much about the film's latter-day acceptance; if "time has sided with a crank minority," the eccentricity that initially distinguished the film is now embraced rather than sneered at.

The horror elements can be identified but so can the auteur's spin on them. Jack Nicholson's performance seems an addition to his gallery of absurdly self-deluded men, rather than a vulgar affront to realistic acting. And given the fate of the horror cycle, which largely ran its course, as Paul notes, by the late 1980s and the dismal fates of virtually all of the many subsequent big-screen adaptations of Stephen King novels, *The Shining* now seems an example of Jauss' principle that a distinctive work can itself change the horizon of expectations. But this does not mean that the world is ready to appreciate post-modern parody or pastiche, that mass audience reviewers are equipped to recognize alternatives to classical realism when

302 ◆ DENNIS BINGHAM

they surface in ostensibly mainstream products like Kubrick's, or that the next Kubrick film won't find new ways to stupefy expectations.

Notes

1. Dudley Andrew, "The Unauthorized Auteur Today," in *Film Theory Goes to the Movies*, ed. Jim Collins, Hilary Radner, and Ava Preacher Collins (New York and London: Routledge, 1993), 77–85. Tim Corrigan, *A Cinema without Walls: Movies and Culture after Vietnam* (New Brunswick, NJ: Rutgers University Press, 1991), 101–136. James Naremore, "Authorship and the Cultural Politics of Film Criticism," *Film Quarterly* 44, no. 2 (Winter 1991): 14–22.

2. Andrew Sarris, "Notes on the Auteur Theory in 1962," in *Film Theory and Criticism: Introductory Readings*, 4th ed., ed. Gerald Mast, Marshall Cohen, Leo Braudy (New York and Oxford: Oxford University Press, 1992): 585–588. Peter Wollen, *Signs and Meaning in the Cinema* 3rd ed. (Bloomington: Indiana University Press, 1972): 74–115. Michel Foucault, "What Is an Author," in *The Foucault Reader* (New York: Pantheon, 1985): 101–20. Roland Barthes, "The Death of the Author," in *Image, Music, Text*, trans. Stephen Heath (New York: Hill and Wang, 1977): 142–148.

3. Corrigan, 105.

4. André Bazin, "The Evolution of the Language of Cinema" (1950–55), in *What Is Cinema*, vol. 1, ed. and trans. Hugh Gray (Berkeley: University of California Press, 1967): 29; "On the politique des auteurs" (1957), in *Cahiers du Cinéma: The 1950s: Neo-Realism, Hollywood, New Wave*, ed. Jim Hillier (Cambridge: Harvard University Press, 1985): 257.

5. Robert Phillip Kolker, *A Cinema of Loneliness: Penn, Kubrick, Scorsese, Spielberg, Altman*, 2nd ed. (New York and Oxford: Oxford University Press, 1988).

6. Andrew, 81.

7. Ed Guerrero, *Framing Blackness: The African American Image in Film* (Philadelphia: Temple University Press, 1993): 115.

8. John Hofsess, "*The Shining*: Stanley Kubrick Is Hoping His Film of Stephen King's Horror Story Will Be a Monster Hit," *The Washington Post*, 1 June 1980, H11.

9. Richard Schickel, "Red Herrings and Refusals," *Time*, 2 June 1980, 69.

10. Kolker, 151.

11. Robert Kapsis, *Hitchcock: The Making of a Reputation* (Chicago: University of Chicago, 1992): 208.

12. Stephen Mamber, "In Search of Radical Metacinema," in *Comedy/Cinema/Theory*, ed. Andrew Horton (Berkeley: University of California Press, 1991), 84.

13. Myron Meisel, "The Sixth Annual Grosses Gloss," *Film Comment*, (March-April 1981): 69.

14. Richard T. Jameson, "Kubrick's Shining," *Film Comment* (July-August 1980): 28–29.

15. Dennis Bingham, "Masculinity and Hallucination: *The Shining*." Chap. 11 in *Acting Male: Masculinities in the Films of James Stewart, Jack Nicholson, and Clint Eastwood* (New Brunswick, NJ: Rutgers University Press, 1994): 136–148.

16. Janet Staiger, *Interpreting Films: Studies in the Historical Reception of American Cinema* (Princeton: Princeton University Press, 1992): 9.

17. Robert C. Holub, *Reception Theory: A Critical Introduction* (1984) (London and New York: Routledge, 1989): 59–60.

18. Charles Maland, *Chaplin and American Culture* (Princeton: Princeton University Press, 1989): 331. This explanation comes up in the reception history of *Monsieur Verdoux* (1947), a bitter black comedy whose disastrous critical and commercial reception helped wreck the fortunes of Chaplin as an American filmmaker. After seventeen years out of circulation, however, the film met with great acclaim on its 1964 reissue. This demonstrates Jauss's point that a work that is out of step with the audience's expectations can by its

existence change those expectations over time. A process very like this, put on fast-forward in the age of VCRs, appears to have occurred in the case of *The Shining*.

19. Kapsis, 11. Emphasis in the original.

20. Barbara Klinger, "Much Ado about Excess: Genre, Mise-en-Scène and the Woman in *Written on the Wind*," *Wide Angle* 11, no. 4 (Fall 1989): 4–22. See also Cynthia Erb, "Film and Reception: A Contextual and Reading Formation Study of '*King Kong*' (1933), (Ph.D. diss., Indiana University, 1991).

21. Kolker, 78.

22. Colin Young, "The Hollywood War of Independence," *Film Quarterly* 12, no. 2 (Winter 1959): 10–11.

23. Robert Sklar, "Stanley Kubrick and the American Film Industry," *Current Research in Film: Audiences, Economics, and Law*, vol. 4 ed. Bruce A. Austin (Norwood, NJ: Ablex, 1988): 118.

24. For a strong critique of the New Critical and anti-audience orientations of auteurism, see Nick Roddick, *A New Deal in Entertainment: Warner Brothers in the 1930s* (London: BFI, 1983), 12–14.

25. Judy Lee Kinney, "Mastering the Maze," *Quarterly Review of Film Studies* 9 (Spring 1984): 138.

26. Foucault, 104.

27. Andrew, 85.

28. Richard Jameson, 28.

29. Sklar, 122.

30. Hofsess, H11.

31. Jim Albertson and Peter S. Perakos, "*The Shining*," Cinefantastique 7, no. 3–4 (Fall 1978): 74.

32. Aljean Harmetz, "Kubrick Films *The Shining* In Secrecy in English Studio," *The New York Times*, 6 November 1978, 72.

33. Hofsess, H11.

34. David Denby, "Death Warmed Over," *New York*, 9 June 1980, 60.

35. "The Shining: But Not Bright," *Variety*, 28 May 1980, 14.

36. Tom Allen, "Hatchet Job," *The Village Voice*, 2 June 1980, 42.

37. Stanley Kauffmann, "The Dulling," *The New Republic*, 14 June 1980, 27.

38. Kauffmann, 26–27.

39. Stephen Harvey, "'Shining' It Isn't," *Saturday Review* (July 1980): 64.

40. Jack Kroll, "Stanley Kubrick's Horror Show," *Newsweek*, 26 May 1980, 96.

41. Schickel, 69. William Wolf, "The Dream Master," *New York*, 9 June 1980, 63.

42. Janet Maslin, "Flaws Don't Dim The Shining," *The New York Times*, 8 June 1980, C1.

43. Janet Maslin, "Nicholson and Shelley Duvall in Kubrick's *The Shining*," *The New York Times*, 23 May 1980, C8.

44. Andrew Sarris, "We Are Family," *The Village Voice*, 5 November 1980, 49.

45. Richard T. Jameson, 29.

46. Flo Leibowitz and Lynn Jeffries, "*The Shining*," *Film Quarterly* 34, no. 2 (Winter 1981): 48–50. For further treatment of sociological issues in the film, see David A. Cook, "*The Shining*: American Horror," *Literature/Film Quarterly* 12, no. 1 (Fall 1984): 2–4.

47. Larry W. Caldwell and Samuel J. Umland, "'Come and Play with Us': The Play Metaphor in Kubrick's *The Shining*," *Literature/Film Quarterly* 14, no. 2 (Winter 1986): 106, 110–111.

48. Kroll's *Newsweek* review is followed by a production story which details the painstaking lengths to which Kubrick went. Scatman Crothers, who played Halloran, said, "In one scene I had to get out of a Sno-Cat and walk across the street, no dialogue. Forty takes. He had Jack Nicholson walk across the street, no dialogue. Fifty takes. He had Shelley, Jack and the kid walk across the street. Eighty-seven takes, man, he always wants something new and he doesn't stop until he gets it" (97–99).

49. Mario Falsetto, "The Mad and the Beautiful: A Look at Two Performances in the Films of Stanley Kubrick," *Making Visible the Invisible: An Anthology of Original Essays on Film Acting*, ed. Carole Zucker (Metuchen, NJ: Scarecrow Press, 1990): 343.

50. Paul Mayersberg, "The Overlook Hotel," *Sight and Sound* (Winter 1980–81): 57.

51. Mamber, 88–89.

52. Ibid., 80.

53. Ibid., 81.

54. Mayersberg, 57.

55. King said in 1980: "Horror's basic theme is the confirmation of our feelings of normality. 'The outsider must be stamped out.' 'If you're different you're bad.' Horror movies are as Republican as Gerald Ford, and the really interesting ones play with that theme." William Wilson, "Riding the Crest of the Horror Craze," *The New York Times Magazine*, 11 May 1980, 46.

56. Linda Hutcheon, *A Theory of Parody: The Teachings of Twentieth-Century Art Forms* (New York and London: Methuen, 1985): 74.

57. Linda Hutcheon, "An Epilogue: Postmodern Parody: History, Subjectivity, and Ideology," *Quarterly Review of Film and Video* 12 (1990): 125.

58. Ibid., 129.

59. Fredric Jameson, "Historicism in *The Shining*" (1981), *Signatures of the Visible* (New York and London: Routledge, 1990): 82.

60. Fredric Jameson, *Postmodernism, or, The Cultural Logic of Late Capitalism* (Durham, NC: Duke University Press, 1991): 17.

61. Jameson, "Historicism in *The Shining*," 84.

62. Ibid., 90.

63. Hutcheon, *A Theory of Parody*, 104.

64. P. L. Titterington, "Kubrick and *The Shining*," *Sight and Sound*, (Spring 1981): 120–121.

65. Mamber, 85.

66. Vivian Sobchack, "Child/Alien/Father: Patriarchal Crisis and Generic Exchange," *Camera Obscura* 15 (Fall 1986): 15. Emphasis in the original.

67. Ibid., 15; Greg Keeler, "*The Shining*: Ted Kramer Has a Nightmare," *The Journal of Popular Film and Television* 8, no. 4 (Winter 1981): 8.

68. William Paul, *Laughing, Screaming: Modern Hollywood Horror and Comedy* (New York: Columbia University Press, 1994): 342.

69. Christopher Hoile, "The Uncanny and the Fairy Tale in Kubrick's *The Shining*," *Literature/Film Quarterly* 12, no. 1 (Fall 1984): 5.

70. Ibid., 8.

71. Sigmund Freud, "The Uncanny," *Studies of Parapsychology*, ed. Philip Rieff (New York: Collier, 1963), 28.

72. Bingham, 144–147.

73. Hoile, 6–7. Animism, as defined by Hoile—"the language of the child's, the neurotic's, and our own primitive mind" (8)—brings up the troubling treatment of race in the character of Hallorann, the black chef played by Scatman Crothers: "When Torrance kills Hallorann, who has come to rescue the family, he kills Danny's good guardian and contact in the animistic world" (10). I can't find any criticism which discusses the film's racial politics in much detail. Race functions importantly, however, in two senses. One seems very conscious: the "trace" of racial genocide in America to which the murdering white man is recalled in this hotel "built on an Indian burial ground." It is thus no accident that Kubrick puts the explanation of "traces" of the past in the mouth of a black man, who would know. It is also no accident that Grady, Jack's "double" from the past, calls Hallorann "a nigger cook," while the hotel manager Ullman, had called him, in the "colorblind" usage of a culture that has repressed its racism, "our chef."

The other, much less conscious sense, comes from the King novel, and Kubrick, unfortunately, appears to have left it more or less intact. This connects to the racial iconography of "house Negroes" such as cooks as "good guardians," protectors of the white folks, a convention which runs back through the Shirley Temple-Bill "Bojangles" Robinson films of the 1930s and *The Birth of a Nation* (1915) to *Uncle Tom's Cabin*. "Shining" appears to be a gift given to children and blacks because they are presumably closer to an "animistic," primitive life. "Animism" is connected to "atavism," as Richard Dyer discusses the connotative connection of black stars such as Paul Robeson to African "savagery." Atavism "implies the recovery of qualities that have been carried in the blood from generation to generation, and this may be crossed with a certain kind of Freudianism, suggesting taboo impulses and emotions that may be recovered. It also suggests raw, violent, chaotic, and 'primitive' emotions." *Heavenly Bodies: Film Stars and Society* (New York: St. Martin's, 1986), 89.

Thus the irony of the trap in which Kubrick gets snared is clear. This "recovery . . . crossed with a certain kind of Freudianism" pertains exactly to Kubrick's notion of the evolution of the white male power structure, with the "Dawn of Man" and its discovery of weaponry and battle never far behind. In Kubrick it is white men who are both animistic and atavistic, in spite of both the advance of civilization and a homogenized, de-tribalized culture. Nonetheless, the presentation of the black character as a collection of deep-seated stereotypes exemplifies the danger of Kubrick's cryptic, elliptical style of exposition and signification, once again moving critics to misread (perhaps) his intentions: Pauline Kael wrote in 1980, "The awful suspicion pops into the mind that since we don't want Wendy or Danny hurt and there's no one else alive around for Jack to get at, he's given the black man." "Devolution," *The New Yorker*, 9 June 1980, in *Taking It All In* (New York: Holt, Rinehart, Winston, 1984), 6.

There is little racial signification in Kubrick's films before *The Shining*, except for an extraordinary scene in *The Killing* with James Edwards and Tim Carey in which fate ironically appears to have wreaked vengeance on behalf of a black man. It is more likely that Kubrick has an ironic reverse atavism mixed up with the satiric attitude toward the noble images of 1950s and 1960s white liberalism that moved him to cast James Earl Jones as Major Kong's bombardier in Dr. Strangelove, knowing the confusion such signfication would wreak in well-meaning white souls. But even this is not clear. At times Hallorann, albeit played with "dignity" (itself a trap) by Scatman Crothers, recalls what is perhaps the most embarrassing scene Kubrick ever filmed: the uncomfortable slapstick over a collapsable bed between Humbert and a black bellhop in *Lolita*. Moreover, the fetishistic paintings of nude black women in Hallorann's apartment come uncomfortably close to the nudes on the Catwoman's walls in *A Clockwork Orange*.

Thus Kubrick's confused attitude toward women is compounded with his confused attitude toward blacks: he seems not to have thought very much about either (perhaps the only modern issues he hasn't thought about very much). This blind spot is most noticeable in *2001*, which predicted that by the millenium Russians and Americans would be allies, but judging from Kubrick's all-white American space teams, failed to anticipate even the appearance of racial progress in the future (a lapse which put it behind TV's Star Trek, with its African American crew member). More recently, *Full Metal Jacket*, like *The Shining*, placed racism as part of the American social topography, with blacks fighting Vietnamese in a distinctly white war ethic. However, in avoiding negative signification of blacks, Kubrick omitted signifying them at all, except as "real people." This of course is problematic since Kubrick finds all "reality" to be heavily codified and contrived. Therefore, blackness in *Full Metal Jacket* comes off as nothing more than an anti-stereotype (or an anti-stereotypical stereotype): thus it is invisible. The consequent invisibility of these issues in criticism on Kubrick may have helped dismiss him as a white male auteur for white male critics.

74. Bruno Bettelheim, The Uses of Enchantment (New York: Knopf, 1976): 72.

75. Kolker, 155.

76. See Bettelheim, 71–72, on the fairy-tale motif of "The Three Wishes."

77. Bettelheim, 62.

78. Hoile, 11.

79. Paul, 338–339; Hoile, 11.

80. Paul, 342–343.

81. David Bordwell, Janet Staiger, and Kristin Thompson, *The Classical Hollywood Cinema: Film Style and Mode of Production to 1960* (New York: Columbia University Press, 1985): 373.

82. Michael Bérubé, *Public Access: Literary Theory and American Cultural Politics* (London and New York: Verso, 1994): 190.

83. Ibid., 182.

84. Ibid., 190.

85. Mamber, 88.

86. Patrick McGilligan, *Jack's Life: A Biography of Jack Nicholson* (New York: Norton, 1994), 320–321.

Full Metal Genre: Stanley Kubrick's Vietnam Combat Movie

THOMAS DOHERTY

Since 1977, Hollywood has been succeeding where Washington consistently failed: namely, in selling Vietnam to the American public. To be fair, the motion picture industry enjoys a crucial edge. If the military's classic mistake is to fight with the tactics of the last war, the moviemaker's decisive prerogative is the license to fight the same war over and over again. Whatever the historical uniqueness of what *Time-Life* Books calls "the Vietnam experience," the conventions of the Hollywood combat film have proven flexible enough to accommodate America's outcast war even as Vietnam has in turn reinvigorated a moribund Hollywood genre.

Released in the wake of Oliver Stone's *Platoon* and sharing marquee space with *Hamburger Hill* and *The Hanoi Hilton,* Stanley Kubrick's *Full Metal Jacket* exemplifies the Vietnam War film in its mature stage, a stage whose distinguishing quality is its reliance on cinematic, not historical, experience. The Vietnam film has not yet settled into the ripe generic dotage of the private eye or western genre, but it has reached the point where previous Vietnam films as much as Vietnam memory determine its rough outlines. As with any genre, a recurrent set of visual motifs, narrative patterns, and thematic concerns has emerged. For better and worse, these conventions are the immediate and unavoidable referents for *Full Metal Jacket,* a cinematic usurpation of the historical record that reaffirms the vital cultural function of genre: to ease division and reconcile conflict through myth. Like the Vietnam War Memorial on the Washington Mall, the Vietnam combat film is the occasion for a soothing ritual of atonement and celebration, a screen that reflects back the two faces of American regret and pride.

That range of reaction is neatly encompassed by Michael Herr and Gustav Hasford, Kubrick's co-screenwriters for *Full Metal Jacket.* Both were participant-observers in the war, Herr as a civilian journalist, Hasford as a combat correspondent for the Marines; both wrote estimable accounts of their tours of duty, Herr in the crystalline memoir *Dispatches* (1978) and Hasford in the phantasmagorical war-novel that serves as the source for Kubrick's film, *The Short Timers* (1979). Herr's book is a kaleidoscopic series of snapshots alternately—simultaneously—positive and negative.

Copyright the Regents of the University of California. From *Film Quarterly*, 42, no. 2 (1988–89), pp. 24–30. Reprinted by permission.

Despite everything, Herr finds the Vietnam ground at once immoral and holy, glorious and horrible. Its penultimate image is darkly ironic. A wounded wreck of a war correspondent, crippled in mind and body, raves about the impossibility of fulfilling a publisher's mandate to write a book "whose purpose would be to once and for all take the glamor out of war." He shrieks out a question that antiwar film-makers have agonized over since *The Big Parade:* "Take the glamor out of war! I mean how the bloody hell can you do *that?*"

Hasford supplies the answer. Where Herr is sentimental, and mythopoetic, Hasford is searing and ruthless—above all, toward the celluloid-sustained image of Men at War. In *The Short Timers* Hollywood's combat dreams run headlong into Vietnam's charnel reality. "Harry S. Truman once said that the Marine Corps has a propaganda machine almost equal to Stalin's," observes the Information Service Officer in Hasford's book, and the "crap civilians have seen in Jack Webb's *The D.I.* and Mr. John Wayne's *The Sands of Iwo Jima*" helps power the engine. An elite, all-volunteer service, the Marines boast a set of elaborate rituals and a history of bloody combat that make them the most cultish, celebrated, and cinematic of the American armed forces. Not for nothing is the signature photograph from World War II a Marine moment, the flag-raising on Mount Surabachi, Iwo Jima. "Grunts are good show business, but we make them what they are," boasts Hasford's ISO, "Marines fight harder because Marines have bigger legends to live up to." Hasford defaces that recruiting poster portrait of warfare and debunks a military code of honor rendered alternately immoral and inane by Vietnam—though "debunk" is probably too soft a word for Hasford's venomous attack on the brotherhood he once served.

In Kubrick, who launched his own blitzkrieg assault on the military in wars hot [*Paths of Glory* (1957)] and cold [*Dr. Strangelove* (1964)], Hasford's bitter, subversive vision might seem to have found a sympathetic interpreter, just as the Vietnam war had finally met up with the director best equipped to do it proper injustice. In the transference from novel to film, however, the Marine machine emerges in pretty good working order. Negotiating the space between Herr's mythic shadings and Hasford's black hatred, Kubrick opts for accommodation and continuity. Even for the expatriate film-maker, it seems, the combat film has a code of conduct as severe, inviolable, and ultimately seductive as the one enforced on Parris Island.

Appropriately, the first rule of engagement for the Vietnam combat film is acknowledgment of its own patrimony. The blood ties between the traditional combat film and its Vietnam descendant cut deeper than the usual anxiety of generic influence. Always, there is the whisper of complicity, the suspicion that Hollywood lent its imagination to the disaster: A true son of Hollywood and television, the Vietnam soldier was weaned on mass-mediated fantasies of World War II combat. Never far from his consciousness are films like *The Sands of Iwo Jima* (1949), *Halls of Montezuma* (1950), and *To Hell and Back* (1955), TV series such as *Combat* and *The Desert Rats,* and comic books like DC's *Sgt. Rock* and Marvel's *Sgt. Fury and His Howling Commandoes.* As if in penance for the excesses and duplicities of the past, the Vietnam combat film embraces a stony narrative authenticity and cynical verisimilitude—or at least it must appear to. Obviously, the fanciful action-adventure pics of Chuck Norris and Sylvester Stallone partake of the old matinee spirit with relish, but reflection and seriousness dominate the genre, and not just the works of the big-gun auteurs. More often than not, a film depicting combat in Vietnam presents itself as no blood-and-guts Hollywood fantasy, but the genuine item, one step removed from actually being in the bush (viz., *Time*'s cover on *Platoon:* "Vietnam As It Really Was").

Tellingly, in Vietnam vernacular an act of reckless courage is "pulling a John Wayne." Almost obsessively, the Vietnam genre returns to the backlot heroics of Wayne, above all his role as steely Marine Sgt. John Stryker in *The Sands of Iwo Jima.* (In addition to *The Short Timers,* the film is singled out by name in Ron Kovic's *Born on the Fourth of July* and Philip Caputo's *A Rumor of War.*) Oddly, it is one of the handful of films in which John Wayne dies and his tough-as-nails sergeant is by no means a character to be naively admired. Alcoholic, divorced, insubordinate, Sgt. Stryker is among the walking wounded; he charges an enemy machinegun nest because he has so little to lose. No dewy-eyed paean to combat glory, *The Sands of Iwo Jima* portrays war as unforgiving and cruel: a thoughtless coffee break causes the death of one's comrades and the Duke himself gets shot in a surprise ending as radically disruptive as anything in the Vietnam film genre. By all accounts, however, such subtleties were lost on the adolescent audience. In what has become a *locus classicus* of the Vietnam war memoir, Ron Kovic describes how he and his friend Castiglia would sit spellbound before *To Hell and Back* and *The Sands of Iwo Jima,* feeding off Hollywood for the raw material of schoolboy daydreams:

> The Marine Corps hymn was playing in the background as we sat glued to our seats, humming the hymn together and watching Stryker, played by John Wayne, charge up the hill and get killed just before he reached the top. And then they showed the men raising the flag on Iwo Jima with the Marines' hymn still playing, and Castiglia and I cried in our seats. I loved the song so much, and every time I heard it I would think of John Wayne and the brave men who raised the flag on Iwo Jima that day. I would think of them and cry. Like Mickey Mantle and the fabulous New York Yankees, John Wayne in *The Sands of Iwo Jima* became one of my heroes.

Exacerbating Wayne's iconic centrality was his infamous foray into Vietnam agit-prop, *The Green Berets* (1968). A memorable scene in *The*

Short Timers has real-life grunts bent over in hysterics at a screening of Wayne's war: "At the end of the movie, John Wayne walks off into the sunset with a spunky little orphan. The grunts laugh and whistle and threaten to pee all over themselves. The sun is setting in the South China Sea—in the East—which makes the end of the movie as accurate as the rest of it."

The Vietnam film consistently makes reference by way of debunking to the on-screen firefights and backlot heroics of the classical Hollywood combat film, as when the gung-ho lieutenant in *Go Tell the Spartans* (1978) learns too late that the VC fire live ammunition. Throughout *Full Metal Jacket*, John Wayne mimic Private Joker (Matthew Modine) harkens back to the matinee dreams of boyhood and voices his adult disillusionment and displacement with drawling impersonations: "Listen up, Pilgrims. . . ."

A proper sense of Vietnam decorum demands the proper language. Nothing captures the Nam better than the Word. Any Vietnam film with pretentions to verisimilitude has faithfully to record and incorporate into its dialogue the unique speech of the Vietnam era soldier. Just as the FNG (fucking new guy) is initiated into the soldierly subculture where "book" is a verb and "dinks" is a noun, so the audience is initially confused with Vietnam-variety vernacular. Needless to say, the creative deployment of obscenity, especially "fuck" and derivatives thereof, has an incantatory function. Likewise, a whole range of military acronyms (AIT, CIB, RPG), bastardized Vietnamese ("most rickeytick"), Japanese ("skosh"), French (the ubiquitous "beaucoup"), broken English, and black English vernacular remains an exotic subcultural dialect, the knowledgeable use of which grants admission to the brotherhood of Vietnam warriors. Like all subcultural slang, its purpose is not only to identify the kindred spirit but to brand the non-conversant as alien—as in *Full Metal Jacket* when a seasoned grunt explains to FNG Rafter Man, and the audience, the meaning of "the thousand-yard stare."

Opposing the richness and directness of the speech of the troops, though often employed ironically by them, is the Orwellian language of euphemism and disguise used by the Armed Forces and the civilian authorities. The arcane military call signs, the stolid bureaucratese, and the forms and statistics that are so much a part of military life reached cavernous depths of obtuseness and impenetrability in Vietnam. The classic is "to terminate with extreme prejudice" immortalized in *Apocalypse Now*, though the editorial instructions given to combat correspondent Joker—to distinguish between an "evacuee" and a "refugee" and to change "search and destroy" to "sweep and clean"—rank a close second.

Both the soldierly slang and the Orwellian language serve an analogous function: emotional insulation. Hence also the troops' consistent replacement of surnames by nicknames—totally so in *Full Metal Jacket*, whose dramatis personae carry monikers like Joker, Rafter Man, Cowboy, Animal

Mother, and Eightball. As Tim O'Brian wrote in his war memoir *If I Die in a Combat Zone*, "the platoon's squad leaders were named Ready Whip, Nestle's Quick, and Shake and Bake. And when two of them—Tom and Arnold—were killed two months later, the tragedy was somehow lessened and depersonalized by telling ourselves that ol' Ready Whip and Quick got themselves wasted by slopes." Ironically, it is the linguistic element, the verbal not the visual, that most clearly distinguishes the Vietnam film from predecessor combat films as well as its contemporary action-adventure competition.

In *Full Metal Jacket,* the language is splendid, a lyric bombardment of raw Marine obscenity—homophobic, misogynistic, sado-masochistic, racist, and exuberantly poetic. Where Clint Eastwood's gunnery sergeant in *Heartbreak Ridge* (1987) was but a colorfully dirty wordsmith, Sgt. Hartman is a poet laureate of verbal vulgarity. Spouting a series of ethnic slurs at the raw recruits (a.k.a. "amphibious shit") and preaching a rank military egalitarianism ("you are all equally worthless"), Hartman is such a virtuoso of vile invective that the main response to his torrents of abuse is delight in a master at work. Screenwriters Kubrick, Herr, and especially Hasford (the film's most memorable phrases are drawn verbatim from his *The Short Timers*) bestow upon Hartman the film's best lines and Lee Ermey, a for-real ex-DI, turns in its most magnetic performance, a portrayal that for all its hard-ass hyperbole never moves from boot camp into Sontag camp. His declamations are so hilarious and he so dominates the long first act—a self-contained, fifty-minute induction into Marine subculture—that you're sorry to see him go.

For all his vocal dominance, Hartman is the most impersonal of cinematic DIs. Outside of his DI persona, we know nothing about him. In following the maggot point of view of Hasford's book, Kubrick departs radically from the Marine Corps indoctrination film of classical Hollywood, a form that consistently subordinated battlefield action to melodramatic revelation, that stripped away layers of military insulation to get to the warm human core beneath the officer corps. The prime narrative movement was not from tranquillity to combat, but from basic training to Marine Membership, a ceremonial rite of passage into the Corps that was more dramatically central than any beachhead landing. The induction and basic training sequences, often shot on location at Parris Island and made with the cooperation of the Marine Corps, outpointed combat footage in both running time and emotional investment. Getting through training was the real initiation rite. The touchstone is Jack Webb's *The D.I.* (1957), which dispenses with battle sequences altogether. Less a combat film than a familial melodrama, *The D.I.* has Marine drill sergeant Jim Moore battling for the soul of a recalcitrant recruit, not an enemy machinegun nest. In the persons of John Wayne, Jack Webb, or Clint Eastwood, the gruff drill sergeant fronted a complex, haunted human being. About Hartman,

Kubrick tells us nothing. The man is his function. Kubrick's impersonality extends to the lower orders: there's none of the economical character delineation and identification that would humanize the recruits, no Warner Brothers-style platoonery. This is a film short on reaction shots and nearly bereft of eyeline matches: the vantage is distancing, almost antiseptic, as scrubbed-down as the squad's ghostly white barracks lavatory.

In spite of—because of—the mechanical treatment of mechanical training, the ritual ballet of basic training (small arms drill, mock combat, obstacle course, inspection, quick-time march) has a synchronized beauty that seduces director and spectator alike. Conjuring the Orwellian union of the masses with Big Brother, Kubrick renders the visceral appeal of being a working cog in a well-oiled machine, of enveloping the private self in a full metal jacket. "The marines want killers, not robots," Joker's narrative voice-over observes, but getting in lockstep is the necessary first step.

The quagmire that was Vietnam finds apt expression in the imagistic and thematic concentration on the literal and metaphoric grossness of "life in country," a veritable fecal obsession wallowed in most vividly in Stallone's sewage immersion scene in *Rambo*. The line repeated most often, *Full Metal Jacket*'s mock benediction, is the description of earthly life as a "world of shit," an existential state the military and Vietnam cannot be held totally responsible for. Plunged deepest into the cesspool is recruit Leonard (Vincent D'Onofrio), a good-natured goober Hartman labels "Private Pyle." Pudgy, slack-jawed, totally lacking in motor skills, he is the platoon goat. Hartman ritually humiliates him, first by forcing him to march behind the platoon, thumb in mouth, pants around his ankles, and later by demanding he scarf a jelly doughnut while his comrades pay the price of his gluttony with push-ups at his feet. Urged by Hartman to give Leonard the "proper motivation," the recruits stage a nighttime, nightmarish raid on the sleeping baby. One by one, they close in for an assault, savagely whacking him with soap wrapped tightly in towels. Joker, who passes for an audience point of identification, joins in first reluctantly and then with brutal enthusiasm. When we next see Leonard in stark close-up, he is a new, or rather a non, man. Eyeballs rolled high, mouth back in a ghastly grin, he has gone over the edge. No one fixes an actor's gaze like Kubrick—think of Jack Nicholson leering demonically in *The Shining*—and Leonard's face holds a terror more potent than anything awaiting the boys in the Nam. He truly looks to be, as he says, in a world of shit.

It is in the barracks lavatory that he freaks out, that the violent rite of passage comes to a head. For this sequence, Kubrick's set design bears comment because it is reportedly his only liberty with authentic Marine interior decor. Stark white, two rows of open toilets face each other, with Leonard, himself in white underwear and astride a john, smack dab in this literal world of shit. On fire watch, Joker enters and Leonard explains that his M-14 is indeed being loaded with live rounds ("7.62 mm, full metal jacket"). Hartman bursts in on the commotion, totally unintimidated by the live weapon, and bellows, "What is your major malfunction, numbnuts?" A patented slo-mo impact shot records Leonard's high-velocity answer: Hartman's chest explodes and he falls lifeless to the immaculate floor. After a tense consideration of Joker, Leonard sits down, turns the barrel into his mouth, and blows himself against the bathroom wall. His red blood splatters against the pure white tile. After this, Vietnam is redundant.

The first glimpse of life "in country" is the chassis of a leather-skirted hooker sashaying down the streets of Saigon. Nancy Sinatra's "These Boots" provides ironic sound-track accompaniment, the veiled S&M undertones of the title footwear conjuring also the forward march of military escalation. Like the 1966 pop hit, double meanings and metaphorical associations tend to proliferate in the context of Vietnam—sex and violence, johns and soldiers, the screwing of the Vietnamese. Both playground and killing ground, Vietnam is a landscape for American projections.

That the Vietnam war was an imperialist extension of the American frontier mythos, especially in the campaign waged against the native population, has long been an article of faith for New Left historians. The extension of the American frontier myth to the jungles of Southeast Asia is also explicit in novels such as Mailer's *Why Are We in Vietnam?* and the Leatherstocking-inspired film, *The Deer Hunter* (1978). As a sort of surrogate western, the Vietnam film offers a convenient new territory for interracial firefights. Among other reasons for the decline of the classical Hollywood western is surely the inadmissibility of guilt-free cowboy-and-Indian play—the conspicuously absent element in two contemporaneous attempts at genre resuscitation, *Silverado* (1985) and *Pale Rider* (1985), being the native population. The Vietnam cowboy has it both ways, alternately battling the Indian-like VC or, as in *Rambo* and *Missing in Action*, assuming himself the guise of the Apache warrior. In *Full Metal Jacket*, the connection is articulated for the cogniscenti during a tracking shot where the grunts face a network camera crew and call out in sequence a related screen fantasy called *Vietnam: The Movie* for the folks back home. "We'll let the gooks play the Indians," suggests a soldier.

The frontier ethos was not without compensations. In good Leslie Fiedler fashion, the American dream of homoerotic interracial brotherhood is played out in the jungles of Vietnam no less than on the waters of the Mississippi. If racial animosities remain acute in the rear echelon, racism is a dangerous indulgence in the bush. Propelled both by good Hollywood liberalism and the box-office power of the inner-city black audience, blacks appear as featured and secondary players, always among the grunt ensemble, often as non-com lifers and grizzled majors. In *Full Metal Jacket*, for example, the huge white grunt Animal Mother hassles and slurs his black comrade Eightball. But when Eightball lies wounded, stranded in an open field, it is Animal Mother who disobeys orders and makes a heroic rescue charge.

Though the black-white relation remains primary, two other ethnics are featured up front in the Vietnam combat film. Contrary to popular belief, Hispanic Americans, not black Americans, served and died out of all proportion to their numbers in Vietnam. (The recognition of the Hispanic American is also symbolized by his representation in the statue at the entrance of the Vietnam War Memorial on the Washington Mall.) The roots here in the classical combat film—with the obligatory Bronx Jew, Brooklyn Italian, and Iowa Farm Boy issued to each squad—are self-evident. The portrayal of the Vietnam platoon often deploys the same cozy clichés of ethnic representation and tolerant camaraderie as its predecessor.

By contrast, the South Vietnamese troops, and by implication America's latest prominent immigrant group, are the object of derision and disdain. Reflecting a widespread contempt toward the ARVN forces by American combat units, the nominal allies come in for consistently bad treatment. Typical is the establishing sequence in *Go Tell the Spartans* (1978) which features ARVN forces torturing a captured VC. The screenplay of *Full Metal Jacket* is even harder on the South Vietnamese than Hasford's source novel. Cowboy complains of how he keeps running into ARVN troops "coming the other way" [retreating] and opines that "we're shooting the wrong gooks." To a man (and woman), the natives are whores, pimps, thieves, and cowards. One troop offers to sell an ARVN rifle with the old line "never been fired, only been dropped once." Thus, the introductory violent "action" for the Vietnam section of *Full Metal Jacket:* Saigon street punks stealing a camera from Joker and Rafter Man. After being ripped off, Rafter Man complains, "We're supposed to be helping them and they shit all over us." The punks respond by flipping the Americans the finger. Only rarely are the ARVN granted a degree of respect and equality with Americans, as in *The Green Berets* or in the person of Stallone's female sidekick in *Rambo*. By way of pointed comparison, the VC are consistently presented as the superior Vietnamese species: ruthlessly efficient, coldly determined, and authentically heroic. In the centerpiece action climax of *Full Metal Jacket*, a lone VC sniper (who turns out to be a woman) pins down and tears apart an entire squad of bewildered and desperate American Marines.

The director of *2001* pays his usual clinical attention to forensic detail. The crucible of combat is rendered with state-of-the-art technology and showcased for maximum effect. Advances in battlefield verisimilitude (gasoline explosions, timed charges, mock-ups, mattes, and miniatures) and stunt choreography (above all the trademark helicopter assaults and dustoffs, often piloted by veterans turned stuntmen) make any Vietnam combat film an exhilarating special-effects rollercoaster. The vivid depiction of the gruesome effect of sophisticated weapons on human flesh is not neglected, as in the ghastly appearance of the armless troop or the infamous brain-smashing sequence in *Platoon.*

Kubrick's most impressive special-effects achievement is his re-creation of the bombed-out city of Hue on a Pinewood backstage. Drawing on network videotape, the *Life* magazine photos of John Olsen, and Herr's eyewitness descriptions, Kubrick built the set from the ground up, utilizing a British industrial site slated for destruction. For all the painstaking reconstruction of the burned shell of the city, however, the tableau functions mainly as a hallucinatory dreamscape, not a geographical space. The stylization in the set design (even the bullets in the brick walls seem distributed with mathematical randomness) and the textbook flourish of the combat montages (the waist-level advance of the Steadicam, the studied entrapments of the *mise-en-scène,* the slo-mo rending of flesh) are calculated compromises. Kubrick chooses imagistic control over location verisimilitude or documentary realism. His Hue looks nothing like Vietnam—not even Thailand, the Philippines, or Mexico, the usual scenic backdrops for the Vietnam genre. Lacking the authority of the participant-observer, Kubrick won't compete with Oliver Stone on his own turf. *Full Metal Jacket* is not Vietnam As It Really Was, but as Kubrick realized it. For him, the odyssey through whatever space will always lead back to the self.

Or selves. The inside joke in this antiwar war film is its own double-dealing nature. With a peace symbol adorning his combat helmet, Joker himself is the bearer of the schizophrenic sensibility. "I was trying to suggest the duality of man," he observes a little too smartly to his superiors, "You know, the Jungian thing." Just as the Vietnam combat film depicts the absurdity and immorality of the war even as it exalts the courage and nobility in the American presence, Joker embodies mutually exclusive features. Like the Memorial on the DC Mall, he reflects no single face of the Vietnam War.

In that acceptance of options, *Full Metal Jacket* becomes far more complex and, yes, affirmative than Hasford's bitter novel. Hasford's nihilism knows no depths: his novel climaxes with an appalling bloodbath that has his narrator Joker reject finally the sacred Marine oath never to leave his wounded behind. He kills the stranded Cowboy rather than let his squad move forward and "commit suicide for a tradition." The climactic scene in *Full Metal Jacket* gives a similar scenario a different ending. Despite moments of terror and panic, despite the killing damage done them, the squad sustains and lives up to the Marine tradition—the mercy killing is aimed at the VC sniper, not a fellow Marine. Marines have died, but in a way not all that far from *The Sands of Iwo Jima,* the Marine tradition is upheld. Consecrated in the blood of the innocent, Joker attains a kind of purifying transcendence: "I'm in a world of shit, yes, but I am alive and I am not afraid." The final sequence frames the surviving grunts departing Hue at night in a beautiful, bloody haze. They are singing the Mickey Mouse Club theme—carrying Joker, and presumably the spectator, away from Vietnam and back to Hollywood, a movement that the Vietnam combat film has itself completed.

Full Metal Jacket:
The Unravelling of Patriarchy

MICHAEL PURSELL

"In language we create a symbolic model of the world, in which past and present are carried forward into the future."[1]

I want to offer some thoughts about *Full Metal Jacket,* partly in relation to other Vietnam films such as *Platoon* and *Hamburger Hill,* and partly in relation to the cultural context in which the film has appeared.

Quite suddenly, Thatcher's rhetoric has taken a new, religious turn. She is arguing the morality of wealth through doctrines such as "Work hard, save hard, give freely." This regression to Wesleyism is no surprise. On the one hand it cynically pre-empts real discussion about the means of creation and distribution of wealth. It threatens to reduce the media agenda about social ills to the agendum of the morality of wealth, thus, in effect, de-politicising populist discussion. On the other hand, the re-living of history is a British habit, steeped as we are in the regressive imperatives of a patriarchal culture. This is why, with no sense of strain, Thatcher can attend a militaristic Remembrance Sunday parade and drone about self-sacrifice while presiding over a yuppie culture. To such imperatives Thatcher must, by the nature of her politics, be commited.

I speak then, from a time-warp. It isn't that Thatcher has re-established Victorian values—that puerile endeavour continues—but that she is reverting to the ethical climate of the nineteenth century where, as now, Church and State were at odds over just this issue of wealth. In that context, how can I teach *Hard Times,* as required, without being political? The answer is that I can't and shouldn't.

In themselves ludicrous, Thatcher's posturings are indications of serious political intentions. To satisfy one such, the Secretary of State for Education, Kenneth Baker, set up a Committee of Enquiry into the Teaching of English Language under the chairmanship of Sir John Kingman FRS. To be fair to the Kingman Committee they did not conveniently produce exactly what the government wanted. Even so, the intention was clear enough: What was at stake was the control of the language and the transmission of knowledge about it; in other words, cultural politics. For this reason, if for no other, *Full Metal Jacket* is a timely film, for

From *Literature/Film Quarterly*, 16, no. 4 (1988), 218–225. Copyright © Salisbury State University. Reprinted by permission one of its concerns, though in a depth unguessed at by Kingman, is the politics of language. The language in *Full Metal Jacket* is of a very specific kind with profound cultural implications.

In the first paragraph of Chapter Two of the Kingman Report there is this;

> "In language we create a symbolic model of the world, in which past and present are carried forward into the future."

If we think about this in relation to *Full Metal Jacket* the film's implications become frighteningly clear, but for Kingman these symbolic models are offered as wholly, almost naively positive. There is a constant demand in the Report, for example, to re-instate Standard English—a written form which the Report confusedly ascribes to speech—as one aspect of a student's linguistic repertoire. It suggests that this will help to make available to the student "the best that has been thought and said in our language".[2] This may well happen, but behind this liberal paternalist plea for Standard English lies the government's Utilitarian desire for standardised English which will facilitate production and consumption in the upwardly mobile future it holds out to us. Behind that lurks a desire for a metropolitan orthodoxy and the implicit redundancy of regional variation under the linguistic hegemony of the Home Counties, exactly, in other words, Dickens' own attitude in *Hard Times*.[3] Behind all that lies Kingman's ignorance of, or unwillingness to engage, the idea that the spirit of Empire soldiers on.[4] One is left with the feeling that the Kingman Committee hardly seems to know what some of the questions might be, much less the answers. Again, the Report advocates the teaching of discourse structure to clarify received misinformation from "family and friends, work mates, advertisers, journalists, priests, politicians and pressure groups." This might seem to strike at the heart of patriarchy until it emerges that on the one hand the ideal student produces language that is concise and unambiguous and on the other that the Report itself is riddled with the abuse of the passive voice so characteristic of liberal-paternalist/patriarchal discourse. What kind of language report is it that fails to reflect and act upon its own practice in this way? To what extent does it really seek to impart to students the linguistic skills demanded by the ravelling or the unravelling of great cultural lies? It is such lies, of course, that *Full Metal Jacket* so unswervingly exposes. Kingman, however, prefers to dream on, about as connected with political reality as Gonzalo's dream of the ideal state.

Kingman's contributors, though writers, academics and journalists, don't seem to know what language actually does. "Language," they say, "confers freedom."[5] Perhaps they should impart this cheering news to Nelson Mandela. More revealing are the paternalist/patriarchal assumptions in that word "confers" and the erasure of a human grammatical subject doing the conferring. They continue;

"Language is the naming of experience, and what we name we have power over."[6]

In one sense this is patently silly: Naming God, the Inland Revenue and myocardial infarction does not give me power over these things. More pertinently, the "we" in that statement represents a spurious universality. When Caesar declares "Gallia est omnis divisa in partes tres" his use of the present tense and passive construction erase the fact that his division and naming of tribes is consequent upon the exercise of non-linguistic, primarily military, power. This is the forerunner of the liberal-paternalist erasures of Kingman. As important, however, is the role of the Auitani and the Belgae, for what Caesar will have them named, even that they are.[7]

That last phrase is, appropriately, borrowed from that crucial scene in *The Taming Of The Shrew* where Kate, to demonstrate her tractability, agrees to call the sun the moon as Petruchio insists. Kate's naming of the sun as the moon does not confer power upon her (unless by some patriarchal wrench we are ready to see entry into submissive wifehood as an access to power); in this naming she surrenders her power to another. Like Petruchio's moon, Kate herself becomes one of the named—a wife— in an act of compromise within the sexual power politics of her time. One wonders about the reactions of the Aquitani and the Belgae to Caesar's sweeping classification; there are plenty of lowland Scots who would be affronted to be called English, even though they speak it. They don't speak Standard English, though Kingman would have it so, and in that standardisation that gathers us into the universal "we" lies the really insidious erasure; the disappearance of the fact that participating in a linguistic and thus philosophical, intellectual and ethical system, is to surrender one's power to an establishment or, which is the same thing, to be empowered by it. Language confers *some* freedoms just as it withholds others.

This is certainly the effect of Hartman's training programme. The recruits have no power over the rifles Hartman insists they name; quite the reverse. Any power they have over themselves is thoroughly destroyed by Hartman's process of naming. Joker holds out longer than most but even he succumbs to the identity change he's half ready for at the start: "Is that you John Wayne? Is this me?" The recruits emerge as Marines because Hartman's language is not just nominative, it is constitutive: it is not random abuse but purposive discourse. Like Datherina, like the Belgae, the recruits are as they are spoken of, the final proof being their adoption, like Katharina and perhaps the Belgae too, of the language of their master.

Kingman, ironically named, doesn't begin to address such issues. Ideologies are the more potent for being invisible and for that reason alone *Full Metal Jacket* is an important film. Unlike *Hamburger Hill* and even *Platoon,* it doesn't revel in patriarchal values; it unravels and reveals them. In this culture, as Kingman shows, such an effort is desperately needed.

If that seems like overstatement, think of what literature students are taught. Tragedy, for example, is a patriarchal mode that operates through a form of psychological terrorism. When Hartman accuses Pyle of being as ugly as a modern art masterpiece, he's practising a familiar patriarchal reversal. It is Hartman who is ugly; as ugly as an old masterpiece. His method, though more extreme, is Shakespeare's as well as Aeschylus's and Arthur Miller's.

I am not suggesting that students emerge from a Shakespeare course believing in the divine right of kings. On the other hand, there are questions which they are often not encouraged to ask. Why is it that in *Macbeth* the Weird Sisters are given the doggerel to speak in an age when the iambic pentameter was the courtly mode for projecting an egocentric male perspective as natural?[8] Why do the Sisters in their spells sadistically re-enact the torture of witches? Why is Macbeth himself seen as anything other than a stupid warrior who confuses phallocracy with aristocracy; a psychopomp rather than a psychopath? Questions of Macbeth's tragic consciousness obscure more urgent political ones. Macbeth is a killing machine praying for war, to adapt Hartman's phrase. What Kubrick reveals and Shakespeare re-veils is that this presupposes a head full of shit.

The Jacobean message is clear enough—admire your leader come what may and don't attempt to seize the crown for yourself because you won't be able to hack it. The real terror though, is not of a bad king, but of no king at all. After Duncan's death the nobility of Scotland are in such a panic about who should be crowned that they make Macbeth king. No-one suggests forming a steering committee, or that they don't need a king—a fact clear from the play, for Duncan was as useless as Macbeth will be destructive. The terror is the absence of male authority. James I must have been delighted.

Not to raise such questions is, in a sense, to validate the "naturalness" of certain attitudes and assumptions. This is true not just in Shakespeare but in Aeschylus, who terrorises us with visions of what will happen if the male line is broken. It is true of Arthur Miller, who offers a vision of what happens to us if we don't get out there and sell. To say that *Death of A Salesman* promotes yuppie values doesn't trivialise the play, quite the contrary; it suggests that it re-enacts patriarchal values. It is those values that *Full Metal Jacket* confronts, in a way that *Hamburger Hill* doesn't want, and *Platoon* fails to do.

Much of this has to do with Kubrick's avoidance of certain genre conventions. Consider the Hue City settings. There is no richly photographed jungle in *Full Metal Jacket,* no visual recourse to Nature or the Pastoral, however blighted. To be in the shit is to be in a strictly man-made world.

As so often in Kubrick we seem outside real space and time. There are good reasons for this, as we shall see. The point is that this re-location of the war visually doesn't leave us in a political vacuum, though it might seem to. The Hue settings collapse together images of World War II, New York dereliction and *1984*. This is possible because it doesn't matter where the film is set in a sense; the phenomenon we witness is planet-wide and culture-long. We are in ethical as much as documentary space. This isn't aesthetic detachment or a failure to get into the shit; the shit is everywhere because our heads, like the Marines' language, are full of it. Why else would the designer violence of *Miami Vice* be so popular? The perennial unnaturalness of war is a transcendent political theme.

Again, the absence of a conventional angle character and the emotional separation of audience from characters is a familiar Kubrick inflection. Here, though, Kubrick has moved beyond the misanthropy of the previous films. The absence of conventional presentation in *Full Metal Jacket* is a political decision. It is an eschewal of the seductive nostalgia to which that otherwise worthy film, *Platoon*, falls prey. Kubrick is rightly uncompromising over this. A conventional plot with conventional characterisations would simply re-inscribe patriarchal values, as *Platoon* ultimately does. Besides, the combat violence when it does occur is so horrific that it generates all the sympathy and identity needed. I don't need to know a man to feel that his slaughter is barbaric. To see these men as protagonists in their own drama we would have to stop seeing them as victims of the roles and values dinned into them by Hartman. Similarly, in the first half of the film, Hartman's verbal and psychological assault, the paradigm of the slow motion shootings, is so intense and levelling that no angle character is required to generate empathy. Hartman tells them they are maggots, destroying individual differences to create the patriarchal plurality of comradeship where every Marine is a brother, for which read, clone. Even the male mothering that goes on is emotionless, a sterile substitute for something, or someone, real. To be caught up emotionally with a character would diffuse and de-fuse this essential outside view.

Essential because the culture shock of being plunged in Hartman's diatribe is the shock of our own culture made visible. When Hartman announces that their rifles will be the only pussy they'll get from now on, he isn't just commenting on the exclusion of women from a male group, he's talking about the process of expunging women psychologically. His language dismembers women, absenting them even from the sexual act. He addresses the platoon as "ladies," using the female label as a sign of contempt until they qualify, at which point they are suddenly told they are brothers. In a book called *Sexual Suicide,* George Gilder writes of Marine training;

> "The good things are manly and collective; the despicable are feminine and individual . . . when you want to create a group of male killers, that is what you do, you kill the women in them. That is the lesson of the Marines."[9]

This requires precisely the degradation of women that informs Hartman's language. This killing of the women in the recruits is the gynocide that facilitates the genocide. It is that genocide that *Hamburger Hill, Apocalypse Now* and *Platoon* never quite get to grips with, let alone what lies behind it. *Platoon* tries; it very honestly presents the war as various kinds of rape, but the effort is re-absorbed into spectacles of heroic patriarchy through figures such as Elias, whose death is presented in a vastly overblown symbolic moment of martyrdom. Moreover, the film is at least equally concerned to see Vietnam as an extension of American internal dissentions, an approach openly exploited by the television version of *M.A.S.H.* In that sense it reflects a continuing American insanity, but against this is set the nostalgic, unironic photography and the closing adagio that forces identification with the hero and his perspective on events: First, his seeing of Elias and his rival as twin father figures (i.e. patriarchy incarnate) so that the emotion is to do with lost male bonding; second, his American-ness which produces a lament for lost American bonding; third his youth, which produces what one might call a nostalgia for the future. Except as targets, the Vietnamese scarcely exist; they are absent as people—as absent as their not wholly unreasonable anti-colonial politics. To be fair, *Platoon* does more than any other Vietnam film I've seen to reinstate the gook as human (*The Killing Fields* is a rather different case) but like all the other films it remains politically safe, thus attracting first the money and last the Oscars.

Kubrick will have none of all this. Where the plot of *Platoon* suggests the possibilities of moral choice and justice, no such opportunities arise in *Full Metal Jacket* (the attempted rescue of Doc Jay and Eightball is not a moral choice as we shall see). Where the hero of *Platoon* can be airlifted out of the war, the squad in *Full Metal Jacket* are sealed within it: Joker at the end has become John Wayne, solving his own schizoid riddle. Nor is there the choice of a convenient wound; in Kubrick's Hue City you live or you die. The narrative climax in *Full Metal Jacket* is not the taking of a neutral, if useless objective like a hill, nor the enactment of justice in the manner of a western, but the group killing of a woman. The psychological genocide of Parris Island emerges in Hue on the level of action. The symbolic and linguistic universes create the physical one, and it is the slaughter of the woman that turns Joker into a full Marine, living out the "Born To Kill" slogan written across his head.

The enemy might seem even more absent here than in *Hamburger Hill,* but Kubrick is making a point very different from John Irvin's. Kubrick's assertion is that there is only one enemy, figuratively and literally, within the film; the gynocidal act informs all other cultural barbarities. This isn't Kubrick standing outside politics; it's a reassessment of what they are. *Full Metal Jacket* is only a safe film for those locked into conventionally political, patriarchal modes.

Kubrick points to the difficulty of making a film about Vietnam and the sheer silliness of some filmmakers when he has the documentary crew arrive in Hue. The organised incoherence of the soundtrack music and the absurd sideways creep of the crew are comment enough on the Vietnam genre and its pseudo-documentary posture. After offerings like *Uncommon Valor* and *Hamburger Hill* I can see his point: This crew will gather no truth through their lens. The squad's instant reaction is to play movies, asking who gets to be John Wayne and who the Indians. I don't think this sequence is a self-deprecatory gesture on Kubrick's part; it is rather a suggestion that these are not the kinds of film that he wishes to make. The sideways creep is, of course, a re-run of that famous tracking shot in *Paths of Glory,* while the on-camera interviews which are part of the fictional documentary dovetail into Kubrick's own text at the same time as they violate one of the most basic ground rules of television by letting the interviewee look into the camera. What all this adds up to is a recognition of the limitations implicit in making a Vietnam or any other war movie, and a determination not to let such limitations shape the discourse.

As I've suggested, Kubrick uncompromisingly avoids the characters, situations and techniques of the genre in order to cut through the role-playing and the clichés. For example, it is a commonplace of war films that disciplined training creates, under fire, disciplined and effective action. Not so in *Full Metal Jacket.* Once off base, where the attack on Da Nang is repulsed in an orderly manner not quite evident in some actual accounts, the squad are off-base in the other sense. Their training has produced a disorganised, ill-disciplined, lost, careless rabble. This may be realism but that is beside the point. The point is what the symbolic universe of their training actually produces in the combat zone.

The attempt by Doc Jay to rescue Eightball and Animal Mother's attempt to rescue them might look like John Wayne style comradely heroics but they aren't. They behave with the same reflex with which they use words like "shit" or "fuck." This is an important point, because one could see this rescue as a glimmer of optimism on Kubrick's part, a hint of redemption for the brutalised squad; Hartman might not, after all, have completely lobotomised their humanity.

In fact, this suicidal effort is the culmination of their training, hinted at at the end of the film's first section. Just before the first fade we see the squad wading and stumbling in a thick mud-splash. They're getting into the shit alright, but Pyle stumbles, bringing down Joker and Cowboy who try to keep going. Their helping gestures are part self-preservation, part the male mothering that runs through the Parris Island section and part the most successful entry into the shit. Pyle's fall, like his suicide, comes first, but no-one stops running. In their own ways, both Cowboy and Joker show the same suicidal, gung-ho attitudes in the combat zone. This charge

mentality is shown again at the end of their training, when the now uni-
formed squad charges the camera in the same way and in the same slow
motion as before. The slow motion deaths of Doc Jay, Eightball and Joker
are the visual and logical conclusion of those earlier charges. Joker's voice-
over comment during the second charge is that they are breaking out of
their instructor's control, but this rush into the shit *is* his control—he does
it himself trying to disarm Pyle. The rescue attempt is male mothering at
best, thus part of the gynocide, and so a programmed reflex. It is futile in
any case.

This collapsing of one incident into another, one place into another is a
clue to one of the film's major techniques. Its visual language moves it
beyond the unreality of *Platoon,* beyond *Hamburger Hill's* efforts to be a
remake of *All Quiet on the Western Front* towards the supra-real, a mode
Kubrick is familiar with.

Consider the slaughter of the sniper. This is presented in overtly sexual
terms. The victim lies on the floor, gasping with pain in an obscene parody
of sexual excitement while men stand round and watch. This is quite consistent with the portrayal elsewhere in the film of war and pornography as
facets of the same system. Our first sight of Vietnam is a prostitute's back-
side, while the music (*These Boots Are Made For Walking*) refers ironically
to Marines fresh from boot camp and the masochistic nature of the bargain
they strike. Later, Joker describes the war as "just business", another way
of referring to the same sick culture.

When Joker asks what to do with the sniper, Animal answers, "Fuck
her." Joker does, but in a manner appropriate to a Marine: He shoots her.
We hear the off-screen response of one of the men—"Hard core, man,
fucking hard core." The killing of the sniper is thus rape. With this act,
Joker elevates himself to heroic status. As they move off, he comments,
"We have nailed our names in the pages of history enough for one day." In
one sense absurd, this is in another sense true: One rape/murder a day
keeps the gynocide/genocide rolling. The deep irony is that Joker has not
killed only a woman because the sniper, though female, is herself enacting
the patriarchal values of war. Joker has shot himself in her just as surely as
Pyle killed himself. The final gunshot is gynocide/genocide/suicide. Joker is
phony tough because he's killed, in one sense, a phony woman; his survival is his death in every other way. He ends the film locked into the ideology of the Corps, singing of Mickey Mouse, just as Hartman made his
fatal entrance to the latrine asking "What's this Mickey Mouse shit? Just
what are you doing in my head?" The two parts of the film constantly inter-
act in this way, the structure pointing the parallels. The failure of Joker's
rifle at the crucial moment is a reprise of his purpose tremor in attacking
Pyle with the towel. The dying sniper is also the beaten Pyle, her request
("Shoot me.") a form of suicide that is consequent upon the death of her
tormentor. There is an almost Roegian interconnectedness here, though

without the flashiness.[10] The sniper is also their dead comrade Hand Job (Joker shoots the sniper with a hand gun and the onanistic reference is surely appropriate), likewise encircled as the squad exchange comments. The wrecked building where this occurs, as well as being part of Kubrick's discourse on cinema, is the ethically envisioned version of Parris Island barracks, where no amount of scrubbing can remove the shit in the head. Again, think of that verb "nailed": Diagrammatically sexual, it evokes the whole sadistic/masochistic male-centered necrophilia of Christianity, already disturbingly triggered by the one really bright image in the film's first half—the blood red sunset behind the training scaffold, an image later picked up in Joker's remark, "A day without blood is like a day without sunshine." The colour scheme of blood red, grey and olive drab pervades the film, signalling, like the slow motion, the paradigms arising from the minimal narrative. Religion is part of the training; as Hartman tells them, "God has a hard-on for Marines." It is no surprise then to hear Joker follow his nailing statement (and what a different martyrdom from Elias's that is) with "We humped down to the river."

The religion is part of the male motherhood that runs through the film and which is itself the enactment of the symbolic universe of Christianity where the Divine father begets first the son and then, through the totality of their love, the Holy Spirit. This mystical male begetting has its counterpart in Hartman's disgusting description of Cowboy's birth, and in the rebirth that turns Cowboy into a Marine. Thus, whether we look at the religious language, the scatological language or the obscene language (frequently impossible to separate), we are led to the conclusion that this symbolic universe is founded on gynophobia. That the film's two climaxes take place in the head, once literally, once figuratively, if such a separation is possible, is a comment about setting, theme and method. This is what pushes the film beyond its genre rivals. The aggression, Kubrick shows, emerges on the physical level only after it has been established in the symbolic universe of thought, language and behaviour. The symbolic model of the world that Kingman naively prattles about really does carry the past and present forward into the future.

The climax in Hue City is this symbolic universe in action; "Clearly, the primary and essential object of aggression is not the opposing military force. The members of the opposing teams share the same values and play the same war games. The secret bond that binds the warriors together, energizing them, is the violation of women, acted out physically and constantly replayed on the level of language and shared fantasies. In the absence of women, defeating the enemy is envisaged as making him a woman. Yet the warriors always attempt to seal the ultimate victory by actual rape, murder or dismemberment of women."[11]

Full Metal Jacket confronts us with just such conclusions, sparing us nothing, optimistic about nothing. If Terence Rafferty in *Sight and Sound* complains that it's all going on in Kubrick's head, he's missed the point; it's there in everyone's head.[12] Hartman (think of the implications of that name) doesn't invent an ideology to stuff the recruits' heads with; he simply extends what's already there to its limit. Rafferty complains that Kubrick can't get into the shit when it comes to it. Well no, he can't or won't; he leaves that to John Irvin and Oliver Stone. Unlike them, he recognises the real shit when he sees it. Kubrick knows what he believes and says it. From within the time-warp, we all need to listen.[13]

Notes

1. Sir John Kingman FRS (Chairman), *Report of the Committee of Inquiry into the Teaching of English Language.* (Her Majesty's Stationary Office, March 1988), p.7.

2. Kingman, p. 11.

3. Despite its radical posture, *Hard Times* remains a metropolitan novel; the cultureless dullness of Coketown is a Londoner's view of the provinces. One only has to compare Coketown with Dickens's London to see the bias.

4. Leicestershire is being colonised by yuppies from the South-East. One developer is offering homes in a purpose-built rural village at prices only affordable by affluent South-Easterners. The local population are priced out.

5. Kingman, p. 7.

6. Kingman, p. 7.

7. *The Taming of the Shrew,* IV,5,21, (London: Penguin, 1968).

8. A point I owe to a forthcoming article by my colleague M. A. Williams.

9. George F. Gilder, *Sexual Suicide,* (New York: Quadrangle Books, 1973) pp. 258–259. Also quoted in Daly.

10. For a fuller account of this diagenetic structure in Roeg's work, see this author's "From Gold Nugget to Ice Crystal: The Diagenetic Structure of Roeg's *Eureka,*" *Literature/Film Quarterly,* 11, No. 4, 1983.

11. Mary Daly, *Gyn/Ecology,* (London: The Women's Press, 1987), p. 357.

12. Terence Rafferty, "Remote Control," *Sight and Sound,* 56, No. 4 Autumn 1987, pp. 256–259.

13. The British censor has certified *Full Metal Jacket* as 18. This can't be because of the violence—*Hamburger Hill* is rated 15; nor can it be because the film is, however obliquely, sexually explicit in visual terms—*An Officer and A Gentleman* and *The Honorary Consul* have both been screened on British television. *Jacket's* danger is in its language.

Kubrick Filmography

SHORT FILMS

1951: *Day of the Fight*
DIRECTION, PHOTOGRAPHY, EDITING, SOUND: Stanley Kubrick
ASSISTANT: Alexander Singer
MUSIC: Gerald Fried
COMMENTARY: Douglas Edwards
LENGTH: 16 minutes
DISTRIBUTOR: RKO Radio

1951: *Flying Padre*
DIRECTION, PHOTOGRAPHY, EDITING, SOUND: Stanley Kubrick
MUSIC: Nathaniel Shilkret
LENGTH: 9 minutes
DISTRIBUTOR: RKO Radio

1953: *The Seafarers*
DIRECTION, PHOTOGRAPHY, EDITING: Stanley Kubrick
SCRIPT: Will Chasen
NARRATOR: Don Hollenbeck
LENGTH: 30 minutes
DISTRIBUTOR: Seafarers International Union, Atlantic and Gulf Coast District American Federation of Labor

FEATURE FILMS

1953: *Fear and Desire*
PRODUCER: Stanley Kubrick
DIRECTOR, PHOTOGRAPHY, EDITING: Stanley Kubrick
SCREENPLAY: Howard O. Sackler
MUSIC: Gerald Fried
CAST: Frank Silvera (Mac), Kenneth Harp (Corby), Virginia Leith (the girl), Paul Mazursky (Sidney), Steve Coit (Fletcher), David Allen (Narrator)

LENGTH: 68 minutes
DISTRIBUTOR: Joseph Burstyn

1955: *Killer's Kiss*

PRODUCTION COMPANY: Minotaur
PRODUCERS: Stanley Kubrick and Morris Bousel
DIRECTOR, PHOTOGRAPHY, EDITING: Stanley Kubrick
SCREENPLAY: Stanley Kubrick, Howard O. Sackler
MUSIC: Gerald Fried
CHOREOGRAPHY: David Vaughan
CAST: Jamie Smith (Davy Gordon), Frank Silvera (Vincent Rapallo), Irene Kane (Gloria), Jerry Jarret (Albert), Ruth Sobotka (Iris)
LENGTH: 67 minutes
DISTRIBUTOR: United Artists

1956: *The Killing*

PRODUCTION COMPANY: Harris-Kubrick Productions
PRODUCER: James B. Harris
DIRECTOR: Stanley Kubrick
SCREENPLAY: Stanley Kubrick, based on the novel *The Clean Break* by Lionel White
ADDITIONAL DIALOGUE: Jim Thompson
PHOTOGRAPHY: Lucien Ballard
MUSIC: Gerald Fried
EDITOR: Betty Steinberg
SOUND: Earl Snyder
ART DIRECTOR: Ruth Sobotka Kubrick
CAST: Sterling Hayden (Johnny Clay), Colleen Gray (Fay), Jay C. Flippen (Marv Unger), Marie Windsor (Sherry Peatty), Elisha Cook (George Peatty), Ted de Corsia (Randy Kennan), Joe Sawyer (Mike O'Reilly), James Edwards (parking lot attendant), Timothy Carey (Nikki), Vince Edwards (Val), Joseph Turkel (Tiny), Kola Kwariani (Maurice)
LENGTH: 83 minutes
DISTRIBUTOR: United Artists

1957: *Paths of Glory*

PRODUCTION COMPANY: Harris-Kubrick Productions
PRODUCER: James B. Harris
DIRECTOR: Stanley Kubrick
SCREENPLAY: Stanley Kubrick, Jim Thompson, Calder Willingham, based on the novel by Humphrey Cobb
PHOTOGRAPHY: George Krause
MUSIC: Gerald Fried

EDITOR: Eva Kroll

SOUND: Martin Muller

ART DIRECTOR: Ludwig Reiber

CAST: Kirk Douglas (Colonel Dax), Ralph Meeker (Captain Paris), Adolphe Menjou (General Broulard), George Macready (General Mireau), Wayne Morris (Lieutenant Roget), Richard Anderson (Major Saint-Aubain), Joseph Turkel (Private Arnaud), Timothy Carey (Private Ferol), Peter Cappel (Judge), Susanne Christian (German girl), Bert Freed (Sergeant Boulanger), Emile Meyer (priest), John Stein (Captain Rousseau)

LENGTH: 86 minutes

DISTRIBUTOR: United Artists (Presented by Bryna Productions)

1960: *Spartacus*

PRODUCTION COMPANY: Bryna Productions

PRODUCER: Edward Lewis

EXECUTIVE PRODUCER: Kirk Douglas

DIRECTOR: Stanley Kubrick

SCREENPLAY: Dalton Trumbo, from the novel by Howard Fast

PHOTOGRAPHY: Russell Metty

ADDITIONAL PHOTOGRAPHY: Clifford Stine

PROCESS: Super Technirama, 70 mm. Technicolor

EDITORS: Robert Lawrence, Robert Schultz, Fred Chulack

SECOND UNIT: Irving Lerner

MUSIC: Alex North

MUSIC DIRECTOR: Joseph Gershenson

PRODUCTION DESIGNER: Alexander Golitzen

SET DECORATION: Russell Gausman, Julia Heron

ART DIRECTOR: Eric Orbom

TITLES: Saul Bass

SOUND: Waldo Watson, Joe Lapis, Murray Spivack, Ronald Pierce

CAST: Kirk Douglas (Spartacus), Laurence Olivier (Marcus Crassus), Jean Simmons (Varinia), Charles Laughton (Gracchus), Peter Ustinov (Batiatus), Tony Curtis (Antoninus), John Gavin (Julius Caesar), Nina Foch (Helena), Herbert Lom (Tigranes), John Ireland (Crixus), John Dall (Glabrus), Charles McGraw (Marcellus), Woody Strode (Draba)

LENGTH: 196 minutes

DISTRIBUTOR: Universal Pictures

1962: *Lolita*

PRODUCTION COMPANIES: Seven Arts/Anya/Transworld

PRODUCER: James B. Harris

DIRECTOR: Stanley Kubrick

SCREENPLAY: Vladimir Nabokov, based on his novel (Stanley Kubrick, uncredited)

PHOTOGRAPHY: Oswald Morris

EDITOR: Anthony Harvey

ART DIRECTOR: Bill Andrews

ASSOCIATE ART DIRECTOR: Sid Cain

MUSIC: Nelson Riddle

LOLITA THEME: Bob Harris

ORCHESTRATIONS: Gil Grau

PRODUCTION SUPERVISOR: Raymond Anzarut

SOUND RECORDISTS: H. L. Bird, Len Shilton

CAST: James Mason (Humbert Humbert), Peter Sellers (Clare Quilty), Shelley Winters (Charlotte Haze), Sue Lyon (Lolita), Marianne Stone (Vivian Darkbloom), Jerr Stovin (John Farlow), Diana Decker (Jean Farlow), Gary Cockrell (Dick Schiller), Suzanne Gibbs (Mona Farlow), William Greene (Mr. Swine)

LENGTH: 152 minutes

DISTRIBUTOR: Metro Goldwyn Mayer

1964: *Dr. Strangelove, or How I Learned to Stop Worrying and Love the Bomb*

PRODUCTION COMPANY: Hawk Films

PRODUCER/DIRECTOR: Stanley Kubrick

SCREENPLAY: Stanley Kubrick, Terry Southern, Peter George, based on the book *Red Alert* by Peter George

PHOTOGRAPHY: Gilbert Taylor

EDITOR: Anthony Harvey

PRODUCTION DESIGNER: Ken Adam

MUSIC: Laurie Johnson

ART DIRECTOR: Peter Murton

SPECIAL EFFECTS: Wally Veevers

SOUND RECORDIST: Richard Bird

ASSISTANT EDITOR: Ray Lovejoy

ASSOCIATE PRODUCER: Victor Lyndon

CAST: Peter Sellers (Group Captain Mandrake, President Muffley, Dr. Strangelove), George C. Scott (General "Buck" Turgidson), Sterling Hayden (General Jack D. Ripper), Keenan Wynn (Colonel "Bat" Guano), Slim Pickens (Major T. J. "King" Kong), Peter Bull (Ambassador de Sadesky), James Earl Jones (Lieutenant Lothar Zogg), Tracy Reed (Miss Scott), Jack Creley (Mr. Staines), Frank Berry (Lieutenant Dietrich), Glenn Beck (Lieutenant Kivel), Shane Rimmer (Captain Ace Owens), Paul Tamarin (Lieutenant Goldberg)

LENGTH: 94 minutes

DISTRIBUTOR: Columbia Pictures

1968: *2001: A Space Odyssey*

PRODUCTION COMPANY: Metro Goldwyn Mayer

PRODUCER/DIRECTOR: Stanley Kubrick

SCREENPLAY: Stanley Kubrick, Arthur C. Clarke, based on Clarke's short story "The Sentinel."

PHOTOGRAPHY: Geoffrey Unsworth

PROCESS: Super Panavision

ADDITIONAL PHOTOGRAPHY: John Alcott

PRODUCTION DESIGNERS: Tony Masters, Harry Lange, Ernie Archer

EDITOR: Ray Lovejoy

SPECIAL PHOTOGRAPHIC EFFECTS DESIGNER/DIRECTOR: Stanley Kubrick

SPECIAL PHOTOGRAPHIC EFFECTS SUPERVISORS: Wally Veevers, Douglas Trumbell, Con Pederson, Tom Howard

MUSIC: Richard Strauss, Johann Strauss, Aram Khachaturian, Gyorgy Ligeti

COSTUMES: Hardy Amies

CAST: Keir Dullea (Dave Bowman), Gary Lockwood (Frank Poole), William Sylvester (Dr. Heywood Floyd), Douglas Rain (voice of HAL), Daniel Richter (Moonwatcher), Leonard Rossiter (Smylov), Margaret Tyzack (Elena), Robert Beatty (Halvorsen)

LENGTH: 141 minutes (originally 160 minutes)

DISTRIBUTOR: Metro Goldwyn Mayer

1971: *A Clockwork Orange*

PRODUCTION COMPANY: Warner Bros./Hawk Films

PRODUCER/DIRECTOR: Stanley Kubrick

EXECUTIVE PRODUCERS: Max Raab, Si Litvinoff

SCREENPLAY: Stanley Kubrick, based on the novel by Anthony Burgess

PHOTOGRAPHY: John Alcott

EDITOR: Bill Butler

PRODUCTION DESIGN: John Barry

ART DIRECTORS: Russell Hagg, Peter Shields

ELECTRONIC MUSIC: Walter (Wendy) Carlos

MUSIC: Ludwig van Beethoven, Edward Elgar, Gioacchino Rossini, Nikolai Rimsky-Korsakov, Henry Purcell, Terry Tucker, Arthur Freed, Nacio Herb Brown, James Yorkston, Erica Eigen

COSTUMES: Milena Canonero

ASSISTANT TO PRODUCER: Jan Harlan

CAST: Malcolm McDowell (Alex), Patrick Magee (Mr. Alexander), Michael Bates (Chief Guard), Anthony Sharp (Minister of the Interior), Godfrey Quigley (Prison Chaplain), Adrienne Corri (Mrs. Alexander), Warren Clarke (Dim), Miriam Karlin (Cat Lady), Paul Farrell (tramp), Philip Stone (Dad), Sheila Raynor (Mum), Aubrey Morris (Mr. Deltoid), Carl Duering (Dr. Brodsky), John Clive (stage actor), Madge Ryan (Dr. Branom), Pauline Taylor (psychiatrist), Margaret Tyzack (conspirator)

LENGTH: 137 minutes

DISTRIBUTOR: Warner Bros.

1975: *Barry Lyndon*

PRODUCTION COMPANY: Hawk/Peregrine Films for Warner Bros.

PRODUCER/DIRECTOR: Stanley Kubrick

EXECUTIVE PRODUCER: Jan Harlan

SCREENPLAY: Stanley Kubrick, based on the novel *The Luck of Barry Lyndon* by William Makepeace Thackeray

PHOTOGRAPHY: John Alcott

EDITOR: Tony Lawson

PRODUCTION DESIGNER: Ken Adam

ART DIRECTOR: Roy Walker

COSTUMES: Ulla-Britt Søderlund, Milena Canonero

MUSIC: J. S. Bach, Frederick the Great, W. A. Mozart, G. F. Handel, Franz Schubert, Giovanni Paisiello, Antonio Vivaldi, traditional Irish music played by The Chieftains

MUSIC ADAPTATION: Leonard Rosenman

CAST: Ryan O'Neal (Redmond Barry/Barry Lyndon), Marisa Berenson (Lady Lyndon), Patrick Magee (Chevalier de Balibari), Hardy Kruger (Captain Potzdorf), Steven Berkoff (Lord Ludd), Gay Hamilton (Nora Brady), Marie Kean (Mrs. Barry), Murray Melvin (Reverend Runt), Godfrey Quigley (Captain Grogan), Leon Vitali (Lord Bullingdon), Diana Koerner (Lischen), Frank Middlemass (Sir Charles Lyndon), André Morell (Lord Wendover), Philip Stone (Graham), Anthony Sharp (Lord Hallum), Michael Hordern (Narrator)

LENGTH: 185 minutes

DISTRIBUTOR: Warner Bros.

1980: *The Shining*

PRODUCTION COMPANY: Hawk/Peregrine Films (in association with The Producer Circle Company) for Warner Bros.

PRODUCER/DIRECTOR: Stanley Kubrick

EXECUTIVE PRODUCER: Jan Harlan

SCREENPLAY: Stanley Kubrick, Diane Johnson, based on the novel by Stephen King

PHOTOGRAPHY: John Alcott

STEADICAM OPERATOR: Garrett Brown

EDITOR: Ray Lovejoy

PRODUCTION DESIGNER: Roy Walker

ART DIRECTOR: Les Tompkins

MUSIC: Béla Bartók, Gyorgy Ligeti, Krzysztof Penderecki, Wendy Carlos, Rachel Elkind, Henry Hall

COSTUMES: Milena Canonero

SOUND: Ivan Sharrock

SECOND UNIT PHOTOGRAPHY: Douglas Milsome, Gregg Macgillivray

PERSONAL ASSISTANT TO STANLEY KUBRICK: Leon Vitali

CAST: Jack Nicholson (Jack Torrance), Shelley Duvall (Wendy Torrance), Danny Lloyd (Danny Torrance), Scatman Crothers (Halloran), Philip Stone (Delbert Grady), Joe Turkel (Lloyd), Barry Nelson (Ullman), Anne Jackson (Doctor), Lia Beldam (young woman in bath), Billie Gibson (old woman in bath), Lisa and Louise Burns (the Grady girls)

LENGTH: 144 minutes

DISTRIBUTOR: Warner Bros.

1987: *Full Metal Jacket*

PRODUCTION COMPANY: Puffin Films for Warner Bros.

EXECUTIVE PRODUCER: Jan Harlan

PRODUCER/DIRECTOR: Stanley Kubrick

SCREENPLAY: Stanley Kubrick, Michael Herr, Gustav Hasford, based on Hasford's novel *The Short-Timers*

LIGHTING CAMERAMAN: Douglas Milsome

PRODUCTION DESIGNER: Anton Furst

EDITOR: Martin Hunter

ORIGINAL MUSIC: Abigail Mead (plus songs: "Hello Vietnam," performed by Johnny Wright; "The Marines Hymn," performed by the Goldman Band; "These Boots Are Made for Walking," performed by Nancy Sinatra; "Chapel of Love," performed by the Dixie Cups; "Wooly Bully," performed by Sam the Sham and the Pharaohs; and "Paint It Black," performed by the Rolling Stones).

SOUND RECORDING: Edward Tise

SPECIAL EFFECTS SUPERVISOR: John Evans

CAST: Matthew Modine (Private Joker), Lee Ermey (Sergeant Hartman), Vincent D'Onofrio (Private Pyle), Adam Baldwin (Animal Mother), Arliss Howard (Private Cowboy), Dorian Harewood (Eightball), Kevyn Major Howard (Rafterman), Ed O'Ross (Lt. Touchdown), John Terry (Lt. Lockhart), Ngoc Le (V.C. Sniper)

LENGTH: 118 minutes

DISTRIBUTOR: Warner Bros.

Selected Bibliography

Agel, Jerome, ed. *The Making of Kubrick's 2001*. New York: New American Library, 1970.

Alcott, John. "Photographing Stanley Kubrick's *Barry Lyndon*." *American Cinematographer* (March 1976): 268.

Appel, Alfred, Jr., ed. *The Annotated Lolita*, by Vladimir Nabokov. New York: McGraw-Hill, 1970.

Barr, Charles. "*Straw Dogs, A Clockwork Orange* and the Critics." *Screen* (Summer 1972): 17–31.

Bernstein, Jeremy. "How About a Little Game?" *New Yorker*, 12 November 1966, 70–110.

Boyers, Robert. "*A Clockwork Orange*: Some Observations." *Film Heritage* (Summer 1972): 1–6.

Brown, Garrett. "The Steadicam and *The Shining*." *American Cinematographer* (August 1980): 786.

Brustein, Robert. "Out of this World." *New York Review of Books*, 6 February 1964, 3–4.

Burgess, Anthony. *A Clockwork Orange*. New York: Ballantine, 1965.

———. "Juice from *A Clockwork Orange*." *Rolling Stone*, 8 June 1972, 52–53.

Burke, Tom. "Malcolm McDowell: The Liberals, They Hate *Clockwork*." *New York Times*, 30 January 1972, 13.

Cahill, Tim. "The Rolling Stone Interview: Stanley Kubrick." *Rolling Stone*, 27 August 1987.

Ciment, Michel. *Kubrick*. Trans. Gilbert Adair. London: Collins, 1983.

Clarke, Arthur C. *2001: A Space Odyssey*. New York: New American Library, 1968.

Cobb, Humphrey. *Paths of Glory*. New York: Viking Press, 1935.

Coyle, Wallace. *Stanley Kubrick: A Guide to References and Resources*. Boston: G. K. Hall, 1980.

Daniels, Don. "Skeleton Key to *2001*," *Sight and Sound* (Winter 1970/71): 28–33.

Deer, Harriet and Irving Deer. "Kubrick and the Structures of Popular Culture." *Journal of Popular Film* 3, no. 3 (Summer 1979): 233–244.

Dempsey, Michael. "*Barry Lyndon*." *Film Quarterly* 30: no. 1 (Fall 1976): 49–54.

Doherty, Thomas. "Full Metal Genre: Kubrick's Vietnam Combat Movie." *Film Quarterly*, 42: no. 2 (1988–89): 24–30.

Dumont, J. P. and J. Monod. "Beyond the Infinite: A Structural Analysis of *2001: A Space Odyssey*." Trans. Susan Thomos. *Quarterly Review of Film Studies* 3 (1978): 297–316.

Durgnat, Raymond. "*Lolita*." *Films and Filming*, (November 1962): 35.

Falsetto, Mario. *Stanley Kubrick: A Narrative and Stylistic Analysis*. Westport, Conn.: Greenwood Press, 1994.

Feldmann, Hans. "Kubrick and His Discontents." *Film Quarterly* 30 (Fall 1976): 12–19.

Forbes, Bryan. "*Dr. Strangelove*" *Films and Filming* 10: no. 5 (February 1964): 26.

Geduld, Carolyn. *Filmguide to 2001: A Space Odyssey*. Bloomington: Indiana University Press, 1973.

Gelmis, Joseph. *The Film Director as Superstar*. Garden City, N.Y.: Doubleday, 1970.

George, Peter. *Dr. Strangelove*. New York: Bantam, 1963.

Hoch, David G. "Mythic Patterns in *2001: A Space Odyssey*." *Journal of Popular Culture* (Summer 1970): 961–965.

Houston, Penelope. "Kubrick Country." *Saturday Review*, 25 December 1971: 42–44.

Jameson, Fredric. "Historicism in *The Shining*" (1981), in *Signatures of the Visible*. New York and London: Routledge, 1990.

Jameson, Richard T. "Kubrick's Shining." *Film Comment* 16: no. 4 (July-August 1980): 28–32.

Kagan, Norman. *The Cinema of Stanley Kubrick*. New York: Holt, Rinehart, and Winston, 1972.

Kauffmann, Stanley. "It Needn't Be Bad if it's Big." *The New Republic*, 14 November 1960, 19.

King, Stephen. *The Shining*. New York: Signet, 1977.

Kinney, Judy Lee. *Text and Pretext: Stanley Kubrick's Adaptations*. Ph.D. diss., University of California, Los Angeles, 1983.

Kolker, Robert Philip. *A Cinema of Loneliness: Penn, Kubrick, Scorsese, Spielberg, Altman*. 2d ed. New York: Oxford University Press, 1988.

Kubrick, Stanley. "Director's Notes: Stanley Kubrick Movie Maker." *The Observer* (London), 4 December 1960.

———. "Words and Movies." *Sight and Sound* (Winter 1960/61): 14.

———. "How I Learned to Stop Worrying and Love the Cinema." *Films and Filming* 9, no. 9 (June 1963): 12–13.

———. *A Clockwork Orange: A Screenplay*. New York: Ballantine Books, 1972.

———. Michael Herr, and Gustav Hasford. *Full Metal Jacket: The Screenplay*. New York: Alfred A. Knopf, 1987.

Lambert, Gavin. "*Paths of Glory*." *Sight and Sound* (Winter 1958): 144.

Lightman, Herb. "Filming *2001: A Space Odyssey*." *American Cinematographer* (June 1968): 3–10.

———. "Photographing Stanley Kubrick's *The Shining*: An Interview with John Alcott." *American Cinematographer* (August 1980): 760.

Maland, Charles. "*Dr. Strangelove* (1964): Nightmare Comedy and the Ideology of Liberal Consensus." *American Quarterly* (Winter 1979): 697–717.

Mamber, Stephen. "*A Clockwork Orange*." *Cinema* (USA), (Winter 1972–1973): 48–57.

Mayersberg, Paul. "The Overlook Hotel." *Sight and Sound* (Winter 1980/81): 54–57.

McCracken, Samuel. "Novel into Film; Novelist into Critic: *A Clockwork Orange* . . . Again." *Antioch Review* 32, no. 3 (1978): 427–36.

Miller, Mark Crispin. "Kubrick's Anti-Reading of *The Luck of Barry Lyndon*." *Modern Language Notes* 91 (1976): 1360–79.

Milne, Tom. "Stanley Kubrick: How I Learned to Stop Worrying and Love Stanley Kubrick." *Sight and Sound* (Spring 1964): 68–72.

Nabokov, Vladimir. *Lolita: A Screenplay*. New York: McGraw-Hill, 1974.

Nelson, Thomas Allen. *Kubrick: Inside a Film Artist's Maze*. Bloomington: Indiana University Press, 1982.

Phillips, Gene D. "Interview with Stanley Kubrick." *Film Comment* (Winter 1971/72): 30–35.

———. *Stanley Kubrick: A Film Odyssey*. New York: Popular Library, 1975.

Pursell, Michael. "*Full Metal Jacket*: The Unravelling of Patriarchy." *Literature/Film Quarterly* 16, no. 4 (1988): 218–25.

Rapf, Maurice. "A Talk with Stanley Kubrick." *Action* (January/February 1969): 15–18.

Salt, Barry. *Film Style and Technology: History and Analysis*. London: Starword, 1983.

Spiegel, Alan. "Kubrick's *Barry Lyndon*." *Salmagundi* (Fall 1977): 194–208.

Switzer, Judith Anne. *Stanley Kubrick: The Filmmaker As Satirist*. Ph.D. diss., New York University, 1983.

Thackeray, William Makepeace. *The Luck of Barry Lyndon*. Middlesex, England: Penguin Books, 1975.

Titterington, P. L. "Kubrick and *The Shining*." *Sight and Sound* (Spring 1981): 117–21.

Trumbull, Douglas. "Creating Special Effects for *2001*." *American Cinematographer* (June 1968): 15–21.

Walker, Alexander. *Stanley Kubrick Directs*. Expanded edition. New York: Harcourt Brace Jovanovich, 1972.

Weinraub, Bernard. "Kubrick Tells What Makes *Clockwork* Tick." *New York Times*, 4 January 1972, 26.

White, Lionel. *The Clean Break*. New York: E. P. Dutton, 1955.

Wolfe, Gary K. "*Dr. Strangelove, Red Alert*, and Patterns of Paranoia in the 1950s." *Journal of Popular Film* (Winter 1976): 57–67.

Index

Wild Bunch, The (Peckinpah), 178, 201
Willingham, Calder, 44
Windsor, Marie, 101
Winters, Shelley, 111, 114
Wizard of Oz, The (Fleming), 182
Wollen, Peter, 284
Woolf, Virginia, 210

Wright of Darby, 205

Yates, Peter, 105
Youngblood, Gene, 146
Young Frankenstein (Brooks), 296

Zucker, Bert, 45